PITTSBURGH SERIES IN SOCIAL
AND LABOR HISTORY

Distribution of Wealth and Income in the United States in 1798

LEE SOLTOW

University of Pittsburgh Press

Published by the University of Pittsburgh Press, Pittsburgh, Pa., 15260
Copyright © 1989, University of Pittsburgh Press
All rights reserved
Baker & Taylor International, London
Manufactured in the United States of America

Library of Congress Cataloging in Publication Data

Soltow, Lee.
    Distribution of wealth and income in the United States in 1798 /
Lee Soltow.
        p.   cm.
    Includes index.
    ISBN 0-8229-3620-8
    1. Wealth—United States—History—18th century.   2. Income
distribution—United States—History—18th century.   I. Title.
HC110.W4S63   1989   89-4744
339.2′0973—dc19   CIP

Contents

1   THE OBSERVATION OF INEQUALITY   9

> *A Counter Hypothesis / The Problem of the Life Cycle / A Statistical Approach / John Adams / Shares of Wealth / The Lognormal Configuration / The Franklin and Adams Hypotheses / Other Alternatives / Reasons for Believing in American Equality / Census Counts / Consumption and Inequality / Income and Inequality*

2   DISTRIBUTION OF WEALTH   35

> *The Statistical Data / Sampling Procedure / The Sample: Data and Problems / Distribution Among Property Holders in 1798 and 1860 / Biases / Changes in the Inequality of Wealth Between 1798 and 1860*

3   DISTRIBUTION OF INCOME   49

> *The Housing Data / Distribution of Housing / Crowding / Elasticities / Dwelling-Derived Income*

Tables

Appendix Tables

Figures

Acknowledgments

THE STUDY that has resulted in this book was supported in large part by grants from the National Science Foundation. In addition, the Department of Economics at Ohio University offered strong assistance by reducing my teaching load.

My thanks to Ekkehart Schlicht, Robert Gallman, William Parker, Stanley Lebergott, Van Beck Hall, Meno Lovenstein, Joseph Sligo, Carole Shammas, Vishwa Shukla, and Judy Klare for reading all or parts of my manuscript and offering constructive criticisms. I am particularly grateful to two unknown readers, for the University of Pittsburgh Press, for their meticulous readings and their suggestions which have added new dimensions to the manuscript. I also thank my wife, Margaret, for her research help in the various archives and libraries in which we have worked during the last decade and for her valuable assistance in editing and manuscript preparation. However, the conclusions, opinions, and other statements in this book are mine and not necessarily those of any of the persons or groups mentioned above.

Distribution of Wealth and Income
in the United States in 1798

Introduction

THIS MONOGRAPH analyzes the findings from a unique census of wealth at the end of the eighteenth century in the United States. Legislation passed in 1798 governed the First Direct Tax at the federal level. It set in motion an inventory of every dwelling in the country, every mill, barn, and wharf. The value of each was listed by the owner's and the occupant's name, and totals were derived for most counties and all states in the new nation. Grand totals of value are available, as are manuscripts or descriptions of individual ownership for 62 of the nation's 359 counties.

I have coupled these records with data from the censuses of population in 1790 and 1800 in order to determine the wealth position of individuals. My estimates yield the distribution of wealth in America at the time, consisting of 433,000 owners of land in a country with 877,000 free males 21 and older.

This analysis fills a gap in our knowledge of inequality in America between the estimates that Alice Hanson Jones made for 1774, as determined from a sample of a thousand estates, and my own estimates for 1850–1870, determined from samples drawn from the censuses of wealth in those years. My data for 1798 consist of about 60,000 properties and 40,000 owners. The sample is sufficiently large to serve as a basis for the determination of the levels of wealth and inequality for all states and 687 tax districts. Further, the sample allows for an analysis not only of wealth but also of housing values. Since housing consumption can serve as a proxy for income, I have made an estimate of income distribution for 1798.

An appreciation of the significance of inequality in the early federal period permits a better understanding of those strategic issues still governing our society. This was a time when basic laws were being drafted, state constitutions formulated, and the federal Constitution adopted. Views concerning inequality found expression in at least four kinds of legislation. One, land laws were drafted with an eye to price policies, since they could affect not only the poor but also the affluent. The rich conceivably could monopolize landownership, as had happened in Europe. Two, credit for the poor, poor laws, and debtors' prisons were topics of vital concern. Paradoxically, the establishment of banks to facilitate credit were viewed by some as an avenue for creating a policy of "paper-money" wealth.

A third issue, with obvious implications for distribution, was how to raise revenues. The First Direct Tax was, in some ways, quite amazing, since it was a strongly progressive tax, applicable not directly to income, but also to wealth, albeit wealth in housing—in effect, to income! As a fourth and final kind of legislation, we note the emphasis on suffrage. At what level in the distribution of income were adult free males allowed to vote? How permissive was America to be in allowing political participation? Was there to be a bicameral legislature, with a senate to guard the interests of a property holder class? Deliberations were replete with references to people's views about the rich and the poor. Equality and inequality were important theoretical concerns in this era of constitution making, perceptions we still live with today. A quantitative analysis of the distribution of wealth at that time is most important to our actions even now.

This study should be considered as part of a larger analysis of inequality, both in Europe and in America. The end of the eighteenth century was an exciting time, not only because of the French Revolution, but also because of incipient movement away from traditional patterns taking place in other countries. R. R. Palmer, in *The Age of the Democratic Revolution,* discusses such activities in at least four other countries. These transformations are often tied to the American experience in demonstrating the universality of change. I have attempted to quantify aspects of wealth distribution on both sides of the Atlantic in 1800 by using data for the four Scandinavian countries and Scotland for comparison. I state average wealth for England, Scotland, Scandinavia, and America in order to provide an understanding of our general well-being compared to that of the populations of Europe.

The end of the eighteenth century was a time of census taking. The 1749 census of Sweden, along with the country's remarkable elaborations of labor-force counts by 1810, set the standard. U.S. censuses of 1790 and 1800 included some age details; the British census of 1801 provided new perspectives. By means of these summaries, societies could now view themselves in a broader sense, not just in terms of the rich and somewhat rich in the upper tail of the income distribution. The masses of the poor and destitute were now being properly considered in data gathering. In Sweden authorities went so far as to count the numbers of families in four classes: the rich, the somewhat rich, the poor, and the destitute!

The quantification of inequality for 1800 is strategically important from another standpoint. Those years were part of the last phase of the traditional period before the onset of the Industrial Revolution, said to have begun by the turn of the century, if not earlier, in England. Modernization brought a quickening in the pace of activity in America by 1830 or later; Scotland lagged by a decade, but preceded the change in Sweden.

Did the Industrial Revolution increase or reduce inequality? There is controversy over this matter, with Jeffrey Williamson and Peter Lindert leading the way by arguing that industrialization brought increased inequality. For many years I have felt that the Industrial Revolution had the opposite effect, that the factory revolution offered greater employment opportunities to the masses than they had ever experienced. I concede that my analysis rested largely on my studies of Scandinavia, and more particularly of Norway. A thorough study of inequality in the traditional period before the takeoff of industrialization should be a first step in trying to establish what actually happened. Did the American experience begin from a position of high or of low inequality? This monograph addresses that basic question.

The figures for 1798 permit me to deal with the period 1798–1850–1870 in testing the view of Lindert and Williamson. But they also permit me to look at the 1774–1798 period, a really chaotic time, covering the war, the expulsion of the Tories, the passage of the Articles of Confederation, and the framing and adoption of the Constitution.

Chapter 1 proposes several hypotheses concerning inequality in America in 1800. These hypotheses are based on generalizations made at the time by those sages who had observed economic conditions on both sides of the Atlantic. I focus on a hypothesis of relative inequality—or the "happy mediocrity" postulated by Benjamin Franklin—as well as on the contrasting hypothesis of substantial inequality stated by John Adams. The observations of La Rochefoucauld and Michaux centered on the very poor, at the lower tail of the income distribution.

The 1798 census of wealth in real estate is introduced in chapter 2, which describes the distribution of wealth among 433,000 wealth holders in that year. I highlight the shares held by the rich, middle, and low wealth classes. A decision is made as to whether the Franklin or Adams hypothesis was closer to reality. I also present some initial comparisons of inequality in 1798 and 1860.

Chapters 3 and 4 center on the idea that housing consumption was closely related to income and that the distribution of housing is most revealing with respect to inequality of *all* people. The focal point of the material is an estimate of income distribution, or at least the relative income distribution in the United States in 1798. It is based on the "crowding" of 715,000 families into 577,000 houses as well as on certain assumptions about the elasticity of housing with respect to income. I have prepared distributions for each of the states, counties, and 687 tax districts of the country by using housing values. Housing and income in 1798 are compared to similar data for 1980. The results prove to be a dramatic test of the hypothesis of Tocqueville, that equality was on the rise in the new nation.

Chapter 5 continues the housing data and introduces a possibly powerful revelation. In 1798, the authorities in Philadelphia made estimates of the housing distribution in their city *prior to* gathering the data. The accuracy of their estimates is important in judging whether these men really understood the extent of inequality in the country. There is another compelling notion revealed in the estimates. Possibly the authorities used the notion of a lognormal curve in deriving their estimates, a creation that would have been a startling advance, one anticipating model-building techniques employed today. One cannot prove this assertion of originality in intellectual thought, but the idea is nevertheless intriguing. The prognostication, as a minimum, reveals beliefs about the two tails of the curve that represent the very rich and the very poor in Philadelphia.

We know that in the late eighteenth century the wealth distribution in the United States showed a certain degree of inequality. How can we judge whether inequality was large or small? We can compare it with the degrees of inequality in Europe at the time or with inequality levels in the United States either earlier or later than 1798. These comparisons are the subjects of chapters 6, 7, and 8. In chapter 6 I compare the distributions for Denmark, Sweden, Norway, and Finland, along with one I have completed for Scotland, with that for the United States. The subsequent time comparisons use data not only for 1771, 1774, and 1798, but also for 1798, 1850–1860, and 1983. These data form the basis for further judging the Franklin and Adams hypotheses and the observations of La Rochefoucauld and Michaux.

What was the reason for the degree of inequality of wealth in the country in 1798? What policies had our new government introduced that would alter disparities between rich and poor? Was the Western world's most effective democracy then setting a standard for inequality that was clearly different from the past? These are the questions with which I grapple in chapters 7, 8, and 9. I approach the subject from a perspective of time— a generation—to measure the differences in inequality before and after 1798. A dozen or so aspects of changes are considered: the forfeiture of Loyalist estates, the demise of entail and primogeniture, and the rise of banking and speculation in government securities. In his *Democracy in America,* Alexis de Tocqueville hypothesized that equality of condition, including equality of land and wealth, was strengthened after America's break with the colonial system. I test this idea by considering the distribution of slaves in various periods and the effects of changes in rural/urban residence and nativity. Backward extrapolations to 1800, based on the censuses of 1850, 1860, and 1870, prove fruitful in this respect. These extrapolations focus on the data sets for males 70 and older in 1850, men who had been 20 years old in 1800.

Economic developments at the end of the eighteenth century, as well as from 1760 to 1860, are highlighted in chapter 9. I have made various estimates of change based on the average values of wealth in 1798 in frontier and settled regions, and between per capita values in 1798 and 1860. Deeds of sale and land grants are examined for long periods. The dynamics of change in the early decades of the federal period emphasize the fact that 1798 was not a dormant economic period. These changes are strategic in understanding inequality levels then and at various other times in U.S. history.

Chapter 10, as a substantial change in focus, attempts to place inequality in a wider perspective of socioeconomic and cultural activity at the end of the eighteenth century. It is admittedly speculative. In it, I explore a possible application of the housing data to a field allied to economics, namely, politics. I pose the question: "Would a general plebiscite of all males 21 and older in 1788 have ratified the Constitution?" Would such a plebiscite have rejected the Constitution? To answer this question, I have compiled information concerning the votes of delegates and the values of their housing and the number of slaves they owned. The argument that the Constitution would have been rejected is based on the idea that a minority of persons with higher income and wealth naturally had greater fervor for ratification than did the majority of ordinary people, that delegates tended to be either rich or somewhat rich relative to the mass of individuals. One's view about the outcome of the theoretical plebiscite depends partly on the degree of inequality in, or the shape of, the housing distribution—on the extent of the differences in well-being between the affluent, middling, and poor classes in the new country.

Chapter 11 is a summary and critique of inequality. I consider all of the evidence garnered from various sources, including results of comparisons for the United States in 1774, 1798, and 1850–1870, and of comparisons between the United States and Europe at the end of the eighteenth century. I then judge whether our land was one of equality or inequality in 1798.

1

The Observation of Inequality

A MERICANS AND EUROPEANS who had observed economic conditions on both sides of the Atlantic at the end of the eighteenth century generally agreed that there was greater equality in America. Yet there were differences regarding the degree of dispersion in wealth and income, depending in part on whether the observer focused on the rich or the poor. Europeans, particularly the affluent, found a paucity of large estates and great landowners in America. American travelers, on the other hand, often emphasized the plight of the poor they saw in Europe. The overriding consideration was the abundance of land in America, as contrasted to limited land supplies in Great Britain and on the Continent. Whereas there was a tendency to minimize distinctions between great landowners, tenants, land managers, crofters, cotters, day laborers, and the poor and destitute in America, it is of greater interest to note the range of opinion about the degree of inequality in the country during the age of revolution.

Many of America's political leaders spent months, if not years, in Europe and then recorded their sensitive feelings about socioeconomic differences. Their expert opinions provide valuable insights into the broader ramifications of inequality. Their thinking inevitably became embedded in the administrative and legal processes instituted in the new nation. Benjamin Franklin, Thomas Jefferson, and James Madison, but most particularly John Adams, all had arrived at firm convictions about these matters. Their European counterparts are best exemplified by the duc de La Rochefoucauld and the Count Francesco dal Verme from the noble or upper classes, Thomas Paine, and André Michaux from among the more ordinary people, and Henry Wansey, representing the middle class. It is more difficult to obtain observations made by ordinary Americans who had had the opportunity to travel in Europe. Obviously, a person had to possess considerable resources and have the leisure to travel abroad; only if such an individual had been exceptionally affected by the plight of the poor are we likely to find a contemporary observation about that part of society in Europe.

Benjamin Franklin observed poverty in Europe in the 1770s and 1780s, and could not refrain from contrasting it to what he perceived to be the condition in America. He wrote to Joshua Babcock:

> I have lately made a Tour thro' Ireland and Scotland. In those Countries a small Part of Society are Landlords, great Noblemen, and Gentlemen, extreamly [sic] opulent, living in the highest Affluence and Magnificence: The Bulk of the People Tenants, extreamly poor, living in the most sordid Wretchedness, in dirty Hovels of Mud and Straw, and cloathed only in rags. I thought often of the Happiness of New England, where every Man is a Freeholder, has a Vote in publick Affairs, lives in a tidy, warm House. . . .
>
> Whoever has travelled through the various parts of Europe, and observed how small is the proportion of people in affluence or easy circumstances there, compared with those in poverty and misery; the few rich and haughty landlords, the multitude of poor, abject, rack-rented, tithe-paying tenants and half-paid and half-starved ragged laborers; and views here the happy mediocrity that so generally prevails throughout these States, where the cultivator works for himself, and supports his family in decent plenty, will, methinks, see abundant reason to bless Divine Providence for the evident and great difference in our favor, and be convinced that no nation known to us enjoys a greater share of human felicity.[1]

John Adams's travels to Spain in 1779 led him to observe, "I see nothing but signs of poverty and misery among the people. A fertile country, not half cultivated, people ragged and dirty, and the houses universally nothing but mire, smoke, fleas and lice."[2] Yet in 1786 Adams summarily dismissed a European's question concerning the extent of poverty and dejection in America.

> As to poverty, there is hardly a beggar in the country. As to dejection, I never saw, even at the time of our greatest danger and perplexity, so much of it as appears in England or France upon every intelligence of a disastrous event.
>
> The greatest source of grief and affliction is the fluctuation of the paper money; but this, although it occasions unhappiness, has no violent or fatal effects.[3]

Thomas Jefferson, too, left his deep impressions of the plight of lower-class Europeans in this perceptive observation made during a trip in 1785 to Fontainebleau, the summer residence of French kings:

> This being the first trip, I set out yesterday morning to take a view of the place. . . .
> I fell in with a poor woman walking at the same rate with myself and going the

same course. Wishing to know the condition of the labouring poor I entered into conversation with her. . . . She told me she was a day labourer, . . . that often she could get no emploiment [*sic*], and of course was without bread. . . . I gave her, on parting, 24 sous. . . . She had probably never received so great an aid. This little attendrissement, with the solitude of my walk led me into a train of reflections on that unequal division of property which occasions the numberless instances of wretchedness which I had observed in this country and which is to be observed all over Europe. The property of this country is absolutely concentered in a very few hands. . . . The earth is given as a common stock for man to labour and live on. . . . It is too soon yet in our country to say that every man who cannot find employment but who can find uncultivated land, shall be at liberty to cultivate it, paying a moderate rent. But it is not too soon to provide by every possible means that as few as possible shall be without a little portion of land. The small landholders are the most precious part of a state.[4]

In his *Notes on the State of Virginia* (1781), Jefferson wrote, not as an observer in Paris, but as a Virginian in his native land,

Vagabonds, without visible property or vocation are placed in workhouses, where they are well cloathed [*sic*], fed, lodged, and made to labour. Nearly the same method of providing for the poor prevails through all our states; and from Savannah to Portsmouth you will seldom meet a beggar. In the larger towns indeed they sometimes present themselves. These are usually foreigners, who have never obtained a settlement in any parish. I never yet saw a native American begging in the streets or highways. A subsistence is easily gained here: and if, by misfortunes, they are thrown on the charities of the world, those provided by their own country are so comfortable and so certain, that they never think of relinquishing them to becoming strolling beggars.[5]

Franklin, Adams, and Jefferson undoubtedly were correct in their observations of Europe; Franklin, especially, had seen barefooted and ragged boys in the midlands of England and in Scotland. But had he visited the mountains of central and western Pennsylvania or, for that matter, had he deviated from the main roads on his trips between Boston and Philadelphia?[6] One also wonders if Jefferson in fact had made a concerted effort to walk the back roads of his native Albemarle County in Virginia. Had he ascertained the proportions of free men who owned no property— the proportions of men who could neither read nor write—the proportions of men who owned no horses, let alone chariots?[7]

Though he did not travel so widely as did some of his contemporaries, and though his knowledge of the poor in Europe therefore was seen only through the eyes of others, James Madison's experiences in America and his general sensitivities gave him a remarkable understanding of the plight of the poor.[8] In Madison's reply to Jefferson's Fontainebleau letter of 1786, he urged Jefferson to observe the wretchedness and conditions of indigent peoples in other regions of Europe. At this point he seemed to anticipate his famous Federalist Paper No. 10, dated 1787, in the following noteworthy observations:

> I have no doubt but that the misery of the lower classes will be found to abate wherever the Government assumes a freer aspect, & the laws favor a subdivision of property, yet I suspect that the difference will not fully account for the comparative comfort of the mass of people in the United States. Our limited population has probably as large a share in producing this effect as the political advantages which distinguish us. A certain degree of misery seems inseparable from a high degree of populousness. If the lands in Europe which are now dedicated to the amusement of the idle rich, were parcelled out among the idle poor, I readily conceive the happy revolution which would be experienced by a certain proportion of the latter. But still would there not remain a great proportion unrelieved?[9]

A year later, Madison presented his views more fully in his reports of the federal convention which gave the most comprehensive opinion about equality at that time.

> If equality is as I contend the leading feature of the U. States, where then are the riches & wealth whose representation & proportion is the peculiar province of this permanent body. Are they in the hands of the few who may be called rich; in the possession of less than a hundred citizens? Certainly not. They are in the great body of the people, among whom there are no men of wealth, and very few of real poverty.[10]

We should not neglect the views on inequality held by the father of our country. Even though he had no occasion to travel in Europe, Washington was keenly aware of the "habitual distinctions" in the southern states, and of the paradox that it was southerners who most feared monarchial government. Washington presumed that the region with the smallest class distinctions was New England, and he felt that there the citizens displayed less antipathy to strong government.[11] Washington's general view of the United States was that its vast, undeveloped frontiers mitigated inequality not only among residents, but also among the peoples of the world. "Rather than quarrel about the territory, let the poor, the needy, and oppressed of the earth, and those who want land, resort to the fertile lands of our western country."[12]

A COUNTER HYPOTHESIS

In addition to the assertions of our great leaders, what information is necessary to defend a hypothesis of equality in early America? Three of those leaders were to become members of the most learned coterie in America, the American Philosophical Society, dedicated to proper scientific classification. These men had observed conditions in both worlds, not just one, and in this sense they were using procedures like the matched sampling and controls employed in modern statistical methods. So we must turn to the observations made by the dozens of Europeans who had visited the United States if we are to complete the matching process. The most prominent of the European counterparts to our country's leaders was the duc de La Rochefoucauld-Liancourt, a man experienced in making comparisons between France, England, and the United States. As a friend of Arthur Young, La Rochefoucauld was able to extend his comparative studies to Ireland as well. We select a few of the numerous passages dealing with inequality from his four volumes on the subject of America.

During a trip from Philadelphia, to Chester, Wilmington, and Federal City (Washington) in 1797, La Rochefoucauld expressed his reaction in this revealing passage:

> Huts formed of logs and planks of wood, as miserable as any that are to be seen in the poorest parts of France, cover the country. The inhabitant here is proprietor and cultivator; that he lives as he pleases, must be admitted; but in the most remote and uninhabited parts of America that I have visited, I have never seen a greater proportion of wretched habitations. The men and women who are seen issuing from their huts are badly clothed, and bear every mark of poverty. The children are in rags, and almost naked.[13]

In his notes on travel to Virginia, La Rochefoucauld stated, "In the space of sixty miles which I yesterday traveled from Williamsburg to Richmond, I did not see twenty houses; and such as I saw were mean and wretched. . . . In a country [Virginia] where slavery prevails and where the possession of the soil is vested in so few hands, that class of whites who do not possess landed property are more indigent than elsewhere." In yet another passage, he presented a view of hopelessness quite contrary to that expressed by America's leaders: "Indeed it must be confessed that under the present mediocrity of wealth in the state of Virginia, the paucity of her population in proportion to her extent, and her backwardness in point of agricultural improvement, the inhabitants could not reasonably entertain a desire of such an event [improvement]."[14]

La Rochefoucauld was not alone in assaying Pennsylvania and Virginia as he did. Isaac Weld, another observer-traveler in the 1790s, wrote:

> Among the inhabitants here, and in the lower parts of Virginia, there is a disparity unknown elsewhere in America, excepting in the large towns. Instead of the lands

being equally divided, immense estates are held by a few individuals, who derive large incomes from them, whilst the generality of the people are but in a state of mediocrity. Most of the men also, who possess these large estates having received liberal educations, which the others have not, the distinction between them is still more observable.[15]

We must not neglect the American West as the main frontier. The ever attentive François Michaux visited many families from all economic strata, apparently. He describes an 1802 meeting, near Knoxville, with two emigrant families, numbering 10–12 persons who were going to settle in Tennessee.

Their ragged clothes and the miserable appearance of their children, who were bare-footed and in their shirts, was a plain indication of their poverty, a circumstance by no means uncommon in the United States. At the same time it is not in the western country that the riches of the inhabitants consist in specie; for I am persuaded that not one in ten of them are in possession of a single dollar; still each enjoys himself at home with the produce of his estate, and the money arising from the sale of a horse or a few cows is always more than sufficient to procure him the secondary articles that come from England.[16]

Objective descriptions of the rich and poor are difficult to obtain from travel accounts so we should be on our guard. By looking only at the extremes of the range, we develop no feeling for the proportions of the population living in conditions of either opulence or abject poverty. The cited examples may be rare exceptions that could be quite misleading for several reasons. For one thing, we tend to become inured to local conditions and observe only those people and environments in contrast to our own norm. It is not uncommon to observe poverty, even when not purposefully looking for it, in an unfamiliar area.

An extension of the familiarity principle arises particularly in the case of America. A traveler to this continent whose journey had begun in Canada no doubt would have experienced differing reactions to his sur-roundings than did a traveler whose journey had begun in Philadelphia. One perspicacious observer noted his own differing reactions on two trips to America, one preceded by moderate living and the other by relative affluence.[17]

Alexis de Tocqueville suggested that an American, on the other hand, may have been vindictive in his views of Europe. "On arriving in Europe, he at once finds that we are not as engrossed by the United States and the great people who inhabit them as he had supposed; and this begins to annoy him."[18] We might turn the statement around and ask if Tocqueville had eyed his own France as meticulously and critically in his book on the French Revolution as he did when writing about America.

THE PROBLEM OF THE LIFE CYCLE

An American reader may be uneasy at this stage of the description. Why wouldn't an American child be barefooted and in torn clothes in the summertime in the wilderness? Tom Sawyer went barefoot whenever he could—and he was not poor. The hovels inhabited by many people on the frontier and elsewhere may have been worse than those in Europe, but they were only temporary. Conventional wisdom dictates that most Americans began with very little but made rapid improvements. The life-cycle pattern of individuals showed a strong improvement from age 21 to age 50 or 60, particularly in wealth in housing.

Yet we cannot wish relative poverty away; nor can we say that we should not count these poor because someday they would be rich. The fact that my grandfather lived in a sod hut during his first years in America and in a fine home as an older man did not preclude his being counted in the census at a lower wealth level when he was young. The problem of teenage unemployment cannot be disregarded by stating that these young people probably will find employment in the future. Furthermore, the evidence from censuses indicates that relative inequality of wealth within specific age groups was, on the average, not much less than overall inequality.[19]

A STATISTICAL APPROACH

One traveler's comments on America technically reflect only those variables he chose to observe, not a larger set. Furthermore, the lower and upper limits of each variable—the perceived extent of poverty or affluence exhibited in housing, clothing, or estate values—depended on his diligence in seeking to find them. The traveler may have been completely biased with regard to certain aspects of American life. For example, Count Francesco dal Verme visited the United States in 1784, when he had occasion to dine with President Washington and with Robert Morris, among others. He felt that while the large cities of the North and Charleston in the South were worthy of his attention, preferably one should make the trip from Philadelphia to Charleston by sea, since "everything beyond this is sterile uniformity."[20]

How could he have known this to be true? Was it possible that there was a great deal of relative inequality among people in that unobserved region of "sterile uniformity"? A wealthy nobleman may have been unable to make accurate assessments of significant differences between houses whose values were $20, $40, $80, or even $160. The occasional log cabin worth $5, or a substantial stone home worth $320, $640, or even $1,280 may not have been visible from the ordinary road even if the count had traversed thoroughly the region in question. Nor might a nobleman have taken the trouble to note various qualities and amounts of clothing, food, furniture, domestic animals, and so forth, owned by the residents. After all, he was neither census taker nor tax collector—and not interested in minute details. Thus, he may have inadvertently failed to see or make note of a large part of existing relative inequality.

We must be cautious in judging the degree of objectivity in the observations made by the 70-odd foreign-born visitors to this young country who recorded their travels during the quarter century after Independence. This need for discretion also applies to our interpretation of those writers who warned us that any one person's perceptions may not have been the same as those of another onlooker. Henry Wansey's 1794 tract on America is one such case. After criticizing other writers' judgments, he provided his own categorical conclusions. He stated that America provided a new system, "without Kings, without Nobles, without a hierarchy."[21] This fact led him to make assertions about a homogeneity in condition. "You behold a certain plainness and simplicity of manners, which bespeak temperance, equality of condition, and a sober use of the faculties of the mind."[22] Tocqueville described America in strikingly similar terms a generation later.[23]

Was Wansey correct in his assessment of a happy mediocrity? We know that he was an English middle-class textile manufacturer, a fact that makes us somewhat uncomfortable when reading his observations about poverty, just as we are uneasy when considering that Tocqueville was the son of aristocratic parents. Could anyone who enjoyed relatively high consumption standards perceive effectively the shades of difference in well-being among persons having lower consumption standards without scientific measurement? To be fair, Wansey must be given credit for his attempts at such measurement when he tried to find the destitute. In Hartford he noted, "I never observed a single person in rags or with any appearance of distress or poverty; yet I looked into all the poor habitations I could find, which were few indeed."[24]

It may be that few among America's free population lived in poverty, with the destitute family being a rarity. On the other hand, is it possible that there were relatively few rich persons in the country, with the truly wealthy family also being a rarity? Here we are on firmer ground in accepting the observations about America's rich, as noted by approximately 70 foreign authors. Generally, these persons were guests in one, two, or three or more of the 25 most elegant homes in the United States. Such homes would be a stark contrast to the country's 25 worst shacks, which these visitors would probably never have seen, let alone visited.

In the 1790s, it seems that Philadelphia was on the route of all travelers. The most prominent home in the city belonged to William and Anne Bingham, an edifice described by Wansey as follows:

> I found a magnificent house and gardens in the best English style, with elegant and even superb furniture. The chairs of the drawing room were from Seddon's in London, of the newest taste; the back in the form of a lyre, with festoons of crimson and yellow silk. The curtains of the room a festoon of the same. The carpet one of Moore's most expensive patterns.[25]

Many had viewed the home, since the Binghams were known for their elegant life style and lavish entertaining. Their guests included not only Philadelphians, but also politicians—especially when the city was the seat of government—as well as a wide circle of friends and relatives from more distant parts of this country; in addition, numerous travelers from abroad enjoyed the Bingham hospitality.

There is the possibility, therefore, that writings about America suffered as much from overexposure to the rich as from underexposure to the poor. The foreign visitor may have missed a visit to the elegant home of Elias Hasket Derby in Salem, Massachusetts, or to the more distant Ramsey house near Knoxville, Tennessee, but a visit to the Philadelphia Bingham residence would have had a profound effect on his feeling about the highest standards of living.[26] Anyone who had viewed such a luxurious establishment near the beginning of his American visit indeed might have found the rest of America by contrast to be in a condition of "sterile uniformity." George Logan, an affluent doctor and farmer who lived on the outskirts of Philadelphia, found the Binghams to be leaders in the Federalist social life; it was Logan's judgment that such high living would lead to the corruption of America.[27] Further evidence of the Binghams' social aspirations is that in their European travels they managed to be presented at the courts of Louis XVI in France, and of George III in England.[28]

There is enough negative evidence to cast a shadow over the veracity of the four volumes written by the duc de La Rochefoucauld-Liancourt, the ultimate in American travel journals in the early federal period. Was his picture of America an adequate one? Were the best homes he saw in America only middling by European standards? Where did he reside during his travels? Which routes did he follow? More likely than not, the main routes of travel included homes, in view from the roads, which were likely to have been atypical. On maps of the 1790s, dots that represent homes generally appear only along major routes. It seems unlikely that most travelers ventured far from the main highways, if at all.

Before we describe the European and American statistics available at the turn of the eighteenth century, we should consider the writings of our more sagacious American thinkers. Since statistical counts are far from complete, it is possible that some remarkable insights might come from native-born observers less exposed to the extremes of wealth in Europe or at least more attuned to American standards. Two sources appear to be especially fruitful: one is, surprisingly, the writings of John Adams; the other is a mathematical model of the lognormal distribution of wealth presented to Congress in 1798 by Oliver Wolcott, but perhaps developed by David Rittenhouse. Adams provides specific testable hypotheses concerning the rich and the poor in America; Wolcott's lognormal distribution allows us to generalize about the shares of total wealth associated with various percentiles of the labor force.

VIEWS OF JOHN ADAMS

One man who gave a great deal of thought to the prevalence of the poor and the rich in society was John Adams. In his thinking, each group was vital to the whole because of its possible dominance, or tyranny, over society; these forces were strategic in determining the design of governments so that each group had proper representation but could not exercise a dominating influence.

Adams's logic for a bicameral legislature hinged on the argument that a house of representatives would represent all men, but that a senate would reflect the interests of the minority who owned property. In his view, it was quite important that less than half of the population of adult males owned property. If more than half had owned property, then general representation of the population would both reflect and protect the property holders' interests; in this event, the need for two legislative bodies would be much less urgent.

John Adams stated his views in many treatises and speculated about population counts in at least two passages, one written in 1787 and the other in 1817. The first reference apparently focused on England, but perhaps pertains to the United States.

> Suppose a nation, rich and poor, high and low, ten millions in number, all assembled together; not more than one or two millions will have lands, houses, or any personal property; if we take into account the women and children, or even if we leave them out of the question, a great majority of every nation is wholly destitute of property, except a small quantity of clothes, and a few trifles of other movables. Would Mr. Nedham be responsible that, if all were to be decided by a vote of the majority, the eight or nine millions who have no property, would not think of usurping over the rights of the one or two millions who have? Property is surely a right of mankind as really as liberty. Perhaps, at first, prejudice, habit, shame or fear, principle or religion, would restrain the poor from attacking the rich, and the idle from usurping on the industrious; but the time would not be long before courage and enterprise would come, and pretexts be invented by degrees, to countenance the majority in dividing all the property among them, or at least, in sharing it equally with its present possessors. Debts would be abolished first; taxes laid heavy on the rich, and not at all on the others; and at last a downright equal division of every thing be demanded, and voted.[29]

In this statement, made just before the French Revolution, there is a clear expression of the reasoning for the design of government. Such a government is based on presumed facts regarding the distribution of wealth within a society. Interests of the alleged minority of wealth holders, 10 to 20 percent of the population, must be protected from the will of the majority, the other 80 to 90 percent of the people. It would be extremely interesting to find the statistical information on which Adams based his assessment of the population. It was an uncanny guess in the case of England, as a recent study of property distribution for that country shows. The proportion of properties that were owner-occupied in England and Wales was .221 in rural districts, .162 for urban areas, and .204 for all entries reported in the 121 volumes of land tax records for 1798.[30]

What is surprising about the passage cited above is that Adams made no mention of the United States as an exception to his generalization that the "great majority of every nation is wholly destitute of property," and this was only two years before he would become vice-president. Just how he perceived the American distribution of wealth during his years as president is open to debate, but we do have an expression of his views 30 years later, this time clearly distinguishing Europe from America.

> In all the nations of Europe, the number of persons, who have a penny, is double those who have a groat; admit all these to an equality of power, and you would soon see how the groats would be divided. Yet, in a few days, the party of the pennies

and the party of the groats would be found to exist again, and a new revolution and a new division must ensue.

If there is anywhere an exception from this reasoning it is in America; nevertheless, there is in these United States a majority of persons who have no property, over those who have any.[31]

Certainly the intent of the passage is that the proportion of property holders was less than one-third in Europe, but perhaps only half of this, or one-sixth, if we distinguish a groat from property. However, Adams's assertion that less than half of Americans owned property is rather astounding. I believe we can view this as a serious statement of perceived fact and not as a passing remark. Adams made the estimate in a letter from Quincy dated 17 June 1817 to James Madison, who had just retired as president and was returning to his interest in agriculture, landholding, and the landless.[32] Adams was very familiar with landownership patterns and had himself an estate consisting largely of land valued at about $100,000.[33]

It is possible that Adams based his guesstimate on the Boston area, or perhaps on Virginia, since he addressed his remarks to Madison of Orange County, Virginia. I will show that less than 50 percent of the people of Boston owned real estate (1,999 of 4,500 adult males in 1798) and that slaves (held by one-third of southern white families in 1800) might have enhanced concentration to the point where landowners were in the minority in certain areas.[34]

In any case, the hypothesis that landowners were a minority among freemen of voting age is one of the major propositions to be tested in this volume. The hypothesis is far different from the idea of free land, which would give rise to the assertion that 90 percent of Americans were farmers and, thus, that 90 percent were freeholders.

SHARES OF WEALTH

Adams did not confine his analysis to the landless alone. He considered the power of the aristocracy in some quantitative statements concerning the shares of total wealth held by the rich. This is an issue of continuing interest today. Did the top 10 percent of potential voters own half of the wealth? Did the top 1 percent own one-third of the land, buildings, wharves, ships, farm animals, and slaves? More specifically, given that the number of free adult males 21 and over in the United States in 1800 was about 880,000, we would like to know the shares of wealth held by the wealthiest 88, or 880, or even the top 8.8 men.

Here again, Adams astounds us with his assertions that a wealthy aristocracy did prevail in America and that it was of great importance. He even intimated that the group was comparable to the aristocracy in England. In a manuscript penned in 1808, presumably from his home in Quincy, Massachusetts, Adams made an extensive analysis.

> Infinite art and chicanery have been employed in this country to deceive the people in their understanding of this term *aristocracy,* as well as that of being *well-born,* as if aristocracy could not exist without hereditary power and exclusive privileges; and as if a man could not be well-born, without being a hereditary nobleman and a peer of the realm.
>
> Chancellor Livingston inherited a name, numerous and wealthy family connections, and a fine manor. These are all hereditary privileges, and have given him more influence in this country than all the titles and immense landed estates of the Duke of Norfolk, with all the hereditary rank and seat in the house of lords, have given him in England. Mr. John Randolph inherited his name, family connections, his fine plantations and thousand negroes, which have given him more power in this country than the Duke of Bedford has in England, and more than he would have, if he possessed all the brilliant wit, fine imagination, and flowing eloquence of that celebrated Virginian. Were not, then, Mr. Livingston and Mr. Randolph well-born? The state of Connecticut has always been governed by an aristocracy, more decisively than the empire of Great Britain. Half a dozen or, at most, a dozen families, have controlled that country when a colony, as well as since it has been a state.[35]

The comparison between Randolph and Bedford is striking because the duke of Bedford was the richest man in England, at least as recorded in the land tax records for England and Wales in 1798. The duke's 319 properties in Bedford County accounted for 8 percent of the county's total valuation, and his thousands of properties in Devon, Southampton, Surrey, and Middlesex, and even many solid city blocks in London, accounted for even more of the country's real estate. Yet the duke's property was only about 1,400 times the average wealth per family in England and Wales. If Randolph had 1,000 slaves, perhaps it is conceivable that the Adams assertion was correct; but we must investigate land and other values before coming to a conclusion.

If we grant that slavery in the South produced substantial inequality, we might be unconvinced that Connecticut's aristocracy rested on vast accumulations of wealth, particularly since Adams suggested neither names of the wealthy nor examples of holdings. Nevertheless, he asserted that an aristocracy may arise among merchants, manufacturers, shippers, and the "moneyed interest." And he does give us a spectacular example for Massachusetts, as stated in a letter to John Taylor of Virginia.

> I remember the time, Mr. Taylor, when one thousand families depended on Mr. Hancock for their daily bread; perhaps more. . . . If he could, he was an aristocrat,

according to my definition and conscientious opinion. Let me appeal now to your own experience. . . . Are there not in your own Caroline County in Virginia, two or three, or four, five or six, eight or ten great planters, who, if united, can carry any point in your election? . . . Give me leave to add a few words on this topic. I remember the time when three gentlemen—Thomas Hancock, Charles Apthorp, and Thomas Green, the three most opulent merchants in Boston, all honorable, virtuous, and humane men,—if united, could have carried any election almost unanimously in the town of Boston.[36]

A standard of control of 1,000 men is suggested as the rough rule of superior economic power; its possibility seems most remote in the case of Boston. Yet we shall see that in 1771 John Hancock reported a value for money and stock that was 750 times the value reported by the average tax-payer of Massachusetts, and not all people were taxpayers.[37] We are in-grained with the idea that the ownership of land was so equally distributed that young America had to be an egalitarian nation. Nevertheless, an exami-nation of ownership plats at the turn of the century reveals that William Bingham owned over a million acres of land in Maine. A skeptic might quickly point out that it was relatively worthless land; and, indeed, we must come to grips with the differences in values of land within the country.

Finally, John Adams argued his case for an aristocracy in America based partly on marriage and inheritance.

You [John Taylor] had the honor and felicity to marry the only child of my honest and sincere friend, the Honorable John Penn of North Carolina. From this marriage, you derived, with an amiable consort, a handsome fortune. . . . I will be bolder still, Mr. Taylor. Would Washington have ever been commander of the revolutionary army or president of the United States, if he had not married the rich widow of Mr. Custis? Would Jefferson ever have been president of the United States if he had not married the daughter of Mr. Wales?[38]

The Adams framework of wealth distribution is really quite specific. Its base is the population of free adult males 21 and older, or about 880,000 in 1800. About half of these individuals had very little or no wealth and perhaps 25 to 50 men, about one, two, or three persons from each of the 17 states, had very substantial wealth equivalent to 1,000 times the average. Shortly we shall sketch a possible distribution for all wealth ranges, based on Adams's parameter estimates, the lognormal model.

THE LOGNORMAL CONFIGURATION

A mathematical form called a lognormal frequency curve often ap-pears in the wealth statistics for the end of the eighteenth century; it is the familiar bell-shaped normal curve when the wealth values are expressed in logarithms. The unique feature of a lognormal table is that if one knows the share of wealth of, say, the top 10 percent of wealthholders, then the shares of all other percentile groups can be determined.

Suppose the share of the top 10 percent of people is 50 percent of all wealth $(N_x, A_x) = (.10,.50)$. A search can be made in the set of lognormal tables for the one having this parameter, and the following figures can be recorded immediately:

N_x	A_x
.001	.035
.01	.15
.10	.50
.50	.90
1.00	1.00

The top one person in a thousand would have 3.5 percent of the aggregate wealth of all people; one person in every hundred would have 15 percent of wealth; our chosen 10 percent of persons has, of course, half of the wealth; finally, the top half would control 90 percent of all wealth. What we are asserting is that in a given community where the top 10 percent have half the wealth, it is often true that the top half of the community has 90 percent of the wealth, while the bottom half holds only 10 percent. It is also true that in a series of communities of this type, the share of the top 1 percent varies somewhat, but tends to be about 15 percent.

Benjamin Franklin provides us with an excellent example of the implications of the configuration. He recommended a wealth level of £1,000 as a requirement for voting in elections for the Pennsylvania upper house in 1789.[39] In so doing, he judged that only one person in 50 in the state would be able to qualify, $N_{x> £ 1,000} = .02$. A rough calculation can be made of the share of wealth of this group and it appears to be about 14 percent.[40] If $(N_x, A_x) = (.02,.14)$, we can find Franklin's lognormal table at $G = .50$ (see table 1). Franklin's estimate, in fact, indicates his belief that Pennsylvania was quite egalitarian; the inequality coefficient is quite moderate. Corresponding to each table is a general index of relative dispersion, the Gini coefficient of inequality, G, which varies between 0 (if there is perfect equality) and 1 (if there is perfect inequality). The former case would be one where the top 1 percent would have 1 percent of wealth.[41]

Franklin's estimate for Pennsylvania intriguingly yields a coefficient that is halfway between perfect equality and perfect inequality. We shall test this particular hypothesis in chapter 2.

The statements by John Adams about the shares of the rich also suggest a possible distribution and level of inequality, this time for the United States. The intent of his observations is to suppose that 50 people at the turn of the century had 1,000 times the wealth of the average individual. A general scheme could be concocted by considering that N_x was 50 of 880,000 free males above age 21, for a ratio of .000057, and that their share was 1,000 times as large, implying an $A_x = .057$, or 5.7 percent, of national wealth. A search of the lognormal table in this case suggests a substantially greater concentration of wealth than in the Franklin estimate (see table 2).

Perhaps Adams was suggesting only 10 persons, at most, in this elite group or possibly, at the limit, only Randolph and Hancock; lognormal schedules for these possibilities are also shown. The above three lognormal tables have very large coefficients, of .78–.89, which are interesting from several standpoints. They are (or are nearly) in the range of coefficients for the inequality of wealth found for the United States for the present time

TABLE 1
FRANKLIN'S HYPOTHESIS ABOUT THE DISTRIBUTION OF WEALTH IN PENNSYLVANIA, 1789

Proportion of Persons Having Wealth Exceeding a Given Level (N_x)	Proportion of Wealth Held by the N_x Group (A_x)
.001	.02
.01	.08
.02	.14
.10	.37
.50	.83
1.00	1.00
Inequality, G	.50

Source: Compiled from a computer program generating a lognormal distribution with G=.50. See J. Aitchison and J.A.C. Brown, *The Lognormal Distribution with Special Reference to its Uses in Economics* (Cambridge: Cambridge University Press, 1969), pp. 8–10, 13, 113, 154–55. For the Franklin considerations, see ch. 1, nn. 39–41.

Note: For example, line 4 says that the top 10 percent of persons would have 37 percent of the wealth if the distribution were lognormal with a Gini coefficient of relative inequality (G) of .50 (described in ch. 1, n. 41).

TABLE 2
ADAMS'S HYPOTHESIS ABOUT THE DISTRIBUTION OF WEALTH
IN THE UNITED STATES, 1787: THREE INTERPRETATIONS

50 People		10 People		2 People	
N_x	A_x	N_x	A_x	N_x	A_x
.000057	.057	.000011	.011	.0000022	.0022
.001	.20	.001	.13	.001	.09
.01	.47	.01	.37	.01	.28
.10	.84	.10	.76	.10	.67
.50	.99	.50	.98	.50	.96
1.00	1.00	1.00	1.00	1.00	1.00
G=.89		G=.84		G=.78	

Sources: See table 1 and *The Works of John Adams,* ed. Charles Francis Adams (Boston: Little, Brown, 1856), 6:8–9, 460–62, 506–10, 530.

Note: Adams's first interpretation (G=.89) is a lognormal curve where the top 50 among 880,000 persons had wealth averaging 1,000 times that of the overall average.

N_x = Proportion of persons having wealth exceeding a given level.
A_x = Proportion of wealth held by the N_x group.

as well as for an earlier period (1850 to 1870), thus suggesting that inequality of wealth remained quite constant during the century following federation. We also note that the Adams lognormal schema shows the lower half of the population with almost no wealth. If the bottom half had but 2–4 percent of wealth, it would mean that their average was only 4–8 percent of mean wealth, or less than $50 per person, hardly enough to account for a horse or a few cows.

There is the further ramification from the Adams assertions about the rich in England and America, that he estimated inequality coefficients in Europe to have been .85 or larger. This indeed was the case, as we shall show later.[42] We also should consider the possibility of extreme inequality. John Taylor of Caroline County, Virginia, suggested that a monarchy might consist of the crown, lords, and the people, with each group having one-third of aggregate wealth. This scheme shows some vague consistencies with the lognormal configuration and it demonstrates almost unbelievable inequality. If G = .99, then among 2 million English families, 50 would have one-third, and 1,350 would have two-thirds, of total wealth. The 50 might comprise the entourage of the crown, and the 1,350 figure is reasonably close to the number in the English titled group at the time.

Perhaps royalty in some countries did control such large proportions of total wealth. The most celebrated case might be that of Count Sheremetev of Russia who, in 1798, had 200,000 serfs.[43]

THE FRANKLIN AND ADAMS HYPOTHESES

A review of the literature on the inequality of wealth in eighteenth-century America leads to two quite distinct hypotheses. First, there is the Franklin hypothesis of relative equality, with a Gini coefficient of about .5. Though this level technically pertains only to Pennsylvania, I find it useful to apply it as a minimum statement of inequality for the nation as a whole. Persons subscribing to this hypothesis generally would have in mind a country with abundant land and sparse population. Such a dispersion of wealth would be consistent with a philosophy affirming human equality and the equal rights of men. It would be understood, in this case, that some inequality would naturally exist because of differences in age, nativity, and urban/rural residence. For example, a young man beginning his farming activity on the frontier would own relatively little compared to a man of age 50 who owned a well-established farm. Another factor is that inheritances would lead to some moderate perpetuation of existing wealth differences from generation to generation. Large families would militate against a substantial transfer of wealth; with greater fragmentation of an estate in succeeding generations, each family would re-enter the wealth distribution with a more equal share. Immigrants would be in almost the same economic position as the young native-born in larger families. A few merchants and shippers in urban areas would emerge with wealth, but an essentially rural economy would be dominant; certainly manufacturing would be on a relatively small scale. Some might conceive of Gini levels of wealth inequality as low as .45 or .40 within specific age-nativity-urbanity groups, where the vast majority were landowners; in this case, equality would exist in reality as well as in theory.

The second, clear, alternative is the Adams hypothesis, assuming an inequality of wealth of, say, $G = .8$, or larger. The few would hold large shares of the total wealth at any given time because society contained a small natural aristocracy. This would not arise from ability so much as from ambition on the part of particular groups or persons. Perhaps the rewards to this "aristocracy" in one generation might be passed on to the next generation, at least in part, through inheritance. In 1813 Jefferson succinctly stated his opinion of such an elite group in a letter to Adams: "I agree with you that there is a natural aristocracy among men. The grounds of this are virtue and talents. . . . The artificial aristocracy is a mischievous ingredient in government, and provision should be made to prevent its ascendancy."[44] The subscriber to these ideas might assert that society could begin with a modest inequality level at G = .5 or lower, but that the condition would change rather quickly because of the aristocracy, natural or artificial; the change could cause inequality to rise to a level of G = .8.[45]

A further expansion of these ideas is fruitful, but let us first present the quantitative configuration of the two views boldly, using the lognormal configurations (see table 3). There is a stark contrast between the two levels. One person in 1,000 has the equivalent of 16 shares in the one case, and 100 shares in the other, and this might make the difference between oligarchic control and its absence. A focus on the lower tail, or the lower half of the distribution, becomes a question of whether the poor had 17 percent of wealth or only 3 percent. This difference can be translated into the possession of plots of land, cows, and horses, or even the most humble of log huts as compared to a modest dwelling. The gnawing question is whether almost half of Americans had such small accumulations of wealth.

The average wealth in America per adult free male 21 and older was, roughly, $1,000 in the decade before 1800. When we consider this fact, assuming lognormal distributions and Gini levels of .5 and .8, the results are as shown in table 4. Figure 1 shows that each distribution has a mean of $1,000 but that dispersion is quite different, depending on the level of inequality. There would be about 8 times as many persons with holdings above $10,000 in the one case, as opposed to the other (.0147 instead of

TABLE 3
FRANKLIN'S AND ADAMS'S HYPOTHESES COMPARED

Proportion of Persons Having Wealth Exceeding a Given Level (N_X)	Proportion of Wealth Held (A_X)	
	Franklin G=.5	Adams G=.8
.001	.016	.100
.01	.084	.300
.10	.37	.70
.50	.83	.97
1.00	1.00	1.00

Sources: See tables 1 and 2.

.0019). On the other hand, the concentration of poor, with half of the population below $194, at G = .8, means that many would not have had resources sufficient to purchase land. The two curves shown in figure 1 have equivalent areas above $2,350.

OTHER ALTERNATIVES

It is possible that the two hypotheses presented in figure 1 or in the accompanying tables could withstand a test of statistical verification, using actual wealth data from the end of the eighteenth century. On the one hand, society may have been truly egalitarian, with a Gini coefficient of .5, or, on the other hand, strongly inegalitarian, with a coefficient greater than .8. Or perhaps the true situation was nearer to being halfway between the two hypothetical states.

Furthermore, the distribution of wealth for the United States at that time might not have demonstrated a lognormal shape. Mathematical statisticians and econometricians are able to suggest innumerable alternatives, including the binomial, Poisson, gamma, and beta distributions.[46] Usually, these possibilities are stated with parameters tracing skewed distributions of curves, with lower tails and extended upper tails above the modal class. A prominent alternative is the Pareto curve, one often showing the rich and poor with shares greater than those held by middle groups, at least as

TABLE 4

DISTRIBUTION OF WEALTH IN THE UNITED STATES,
1790–1800: TWO HYPOTHESES
(males 21 and older)

	Proportion Having Wealth Exceeding a Given Level (N_x)	
Average Level of Wealth	G = .5	G = .8
$10,000	.0019	.0147
1,000	.32	.18
100	.97	.64
10	1.00	1.00
Mean	$1,000	$1,000
Median	634	194
Mode	255	7

Sources: Based on tables 1–3.

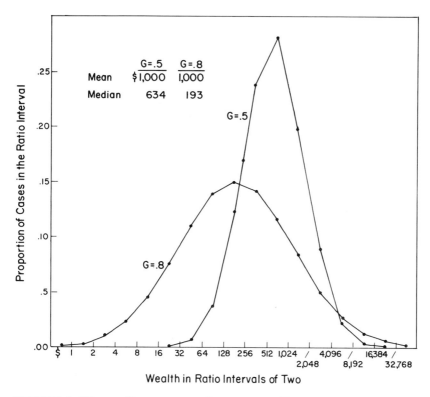

FIGURE 1. WEALTH DISTRIBUTIONS ILLUSTRATING FRANKLIN'S AND ADAMS'S HYPOTHESES

NOTE: The figure exhibits the ratio-scale frequency distributions for the hypotheses about the distribution of wealth suggested by Benjamin Franklin (G = .5) and John Adams (G = .8), assuming that the distributions are lognormal and that average wealth is $1,000.

compared to a lognormal curve with the same Gini coefficient. Unfortunately, the Pareto form is probably unrealistic if accepted through its entire range of wealth.[47] Technically, it has the shape of a reverse-J with no lower tail below the modal class, a configuration not precisely verified by data sets for wealth. Nevertheless, we should be open to the possibility of some variation of this fundamental form.[48]

There is some concrete evidence in the observations regarding the distribution of wealth in 1798 made by America's secretary of the treasury, Oliver Wolcott; his perceptions provide the basis for chapter 5. Rather definite statements can be made as to whether he thought in terms of a two-tail distribution, a reverse-J shape, or whether he even understood the concept of a distribution. Wolcott's 1798 speculation pertains to a most remarkable lognormal curve of dwelling house values. The actual statistics of the 1798 distribution, derived from a tax on dwelling values levied in 1798–1799, also will appear in chapter 3. In addition, the size of the Gini coefficient will be related to the hypotheses posited in figure 1.

EVIDENCE OF AMERICAN EQUALITY

The assertion of equality in this country was based on the relatively plentiful availability of land. Almost any American considering the plight of Europe's masses must have been struck by this reality. The vast amount of acreage in western New York, western Pennsylvania, Georgia, Tennessee, Kentucky, and later in Ohio, must have seemed almost incredible. An American could obtain land cheaply relative to his wage rate; he could become a landowner rather easily. Thus, we can expect the proportion of adult free males owning land to have been much higher here than in Europe. We must use empirical data to ascertain whether the ownership proportion surpassed 50 percent—the Adams hypothesis—but in any case, ownership rates were indeed handsome.

Washington learned from first-hand experience that American tenants and prospective purchasers could be very independent in their thinking and actions because they had so many choices in land settlement; this he learned as the owner of land in western Pennsylvania and in the Kanawha valley of Virginia (now West Virginia).[49] To be sure, the tenant—and possible landowner—was in a much stronger position, with his alternative settlement possibilities, than were the masses of tenants, crofters, and farmhands in Europe.

In the 1780s and 1790s various states offered vast amounts of acreage to prospective buyers at a very low cost per acre. The commonwealth sold land in western Pennsylvania for from less than 3 cents to about 5 cents per acre to persons who were able to show evidence of an intention to settle. Virginia sold its western land at 2 cents an acre, regardless of whether purchasers were speculators or settlers.[50] Similar conditions prevailed from Georgia to Maine. The opportunities for ordinary settlers to purchase land would have strengthened American equality if property transfers had occurred at a rate faster than the growth in the labor force. At the same time, however, large purchases of acreage by speculators (most often absentee owners) may have established patterns of inequality as strong as, or possibly stronger than, those in existence on the east coast.[51]

Some contemporary leaders who saw greater equality in America believed that it would continue for a long period until the country was fully settled. Others thought equality would diminish rather rapidly, while yet others felt that equality had never existed. These feelings were expressed by Madison, Hamilton, and Pinckney at the 1787 Federal Convention. Charles Pinckney reported:

> The people of the U S are perhaps the most singular of any we are acquainted with.—among them there are fewer distinctions of fortune & less of rank; than among the inhabitants of any other nation.—every freeman has a right to the same protection & security and a very moderate share of property entitles them to the possession of all the honors & privileges the public can bestow.—hence arises a greater equality, than is to be found among the people of any other country, and an equality which is more likely to continue.—I say this equality is likely to continue; because in a new country, possessing immense tracts of uncultivated lands—where every temptation is offered to emigration & where industry must be rewarded with competency, there will be few poor & few dependent.[52]

Madison concurred with Pinckney, but felt that coming changes would alter the distribution; he was painfully grappling with the effects of increases in both population and land supply a decade before Malthus wrote his famous tract. Madison wrote:

> We cannot however be regarded even at this time, as one homogeneous mass, in which every thing that affects a part will affect in the same manner the whole. In framing a system which we wish to last for ages, we shd. not lose sight of the changes which ages will produce. An increase of population will of necessity increase the proportion of those who will labour under all the hardships of life, & secretly sigh for a more equal distribution of its blessings. These may in time outnumber those who are placed above the feelings of indigence.[53]

Alexander Hamilton's views came closer to those of Adams in his estimates of actual inequality, but he extended these concepts in forecasting new increases in the disparity. "Real liberty is neither found in despotism or the extremes of democracy, but in moderate governments. . . . But if we incline too much to democracy, we shall soon shoot into a monarchy. The difference of property is already great amongst us. Commerce and industry will still increase the disparity."[54]

Adams gave some credence to the view that inequality may have increased in the generation after 1776, and at the same time offered an explanation of why American inequality may have been as great as that in England.

Have those principles of government which we have discovered, and those institutions which we have invented, which have established a "moral liberty" undiscovered and universal, uninvented by all nations before us, "inhibited monopolies and incorporations?" Is not every bank a monopoly? Are there not more banks in the United States than ever before existed in any nation under heaven? Are not these banks established by law upon a more aristocratical principle than any others under the sun? Are there not more legal corporations . . . than are to be found in any known country of the world?[55]

CENSUS COUNTS

The search for a scientific measure of the shares of aggregate wealth belonging to the rich and poor in a society is an arduous task. Generally speaking, the concept, let alone the reality, of counting all of the people in a nation and recording even one characteristic or determining the socio-economic status for each person did not exist either in Europe or in the United States during this period. Only the detailed Scandinavian censuses of occupations, the Pennsylvania occupational censuses beginning about 1786, and the New York censuses of property holders dating from 1786 were exceptions to the rule.[56]

The first modern British census for 1801 provides tallies of persons employed either in agriculture or in broad categories of trade, manufacturing, or handicraft; that for Pennsylvania was more suggestive in at least some townships and counties, where the terms "tenant" and "landlord" were used. Arthur Young, Sir John Sinclair, and Jeremy Bentham in England clearly considered the possibility of complete enumerations. In 1798 Bentham proposed a magnificent tally sheet, or "Table of Cases Calling for Relief," for eight major classifications and 137 other categories, including physical and mental handicaps, as well as causes of unemployment. Clearly, he hoped to have his table completed within various parishes, but he had little success.[57] On the whole, European data sets are less than complete, except for the Scandinavian data.

If each state or country had conducted a thorough census of wealth at the end of the eighteenth century, we would have a source for definite specifications concerning wealthholding in each land. Since this is not the case, we must make judgments based on partial information. There was no counterpart to the unique censuses of wealth conducted by United States authorities in connection with the censuses of population in 1850, 1860, and 1870. Yet there was a census of the value of real estate conducted in the United States in 1798. This census allows us to make definite statements concerning the distribution of wealth at the end of the century. The summary results of a study of these data appear in chapter 2. The distribution will be compared to the results of studies made of wealthholdings in several European countries at the time.

CONSUMPTION AND INEQUALITY

This book deals almost exclusively with the subject of inequality in America, as measured by differences in wealthholding among the country's population. Inequalities in income, consumption, or even saving receive less attention for two reasons. In the literature, wealth was the concept most often considered to distinguish socioeconomic groups at the end of the eighteenth century. The very terms *rich* and *poor, inheritance, estate,* or even *aristocracy* frequently acquired specific meaning from their associations with wealth. In addition, for this period, the primary data sets demonstrating group disparities are for the most part items of wealth. (U.S. censuses reveal no economic distinctions between the nobility, landowners, crofters, tenants, farm hands, day laborers, or the destitute, as do the Scandinavian censuses for the same era.) Yet, great disparities of wealth, in turn, could lead to substantial disparities in income, consumption, and savings within a society that cannot be ignored. A wealthy man could afford a fine home and still have large net savings if his total earnings, including capital gains in property, were large. His standards of consumption in housing, clothing, carriages, and amusement easily could have been the envy of those below him in economic status. Our eighteenth-century observers were not oblivious to U.S. expenditures for luxury goods, especially those imported from England, that placed the new nation at a trade disadvantage.

We will investigate the inequality among various economic groups of disbursements for food, clothing, furniture, and shelter, and compare these inequality levels with those for wealth. Surely the amounts spent on food would be more equally distributed than was wealth—or probably clothing. Only outlays for housing may have exhibited as much inequality in distribution among the population as did wealth. Characteristically, Adams held views about the elasticity of consumption value with respect to wealth. He felt that eating and drinking would show little variation between groups, with the lowest ranks drinking more ale and porter, and tending to be more intemperate. However, he seemed to feel that proportional increases in expenditures on clothing, furniture, and carts or carriages all rose in about the same ratios as did wealth, in moving from the lowest to the middle, to the top group.[58]

It seems Adams was stating that consumption (C) is related to wealth (W) by the relationship $C = aW^b$, where a and b are parameters. An example in the case of housing expenditures might be $C_H = .15W^{1.0}$, and the housing distribution possibly might be a lognormal distribution, except with values only 15 percent of the original. In the formulation given above, the b is an elasticity coefficient of 1, and Adams judged that this was the case for housing, furniture, and perhaps for clothing. The latter may be a surprising inclusion, but there were many gradations in the dollar value of clothing in that age before ready-made apparel.[59] Food would have had an elasticity coefficient far less than 1; if it were .5 when the Gini coefficient of wealth was .7, then the Gini coefficient for food expenditures would be .4.[60] An example of an elasticity coefficient greater than 1 would be leisure. In 1798, one Massachusetts farmer suggested that only 1 man in 8 could enjoy the luxury of leisure.[61] "Leisure for study must ever be the portion of the few," was the way Adams stated it.[62] Suppose that leisure had an elasticity coefficient of 2.0 with respect to wealth; in this case the Gini coefficient for leisure might be .85.[63]

The purpose of these calculations is to demonstrate that the wealth variable is only a proxy for the style of living of the population in a given economy. Obviously, it is an imperfect measure, since some individuals lived very frugally even if they were rich; others tended to spend all of their incomes; yet others lived better than they could afford, as attested by debtor files.[64]

INCOME AND INEQUALITY

An income distribution in some ways is superior to a wealth distribution in portraying the economic well-being of all people. This is particularly true for the 20 to 70 percent of those who have essentially no wealth at all in real or personal estate but do have income. Differences in incomes of those with little or no wealth display disparities between those in lower middle classes, the poor, and even the destitute that are not adequately measured by wealth statistics. I shall present some estimates of income distribution in chapter 3 that are based on housing data for 1798. These somewhat speculative data will supplement the more solidly based statistics on wealth given in chapter 2.

2

Distribution of Wealth

IT IS SOMETHING of a paradox that the quantifier of American history uncovers more information with which to work, the further back in time one goes. Traditionally, the major sources of information about the wealth of individuals have been the federal censuses from 1850 to 1870; these censuses are invaluable because they provide perhaps the only truly adequate representation of the holding of wealth by all persons. But the data also have limitations because of the somewhat limited span of time they cover. Distributions based on those censuses of wealth have more meaning when they can be viewed from the perspective of change through time. There has been no comprehensive census of wealth since those of the mid-nineteenth century; less complete data sets for more recent periods are based on sample surveys, on inheritances for the rich, and on estates of the deceased.

One major source of data that has not been systematically developed is the inventory of assets in lands, buildings, houses, wharves, and so forth—the real estate owned by individuals—that was the result of the First Direct Tax for the United States in 1798.[1] My work that is based on this tax, described in this chapter as well as in later ones and in appendix 13 has resulted in a statistical summary of this substantial data set in the form of the distribution of wealth in real estate, the predominant form of wealth in 1798. I compare this distribution to its counterpart in 1860 in order to determine in what sense wealth inequality had changed during the first two generations of U.S. nationhood. The results of this comparison are not so clear-cut as I would like them to be. For one thing, there is the problem of a possible measurement error in the 1798 distribution that must be discussed fully.

Comparisons between distributions from the first and second centuries of our country's existence, too, may be flawed, not so much because of measurement error, but because of the many changes that have taken place since the Civil War in all aspects of economic endeavor. Yet, the heritage established after independence and now firmly embedded in our national ideal of equality is a standard that can not be dismissed lightly. Equality among citizens is a cornerstone of both the Constitution and our legal system. The standard of equality is continually being reimposed, to a certain degree, in each generation by means of our established rules of inheritance. It is in this sense that the inequality of wealth existing in 1798 does provide a standard for concepts of equality today.

THE STATISTICAL DATA

While it is an arduous enough procedure to determine the extent of a single individual's wealthholdings, to make such a computation for all individuals in a country is a monumental task. Yet the 1798 census of wealth in the United States accomplished that feat in what amounted to a magnificent display of carefully prepared statistical forms such as initial entries of the number and value of acreage owned or possessed and the value of fixed real estate. The value of housing included various degrees of detail such as plot area, number of stories, windows, and lights, as well as types of building materials; these are described in greater detail in succeeding chapters. Dozens and dozens of enumerators spent countless hours to arrive at totals for the various tax districts of the nation. In most cases, the detailed accounts for real estate only involved filling out at least five forms (labeled A, B, C, D, and E), and sometimes more, all bearing strong evidence of the magnitude of the undertaking.

Examples of the meticulous effort given to the 1798 inventory appear in figures A, B, and C in appendix 13. Here we have the glorious columns of ascertained facts neatly displayed for each of 30 assessment districts in New Hampshire. They purport to display 10-place accuracy in the case of at least one variable and to cover the entire state. The secretary of the treasury of the United States may have had doubts about this degree of precision, yet he did feel the inventories were of sufficient importance that he kept copies as part of his personal papers until his death. These tables can give the reader a preliminary notion of the two essential types of records, "particular" lists B and A, in that order, considered in this and the next chapter. They are worthy of note even though reproduction restrictions make legibility difficult.

In this chapter I choose to proceed directly to my estimate of the inequality of wealth. Its form is very succinct. I shall elaborate upon other elements of this rich data set in succeeding chapters. At this point I can refer to appendixes 1–3, which are broadly related to the 1798 inventory. The first is concerned with the Timothy Pitkin tables listing aggregates of real estate that show a national total of $619,977,245.92 in that year. The total consisted of $479 million in land and houses under $100 in value, and $141 million in houses whose value was above $100; in addition, Pitkin placed a valuation of $140 million on enumerated slaves. It is obvious folly to believe that the tally merited 10-place accuracy, even though accounts were carried to the penny in many cases. Appendix 3 includes a discussion of Pitkin's total and its relationship to a well-known wealth estimate made by Samuel Blodgett for the United States in 1805.

The 1798 inventory, instigated by the secretary of the treasury, Oliver Wolcott, was to serve as a basis for generating revenue for the young government. From this inventory, records for individuals are extant for only 62 of the 357 counties in existence at that time. Furthermore, while there are aggregate summary tables for all 17 states, summary tables exist for only 574 tax districts, of the 687, from only 14 of these states. We must assume that recorded assessments were at or near to market value; Wolcott's investigation in his native state of Connecticut showed that assessment values were within 15 percent of sales value (see appendix 2).

SAMPLING PROCEDURE

My sample of wealth holders for 1798 is derived from the extant records for individuals; it includes 25,975 persons and 43,245 properties in 62 counties, weighted by using the aggregate data for the 687 tax districts in the United States; I constructed an additional data set from the 574 known aggregates plus allocated aggregates for the 113 counties in the three states where there is incomplete detail.[2] My procedure was to weight or "blow up" the disproportionate stratified sample by using the information on aggregate totals from each of the 687 tax districts. The tax districts or county variables are by location: North/South; urban/rural; and distance from one of six major cities or urban locations, with the result that I grouped the data by seven regions or areas.

There were 687 tax districts in 1798; the need for administrative efficiency dictated their sizes. In no case was a district greater than a county, and the number of districts per state varied greatly, from 101 for Massachusetts to as few as 15 for Tennessee or 9 for Delaware. Unfortunately, data for 113 districts (counties) are either incomplete or missing altogether; therefore, I used other kinds of data to allocate wealth values in those cases.[3] The classificatory system appears to be very reasonable in terms of statistical standards, since lognormality appears in (1) the distribution of the 687 acreage aggregates, arrayed from smallest to largest (with only a few being either very large or very small); (2) the arrays of the 687 population totals, as derived from the federal census of 1800; and (3) the 687 wealth averages for adult males, shown in table 5.

The main distribution of wealth in each district is an allocation among free males 21 and older (computed as half of the number in the 16–25 age group, plus all males both in the classes 26–44 and 45 and older, as reported in the 1800 census), resulting in an overall average wealth, for adult white males 21 and older, of $708. This average appears reasonable when compared to the $1,544 average for real estate for males 21 and older in 1860. The average growth rate was 1.9 percent a year in real terms per capita, a rate similar to Raymond Goldsmith's findings of 2.2 percent for reproducible tangible wealth per capita in the period from 1805 to 1850, and the 2.0 percent rate from 1805 to 1950.[4]

THE SAMPLE: DATA AND PROBLEMS

In the 1798 inventory, there were two types of lists, one stating real estate and housing values under $100 (W − H), and the other listing house values of $100 or more (H); most often I found both lists, but in other cases only one or the other; for some Maryland counties I also found a collation of the two lists. I had to abandon an early attempt at collation because of the inordinate time cost. For purposes of this study, I shall use the relative distribution of W − H as my estimate of wealth in rural areas as well as for northern urban areas. (This appears to be a reasonable assumption, as judged from my collations for some Maryland counties, from a complete enumeration and collation I made in the case of Boston, as well as from my partial study of Philadelphia.) For want of a better measure for those areas that suffer most from lack of data, I base the distributions for urban counties in the South on a complete enumeration of collated inventories for Baltimore.[5]

My sample of 45,400 properties and 28,044 owners in 1798 is derived from the list given in table 6, based on samples of 10 percent to 20 percent for the counties in Maine, Massachusetts, Connecticut, and Pennsylvania, and complete enumerations of the available data in the other states. These sample counts are for items drawn from the

TABLE 5
DISTRIBUTION OF AVERAGE WEALTH FOR THE
687 U.S. TAX DISTRICTS, 1798
(males 21 and older)

Average Wealth in Land and Houses[a] (W21)	No. of Districts above W21	Proportion of Adult Males above W21 (N_{W21})	Proportion of Wealth above W21[b] (A_{W21})
$3,000	3	.0014	.007 (.006)
2,000	8	.0084	.029 (.028)
1,000	105	.151	.292 (.293)
500	505	.708	.854 (.850)
200	662	.963	.993 (.988)
100	682	.990	.999 (.998)
50	687	1.000	1.000 (1.000)
Total wealth		$621,138,405	
N		877,756	
Average wealth		$708	
Inequality, G		.271	(.27)

Source: Details of data sources and sampling procedures are given in Lee Soltow: "Wealth Inequality in the United States in 1798 and 1860," *Review of Economics and Statistics* 66, no. 3 (August 1984), 444–52; "The Distribution of Income in the United States in 1798: Estimates Based on the Federal Housing Inventory," *Review of Economics and Statistics* 69, no. 1 (February 1987), 181–85; and "America's First Progressive Tax," *National Tax Journal* 30, no. 1 (1977), 53–58. Appendix 13 provides a description of the 1798 census forms and the location of manuscripts; further details are given in National Archives and Records Service, *United States Direct Tax of 1798: Tax Lists for the State of Pennsylvania,* pamphlet accompanying microcopy no. 372 (Washington, D.C.: GPO, 1963); and *Annals of Congress,* vol. 9, 5th Cong., 3rd sess., Acts of July 9 and 14, Appendix 3757–86.

The Pitkin table (appendix 1) was an integral part of the development of estimtes for 113 of the 687 tax districts described in appendix 4. Other sources for three southern states were the tables for South Carolina for 1794 given in *American States Papers,* Class 3, vol. 1 pp. 462–65; Reports of the Treasurer, General Assembly for 1790–1802, as supplied by Marion Chandler of the S.C. Department of Archives and History. North Carolina information includes *Treasurers' and Comptroller's Papers, County Summaries, 1749–1936* of the N.C. Department of Archives and History, Raleigh. Virginia information includes the commissioners' returns for 1798, Virginia State Library. Georgia information is described in Lee Soltow and Aubrey Land, "Housing and Social Standing in Georgia, 1798," *Georgia Historical Quarterly* 64, no. 4 (Winter 1980), 448–58. Area comparisons for South Carolina, Massachusetts, and Maine are given in Lee Soltow, "Socioeconomic Classes in South Carolina and Massachusetts in the 1790s and the Observations of John Drayton," *South Carolina Historical Magazine* 81, no. 4 (October 1980), 300.

Details of 25,975 persons and 43,245 properties are given in chapter 2 as well as ch. 2, n. 4 and appendix 5.

Basic data for the 687 tax districts and 359 counties are illustrated in the information for New Hampshire given in figures B and C (appendix 13).

Note: It is assumed that all males 21 and older in a district had the district average in the computation of G. No dispersion is assumed within the districts.

a. The 687 averages varied between $3,838 and $59.

b. Figures in parentheses are from a lognormal table with G=.27 and N_{w21} as stated above. Thus 15.1% of all adult males were in the 105 districts with averages of $1,000 or more, and these districts accounted for 29.2% of wealth. a lognormal table with G=.27 shows (N_{w21},A_{w21}) = (.151,.293).

W − H manuscripts; Baltimore City is an exception, since its count is derived from the collated values, W.[6]

My samples from the 62 counties suffer another problem in collation—a major weakness, admittedly. I could and did collate multiple property values (W − H) for any individual within a particular county, since these properties most often were listed on successive lines of the manuscript pages. However, I was unable to collate values for the rich who held properties either in two or more counties or in two or more states, if for no other reason than that I had data sets for only 62 counties, not for all. Furthermore, it was necessary to sample, say, every tenth or twentieth page of the manuscript set for larger counties, again because of time limitations. I can best illustrate the collation problem by an extreme case. George Washington's will, dated 1799, discloses an optimistic estimate of the total value of his real estate, at $508,101; this valuation included land held in at least eight counties in Virginia in addition to holdings in Maryland, Pennsylvania, New York, Kentucky, and the federal city of Washington. Probably America's second-richest man at that time, Washington doubtless owned more widespread holdings than most wealthy men, since he had been granted land in many locations out of respect and in payment for his leadership. I made a study of various other rich men in America: Elias Hasket Derby of Salem, Massachusetts, whose inventory dates from 1799, John Brown of Providence, whose inventory dates from 1805, as well as others in Philadelphia, Baltimore, and Charleston, which is not to

TABLE 6
THE SAMPLED COUNTIES IN 1798, CLASSIFIED BY STATE

	No. of Counties	No. of Owners Sampled
Maine	6	1,393
Massachusetts	10	4,836
Connecticut	5	2,429
New York	1	839
Pennsylvania	24	4,898
Maryland	12	12,159
North Carolina	1	478
Georgia	2	470
Tennessee	1	542
Total	62	28,044

Sources: See table 5 and appendixes 5 and 13.

suggest that one can identify the very wealthy without extremely elaborate collations. Most such men held western properties valued at not more than one-third their total estates. My ultimate distribution—showing the largest total real estate held by an individual to be $290,000, followed by four men owning $200,000 or more—may not seriously understate the holdings of the rich in America.[7] A special study of the distribution of properties among property holders in my sample is of the Pareto form and reveals no discontinuities.

Yet another problem had to be dealt with in moving from the sample distribution to estimating the final distribution for the country. I partitioned each of the 687 districts and each of the 62 sampled counties into seven general areas of the country, as stated in table 7. I determined the relative shares of wealth of different percentile ranges for each sampled county in an area; I then averaged these relative shares and applied this average to all districts in the area. The procedure I used is described in greater detail in appendix 5.

The results for the United States are shown in table 7. The greater concentration, or inequality, in wealth holding was found in urban areas. In rural districts near large cities, inequality was substantially larger in the South. In the hinterland, inequality was about the same, North and South; a surprising finding is that there was greater equality among wealth holders along the eastern seaboard than among landowners on the frontier in the North if not the South. In the northern hinterlands there was a larger proportion of property owners in the labor force, so that overall inequality was less there than in the East.

DISTRIBUTION AMONG PROPERTY HOLDERS IN 1798 AND 1860

In the search for evidence of proportional changes, one should compare the 49 percent of adult males holding property in 1798 with those in 1860, as shown in table 8. Inequality of wealth in real estate in 1800 was substantial (G = .59). The configuration was very close to being a lognormal curve, as determined from a lognormal table, with G = .59 (and a standard deviation in logarithms to the base e of 1.165). This is demonstrated in the second and last columns of table 8, except for the shares above the top percentile. Just why the distribution takes this shape is difficult to explain. For instance, there is evidence that inheritances tend to be divided among children so as to lead to this configuration. The numbers of children in various families also tends to follow a lognormal

TABLE 7

DISTRIBUTION OF WEALTH IN SEVEN AREAS OF THE UNITED STATES, 1798

Region Code	Region	Wealth Holders (W>0)		Males 21 and Older (W≥0)		
		Average Wealth	Gini Inequality	Property Holder Proportion (PHP)	Average Wealth (W)	Gini Inequality G(W)
	Rural North					
1	Within 80 miles	$1,865	.503	.446	$832	.778
2	Outside 80	1,002	.556	.594	595	.736
	Rural South					
3	Within 80	2,314	.641	.310	728	.888
4	Outside 80	883	.525	.581	514	.724
	Urban North					
5	Within 80	3,147	.634	.350	1,103	.872
6	Outside 80	1,753	.545	.444	778	.798
	Urban South					
7	Within 80	3,001	.674	.415	1,247	.865
	Total	1,434	.588	.494	708	.797

Sources: See tables 5, D, and E.

Note: The relative-dispersion pattern for each region has been assumed to be the relative-dispersion pattern of each tax district of that region, as stated in part in table E. The aggregate wealth is that stated in table 5.

curve. The distribution of warrants for land purchases among the military seem to indicate this form, too. A study of land deeds tracing the fragmentation of lands as originally warranted, surveyed, and patented again demonstrates a process tending to produce lognormal forms both in the sizes and the values of parcels of land. Indeed, mathematical models demonstrate that fragmentation often leads to the lognormal form, with Gini coefficients in a range including .59.[8]

Table 8 shows that U.S. inequality was larger in 1860 (as it was in 1850 and 1870) than in 1798. The G in 1860 was .657, not .588—a substantial difference. The 1860 form is also lognormal in shape, which indicates that a simple transformation of the 1800 data is sufficient to generate or duplicate the distribution for 1860. A lognormal theorem states, in effect, that $W_{1860} = a (W_{1798})^{1.15}$, where a is a constant, is sufficient to make the transformation. We can test this assertion of an elasticity coeffi-

TABLE 8
Distribution of Wealth in Real Estate in the United States, 1798 and 1860
(males 21 and over with wealth [W>0])

N_w, the Upper Proportion of Wealth Holders	A_w, the Share of Total Wealth of the N_w Group						Lognormal Table with $G = .59$
	1798			1860			
	All	Rural	Urban	All	Farmer	Nonfarmer	
.0001	.009	.008	.008	.014	.013	.014	.005
.0002	.014	.011	.013	.022	.019	.024	.009
.0005	.024	.020	.024	.038	.033	.042	.017
.001	.036	.031	.038	.050	.047	.065	.027
.002	.054	.046	.059	.080	.070	.092	.043
.005	.090	.079	.099	.13	.11	.16	.079
.01	.13	.11	.15	.19	.16	.23	.12
.02	.19	.17	.22	.27	.23	.33	.19
.05	.31	.29	.35	.40	.36	.49	.32
.10	.45	.43	.49	.53	.49	.63	.45
.20	.62	.60	.67	.69	.65	.76	.63
.30	.74	.72	.77	.79	.75	.84	.74
.40	.82	.81	.85	.85	.83	.89	.82
.50	.88	.87	.91	.90	.89	.93	.88
.60	.92	.92	.94	.94	.93	.95	.92
.70	.96	.95	.97	.96	.96	.97	.95
.80	.98	.98	.99	.98	.98	.99	.98
.90	.99	.99	.99	.99	.99	.99	.99
1.00	1.00	1.00	1.00	1.00	1.00	1.00	1.00
N (in thousands)	433	404	29	2,940	1,910	1,030	
Mean	$1,433	1,315	3,092	3,465	3,342	3,694	
Inequality, G	.588	.569	.638	.657	.616	.722	.59
Property Holder Proportion (PHP)	.494	.507	.359	.446	.586	.308	

Sources: See table 7. The 1860 data are derived from a computer run described in Lee Soltow, Men and Wealth in the United States, 1850–1870 (New Haven, Conn: Yale University Press, 1975), pp. 4, 96 (excluding males 20 years old).

cient of 1.15 by applying a correlation procedure in which various quantiles (percentiles and fractional percentiles) from the 1798 distribution are related to their counterparts in 1860, as shown in figure 2.[9] The results of these comparisons strengthen the assertion of both the logarithmic shapes and the simple transformation:

$$\log W_{1860} = -.0946 + 1.1399 \log W_{1798}$$
$$(.0402) \quad (.0108)$$
$$n = 20 \quad\quad R^2 = .998$$

(standard errors in parentheses). An elasticity coefficient of 1.14 means that differentials widened during the two generations. Two individuals at successive quantile levels who had differentials of 10 percent in 1800 would have a differential of 11.5 percent in 1860.

BIASES

At least five qualifications of the data and statistics presented in table 7 must be pointed out. (1) No consideration has been made for the value of slaves representing about 20 percent of the aggregate value of real estate. Further items of personal estate such as domestic and foreign bonds have not been considered.[10] (2) The data were gathered as part of the tax collection process, and certain assets were either omitted or undervalued. Thus, marginal land in northwestern Pennsylvania was granted tax exemption. A careful study of tax and market values of property in Connecticut in 1798 showed an average undervaluation of 15 percent. (3) Allocating wealth among free males 21 and older was the only practical procedure available. If family enumerations and allocations had been made in both 1798 and 1860, then equality would have been less.[11] (4) Coverage for some regions was unavoidably less than for others, and this means that sampling errors are larger for some areas. Particularly sensitive is the estimate for southern urban regions based only on the extensive Baltimore data.[12] (5) Most important, I am unable to collate the wealth of individuals in more than one county without increasing the sample size to 100 percent and substantially increasing the amount of information collected for each case; even then, a reliable collation would be impossible because the original manuscripts are missing for such a large part of the whole, to say nothing of the staggering difficulties involved in accurate collation.[13]

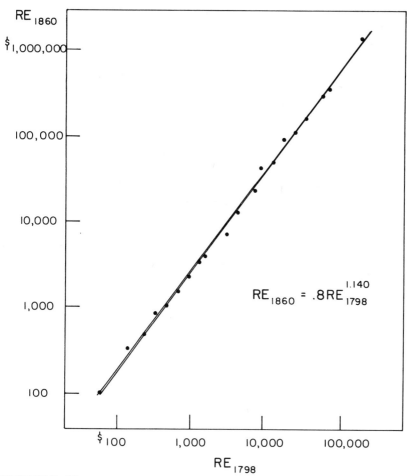

FIGURE 2. WEALTH IN LANDHOLDING, 1798 AND 1860, QUANTILE CORRELATIONS

NOTE: The data are for selected wealth quantiles for adult males in 1798 (RE_{1798}), related to the corresponding quantiles in 1860 (RE_{1860}).

CHANGES IN THE INEQUALITY OF WEALTH BETWEEN 1798 AND 1860

Are we to interpret the changes between 1798 and 1860 as a demonstration of increasing inequality? I am not certain that this transformation was so very large; at least some of the difference could be caused by my inability to collate intercounty and interstate holdings of the rich, referred to above. The distributions presented in table 9 show only one person near $300,000 and four above $200,000, figures that may well understate the holdings of the rich. An informal study of estates of deceased in Boston, Philadelphia, New York, Providence, Baltimore, and Charleston, 1790–1810 (referred to earlier) gives only a rough indication of the understatement of inequality in tables 8 and 9. Estate inventories give only very limited information about the location of properties, but it could well be that one-third of the real estate belonging to a rich person lay outside the county containing his holdings of greatest value, and in which he was most likely to reside. An inventory listing of $200,000 in my sample might more properly be $300,000 if complete collations were possible. A correction of this magnitude would cut the elasticity coefficient from 1.14 to 1.1.[14] This would reduce the size of the transformation somewhat, and almost suggests that there was little or no change in the relative distribution of wealth between 1798 and 1860.

One body of evidence from the end of the eighteenth century enables us to study the degree of understatement caused by the problem just described. Kentucky state tax lists for 1800 fortunately report *all* properties as well as the counties of their location, listed in the county of the owner's residence. I have sampled these data and have constructed two distributions: one collates total wealth, regardless of location ($W_{wherever}$); the other considers him as n owners if he owns properties in n counties (W_{county}). A correlation of quantiles from these two distributions, using the technique employed above, can provide a good estimate of how much of the transformation—with its elasticity of 1.14—may be due to inadequate collation. In the case of Kentucky, the results are:

$$\log W_{wherever} = -.2650 + 1.1101 \log W_{county}$$
$$(.0458) \quad (.0128)$$
$$n = 20 \quad\quad R^2 = .998$$

(standard errors in parentheses). This limited evidence suggests that a large portion of the 1798–1860 difference may be due to measurement error, the lack of intercounty and interstate collation.[15]

One further calculation points to the fact that the measurement error in collation can account for an elasticity of about 1.11. The U.S. distribution shown in table 8 yields the estimate that 90.4 percent of total wealth is accounted for by owner-occupiers and that the complement is owned by nonresidents who were renting to others or were holding unoccupied

TABLE 9
DISTRIBUTION OF WEALTH IN LANDHOLDING IN THE UNITED STATES
FOR THOSE WITH AND WITHOUT WEALTH, 1798
(males 21 and older)

Lower Class Limit	No. Above Lower Class Limit		
	All	*Rural*	*Urban*
$200,000	4	1	3
100,000	29	19	10
50,000	101	41	59
20,000	1,032	556	477
10,000	4,090	2,380	1,720
5,000	20,400	15,700	4,790
2,000	82,900	71,600	11,300
1,000	117,000	156,000	17,000
500	302,000	252,000	21,700
200	369,000	343,000	26,000
100	411,000	383,000	28,100
50	433,000	404,000	29,000
0	877,000	797,000	81,000
Average	$708	667	1,109
Inequality, G	.797	.781	.870
Inequality, G (1860)	.847	.775	.914

Source: Tables 5, 8, and A.

properties in the county. A lognormal theorem gives rise to the following question: if a distribution is lognormal, with G = .588, what transformation ($W_2 = aW^b$) yields a lognormal distribution with a new mean that is (1/.904) times the original mean? The theorem gives an elasticity coefficient of b = 1.101.[16] This correction would mean that a rich man owning, say, property worth $100,000 within his home county would have a total wealth of $133,000 in the United States as a whole; those with less wealth would have smaller percentage increases. The transformation is a distinct possibility as a correction for the noncollation problem. If this correction is applied, it leads to G = .633 instead of .588 for U.S. wealth holders in 1798, and this is only a little less than the .657 found in 1860.

Applying a correction factor should not detract from the general findings of tables 8 and 9. Wealth was distributed lognormally; a prominent finding is that many adults had no wealth at all, a fact that might surprise those with a romantic view of our past. The proportion holding property in 1798 is intriguing for another reason. John Adams, a keen observer of the social scene, and president at the time, had earlier observed that the rationale for a bicameral legislature rested on the proposition that PHP < .5. He felt that limiting senate membership to property owners was an essential protection for the *minority* group holding property. Our perspicacious observer asserted that less than 50 percent of potential voters, free males age 21 and older, belonged to this group. Was he correct in his guesstimate of the size of the PHP? My findings of PHP = .494, of a sample of 26,000, would come close to meeting Adams's estimate of the size of the property holding minority.[17] However, measurement errors in my procedure make me less than certain that I have substantiated the Adams hypothesis. On the other hand, if the sage Adams had been wrong in his evaluation of the proportion holding property, it was by only a small degree.

The conclusion I have reached is that there was extensive inequality of wealth in the United States in 1798, and that this condition continued at a level almost as high two generations later. Of the two hypotheses set out in chapter 1, the Franklin estimate of G = .5 and Adams's of G = .8, I accept the Adams hypothesis.

3

Distribution of Income

A N ESTIMATE of the distribution of income in the United States from its inception would give us a far better perspective on the country's economic direction over the last two centuries. The 1798 census of all housing values provides an excellent opportunity for the study of the rich, middling, and poor groups in America; such a study should include a detailed quantification of the extremes—the very affluent and their mansions as well as the many who lived in humble circumstances—but should also embrace an investigation of the modal group of houses whose value, although not at the bottom of the range, was not much greater than the value of the hovels. This data set shows such surprising inequality that adjustment for crowding (the number of families in each house) and possible income-rent elasticities still leaves substantial inequality. That inequality of income in the United States at the end of the eighteenth century was quite large is a bold hypothesis; yet a careful analysis of the data strongly indicates its plausibility and that it is more tenable than is a hypothesis of mild inequality.

This study is based on the summary statistics for America's 577,000 housing values in 1798, consisting of a frequency table of ten classes essentially compiled at the time when the census was made. I have supplemented this table with data from a sample of 40,000 dwelling values that I drew from scattered extant manuscripts of the original inventory. The ten classes were designed in conjunction with a progressive tax schedule which was applied to the gamut of all dwelling values, from those humble homes worth less than $100 to mansions worth $30,000 or more. At that time there was a feeling that house values were an excellent proxy for personal income. John Adams wrote of emulation and a progression in consumption with a rise in the ranks of classes. More to the point were the congressmen who, in 1798, spoke of housing values as being proportional to "the ability to pay."[1] If rents were 10 percent of house values and/or 10 percent of incomes, then house values might be representative of incomes. One stumbling block in such reasoning is that the number of families living in each dwelling was unknown, except in the case of Boston. Fortunately, the majority of Americans lived in separate houses; moreover, the statistical evidence for Boston indicates that crowding was independent of dwelling value. Thus, one can argue that the distribution of dwelling values did reflect the degree of relative inequality of income, as was true in the censuses reported for 1960, 1970, and 1980.

THE HOUSING DATA

The dwelling inventory made in the years 1798–1800 is remarkable for its comprehensiveness. Detailed correspondence between the hundreds of officials appointed for the task of gathering the information points to the fact that great care was exercised to ensure accuracy, at least in most areas of the country. Assessors spent thousands of hours to obtain information on land area, number of stories, windows, lights, or panes, and the types of construction materials, all of which were used to assign house values. Secretary of the Treasury Oliver Wolcott made a study indicating that assessed values were about 85 percent of market values, which demonstrates a well-ordered frequency distribution devoid of discontinuities.[2] The relative distribution, but not the mean, was anticipated in a remarkable estimate of yields made at the time of the legislative hearings in May 1798, three months prior to the commencement of the data gathering.[3]

In the United States in 1798, there were 576,800 dwellings whose total worth was $151 million, with an average value of $262 and a Gini coefficient of .71. These are the summary results based on aggregates for 10 dwelling classes, $1–100, $101–500, . . . , 30,000 and over, either as reported or estimated for the nation's 17 states, including Vermont, Kentucky, Tennessee, and Maine (as distinguished from Massachusetts), lying in 687 tax districts, within 359 counties. A sample of values for 39,890 dwellings, or 7 percent, was used to estimate dispersion within each of the 10 classes. This monumental accounting of America's housing values provides a meaningful distribution of resources for the end of the eighteenth century.

While the available counts are tantalizingly close to being a complete enumeration, there are some missing counts that are needed to complete the puzzle. I based my overall totals on the following partial information and estimates: (1) The aggregate number and aggregate value of all houses above $100 are known for all 17 states. (2) Totals for houses valued at $1–100 are given for 13 of the 17 states and for 490 of the 687 tax districts. (3) Frequencies and aggregate values of dwellings for *each* of the nine tax classes above $100 are stated for 15 of the 17 states and for 598 of the 687 tax districts. (4) I have made estimates for the missing information for the number and aggregate value of dwellings in order to complete a table of 10 tax classes for each of the 687 tax districts (898 of 6,870 cells). Prominent among the sources of this analysis/estimate are the 1790 and 1800 censuses for families and adults, as well as inventories of acreage and land values for counties in South Carolina in 1794 and 1800 and for North Carolina in 1793, 1808, and 1816. For the totals of the 6,870 cells, the Gini coefficient is .65. Dispersion within some classes, particularly those between $1–100 and $101–500, can be an important factor; estimates for dispersion within cells would raise the coefficient to .71.

Within-class dispersion was determined from a sampling of a limited number of regions in the United States in 1798–1800. (5) The frequencies F_{ij} and average values X_{ij} ($i = 1, . . .,10; j = 1, . . .,7$) were formed for each of the ten tax classes and seven regions of the country. A district was placed in a given region, depending on whether it was rural or urban, in the North or in the South, and whether or not it was under or over 80 miles from a major city. These 70 averages produce a Gini coefficient of .65. (6) A sample of 39,890 dwelling values was derived from extant records of the individual dwellings for 62 of the country's 359 counties in 7 of its 17 states. The unweighted sample mean is about 10 percent larger than the known population mean; certainly, the sample should be adjusted to agree with population aggregates. (7) Each sample value X_{ijk} ($i = 1, . . .,10; j = 1, . . .,7; k = 1, . . .,n_{ij}$) was identified with respect to tax class and region. The constants $f_{ij} = F_{ij}/n_{ij}$ and $b_{ij} = X_{ij}/(\sum_k x_{ijk}/n_{ij})$ allow the sample to represent the population of houses and the exact mean of the population. The resulting $b_{ij}x_{ijk}$, with weights f_{ij}, produce a distribution of 39,890 items having a Gini coefficient of .706. This inequality reflects dispersion between the averages in the 70 cells and the dispersion of values within each cell.[4]

DISTRIBUTION OF HOUSING

The large amount of detail from the U.S. inventory of housing values makes it possible to formulate a rather complete accounting of the distribution, as shown in table 10. The house with the greatest value was owned by Elias Hasket Derby of Salem; designed by Samuel McIntire, it was a magnificent mansion whose furniture, china and ceramics, and silver pieces today exist in the collections of Boston and Philadelphia art museums. At his death in 1799, at age 60, Derby had amassed around a million dollars; a man whose estate was almost the equivalent of 1 percent of the aggregate of the nation's housing value surely could afford the best mansion. With a return of 3 to 6 percent on wealth, the $37,500 value of his new home in 1798 may have been about the same as his average yearly income from 1795 to 1800.[5]

At the other end of the spectrum were the 8 percent of the dwellings valued at less than $10. This group of very rudimentary hovels or log cabins appeared only in rural areas and included some with values below $5. These lowest figures may be questioned as being underrepresentations of market value, but these were at best rough, simple shelters that could be raised and made habitable in a very short time. Many houses in this value range may have been very temporary, and thus were not a true reflection of the owners' incomes. Houses with values of $5 or more can not be dismissed so readily, however, and the modal class of $8 must be treated even more seriously; this value was reported for 2.5 percent of the nation's inventory of houses.

Did a house value of $8 represent an annual income of $8? It is possible that this was the case, especially in the hinterland, say, in Tennessee. Land values in some frontier tax districts averaged little more than $.25 an acre; a cloistered, remote plot of 200 acres may have yielded no cash income, but only a subsistence living for the farmer, with his excess crops having little or no market value in the county of his residence. Testimony by congressmen from Kentucky and Tennessee in 1798 indicated that there was little market for surplus crops. One of them maintained that there was less than $10,000 in coin in the entire state of Kentucky.[6] In 1802, traveler André Michaux rather forcefully characterized the living conditions of two immigrant families who had settled near Knoxville. "Their ragged clothes and the miserable appearance of their children, who were bare-footed and in their shirts, was a plain indication of their poverty, a circumstance by no means uncommon in the United States."[7]

Table 10 distinguishes between urban and rural dwellings. Fifty of the 687 tax districts were classified as urban because they clearly were cities or parts of cities such as Philadelphia or New York; others were classified as urban because the reported number of privately owned acres per adult free male was relatively small. The data of table 10 show that in

TABLE 10
DISTRIBUTION OF HOUSING VALUES IN THE UNITED STATES, 1798

Values (DHV)	No. of Houses		
	All	Rural	Urban
$30,000 and over	3	1	2
20,000–29,999	18	9	9
10,000–19,000	161	31	130
5,000–9,999	1,748	172	1,576
2,000–4,999	7,527	2,222	5,305
1,000–1,999	18,593	8,386	10,207
500–999	46,602	34,999	11,603
200–499	102,784	90,776	12,008
100–199	105,484	100,699	4,785
90–99	10,732	10,643	89
80–89	10,276	10,109	167
70–79	11,169	11,109	60
60–69	15,727	15,487	240
50–59	21,608	21,274	334
40–49	22,008	21,468	540
30–39	32,483	32,066	417
20–29	54,865	54,287	578
10–19	65,937	65,547	390
9–9.99	2,959	2,953	6
8–8.99	13,160	13,149	11
7–7.99	3,342	3,342	0
6–6.99	6,403	6,403	0
5–5.99	3,097	3,097	0
4–4.99	5,148	5,148	0
3–3.99	2,851	2,851	0
2–2.99	4,317	4,317	0
1–1.99	4,694	4,694	0
Below 1	3,102	3,091	11
Total	576,798	528,330	48,468
Mean	$262	181	1,150
Median	96	77	614
Mode	8	8	23
Inequality, G	.706	.655	.564

Sources: Data are taken from a sample of 39,890 dwelling values drawn from housing records in 62 of the country's 359 counties at that time. See method A described in chapter 3 (and for possible alternative methods, ch. 3, n. 4). Further methodology is discussed in Lee Soltow, "Wealth Inequality in the United States in 1798 and 1860," *Review of Economics and Statistics* 66, no. 3 (August 1984), 444–51. See also chapter 3, appendix 13, and table 5.

urban areas the mean dwelling value was considerably larger than in the rural areas. Urban dwellings represented 9 percent of the number of dwellings, but 35 percent of total value, a fact that reflects the importance of locational rents. One congressman at the time suggested that a house of the same quality would cost three times as much in the urban as in the rural sector. Relative dispersion of dwelling values was greater in the rural areas because of the great regional diversity—from Maine, to Georgia, to Tennessee. Yet, it should not be presumed that inequalities were minimal within homogeneous areas of the country. The region of least inequality, the rural North within 80 miles of at least one major city, had a Gini coefficient only 20 percent less than that for all rural areas. In other major rural areas of the country inequality levels were only slightly less than that for the nation as a whole.

The dwelling distribution presented in table 10 shows very strong evidence of being a lognormal curve. A probit analysis of the 28 classes in the table shows

$$\log (\text{DHV}) = 13.86559 + 1.51135Z,$$
$$(.10804) \quad (.06298)$$

where Z is the normal equivalent deviate, and $R^2 = .97$ (standard errors in parentheses).[8] An exact normal curve with the mean and inequality of table 10 would have a median of $86 rather than $96, and a mode of $9 rather than $8. The lognormal characteristics make it easier to transform a distribution with one level of inequality to another lognormal curve with either less or greater inequality. We can make this transformation because of a most intriguing comparison that can be made with the 1798 configuration and one for the present—giving us a perspective of nearly two centuries.

An examination of the distribution of U.S. house values given in the 1980 census shows that it, too, is lognormal in shape, but with a Gini coefficient of only .39. An elasticity coefficient of .5 makes it possible to move from the 1798 distribution to the relative distribution in 1980. This is shown with a correlation of 12 quantile values between the first and 90th percentiles from the top, a strong relationship, with

$$\log \text{DHV}_{1980} = 3.209 + .493 \log (\text{DHV}_{1798}), R^2 = .985$$
$$(.046) \quad (.019)$$

(standard errors in parentheses).[9] Further evidence of the striking transformation is given in table 11.

One other major source of information about housing values is the New York State census of 1865. A sample of 1,000 values from the extant data, covering a little over half of the state's counties, demonstrates an excellent lognormal curve with a mode and lower tail quite like the mathematical form. The relative inequality for the counties in 1865 is somewhat less than for either the state or the same counties in 1798, and is roughly in line with a linear extrapolation of the Gini coefficient from 1798 to 1980. Comparisons of percentile values in 1798 and 1865 show greater gains below the median.[10]

TABLE 11

THE SHARE OF HOUSING VALUES FOR THE TOP PROPORTION OF
U.S. DWELLINGS, 1798 AND 1980

	1798		1980	
N_{DHV}	A_{DHV}	$DHV^{.5}$	A_{DHV}	$Income^a$
.01	.187	.056	.058	.050
.02	.272	.092	.087	.086
.05	.421	.183	.179	.170
.10	.565	.295	.286	.280
.20	.734	.465	.447	.452
.30	.831	.595	.575	.589
.40	.896	.701	.675	.701
.50	.939	.789	.758	.791
.60	.966	.855	.831	.865
.70	.981	.907	.898	.921
.80	.991	.948	.946	.961
.90	.997	.979	.982	.988
1.00	1.000	1.000	1.000	1.000
N	576,798	576,798	69,300,000	87,440,000
Mean	$262	12	43,900	19,900
Inequality, G^b	.706	.416	.388	.417

Sources: See table 10 and ch. 3, n. 9.

Note: The top 10 percent of houses represents 56.5 percent of aggregate house values in 1798 and 28.6 percent of values in 1980. The top 20 percent of families and unrelated individuals had 28.0 percent of all income in 1980. Finally, consider the square roots of all housing values in 1798; the top 20 percent had 29.5 of the aggregate of these transformed values.

N_{DHV} = Top proportion of dwellings.

A_{DHV} = Share of dwelling house value of the N_{DHV} group.

a. Income for families and unrelated individuals as derived from the distribution of 1980 income.

b. Computed for many fewer entries in 1980 than in 1798.

CROWDING

The number of families in 1798 is estimated to have been 715,000, a figure derived both from the counts of families in the 1790 census and from the numbers of free adult males recorded in the censuses of 1790 and 1800. Thus, there is an excess of 138,000 families who had to be crowded into the 577,000 dwellings in order to calculate a rent distribution for all families in the nation. This step demands knowledge, for both rural and urban sectors, of (1) the distribution of the number of families per house, and (2) the relationship between the value of housing and the total number of families. The first of these is based on samples I drew from the federal census of Massachusetts for 1800, and the second is based on the only available data, a study of Boston values and the numbers of "occupiers" in 1798. The distribution of numbers of families per house is approximately Poisson in shape for positive values of the variate in both urban and rural sectors. Furthermore, with slight adjustment, the averages are consistent with the United States totals of 715,000 and 577,000, and with family/dwelling ratios for all of Massachusetts in 1790, as well as for urban and rural sectors of Scotland and England in 1801.[11]

The number of families plus unrelated individuals or "occupiers" per dwelling (OPD) was 1.75 for Boston's 2,452 houses, as stated in a special report.[12] This number was essentially independent of the value of the house except in the case of the top two percent of dwelling values, above $10,000, where there was a drop in the number of families per house. The number of occupiers per dwelling also conforms to a truncated Poisson distribution, a probability density function for nonzero cases. (See table 12.)

No other studies of housing values and numbers of occupants or families are available except for that arising from the New York census of 1865. In this case there is a slightly positive correlation between value and number of males 26 and older, but essentially no correlation between value and number of families. It will be assumed that value was independent of the number of families in deriving income distribution among families. The number of families in a house will be generated randomly from the adjusted Poisson distribution in each sector.

ELASTICITIES

The elasticity of housing values with respect to income ($E_{DHV,Y}$) is crucial in deriving income distribution. Studies of rent-expenditures data for 1874, 1881, and 1922–1924 show elasticities from .81 to 1.24 and, in one case, 1.37, with the average being about 1.0. Williamson has used an

TABLE 12
HOUSING VALUES AND OCCUPANTS PER DWELLING IN BOSTON, 1798

Value of Dwelling	Occupants per Dwelling
$ 100–499	1.77
500–999	1.74
1,000–1,999	1.79
2,000–4,999	1.77
5,000–9,999	1.64
10,000–19,000	1.52
20,000 and over	1.40

Poisson Distribution

	Cumulative proportion of cases	
Occupants per Dwelling	Boston	Poisson
6	.001	.002
5	.004	.013
4	.064	.054
3	.143	.184
2	.540	.498
1	1.000	1.000
Mean	1.75	1.75

Source: Records Commisioners of the City of Boston, *The Statistics of the United States Direct Tax of 1798, as Assessed on Boston* (Boston: Rockwell and Churchill, City Printers, 1890).

elasticity of .83 for Great Britain at the end of the eighteenth century.[13] I shall consider three possibilities, .8, 1.0, and 1.2, as plausible for the United States in 1798.[14]

The extensive decline in housing inequality during the two centuries leads to the suspicion that, in the past, housing was regarded as a luxury good or postponable good.[15] Some indication of this effect is that mean dwelling values in 1798 and 1980, adjusted for consumer price changes, show an average annual change of 1.9 percent, a figure larger than that found by Kuznets for income changes after 1840.[16] The dwelling value/income ratio of 2 to 1 in 1980, in table 11, may have been larger than the ratio in 1798–1800. Part of this long-run sensitivity in housing with respect to income also may have been reflected in housing values of low- and high-income groups both in the United States as a whole and within its regions in 1798.[17]

DWELLING-DERIVED INCOME

The number of families in each urban house in the United States has been generated randomly from a Poisson distribution with nonzero cases having a mean of 1.50, the configuration suggested by the Boston schedule. In randomly assigning families to rural houses, I used a Poisson distribution with a mean of 1.22 for nonzero cases. This process assigned the 715,000 families among all houses, and produced the distributions presented in table 13 for dwelling-derived income (DDY), assuming unit elasticity. Multiple families in a dwelling are assigned equal shares of its value for consumption purposes. An occupier of a dwelling worth $1,000 and occupied by three families is allocated one-third of the house value as a proxy. Rents are assumed to be, say, 10 percent of house values and, likewise, 10 percent of income. Thus, dwelling-derived income is $333 for each of the three families in this example.

Allocating families among houses by the described process leads to the rural and urban distributions presented in table 13. The distributions are potentially important if, indeed, elasticity was about 1. If congressmen

TABLE 13
DISTRIBUTION OF DWELLING-DERIVED INCOME IN THE
UNITED STATES, 1798

Dwelling-Derived Income (DDY) ($E_{DGV,Y}=1$)	No. of Families		
	All	Rural	Urban
$10,000 and up	128	37	95
1,000–9,999	25,000	9,300	15,700
100–999	280,000	233,000	46,000
10–99	318,000	308,000	10,000
Under 10	93,000	91,000	1,000
Total	715,000	642,000	73,000
Mean	$211	$149	$769
Inequality, G	.712	.671	.602
G, if $E_{DHV,Y} = 1.2$	.631	.594	.524
G, if $E_{DHV,Y} = .8$	.807	.766	.701

Source: See table 10.

Note: Further estimates of income distribution using an elasticity of 1.2 are given in chapter 11 and in appendix 8 in discussions of a possible relationship between wealth and income distribution. An elasticity of 1.2 means that if A had 10 percent less income than B, his house would be worth 12 percent less than B's house.

were correct in asserting that housing consumption was proportional to income, then the frequency tables do represent income with $G = .71$. Mean DDY of \$211 seems low by the standards of John Adams. In 1798, ordinary seamen were hired at \$12 a month; in October of that year, John Adams suggested that men could earn \$15 "when they please, by sea, or for common work on the land."[18]

The relative inequality in income in 1798 displayed in table 13 is very substantially larger than that found for income distribution at the present time. Surely one must examine thoroughly the assumptions made when judging the extent of possible biases. If $E_{DHV,Y}$ were 1.2 instead of 1.0, then G is cut significantly, as stated in the table. Even if the elasticity were 1.4, income inequality would have been larger than in 1980. It seems quite impossible that elasticity may have been 2, the level making G in 1798 the same as in 1980. It is true that housing values on the frontier of settlement in 1798 may not have reflected full market value because sizable portions of the labor force had arrived only recently. Life-cycle variation may have been a particularly strong factor. Nevertheless, relative inequality in 1798 generally was as large in the East as in the West; within the rural sectors of the Southeast, the Northwest, and the Southwest, relative inequality was large. Only in the rural Northeast, within 80 miles of Boston, New York, or Philadelphia, was some degree of homogeneity displayed. There, G(DDY) was .55 and .48 for elasticities of 1.0 and 1.2; both were larger than inequality of income in the United States in 1980.

The 1798 inequalities in income demonstrated in this chapter were surprisingly strong. They were significantly larger than inequalities at the present time.

4

Local and Regional Variation in Housing Values

THE DISTRIBUTIONS of wealth and income given in chapters 2 and 3 are rather impersonal. They tell us that there were so many persons, say, with wealth between $500 and $1,000, or with income between $100 and $200; yet these statistics reveal little in terms of the style or manner of living. We need to explore more fully some of the ramifications in consumption standards of Americans at the turn of the century. The housing data prove to be the most promising in this respect. I highlight both these data and information concerning furniture, carriages, and even milk consumption, as measured by ownership of cows, to support the general finding that there was considerable inequality in America.

In 1798 there were markedly different distributions of housing values for any two regions in the United States. Mean values tended to be substantially higher in urban than in adjacent rural areas, higher in the eastern part of a state than in its hinterland to the west, or greater in Pennsylvania than in Tennessee. While one may assume that relative inequality in housing values also may have been larger in urban than rural areas, or in the East, as contrasted to the West, such appraisals must be verified. This chapter begins with a discussion of housing values in two very diverse settings: the city of Boston, and Mifflin County, Pennsylvania, a rural region in the central part of the state. I chose these two districts not only because information about 1798 housing values is readily available for them, but also because of the accessible and relatively complete detailed information about house sizes, building materials, and numbers of stories, windows, and even windowpanes. Knowledge of these characteristics broadens our understanding of the nature of the inequality in economic condition in America. General tables concerning housing inequality, by state and by region, constitute the second part of this chapter. The final section provides a preliminary discussion of the reasons why there was such a surprising degree of inequality in America.

DWELLINGS AS A PROXY FOR INCOME

To emphasize the distribution of wealth in the United States at the end of the eighteenth century perhaps is to highlight only half of a story. Half of free male adults owned no real estate; this group appears as a large mass with zero dollars in the wealth distribution described in chapter 2. The housing data introduced in chapter 3 provide an entering wedge into data touching more intimately the lives of all families. Instead of information on 433,000 wealth holders, we have data on the 577,000 dwellings occupied by the 715,000 free families in the United States at the end of the eighteenth century. Even the difference between these last two figures—138,000 families—is not without meaning; they were "crowded" into (meaning they shared) the dwellings as second, or third, or even more, family-occupants in those dwellings. In one respect a complete analysis of the housing data may tell us more about the well-being of all families than do wealth statistics alone. This is something of a paradox since aggregate housing value accounted for one-quarter of aggregate value in all real estate.[1]

A distribution of dwelling values in a local area, state, or region is a strong indicator of the distribution of *incomes* of an area's families. Obviously such an assertion must be qualified. More than one family may have lived in a house. A poor family may have spent a smaller or larger proportion of its income than a rich family. The dollar value of a house of a given real quality was greater in an urban setting than in a rural environment. These are qualifications that will be dealt with in this chapter and the next. Yet these provisos should not stand in the way of the general proposition that a distribution of housing values in a region or in the country reveals a great deal about the distribution of total expenditures or consumption, total income, and human wealth, as well as assets in real and personal estate.

The material to be presented describes not only housing characteristics but also the allied distributions of furniture and carriages. The wide variation in expenditures that could be made by a rich family compared to a poor one immediately becomes apparent. Plainly, the elasticity of rents compared to income may have been unity or larger. (If unity, then b is 1.0 in the following expression: $rent = a(income)^b$, where a and b are constants.) Housing data are much more strategic in ferreting out income inequality than any other type of consumption. Food consumption would have displayed little variation between persons within a region or between regions, at least relative to housing expenditure. If we had data on clothing expenditures in each family in 1798, we might find surprising inequality in that age before ready-made clothes. Surely clothing would not have displayed as much relative dispersion as was the case for housing.

The end of this chapter will place special emphasis on local, state, and regional housing distributions. These statistics are an introduction to the regional disparities in equality during the early federal period. This analysis comes tantalizingly close to a regional income study. It arises because rents were about 10 percent of dwelling values and families spent about 10 percent of their incomes on housing; therefore one can conclude that house values may be fairly reasonable proxies for incomes in those areas.

Consumption at Its Finest

In 1798, America's most magnificent home was not in Boston, but 20 miles to the North. The Elias Hasket Derby mansion on Essex Street in Salem was designed by Charles Bulfinch of Boston, with adaptations by Samuel McIntire. It was an edifice of three stories, 15 rooms, and 8,757 square feet built between 1795 and June 1798. It featured elaborate interior and exterior carvings and other ornamention. Two noted Boston carvers of ship figureheads were responsible for the Ionic capitals for the exterior carvings as well as other ornamental detail. A 15-page inventory of the furnishings of the home in 1799, taken at the time of Derby's death, gives some idea of the magnitude of the house. The inventory listed 869 books, 26 carpets, 125 chairs, 26 tables, and 105 pieces of silver. The home itself was demolished in 1815.[2]

Such munificence is a startling contrast to the dwelling house of logs and stone, worth $10, owned by John Hamilton in Davidson County, Tennessee, near the Cumberland River. This dwelling measured 14 by 16 feet, one-fortieth the area of the Derby mansion. One must be cautious about attributing only poor housing to frontier regions, however. An exquisite frontier home is to be found in Cragfont in Sumner County, Tennessee, northeast of Nashville, and built in 1798 by General James Winchester. Stone masons and ships' carpenters were brought 700 miles, from the east coast, to build this stone edifice, which includes such refinements as a ballroom and bar on its second floor.

Unfortunately, complete details about all of the houses having great value are no longer available; nevertheless, we do know some of their particulars. The city or county of location and the number of houses among the top 47 in the 15 states are presented in table 14. The house having the second-highest valuation appears to have been that owned by Peter Stuyvesant, located in a suburban area of New York City.[3] The five homes above $20,000 in value located in Boston (shown in table 16, below) were those owned by Patrick Jeffrey, Eliza Bowdoin, Christopher Gore, James Scott, and Morton Perez.[4] The Harrison Gray Otis house on Cambridge Street, built in 1794 and today well restored and open to the public as a museum, was valued in 1798 at only $16,000. Philadelphia's elite included the houses belonging to William Bingham and to Alexander Baring. We must guess that the Albany list surely included the Schuyler home; the leading value for Baltimore apparently was that of a communal home. Richmond's best possibly was the John Marshall house. One can always ask why certain outstanding homes in the country were not assessed at higher values. For example, John Brown's mansion in Providence was valued at only $10,000.

MIFFLIN COUNTY, PENNSYLVANIA, AND BOSTON

The diversity in the quality of homes in a frontier county may be illustrated by examining the data for Mifflin County in central Pennsylva-

TABLE 14
THE MOST VALUABLE U.S. HOUSES, 1798

	$15,000–19,000	*$20,000–29,999*	*$30,000 and Over*
Boston and Chelsea	13	5	
Salem			1
New York City	2	2	1
Albany and Watervliet, N.Y.	1	2	
Philadelphia	2	1	
Baltimore	3	1	
Westmoreland and Richmond Counties, Virginia	1	1	
Richmond and Henrico County, Virginia	1		
Total (N=37)	23	12	2

Sources: See tables 5 and 10 and appendix 13.

Note: North and South Carolina homes are not included.

nia, legally formed 10 years prior to our 1798 date. There, 90 percent of the 545 homes were of log construction; assessments varied between the $2 value for John Allen's house in Wayne Township to the $1,400 brick home owned by William Elliot of Lewiston; the latter had two stories, 21 windows, 498 lights, and measured 45 by 32 feet.[5]

We must look to Mifflin houses for further characteristics of those homes of lower value. (The census inventories rarely provide details of houses whose values were less than $100.) The Lewiston log house owned by Isaac Brush was valued at $105 because it had one window with four panes, and the dimensions of the house were 22 by 18 feet. The home belonging to David Criswell had the same valuation, presumably because even though it was two feet longer, it was graced with only one pane of glass.

With such a multitude of characteristics, the distribution of housing values in Mifflin County unfolded in the same way as in cities and towns. Table 15 shows what these values are for the 315 homes reported for the county. The variation in the characteristics may be viewed from the standpoint of economic necessity to the family. House area would be considered the most basic need to be filled, since it was very difficult for a family of six or seven to live in one small room, the area of the meanest cabin. While a bed might be raised or lowered by ropes to give more space during the day, the living space nevertheless would still be inadequate, particularly in the wintertime. Cabins often had no windows, since windows would be a postponable item, and "lights" were a luxury in many cases. Only as a family had greater income or general wealth could it enjoy such amenities. The more basic the needs, the smaller was the inequality or dispersion in quantity. The Mifflin table for six classes shows that the square footage of the highest value class, $1,000–1,400, was only 1.6 times that in the $100–199 class. The comparable ratio for windows was 9:1, and that for panes, 30:1. It seems reasonable to believe that panes may have been a proxy for other material goods; the term *lights* indeed might signify the presence or absence of such luxuries as books, newspapers, or musical instruments.

By way of further analysis, we can compare the five homes in Boston that were worth $20,000–30,000 with the city's 110 homes of lowest reported value, those worth between $120 and $499. The ratios of the average for the higher group to the average of the lower group were as follows: value, 62; house area (square feet), 6; number of stories, 1.4; area, times number of stories, 9; windows, 7; and area of land (square feet), 51. In this case, the value reflects much more than area or number

TABLE 15
VALUES AND CHARACTERISTICS OF HOUSES IN MIFFLIN COUNTY,
PENNSYLVANIA, 1798

Value ($)	Average Area (sq. ft.)	Average No. of Stories	Average No. of Windows	Average No. of Lights	% Built of Logs
0–99	—	—	—	—	100
100–199	436	1.24	2.1	13	98
200–299	542	1.59	4.5	34	96
300–399	650	1.64	5.4	54	91
400–499	718	1.86	7.1	75	84
500–999	816	1.92	9.1	96	40
1,000 and over	1,146	2.00	18.0	394	0

Sources: John Stroup and Raymond Bell, *The People of Mifflin County, Pennsylvania, 1775–1798* (Lewiston, Pa.: Mifflin County Historical Society, Inc., 1973); Lee Soltow, "Housing Characteristics on the Pennsylvania Frontier: Mifflin County Dwelling Values in 1798," *Pennsylvania History* 46, no. 1 (January 1980), 57–70.

of windows. The mansion was worth 62 times as much as a lower-class house, but it had only seven times the number of windows. It is doubtful that the ratio for panes would have been much higher; thus, the very items to which the frontier was so sensitive were not significant in an established, eastern, city. In fact, there is a reversal of indexes in the sense that lot size was an important distinction in the city—a factor of no consequence on the frontier.

City property comprised much more than one dwelling. It was a complex, consisting of the main residence along with detached outbuildings, as can be seen from the description of Boston's five most valuable properties given in table 16.

Some country estates were in themselves almost small hamlets. The property belonging to Arthur Bryan, of Island Hundred in Talbot County, Maryland, was listed at a total value of $1,175 and consisted of his home of 800 square feet (brick, 2 stories, 8 windows, $800); a small, one-story house of wood ($100); a kitchen 12 by 16 feet ($60); a meat house 12 by 12 feet ($15); a fowl house 30 by 14 feet ($40); a compting house 20 by 16 feet, of wood, with two windows, and another 24 by 20 feet ($80); a living quarter 36 by 22 feet, of wood ($50); and another building ($30).

The various characteristics presented for Boston housing in table 17 display their own relative inequalities and relationships to value in various degrees. While the characteristic most sensitive to value was land size, we

TABLE 16
BOSTON'S FIVE MOST VALUABLE PROPERTIES, 1798

	Owner				
	James Scott	Patrick Jeffrey	Morton Perez	Christopher Gore	Eliza Bowdoin
Value	$25,000	22,500	22,000	20,000	20,000
Materials	stone & wood	wood	brick	brick & wood	brick
House area (sq. ft.)	3,450	1,890	2,106	1,200	2,150
No. of stories	2	2	3	3	3
No. of windows	54	29	21	NA	58
Land area (sq. ft.)	75,625	87,640	8,640	22,500	25,711
Outbuildings	barn (2 stories, brick & wood)	kitchen, barn, greenhouse, etc.	kitchen, woodhouse & barn	kitchen, woodhouse, stable (brick, 650 sq. ft.)	kitchen (393 sq. ft.), barn (2 stories, brick)

Source: Records Commissioners of the City of Boston, *The Statistics of the United States Direct Tax of 1798, as Assessed on Boston* (Boston: Rockwell and Churchill, City Printers, 1890).

degrees. While the characteristic most sensitive to value was land size, we note that its elasticity was less than 1. Windows also were a relatively insensitive measure of value, and relative dispersion for these items was substantially lower. Yet the distribution of windows appears quite log-normal in shape. Not shown in the above table is the importance of building materials in determining house values. The 18 percent of homes built with brick or stone (and not entirely or partially of wood) had values substantially higher.[6]

HOUSING AS A REFLECTION OF PAST WEALTH

One would expect that a man of means during the colonial period would have left his progeny in a relatively high position in the 1798

TABLE 17
CHARACTERISTICS OF BOSTON HOUSES, 1798

	Mean	Inequality, G	Elasticity with Respect to Value	N
Value	$2,284	.457	1.00	2,452
House area (sq. ft.)	836	.31	.48	2,422
No. of stories	2.39	.12	.15	2,425
No. of windows	18.9	.30	.53	2,120
Land area (sq. ft.)	3,790	.55	.78	2,429
Total house area (stories × sq. ft.)	2,180	.39	.63	2,406

Source: Record Commissioners of the City of Boston, *The Statistics of the United States Direct Tax of 1798, as Assessed on Boston* (Boston: Rockwell and Churchill, City Printers, 1890).

Note: A house with 1 percent more value than another had, on the average, .53 percent more windows.

spectrum of wealth, if inheritances were of significant size. The 1798 owner of a fine Boston home may very well have been blessed with a father who, in turn, had owned a fine home in the city in 1771. If the 1798 owner were in his sixties, he may very well have possessed some wealth as early as 1771. Some limited check of this hypothesis can be made by using the distribution for ownership of dwellings in 1798 and the 1771 distribution for wealth in real estate (as discussed in chapter 7), by simply matching names in the two data sets. This procedure is only a first step toward a more solid genealogical study that would involve a thorough analysis of family size, ages, marriages, and so forth, a respectable analysis tracing the wealth of one generation through to the next. The matching of specific names, such as John Adams, Seth Adams, or Ben Austin, in the two years gives evidence only on a probability basis of the link with earlier wealth or inheritance position.

Of 2,275 Boston persons in 1771, I found 279 who also held wealth in real estate in 1798. There was a respectable degree of association in the

FIGURE 3. FRONTIER LOG CABIN

Courtesy of Hubert Wilhelm, Ohio University.

.58 and an R^2 of .14. A person holding 10 percent more wealth than another in 1771 had, on the average, 5.8 percent more wealth than the other in 1798. Of more interest were the 172 cases involving dwelling values in 1798 and real estate values in 1771, as shown in figure 6. In this case, the elasticity coefficient is .36 and $R^2 = .09$. In spite of the wide scatter of points, we can say that there was a tendency for dwelling values in 1798 to reflect the past wealth position of the individual and his family.[7]

EXAMPLES OF RURAL AND URBAN INEQUALITY IN HOUSING

To compare inequality in Mifflin County and Boston may seem far-fetched. There was less crowding in the rural area; the average number of males 26 and older per house was about 1.4 in Mifflin and 1.8 in Boston. The average value of a house was strikingly smaller in Mifflin County. Yet it is fruitful to note the contrasts between the distributions presented in table 18.[8]

It seems strange that relative inequality could have been as great in a small frontier area as it was in each of two major cities of the United States, but such was the case. The difference between log cabins worth $10 and

FIGURE 4. ELIAS HASKET DERBY MANSION, SALEM, MASSACHUSETTS, 1795

Courtesy of the Essex Institute, Salem, Massachusetts.

$100 in central Pennsylvania was as meaningful as was the difference between two houses worth $100 and $1,000 in an eastern urban area. In Mifflin County, the house of greatest value was a $1,400 brick edifice, in marked contrast to several of the county's hovels judged to be worth $2. The descriptions given above demonstrate the phenomenally wide gamut of housing values in the United States, certainly the most apparent embodiment of the staggering inequality that existed in America at the time.

HOUSING, FURNITURE, AND CARRIAGES

The variations in housing range from the bare essentials in a home of log or wood construction to the finest decorative carvings in a large mansion. A most significant fact demonstrating the breadth of variation is the relative distribution of furniture values per home. In 1814, authorities estimated the distribution for the United States in making judgments of tax yields from a furniture tax. (See table 19.) The configuration in table 19 is lognormal in shape, with the *same* probit line as that shown for the 1798 distributions in figure 8, below.[9] Some might feel that such elasticity in furniture expenditures is astounding. Yet the evidence reveals that such a finding is accurate, even if bedding and kitchen furniture had been included. Henry Adams, in *The United States in 1800,* concluded that rooms

FIGURE 5. MOUNT PLEASANT, FAIRMONT PARK, PHILADELPHIA, 1761–1762

SOURCE: Historic American Building Survey, 1939, Library of Congress.

often were quite bare of furniture and that several or many persons might have slept in the same bed.[10] A house having only a few dollars' worth of furniture is certainly a contrast to one whose furniture was worth $9,000. Differences in the value of furniture, then, is a proxy for variations in the niceties in design and the architectural detail in the homes themselves, let alone their size. It certainly seems plausible that $E_{DHV,Y}$ could have been unity.

A further ramification emphasizing the sensitivity of house-related expenditures to income can be shown with data for carriages. A very rich person would have owned a handsome coach, necessitating a coach house—an integral part of dwelling value. The possibility of taxing wealth by imposing duties on conveyances not used for commercial purposes was bluntly stated in 1792. "The progressive increase of rates on the higher numbers has reference to the presumption of greater wealth which arises from the possession of such higher numbers."[11] Progressivity appears in

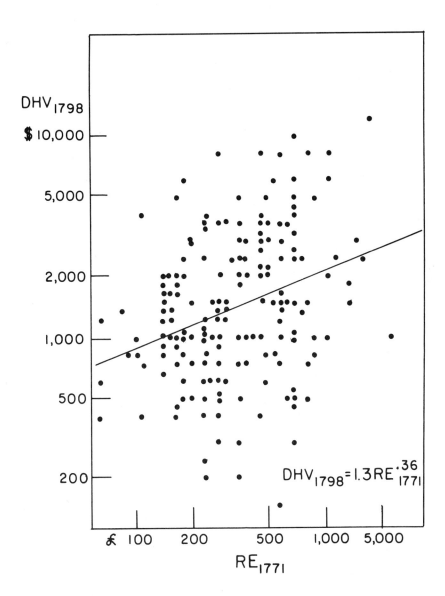

FIGURE 6. WEALTH OF SELECTED PERSONS IN BOSTON, 1771 AND 1798

NOTE: The data are for 173 matches of names with real estate in 1771 and dwelling house value in 1798.

TABLE 18
HOUSING VALUES IN MIFFLIN COUNTY, PENNSYLVANIA,
BOSTON, AND BALTIMORE, 1798

Value of Dwelling	Proportion of all Houses in Class		
(lower class limit)	Mifflin County	Boston	Baltimore
$10,000	—	.020	.012
5,000	—	.083	.085
2,000	—	.308	.245
1,000	.005	.312	.224
500	.070	.230	.214
200	.295	.046	.220
100	.242	.001	—
50	} .205	—	—
20		—	—
10	.138	—	—
5	.026	—	—
2	.017	—	—
1	.002	—	—
	1.000	1.000	1.000
N	542	2,452	3,080
Mean	$177	2,284	1,918
Inequality, G	.549	.457	.509

Sources: John Stroup and Raymond Bell, *The People of Mifflin County, Pennsylvania, 1775–1798* (Lewiston, Pa.: Mifflin County Historical Society, 1973); and Lee Soltow, "Housing Characteristics on the Pennsylvania Frontier: Mifflin County Dwelling Values in 1798," *Pennsylvania History* 46, no. 1 (January 1980), 57–70; Records Commissioners of the City of Boston, *The Statistics of the United States Direct Tax of 1798, as Assessed on Boston* (Boston: Rockwell and Churchill, City Printer, 1890); Maryland Historical Society, Baltimore, *Federal Assessment, 1798,* microfilms 604, 605.

table 20, showing the number and duties on carriages taxed in the United States in 1798.

These data show that fewer than 3 percent of U.S. families enjoyed the luxury of owning a carriage at the end of the eighteenth century. Yet, the existence of the distribution should be stressed, since it demonstrates the possibility of elaborate or higher-level consumption by the rich that was associated with housing values. The upper tail of the housing distribution in many ways was similar to that of the distribution of carriages, and we need not hesitate to use it as a proxy for the distribution of rents and incomes among the affluent.[12]

TABLE 19
U.S. FAMILY WEALTH AS MEASURED BY THE VALUE OF FURNITURE, 1814

Furniture Value[a]	No. of Families
$9,000 and over	1,000
6,000–9,000	5,000
4,000–6,000	10,000
3,000–4,000	10,000
2,000–3,000	10,000
1,500–2,000	15,000
1,000–1,500	25,000
600–1,000	75,000
400–600	100,000
200–400	300,000
Under 200	259,000

Source: American State Papers, 13th Cong., 3d sess., 1814, Class 3, vol. 2, pp. 854–55.
   a. Excludes beds, bedding, kitchen furniture, carpets and curtains of domestic manufacture, and family pictures.

FOOD CONSUMPTION

The distribution of food expenditures in 1800 presumably was some-what egalitarian, but I have very little data as proof. The closest I can come to an approximation is by using the distribution of cows (presumably a proxy for milk consumption) that is given in table 21. It is quite possible that the food coefficient was .35 or .40 within a given region and .40 or .45 for the nation.[13] The variation in consumption between regions probably was substantial. Data presented in appendix 6 for inequalities between the 687 tax districts indicate that the national G could have been .05 to .10 larger than the regional G.

In chapter 3 I argued that for the distribution of income, G may have been .6 or .7. This level of inequality is consistent with that for food, using the hypothetical framework presented in table 22. To construct a distribution of expenditures with a coefficient of about .6 demands very strong coefficients for each of the four. Conceivably, inequality in food consumption was large, and even larger for clothing. Housing inequality was actually at the stated level. Inequality in savings could be expected to be at a level similar to that found for wealth, as distributed among all adult males, to the extent that it dominated wealth formed from inheritances, capital gains, and savings. The scheme given in table 22 must be accepted only as a very rough approximation.[14] Undoubtedly there were transfers

TABLE 20
U.S. FAMILY WEALTH, AS MEASURED BY THE VALUE OF CARRIAGES, 1798

Class	Type of Carriage	N	Duty
1	Coaches	153	$15
2	Chariots, post chariots, post chaises	703	12
3	Phaetons, coaches, other carriages having panel work above, with blinds, glasses, or curtains	1,351	9
4	Four-wheel carriages having framed posts and tops, with steel springs	417	6
5	Four-wheel top carriages with wooden or iron springs or jacks; curricles, chaises, chairs, sulkies with tops; two-wheel carriages with steel or iron springs	10,565	3
6	Other two-wheel carriages; other four-wheel carriages resting upon wooden spars	8,512	2
	Total no. of carriages	21,702	
	Total no. of families	709,000	

Source: American State Papers, 6th Cong., 1st sess., 1800, class 3, vol. 1, p. 620.

of income from the rich to the poor. Inequality in savings may have been .85 or larger before transfer.

A synthetic distribution probably should include the concept of "haves" and "have-nots" for many items of consumption. Only one-half of adult males or families had any permanent savings in the form of real estate, and perhaps 60 percent had savings in personal or total estate.[15] Only 3 percent of families had carriages, and only 50 percent of families in New England owned horses. The distribution of consumption among the "haves" could be quite equal, but quite unequal if we consider all families. If "haves" are 40 percent of the population and if G among them is .3, then G among all is $.3 \times .4 + .6$, or .72. In Connecticut in 1795–1799, the G for a distribution of watches and was only .07 among "haves," but the "haves" constituted only 20 percent of taxpayers; the overall G was $.07 \times .20 + .80 = .81$. Similar statistics might be found for other consumer durables such as bed sheets, imported fabrics, or porcelain teacups. Alexander Hamilton's 1791 report stated that "in a number of districts . . . two-thirds, three-fourths, and even four-fifths, of all the clothing of the inhabitants, are made by themselves."[16]

REGIONAL HOUSING

Given enough time and resources, one could develop a complete distribution of the value of every house in states where records are extant;

TABLE 21
MILK CONSUMPTION IN THE UNITED STATES, 1771–1798
(based on the number of cows reported for tax purposes)

		No. of Males 21 and Over	No. Reporting Cows	Mean	Inequality, G
Massachusetts and Maine	1771	57,257	22,497	2.86	.353
Massachusetts and Maine	1792	—	210	3.43	.379
Connecticut	1798	1,445	837	4.73	.454
Washington County, Pa.	1798	1,331	931	2.06	.287

Source: Data for Maine and Massachusetts are from *Massachusetts Tax Valuation Records, 1771,* Bettye Pruitt, Principal Investigator, Inter-University Consortium for Political and Social Research (Ann Arbor: University of Michigan, 1980), ICP5R 7734. I drew a sample of 362 cases from the Massachusetts assessment lists in 1798, Massachusetts State Archives, Boston; and Latter Day Saints Genealogical Library, Salt Lake City, microfilms 955801, 953998-4000. The towns of Franklin, Hebron, Hartford (partial) and Wolcott, Connecticut, are described in Lee Soltow, "Watches and Clocks in Connecticut, 1800, a Symbol of Socioeconomic Status," *Bulletin of the Connecticut Historical Society* 45, no. 4 (October 1980), 117–19. See also Lee Soltow and Kenneth Keller, "Tenancy and Asset Holding in Late Eighteenth-Century Washington County, Pennsylvania," *Western Pennsylvania Historical Magazine* 65, no. 2 (January 1982), 14.

it then would be possible to study inequality for every county or city, town, and township in the states of Pennsylvania, Maryland, Connecticut, and Massachusetts. My only complete enumerations are for Lancaster and Mifflin County, Pennsylvania, Boston, and Baltimore, partially as reported in this chapter. However, statistics do exist for many areas of the country that can be translated immediately into measures of inequality. These are the *grouped* data for 10 classes for the United States as a whole, already described in chapter 3.

The dwelling tax schedule with its 10 classes—from below $100 to $30,000 and over—forms a frequency table of dwelling values that was available for 15 of the states and for tax districts or larger county units within each state. These distributions make possible a splendid regional analysis for a great part of the country in 1798. One difficulty is that there is no detail about dispersion within the bottom classes, $1–100 and $101–500, where the vast majority of cases lay. Gini coefficients computed from available data understate inequality in these situations. Two procedures will be employed in adjusting for continuity within classes, particularly the two below $500. The first employs a probit analysis in obtaining dispersion within a lognormal curve for an interval with the same character-

TABLE 22
A SYNTHETIC DISTRIBUTION OF POSSIBLE U.S. EXPENDITURES
ON FOOD, CLOTHING, HOUSING, AND SAVINGS, 1798

	Relative Mean	Relative Inequality, G	Elasticity, E (if G = .60)
Food	40	.45	.58
Clothing	25	.60	1.00
Housing	15	.70	1.23
Savings	20	.80	1.53
Total	100	.599	

Source: Author; a computer simulation.

Note: This is a synthetic distribution with G = .599, constructed by assuming four lognormal distributions with guessed parameters.

istics. This procedure is described in table 23, below. A second, much more elaborate, procedure for a study of seven regions within the United States utilizes the data from a sample of 40,000 individual dwelling values drawn from the tax lists for the 62 counties whose 1798 records are extant. As I explained in chapter 3, this method clearly demonstrates lognormality.

DISTRIBUTIONS AMONG THE STATES

We could expect that inequality in housing among free persons in southern states would be larger than among the population of the North. The distribution of slaves in 1790, 1800, and later, introduced in chapter 8, shows that only a minority of southerners were slaveholders and that there was significant inequality in the numbers of slaves owned. Slavery made large farm operations possible, resulting in greater accumulation of wealth in the hands of a few than would have been the case in those areas where individual yeomen farmed without the benefit of hired or chattel labor. Inequality in the value of real estate was larger in the South than in the North, as stated in chapter 2.

At best, wealth inequality explains 60 percent of housing inequality, since there were only 433,000 wealthholders, 577,000 dwellings, and 715,000 families. Was there a greater proportion of homes below $100 in a southern state? Was the average value of a home in the lowest class different in Tennessee from those in Kentucky or Maryland? Did this mean that there was greater relative inequality in the one state as compared to the other? The statistics for the 10 classes provide some evidence in this respect.

One could argue that inequality in a northern state would be counterbalanced by the effects of urbanization. A common belief is that there was greater inequality in urban areas, greater variation in economic conditions in the absence of the great equalizer: *land*. Yet the results of the investigations for Boston, Baltimore, and Mifflin County, Pennsylvania, cast doubt on this judgment. More comprehensive data are needed in order to verify these results.

INEQUALITY AMONG STATES

The inequality levels presented in table 23 confirm general impressions suggested by the literature of the period. The state with the least inequality was Connecticut, while South Carolina had the most. The array of 17 coefficients demonstrates that the Northeast had the lowest inequality, followed by the mid-Atlantic states (with coefficients of .60–.69) and southern states with higher relative dispersion. Of course, there are notable exceptions to this rule.

Inequality was at its lowest in the smaller homogeneous states of Connecticut, Rhode Island, and Vermont. Next above them, with coefficients still below .6, were New Jersey, Maine, and Massachusetts; the New England states account for six of the lowest seven coefficients. Delaware, Virginia, North Carolina, and Tennessee, in the middle of the scale, were followed by the diverse top group—Kentucky, New York, Georgia, and South Carolina—with greatest inequality. One would expect South Carolina to be most heterogeneous. It had the greatest number of slaves per capita, plantations with the largest number of slaves, and the largest relative dispersion of slaves among slaveholders. There were great differences between areas in states characterized by the most fundamental distinction between the lower or coastal counties and upland counties—a difference clearly manifested in administration and politics. New York State had by far the greatest inequality in the North. It, too, had diverse areas—from New York City to counties on Lake Erie and the St. Lawrence. Also prominent was the inequality of holdings in land, including manors or estates with tenants.[17]

Pennsylvania and Virginia, two average states in the array of coefficients, present an interesting contrast. They had the largest free populations (aside from New York) and were the largest in area. Pennsylvania had very sizable inequalities between areas, with the average dwelling value

TABLE 23
AVERAGE VALUES AND INEQUALITY OF HOUSING IN
VARIOUS STATES, 1798

	No. of Houses	Mean Value	No. of Classes Having Frequencies	Inequality, G
Maine	16,072	$ 199	7	.568
New Hampshire	22,778	201	7	.625
Vermont	34,742	84	4	.542
Massachusetts	53,108	426	10	.596
Rhode Island	9,249	329	6	.535
Connecticut	34,557	253	6	.516
New York	73,180	363	10	.760
Pennsylvania	81,848	369	9	.649
New Jersey	31,456	311	5	.562
Delaware	9,183	246	5	.666
Maryland	31,110	360	9	.725
Virginia	65,605	190	9	.683
Georgia	12,461	162	6	.774
Kentucky	15,882	87	6	.748
Tennessee	11,198	41	5	.686
Total, 15 states	502,429	282	10	.683
North Carolina[a]	47,760	84	10	.627
South Carolina[a]	26,427	208	10	.828
Total, 17 states	576,616	262	10	.695

Sources: See table 5 and appendixes 1 and 13.

Note: The basic data for the 10 classes are illustrated in figures B and C (appendix 13) in the case of New Hampshire; here there are 11,648 houses valued at less than $100 and 11,130 reported in the six classes above $100.

a. Estimates for North and South Carolina are based, in part, on supplementary data. The Gini coefficient includes a continuity adjustment in the $1–100 and $101–500 classes using probit slopes and characteristics of the lognormal curve.

in the western part of the state being a fraction of that in the East. Virginia had fewer differences between areas because its population was more essentially rural. Yet slavery remained a force producing inequality. Surprisingly, there was relative equality in Massachusetts. One might expect greater inequality between the eastern and western parts of the state. Particularly striking was the contrast between Massachusetts and South Carolina—a difference greater than I had suspected.[18] Yet the contrast between South Carolina and North Carolina was almost as large. Finally, we note the strong inequality in housing values in the frontier states of

Tennessee and Kentucky. Again, regional differences within Kentucky were more significant than in Tennessee. This shows that the new frontier, too, had experienced inequality of its own.

INEQUALITIES BETWEEN DISTRICTS AND COUNTIES

The inequality measures for housing for all districts and counties in the United States, presented in table 24, display wide variation, with some areas having an inequality coefficient, G, of .6 or .7, and others having coefficients of .4 or even .3. This statistical base allows us to test an important hypothesis concerning the effect of the frontier on equality. Frederick Jackson Turner's thesis was that conditions on the frontier were more likely to foster equality than was the case in more mature areas of settlement.

> The wilderness masters the colonist. It finds him a European in dress, industries, tools, modes of travel, and thought. It takes him from the railroad car and puts him in the birch canoe. It strips off the garments of civilization and arrays him in the hunting shirt and the moccasin.[19]

Turner's thesis is not borne out by the data. Indeed, the frontier environment, or the areas near it, acted as a force producing inequality as long as there was active settlement, as certainly was true at the end of the eighteenth century. As a matter of fact, frontier conditions surely affected a greater proportion of the population in 1800 than they did in 1860, and definitely more than in 1893, when Turner's famous essay appeared.

If the Turner thesis is correct, then America must have been quite egalitarian in 1800. The notion that we were a homogeneous society prior to the industrial revolution receives a strong impetus from Turner's writings. Even the notion of increasing inequality after 1800 fits nicely with his hypothesis. The frontier population withered away in the nineteenth century, at least in relative importance; inequality then became dominant.

The relationship between inequality and its distance from the coast certainly must be tested. I determined the minimum distance in miles between one of six east-coast ports and the center of a county (MILE6) and related this distance to G_{DHV}, or inequality in dwelling house values. An important regression equation is the simple form

$$G_{DHV} = .465 + .000750 \quad MILE6, n = 687, R^2 = .27$$
$$(.006) \quad (.000047)$$

(standard errors in parentheses). Inequality increased from .465 at the coast to .540 at 100 miles from the coast, and to .615 at 200 miles' distance.

This is a direct refutation of the Turner hypothesis. Nor are the results altered if other variables are introduced. The positive slope of the equation remains significant within the northern and southern states and within the rural sector. A significant positive relationship is also found for the relative interdecile-range measures introduced in table 24. The above equation might be the best test of the frontier hypothesis of any that use pre-1900 data. The housing values are a better expression of income than are the wealth data from the censuses for 1850–1870 for those persons having wealth.[20]

Another dimension of timing in settlement is measured by the age of the district. Having found the year each county was established, one can define AGE = 1800 − Year of Settlement, a measure introduced in chapter 3. Now, the age of the community would be expected to vary *directly* with G_{DHV} if inequality were increasing. The older the community, the more one would observe inequalities in ability and inheritances from previous generations. The younger the community, the closer it should be to the Turner ideal. My second important correlation in this respect is

$$G = .623 - .00155 \ \ AGE, n = 687, R^2 = .27.$$
$$\quad (.006) \quad (.00007)$$

TABLE 24

INEQUALITY IN HOUSING VALUES IN U.S. TAX
DISTRICTS AND COUNTIES, 1798

Relative Interdecile Range $\left(\dfrac{D_{90}-D_{10}}{DHV}\right)$	No. of Districts	No. of Counties	Inequality, G with Continuity Adjustment	No. of Districts	No. of Counties
5.0 and over	6	4	.80 and over	15	14
4.0–4.9	77	65	.70–.79	57	49
3.0–3.9	156	101	.60–.69	128	97
2.0–2.9	348	165	.50–.59	222	126
1.0–1.9	100	24	.40–.49	201	61
			.30–.39	56	11
Total	687	359	.20–.29	6	0
			.10–.19	2	1
			Total	687	359
Average inequality	2.81	3.10		.543	.590

Sources: See table 23.

Note: Linear interpolation is used in computing the deciles D_{90} and D_{10}.

The equation says that a newly developed district had a coefficient of .623 and that the coefficient for a 100-year-old district was .468. The older the community, the *less* the inequality. Again, this is a refutation of the frontier thesis, as applied to the end of the eighteenth century. The equation deals with cross-sectional data only for the year 1798. The equation for 1808 or 1818 might lie above it or below it. Yet there is some implication that inequality in housing would drop as the frontier aged, and that inequality in dwellings would be lower, say, in 1860 than in 1798.[21]

FACTORS INFLUENCING INEQUALITY IN HOUSING AND INCOME

I have described in detail characteristics of houses in 1798 for a county in mid-Pennsylvania and for two cities. These characteristics suggest that rich individuals spent large amounts of money on houses and had ample resources for additional expenditures such as furniture and carriages. America's richest citizen in 1798 built a home at a cost of perhaps 10 percent of his average annual wealth from 1793 to 1798. America's affluent class lived in handsome mansions, not as elaborate as the châteaux on the Loire nor as elegant as the majority of manor houses in Britain, Sweden, or Denmark, but certainly respectable by modern American standards. Middle-class housing was much less pretentious, with the average value of houses in the class under $100 being $20 to $30. The relatively poor lived much more humbly, in homes valued at $10, $5, and even less, as demonstrated by the Mifflin County data. The very poor lived in hovels. Some homes were occupied by fresh immigrants from foreign cities. Undoubtedly, there were life-cycle effects in the data. Among families whose breadwinners were in their forties, a distribution for an area would have shown considerably less inequality, with a coefficient of perhaps .35 instead of .50.

There was less relative inequality in a local area than in the nation as a whole; Gini coefficients averaged .54 for districts, .58 for counties, and .65 or larger for the country. Yet there was rather strong inequality in most areas of the country. The housing data provide convincing evidence that inequality of income was substantial, whether in the South, North, East, or West; whether in rural or urban areas; whether the area had been settled recently or had a long history of settlement.

In many ways these results are surprising. Benjamin Franklin's hypothesis of happy mediocrity may have unduly stressed equality, but was it possible to guess at the time that inequality was as severe as the data demonstrate? Even John Adams, so correct in his notions about the distribution of wealth, gave no hints about lower-income groups. It was only La Rochefoucauld and Michaux who indicated that the reality may have been otherwise.

Modern-day hypotheses about income inequality in the early federal period generally portray society as being relatively homogeneous. It is assumed that wage rates for skilled or unskilled persons differed little. The period was traditional in the Rostovian sense, in the time before the takeoff period—an era before the onset of the industrial revolution, with all of its iniquities. Most people who study the period conclude that there was little relative inequality because there was little absolute inequality. Everyone lived in a log cabin, so conditions could not be heterogeneous. Ninety percent of Americans were farmers; each man plowed 10 of his 160 acres. As a corollary, it is assumed that inequality rose with industrialization. Individuals would be pulled or pushed into industries where inequality of income was greater than in agriculture; consumption would shift from food to other things as incomes rose, the so-called Engel effects. New fields of endeavor would demand greater specialization, greater differentiation in the productivity of labor, greater inequality of income. However, this is the type of thinking that seems to be contradicted by the evidence for 1798.

Are there reasons for believing that inequality could have been so large in 1800? At the least, could the industrial revolution have been benign, or even beneficial, in providing strong employment to the masses of individuals? Could inequality of income, if not of wealth, actually have dropped after 1800? Nine factors suggest that the answer was yes.

Isolation

In the early federal period, the country was made up of relatively cloistered, isolated areas. For example, it took several days for the news of Washington's death in 1799 to reach Boston, and travel from Kentucky or Tennessee to the east coast could take three to four weeks. Localized pockets of monopoly arose in mills or stores owned by a few individuals who did well relative to others. There were particularly strong disparities between regions that were not easily negated by ease in travel or shipping.

These disparities are best revealed in the differentials in land prices, shown in table 25. There is no doubt about the statistics shown in column 1, the array of 687 district averages. The average price of land in the most prosperous districts, accounting for 10 percent of all acreage, was $13.61. The average price for the lowest districts in the array, also accounting for 10 percent of all acreage, was $0.177. The Gini coefficient for land prices was .593, as determined by weighting each district's average price by its total acres. It was in this sense that interregional disparities differed little from the inequalities in housing within districts displayed in tables 23 and 24. Improved transportation at the time would have raised prices in western areas, as compared to those in the East, and inequality would thereby have been mitigated. However, there is significant evidence that the West produced much more than it could sell; this was variously ascribed to sparsity of population, lack of urban centers, and lack of facilities for transporting goods to the East. "The people of Kentucky," a congressman from Kentucky said in 1798, "had produce of every kind, in abundance, but they want a market for it. The Mississippi had lately promised a medium through which to transport it, but as yet little advantage has been derived from it."[22]

The industrial revolution brought about the improvement of roads as well as growth in the road network; water transportation was aided immensely by the development of the steamboat. The construction of canals and railroads, too, brought regions closer together. The hypothesis that land prices by 1850 or 1860 exhibited less dispersion than in 1798 proves to be the case. In column 4 of table 25, the Gini coefficient is smaller, and the price ratios in columns 5 and 6 demonstrate the differential price increases. Within the 18 states, districts having the highest land prices, some 16 million acres in 1798 and 18 million acres by 1850, showed a price rise of 250 percent during the half century. The poorest land rose 660 percent in price! Surely this trend produced less inequality of wealth among owners of land and less inequality of income among agricultural employees than otherwise would have been the case.

Quality of Land

Anyone motoring across Pennsylvania or Ohio can see that the best farmhouses and barns are on level or gently rolling land that is extensively cultivated. Surely the diversity in cultivability played a large part in determining wealth and the demand for farm labor. It took a certain amount of luck to be able to settle on the best land or to inherit it. A person whose produce value was 50 to 100 percent larger per acre surely had a larger net income. Yet those with small acreage close to markets and with access to better roads could do as well or better than those with many acres located long distances from markets. By the standard of land productivity, inequalities in America were as great as in Europe. All of the beautiful eighteenth-century manor houses in southern Sweden appear to be located in very productive areas.

There are ample statistical data illustrating the diversity in land types in the United States. The meticulous records kept by Connecticut authorities in 1798 allow us to study with accuracy the ten qualities of land

TABLE 25
LAND PRICES IN THE UNITED STATES, 1798

The Top Proportion of Acres (N_v)	Land (687 Tax Districts) (1)	Land (359 Counties) (2)	Land and Housing (359 Counties) (3)	Cash Value (748 Counties) (4)	(4)/(2) (5)	(4)/(3) (6)
.10	$13.61	$13.22	$19.39	45.90	3.5	2.4
.20	5.21	5.27	6.39	24.43	4.6	3.8
.30	3.21	3.34	3.94	16.62	5.0	4.2
.40	2.31	2.36	2.71	11.67	4.9	4.3
.50	1.73	1.80	1.97	7.99	4.4	4.1
.60	1.25	1.31	1.42	5.92	4.5	4.2
.70	.951	.957	1.033	4.53	4.7	4.4
.80	.755	.764	.824	3.53	4.6	4.3
.90	.450	.452	.487	2.53	5.6	5.2
1.00	.177	.177	.183	1.35	7.6	7.4
No. of acres (millions)	162	162	162	183		
Average price	$2.97	2.97	3.83	12.45	4.20	3.25
Inequality, G	.593	.583	.634	.527		

Average Price Per Acre in Decile Range — 1798 (columns 1–3), 1850 (column 4); Price Ratio (columns 5–6).

Sources: See table 5 and appendixes 1 and 13; see also *Historical Demographic, Economic, and Social Data: The United States, 1790–1970,* Inter-University Consortium for Political and Social Research (Ann Arbor: University of Michigan), data set for 1850.

Note: Basic data for New Hampshire are illustrated in figures A and B (appendix 13). Column 1 says the average value of the land between the 30th and 20th percentiles (from the top) was $3.21.

classified for tax purposes. Table 26 displays the full gamut, from meadowland to unenclosed, third-rate acreage. This frequency table demonstrates an inequality coefficient $G(V_{1\ acre})$ of .45. Such a measure does not translate easily into inequalities among persons, since a given individual could hold many types of land. For example, John Chappel of Hebron owned 6 acres of plowland, 12 of mowing, 5 of boggy meadow, and 62 of bush pasture. Nor does the classification account for location with respect to rivers or urban areas. South Carolina's 1798 tax schedule allowed 24 categories of location. Georgia's was the most elaborate of all, with a schedule of 54 prices, according to location, some of which are shown in figure 7.

The best test of the natural variation in soils and terrain can be obtained from the deeds of sale when the land was on the frontier of settlement. Here, the price per acre essentially was not influenced by improvements. Gini coefficients for prices, weighted by the acreage involved (excluding areas of two acres and less as well as deeds of gift), were between .35 and .56 for four counties in Ohio and Kentucky in the years from 1784 to 1803 and in Bucks County, Pennsylvania, between 1681 and 1689. In Lancaster County, Pennsylvania, and in Charleston District, South Carolina, there was appreciable variation in prices in the early decades of settlement at the end of the seventeenth century as well as later. Thus, the variation in nature's bounty was a prominent element in inequality throughout the traditional period.

Seasonal Variation

A day laborer in the northern part of the country faced a period of four or five months every year when there was little demand for his services. This is in contrast to labor demands after industrialization. The factory provided employment 300 days a year, not just during favorable weather. Certainly, labor disputes interfered with the 300-day expectation, but such strikes resulted in a loss of less than one-third of the year's work. Because of seasonal fluctuations, agriculture was not kind to the person who labored on the land, particularly if he was not a landowner. To be sure, such tasks as clearing land, trapping, cutting timber, and making improvements to buildings could take place during cold weather, but that kind of work generally was less productive economically than if these activities could be conducted in clement weather. La Rochefoucauld lists wages near Albany as being 40 percent more in the summer than in the winter. It should go without saying that there was wide seasonal variation in river traffic and in shipping.[23]

Cycles and Irregularities

Conventional wisdom tells us that the amplitude and duration of business cycles was minimal during the traditional or preindustrial period. Yet we know that there were wide swings in the economic activities of the population in the 1790s. For example, there was a surge in the number of acres granted in 1794, 1795, and 1796, and a relative slackening in 1797 and 1798, at least in the western parts of Virginia and Pennsylvania. By 1798, the land craze had altered considerably. By 1796 Robert Morris probably was America's greatest landowner, but the nature of his business activities is revealed by the fact that he was in debtor's prison two years later. Perhaps such speculative activity was peripheral to the decadal surge

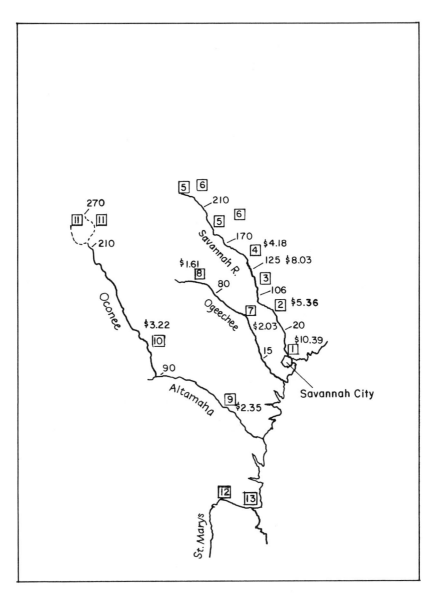

FIGURE 7. Map of Land Prices in Georgia, 1798

Note: The figure presents 13 price areas, as designated in the Georgia Tax Law of 1798, showing the distance in miles from the ocean and some prices of first-class swampland.

TABLE 26
TYPES OF LAND IN CONNECTICUT, 1779, 1798, 1815

	Rated Tax Value, 1798	No. of Acres		
		1779	1798	1815
Meadowland	$2.50	8,010	6,438	6,031
Plowing	1.67	244,699	266,970	260,209
Mowing and clear pasture	1.33	457,858	457,888	436,935
Other meadow	1.25	63,983	61,296	64,938
Bog meadow				
Mowed	.84	30,637	56,305	75,133
Not mowed	.34	4,704	8,665	9,746
Bush pasture	.34	495,287	641,402	852,857
Unenclosed				
1st rate	.34	179,346	87,979	54,725
2nd rate	.17	280,549	263,150	259,258
3rd rate	.09	159,187	307,040	292,574
Total acres		1,924,260	2,157,133	2,312,406
Total value		$1,436,332	1,518,146	1,557,331
Average value per acre		$7.46	7.03	6.73
Polls 21–70 (taxable persons)		29,704	36,432[a]	28,093
Total census population (all persons)		204,000	248,000	268,000
Inequality, G			.45	

Sources: "Return of the Grand List of the State of Connecticut, for August 20, 1798, Combining the returns of the Listers Transmitted in October with the Additional Returns Transmitted in May 1799 Following"; similar titles for 1779 and 1815.
  a. Apparently before "military exempts."

that occurred with the establishment of the federal government, the increase in government securities, and banking. However, such activities were bound to affect some individuals more than others.

Nor were irregularities unimportant. The yellow fever epidemic in Philadelphia in 1793 caused a dramatic increase in the number of administered estates which altered materially the city's inheritance pattern. Finally, we must not forget that the Revolution itself substantially affected personal wealth holdings at the beginning of the 1780s. During the traditional period, dramatic changes took place that left some persons with great resources and others destitute. For example, the number of horses and cattle in Connecticut decreased between 1779 and 1788; and while the population of Kentucky did not even double between 1780 and 1790, it tripled in the decade between 1790 and 1800. The Federal City was only a dream in 1789; by 1798 its total dwelling values were greater than those for the entire state of Tennessee. These activities may not have produced business cycles in the classic manner of the nineteenth and twentieth centuries; nevertheless, the economy was in a state of rapid change. In no way was society stagnant—changes took place in almost every kind of endeavor. Disturbances to the status quo very clearly produced a dynamic society of very rich and poor, and of large inequalities in both wealth and income.[24]

Illiteracy

America was a nation of "haves" and "have-nots" in terms of the ability to read and write. This is evident in the data from army recruitment papers indicating whether or not the enlistee was able to sign his name or had to resort to the use of an X-mark. Consider the information in table 27 for the period before and after the surge accompanying the industrial revolution.

Reading broadsides, newspapers, books, and magazines was a powerful means of learning about economic opportunities. Reading and writing letters provided access to information about markets, prices, property, and new methods in agriculture and manufacturing as well as in business. To the extent that 40 percent of Americans could not participate directly

TABLE 27
ILLITERACY AMONG OCCUPATION GROUPS IN THE
UNITED STATES, 1799–1895

	Illiteracy Rate, 1799–1829	Illiteracy Rate, 1830–1895	N
Blacksmith	.38	.29	90
Carpenter	.25	.15	101
Farmer	.46	.28	587
Laborer	.54	.30	285
Shoemaker	.37	.03	116
Other	.37	.14	623
Total	.42	.21	1,803

Source: A computer run of the sample data described in Lee Soltow and Edward Stevens, The Rise of Mass Literacy and the Common School: A Socioeconomic Study of the United States to 1870 (Chicago: University of Chicago Press, 1981), pp. 51–53; Lee Soltow, "Literacy of the Common Man in the Nineteenth Century, as Judged by Army Enlistment Records," working paper, Dept. of Economics, Ohio University, Athens, Ohio, 45701.

Note: It can be argued that military recruits in the earlier period were more or less likely to have been from the bottom classes of society compared to those in the Civil War period.

in written communication, there was a monopoly—compounded by the geographical isolation previously mentioned. Granted, persons could use the services of others for reading and writing, but those recruits who signed their names with an X, the "marksmen," definitely were disadvantaged. Illiteracy was higher for those born or recruited from the South, relative to those from the North. There is at least some degree of rank correlation between the level of literacy and dwelling value equality for the 18 states.

In 1800, illiteracy was very much a function of the lack of formal schooling for the young. Children of poor and middling families did not attend school to any significant degree. The relationship between the wealth of the parents and the education of the children is of vital importance in ascertaining trends in inequality. If the children of the poor had equal opportunity for advancement, then one might expect inequality to decrease in succeeding generations or, as a minimum, that there would be large intergenerational movement among families, both up and down. The idea that universal education is essential to political democracy has been a basic tenet since the founding of this nation. Education was seen as a fundamental need at the end of the eighteenth century. A letter from "Academicus" to Thomas Jefferson in 1797 finds education to be the key to the current level of inequality.

> It is a matter of the highest importance to a republican government to disseminate knowledge and to keep the evenness of access to it open to all, and especially to the middle, or even the lower class of people. This is the class to which we are to look for improvement in arts and knowledge: and which cultivates learning to its own emolument and the advantage of others. And as the wealth of a republic may be said to consist in the quantity of wisdom and information its citizens are possessed of, it ought therefore to be always kept within their grasp. Wherever it becomes a monopoly in the hands of the rich, the liberties of the state become a boon to the highest bidder.[25]

Inheritance

The inheritance mechanism helps to perpetuate the inequality of wealth and income (above the median) from one generation to the next. This is a theme I have highlighted several times in previous chapters. Dynamic changes take place, of course, but patterns, once established, are renewed every 30 years or so; therefore, assets, particularly in an agricultural society, are strategic in determining income. To a certain extent, the patterns of landownership existing in 1740, 1770, and 1800 were duplicated in 1830 and 1860. The 1860 census reveals the ages of fathers and sons, the wealth of the fathers and the number of sons they had in the

40–45 age group. These data can be coupled with a mortality table to demonstrate that the distribution for sons at specific ages will duplicate the 1860 distribution for males. Thus, the life-cycle patterns for mean wealth and relative inequality are repeated in an attenuated form in the next generation.

Some semblance of this pattern can be demonstrated with the New Jersey estate data for the years 1796–1800. The estates of 1,661 persons manifest a methodical level of inequality, with Gini coefficients between .59 and .62 for each of the five years. The number of children is stated for 576 of the estates; inequality rises from .602 for the deceased to .625 for the 2,915 children, assuming equal distribution within each family. We could devise more complex models to demonstrate that inequality remains constant.[26]

Land Grants

A test for permanence in wealth and income distributions from 1800 to 1860 can be found in the records of land grants issued to persons in Ohio, Indiana, and Illinois in the North, and in Mississippi in the South. Do these grants result in greater or less inequality than existed further east? It appears that they exhibit inequality to the same degree. In Ohio in 1810 and 1825, inequality of wealth was similar to that found in Pennsylvania in 1800. Acreage granted in Illinois produced the pattern shown in table 28. Government policies that resulted in a progressive lowering of acreage sizes that could be purchased, lower prices in general, and the grants to veterans did not materially alter the pattern of ownership.[27] The Gini coefficient of concentration remained about .60, the same as that found for 1798 in chapter 2.

Slavery

The minority of southerners who held slaves were more numerous in 1800 than in 1860. Slaveholders in New York in 1800 constituted a striking 7 percent of the population of adult males; in the state, life-cycle patterns of slaveholding were similar to those in the South.[28] Inequality in slaveholding remained constant from 1790 to 1860.

Inequality on the Frontier

There was greater inequality in dwelling values at the frontier than in more established areas at a time when the recently settled areas were relatively important; this was the condition in 1798, as displayed by the dwelling values in each of the 687 tax districts in table 24, above.

TABLE 28
LAND GRANTS IN ILLINOIS, 1814–1899

	All Land		Nonrailroad Land	
	No. of Owners	Inequality, G in Acreage	No. of Owners	Inequality, G in Acreage
1814–39	72,385	.566	72,383	.566
1840–54	91,174	.592	90,383	.593
1855–99	38,317	.522	10,973	.614
1814–99	177,712	.611	154,255	.610

Source: Lee Soltow, "Progress and Mobility Among Ohio Propertyholders, 1810–1825," *Social Science History* 7, no. 4 (Fall 1983). Illinois data are derived from data supplied by the Illinois State Archives, Springfield. It was possible for an owner's name to appear in more than one period.

Occupational Diversity

One reason for believing that Americans enjoyed relatively equal incomes in 1800 is the perception that everyone's work was the same. If 90 percent of the population were farmers, and each cultivated 10 of 160 acres, how could there be much variation in either housing or income between individuals? This argument implies that economic conditions were the same among all farmers and that farmers carried on very little productive activity other than farming. The most basic need was for food, with either clothing, shelter, or transportation being secondary; purchases of non-necessities, such as watches, clocks, furniture, carriages, or books were inconsequential. This reasoning strongly endorses a hypothesis of homogeneity and equality of income at the end of the eighteenth century. I have argued that there was great diversity within the farm sector by showing there was large variation in size of landholdings and land values as well as the proportion of the population who owned land. Another important dimension in the study of inequality is to examine the diversity in economic activities and occupations.

An 1800 occupational census does exist for the state of Pennsylvania. The septennial census of that year lists complete occupational descriptions for the city of Philadelphia and eleven counties, with only partial listings for five other counties. These lists identify the occupations of 48,463 taxables (persons) in 1800, as shown in table 29. Farming seems to have been a somewhat less common occupation in rural Pennsylvania than one may have supposed. Those census categories most often mentioned were

TABLE 29
OCCUPATIONS AND ECONOMIC GROUPS IN PENNSYLVANIA, 1800
(males 21 and older)

Most Frequently Listed Occupations	N	Economic Sector	N
Farmer	18,097	Agriculture	20,347
Laborer	4,301	Manufacturing and	
Yeoman	2,250	mechanical (artisans)	15,509
Carpenter	2,154	Domestic and personal	
Tailor, hatter, maker of		services	5,028
finished clothing	2,002	Trade and Transportation	2,496
Weaver	1,797	Professional services	934
Blacksmith	1,652	Other	4,149
Merchant, shopkeeper	1,457		
Widow, spinster	1,390	Total	48,463
Miller	1,170		
Cooper	769		
Ropemaker	769		
Gentleman, esquire	731		
Mason, bricklayer	707		
Innkeeper, tavernkeeper	677		
Shoemaker	671		
Metalworker	525		
Brewer, distiller	445		
Doctor, dentist	394		
Wagonmaker, wheelwright	363		

Source: Lee Soltow and Kenneth Keller, "Rural Pennsylvania in 1800: A Portrait from the Septennial Census," *Pennsylvania History* 49, no. 1 (January 1982), 34–37.

Note: These estimates are based on a sample of 970 occupations drawn from every fiftieth page of those counties listing occupations in the Septennial Census of 1800 (Division of Archives and Manuscripts, State Archives, Harrisburg). Not shown are listings for 115 persons without occupational titles.

farmers (18,097), laborers (4,301), and yeomen (2,250). Among the total of 48,463, "farmer" appears 37 percent of the time, while "laborer" constitutes 9 percent of the total. The broad categories in the second column of the table show that about 42 percent of taxable persons (males 21 and older) were engaged in agriculture, 32 percent were in manufacturing and mechanical enterprises, and about 10 percent performed domestic and personal services. In Pennsylvania as a whole, then, one in every three persons was an artisan, and there were almost as many artisans as there were farmers. The labor force was far from being a homogeneous entity. There was ample opportunity for a diversity of income.[29]

This sketch of factors and institutions influencing the permanence of and change in wealth and income is obviously incomplete. While I have focused particular attention on the one year, 1798, and to a lesser degree on the years 1770–1810 and 1850–1860, a more dynamic approach would be to analyze changes before 1770 and after 1820. Such a study would incorporate the findings of Alice Hanson Jones for 1774 and would analyze the work of Charles Beard and others that deals with the rise of a "paper-money" class during the 1790s; additionally, it would entail the analysis of a long cycle in economic development far before 1820, as opposed to that of Williamson and Lindert, which posits a surge, essentially after 1820, accompanied by increasing diversification of occupations.[30]

I have stressed eleven influences on the inequality of wealth at the end of chapter 7, and in this chapter, ten factors affecting inequality of housing and income. The two approaches to inequality obviously overlap; moreover, neither adequately distinguishes wealth from income. In addition, the various economic classes among persons who did not own real estate are not adequately differentiated. A possible solution to this problem would be to discuss those deemed to be poor enough to receive help—the destitute, as compared to the poor who were able to survive without help from others. In America this group never was large, and accounted for not more than 1 or 2 percent of the population. Tax rolls for Boston in the early 1790s classify 10 percent or more as poor, but this urban environment was hardly typical of the whole country. Perhaps illiteracy data provide the best means for measuring the size of the lowest group. Illiteracy rates were correlated with physical height, and stature in turn was related to economic condition.[31] Research in this field is expanding dramatically and includes the study of demography, death rates, marriage rates, and fertility. The focus of this volume, however, must be on the distribution of economic well-being as revealed in the 1798 census of real estate.

5

Inequality in Philadelphia

Treasury Department, May 25, 1798

5th Congress, 2d Session

Sir:

Having been requested to exhibit a calculation . . . I submit the following results and observations:

Of dwelling houses.

1st Class.	Exceeding $ 80 and not exceeding $ 200,	150,000	houses
2nd Class.	Exceeding $ 200 and not exceeding $ 600,	200,000	houses
3rd Class.	Exceeding $ 600 and not exceeding $ 1,200,	100,000	houses
4th Class.	Exceeding $ 1,200 and not exceeding $ 2,000,	30,000	houses
5th Class.	Exceeding $ 2,000 and not exceeding $ 4,000,	10,000	houses
6th Class.	Exceeding $ 4,000 and not exceeding $ 6,000,	5,000	houses
7th Class.	Exceeding $ 6,000 and not exceeding $10,000,	3,000	houses
8th Class.	Exceeding $10,000 and not exceeding $25,000,	1,500	houses
9th Class.	Exceeding $25,000	500	houses
		500,000	

I have the honor to be, with perfect respect, sir, your obedient servant,
OLIVER WOLCOTT

The Hon. Robert Goodloe Harper
Chairman of the Committee of Ways and Means

AMERICA'S FOREBEARS were well aware of the concepts of inequality and equality and did not hesitate to make generalizations about their extent in various countries. Thus, Benjamin Franklin observed: "Whoever has travelled through the various parts of Europe, and observed how small is the proportion of people in affluence . . . the few rich and haughty landlords, the multitude of poor . . . and views the happy mediocrity that so generally prevails throughout these States [of America], where the cultivator works for himself, and supports his family in decent plenty, will . . . be convinced that no nation known to us enjoys a greater share of human felicity."[1]

The gnawing statistical question is whether Franklin or other scientists of his period understood the concept of a frequency distribution and some of its characteristics. Perhaps he thought in vague terms of some histogram with a homogeneous mass of poor, a small group of nobles and industrialists at the top, and some little-defined middle class—at least in Europe's case. But how did he or other scientists view that group of "happy mediocrity" in America? Was it merely an ill-defined rectangular distribution of limited range?

Knowledge of wealth or income distributions could have been of fundamental importance in framing the federal and various state constitutions in the 1780s and 1790s on such points as property qualifications for voting, the need for a senate or upper chamber to guard minority property rights,[2] land sales, and tax legislation, and, more fundamentally, the rights of individuals—to the extent that such rights could be influenced by the dispersion of income and wealth. Were there at least some experts who understood the concepts of frequency distributions, or was there only statistical ignorance? I, for one, accepted the view that none of our Founding Fathers was applying mathematical notions of distributions to economic variables until I happened to stumble upon the profound report appearing in the *American State Papers* for 1798. Here is evidence that not only was the frequency table known at that time, but also the normal curve, as explained by Quetelet in the 1840s and by Galton in the 1870s.[3] The hypothesis I shall defend in this chapter is that the 1798 report was a unique presentation of a statistical distribution and that it came, not from the centers of European intellectual thought, but from within America's capital.

THE MAY REPORT

On 25 May 1798, Oliver Wolcott, secretary of the treasury, submitted to the House of Representatives a remarkable estimate of the frequency distribution of dwelling house values in the United States (see table 30). The purpose of the exercise was to demonstrate the possibilities for imposing a federal tax on wealth; indeed, within a month legislation was passed leading to the First Direct Tax of the United States. Wolcott's intent, and that of his predecessor, Alexander Hamilton, was to introduce a progressive tax whereby owners of valuable properties paid proportionately higher rates. It was crucial to know frequencies at various levels of housing value in order to assign the amounts of revenue to be raised; the Treasury Department had to consider the entire gamut of housing values in the United States, from a meager log cabin worth only a few dollars to the most elegant of mansions. Evidence was available; for instance, it was known that in 1797 and 1798 Robert Morris of Philadelphia and Elias Hasket Derby of Salem had begun building houses whose values were between $30,000 and $50,000.

Wolcott established a range of nine value classes that was presented to the House of Representatives and published in the *American State Papers*. Table 30 shows that a surprisingly large number of houses in the United States—500—were thought to be worth more than $25,000; such mansions today would sell for many times that value. At the other extreme were 70,000 dwellings, including log cabins, valued at less than $80; this

TABLE 30
WOLCOTT'S SCHEDULE OF DWELLING VALUES FOR 570,000
HOUSES IN THE UNITED STATES, MAY 25, 1798

Class	Lower Limit of Class (X)	No. of Dwellings in Class	Proportion of Houses above X (N_X)	Frequencies Suggested from Lognormal Computer Program
9	$25,000	500	.000877	182
8	10,000	1,500	.00350	1,704
7	6,000	3,000	.00877	3,829
6	4,000	5,000	.0175	6,792
5	2,000	10,000	.0350	26,821
4	1,200	30,000	.0877	39,337
3	600	100,000	.263	87,316
2	200	200,000	.614	193,148
1	80	150,000	.877	140,868
Below $80		70,000	1.000	(70,000)
Total		570,000		570,000

Source: Oliver Wolcott, "Direct Taxes," *American State Papers*, Finance, 5th Cong. 2d sess., 1798, class 3, vol. 1, pp. 588–90. The data are presented in reverse of the order used by Wolcott. The class below $80 is implied from Wolcott's letter, since he stated that there were 570,000 housed in total.

was a group not to be considered for taxation in Wolcott's scheme of classes. Next, we note that frequency numbers increase methodically, from the highest or ninth class (Wolcott's term) to the second class consisting of 200,000 houses, and then decreases to a number less than the first class. The class limits also display the application of a methodical process, with each class being about one-half of the preceding value as one descends from the ninth to the first class. We can argue that these ranges were considered as ratio classes spanning a distance of a ratio of about two (the upper-class limit, divided by the lower-class limit) and that the second class is the modal class in this sense.

It is important to note that the first class in table 30 has a frequency of only 150,000, a number that does not conform to the pattern established in the eight higher classes. This fact suggests that the third class is a shoulder class tapering into the second, or modal class, and that as values fall below $200, house values are arrayed as in the lower half of a bell-shaped curve. This could be the most startling concept of all—the idea that the lower mass of houses do not continue to increase monotonically in ratio scales to a value of $1, but start a downward descent in terms of frequency of occurrence. This means that the very poor were fewer in number than those above them, not greater. This finding makes it possible to single out a minority of people for special attention, as was the case in the dwelling house tax legislation that was passed in June and July 1798.

Readers may feel that this view of reality, a bell-shaped curve, with or without the technical aspects of a ratio or logarithmic scale, is not novel. They have known about this curve from the time they examined a grade distribution in school, "the curve," unless they were part of a very selective group, one with very few students with grades in the lower tail of a distribution. The literature indicates that Abraham De Moivre first proposed the formula for the normal curve in 1733 but that he took no interest in applying the concept to empirical data, aside from a study of errors of measurement. It was left to Quetelet in the 1830s and 1840s to suggest the idea of using the curve to analyze social and economic data; but even he offered very little applied evidence, claiming that there were no adequate data at that time. According to Walker, the first table employing the normal curve was published by a French physicist named Kramp either in 1799 or 1798, doubtless unknown to Oliver Wolcott.[4]

PREVIOUSLY PUBLISHED FREQUENCY DISTRIBUTIONS

The frequency formulation prepared by Wolcott, so far as I can determine from an examination of American and European publications before 1798, was the first published distribution showing a modal class with a lower tail below it. Frequency tables for the ages of living and deceased persons date from at least 1750, for windows in larger houses from 1759, and for hearths in all homes from 1787. None of these tables shows either a lower tail or a well-formulated schedule of class frequencies with lower limits indicating a ratio scale.

The distributions of living populations, classified by age, generally were in the shape of a reverse-J, with the modal class being the lowest class. Thus, Swedish males in 1750 were more numerous between the ages of 5 and 9 than in ages 10–14, and in 0–4 more than in 5–9.[5] An exception to the J-shape would arise if there were a famine or disease specifically causing infant mortality from time to time. The Icelandic census for 1703 demonstrates an age distribution with a modal class for ages 15–19; the most frequent age if not the concept of a *modal* class must have been understood by Professor Arni Magnusson when he directed the enumeration in that year, but there is no evidence to prove the point.[6]

The distribution of the number of deaths occurring in a given time interval can lead to age distributions in several different forms, but generally they are thought to be unimodal, with two tails. In his generalizations, De Moivre found it convenient to describe the distributions as rectangular in shape.[7] High infant mortality rates usually dominate, but one or two other classes may be prominent. The earliest authoritative count of deaths was that for Sweden, Finland, and Pomerania in 1749, available in the Archives of the Central Bureau of Statistics in Stockholm. It shows a mode for males from ages 0–1 and again at ages 10–64.

The first distributions employing an economic variable, aside from age configurations of the living and dead, appeared in published form as housing statistics. The earliest important proxy for the upper tail of a wealth distribution was for houses, classified by number of windows, in England and Wales in 1759 and published in the *Parliamentary Papers* in 1781. (See table 31.) Because details for the 60 percent of all houses with six or more windows are sparse, they are insufficient evidence to ascertain the general shape of the frequency curve, the modal class, and a lower tail. The largest number of cottages may mean that the mode was at zero or one window. Thus because the number of windows per house may be an imperfect index of housing values and/or wealth of the population, there is little to be learned from the 1759, 1777, or 1781 window data.[8]

In 1792, Richard Price published an essentially complete distribution of hearths in Irish houses enumerated in 1787. (See table 32.) Unfortu-

TABLE 31
HOUSING VALUES IN ENGLAND AND WALES, AS MEASURED BY
NUMBER OF WINDOWS, 1759

No. of Windows[a]	No. of Houses
80 and over	1,502
60–80	1,692
50–60	2,143
40–50	4,274
30–40	9,719
20–30	27,109
15–19	46,708
10–14	113,133
6–9	383,513
0–6[b]	114,751
Cottages[c]	276,148

Source: British Sessional Papers, House of Commons, Accounts and Papers, vol. 11, 1780–1781, nos. 15–17, 20; Accounts and Papers, vol. 5, 1784, nos. 54b–59, appendix table, penciled, p. 4; Richard Price, *Observations on Reversionary Payments* (London: T. Cadell, 1783), p. 277.

   a. Taxable.
   b. Chargeable (taxable).
   c. Non taxable.

nately, this reverse-J pattern is neither lognormal nor Pareto in shape except above the top quartile. Ninety percent of homes had one hearth, representing an overwhelming modal class at the bottom. This frequency distribution is important, however, in conveying the concept of an empirically derived frequency curve, and it is possible that this information was available in America.[9] In all likelihood, Benjamin Franklin was acquainted with the statistical work of Price and others; a chapter in one of Price's books was devoted to correspondence with Franklin on the doubling of the population in America.[10]

The distribution of hearths may be unique, since there appear to be no other published examples of complete distributions. The printers' plates of the *Encyclopædia Britannica* were used to publish 18 volumes in Philadelphia, in 1798, titled the *Encyclopædia: or, a Dictionary of Arts, Sciences and Miscellaneous.* I have looked through its approximately 14,000 pages of learned articles and can find no bell-shaped curve. Nor can I find any examples of a frequency curve for a continuous variable. While there are some semblances of counts involving qualitative variables, there are

TABLE 32
HOUSING VALUES IN IRELAND, AS MEASURED BY
NUMBER OF HEARTHS, 1787

No. of Hearths	No. of Houses
112	1
50–92	7
20–49	224
5–19	16,148
2–4	37,135
1	397,644
Total	451,159

Source: Richard Price, Observations on Reversionary Payments, 5th ed. (London: T. Cadell, 1792), p. 342.

none with a quantitative variable even remotely similar to the housing values given in Wolcott's May 1798 report.[11]

My argument to this point is that Wolcott's table is unique because its data present a bell-shaped curve and because each ratio class has an upper limit about double the amount of its lower limit. While I do not assert that the bell shape is specifically a lognormal curve, there is a strong suggestion that this is true. First, by using a probit analysis, I shall demonstrate that Wolcott's table was truly logarithmic. I continue with an explanation of how the Philadelphia group, by considering the binomial expansion, *may* have derived such a distribution mathematically. Finally, I must consider the possibility that Wolcott derived the table from empirical observations of his own and of others; however, I consider this unlikely.

LOGNORMALITY

It is well known that a ratio scale becomes arithmetic if logarithms are applied. There is a lengthy article (30 pages) on logarithms, including a voluminous logarithm table, as well as other logarithm examples in the 1798 Encyclopædia. David Rittenhouse published an article in the 1795 Transactions of the American Philosophical Society entitled, "Method of Raising the Common Logarithm of any Number." Articles published in various years demonstrate the use of logarithms in astronomical applications.[12] What was not known was that the lognormal curve is uniquely determined by the value of its standard deviation when the variable is expressed in logarithms. This value can be estimated as follows: determine the number of standard deviations from the mean (the probit) corresponding to the N_x of table 30 by examining the standard normal distribution; plot each probit against the logarithms of its lower class limit; the resulting nine points will plot as a straight line if the data are lognormal. This comes close to being true for the Wolcott data, as shown with the top line and points in figure 8. The resulting squared correlation coefficient is a remarkable .9813. The slope of the line determines the standard deviation of the log of the variable, and this can be used directly in a simple computer run to generate the frequencies shown in the last column of table 30, above. If the Wolcott frequencies had been the same as those in the last column of the table, then we could say there was overwhelming evidence that the Treasury group had employed a table similar to a lognormal table.

Statistical tests of the differences between Wolcott's report and the computer columns of table 30 demonstrate that it is a reasonable hypothesis that the two columns come from the same frequency curve.[13] This is shown in figure 8. More important is the idea that when the computer-run entries are rounded to two significant digits, with the second digit being either a zero or a five, with the total being 570,000, the procedure *perforce* generates numbers almost identical to those of the Wolcott column. I informally tested this procedure by asking a CPA friend to round the computer-column numbers by applying the rules stated above, without his having seen the Wolcott column. I asked him to make a "fair" presentation, as if to congressmen, and in the realization that the computer-column procedure might be quite far from reality. Obviously, he was forced to use a 500 and 1,500 for the first two frequencies, and the remaining entries of 2,500, 5,500, 20,000, 35,000, 85,000, 200,000, and 150,000 tell us what we need to know, that a little further rounding produces the figures used in the May 1798 report.[14]

How did the Treasury Department develop its idea of a lognormal table if it had no access to a statistics textbook or to the computer commands, "probnorm" or "probit"? The table must have been developed as had been done, in part, by De Moivre—by considering the coefficients generated by the expansion of $(a + b)^N$. We are well aware that the following numbers are generated by this procedure and that it produces a normal curve for large N, as shown in table 33. The arrangement for an N of 14 has nine classes if one counts the first class below the modal class and all those above it. This scheme, coupled with lower class limits that double as we proceed up the ladder, is, to my mind, the technique Wolcott used. Its standard deviation in logarithms to the base 10 is .5261 for the top nine classes, while that for Wolcott's classes was .5624. Rounding to frequencies can explain the differences.

Today's scholar might well question whether Wolcott possessed the

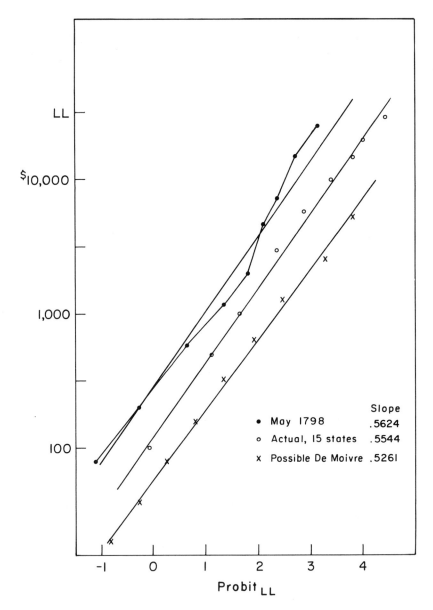

FIGURE 8. THREE LOGNORMAL DISTRIBUTIONS OF HOUSING VALUES IN THE UNITED STATES, 1798

NOTE: The figure exhibits the lower limit of the dwelling house class (LL) and the number of standard deviations of a normal table corresponding to frequencies above LL (Probit$_{LL}$) for nine classes. See tables 30, 33, and 35.

TABLE 33
HOW PASCAL'S TRIANGLE SUGGESTS THE WOLCOTT TABLE

No. of classes (N+1)	
1	1
2	1 1
3	1 2 1
4	1 3 3 1
5	1 4 6 4 1
.	
.	
.	
14	1 13 78 286 715 1,287 1,716 1,716 1,287 715 186 78 13 1
15	1 14 91 364 1,001 2,002 3,003 3,432 3,003 2,002 1,001 364 91 14 1

technical knowledge necessary to construct the table. However, the Treasury Department could have used the assistance of someone like David Rittenhouse and Alexander Hamilton, listed with his former title as secretary of the treasury. They both were members of the American Philosophical Society, a most prestigious learned society whose presidents included Rittenhouse until his death in 1799, followed by Thomas Jefferson.

Earlier, Rittenhouse had been appointed to a government position at the urging of both Hamilton and Jefferson. Jefferson himself was keenly interested in the fiscal reports presented by his secretary of the treasury, Albert Gallatin, who had been leader of the House at the time of the Wolcott report. Nevertheless, it appears that it was Wolcott who was so enamored with the concept of the housing tax. As long as two decades later, while he served as governor of Connecticut, Wolcott's notes show numerous pages of calculations he used in the preparation of an 1820 tax proposal. Another notable personage at the time of the 1798 report was Benjamin Rush, a Philadelphia physician and director of the Mint. Someone in that group of leaders had the flash of brilliance necessary to realize that a wealth distribution might be represented by the lognormal curve. (The idea would not appear again for two generations or more.)

POSSIBLE EMPIRICAL DERIVATION OF THE RATIO SCALE

We face the issue of whether the distribution was designed from empirical data or from mathematical considerations by coupling the coefficients of the binomial expansion with a ratio scale. The dwelling house distribution very well could have been a rounding from an empirical frequency distribution. This I cannot deny. The county tax ledgers for Philadelphia from 1780 to 1798 contain listings of the assessed values of all dwellings, and these reveal unimodal curves whose intervals are geometric in scale. See the 167 values for the city's High Street Ward in 1796 given in table 34. Such an arrangement almost certainly suggests a ratio scale rather than an arithmetic scale if one were to array the values and then struggle to form class frequencies. The data very definitely indicate a lower tail, consisting perhaps of a group of persons in relative poverty, with a few who were living in destitution. The number in the lower tail was relatively small—a few houses or families—not the one large and homogeneous mass at the bottom suggested by the lowest class in the hearth data. Yet, I find no evidence from manuscripts in Philadelphia archives and libraries that anyone had formed a frequency count, with class frequencies. We have only the tables for ages, windows (upper tail), and hearths previously noted.[15]

Suppose the Wolcott group did develop its distribution empirically from Philadelphia housing data; also suppose they formed classes where the lower class limit of one class was a multiple of the lower limit of the next class or where a ratio scale pattern of progression was employed. Their tally would show a peak or modal class, with classes on either side forming tails and tracing the bell-shaped curve as we know it. If this occurred, I would assert that they were performing a unique statistical experiment not achieved before. The frequency table would reveal something about the conditions of the poor in the lower tail—the degrees of relative poverty.

TABLE 34

HOUSING VALUES IN THE HIGH STREET WARD, PHILADELPHIA, 1796

Class	Frequency
$4,000 and over	2
2,000–3,999	37
1,000–1,999	50
500–999	20
250–499	31
125–249	17
62–124	9
Under 62	1

Source: Philadelphia City Archives, City Hall Annex, Philadelphia.

A more appealing theory is that the 1798 report was based on knowledge of the binomial expansion. The Pascal triangle dates from the seventeenth century, and elegant statements of its configurations appeared prior to the 1798 table, sometimes in treatises also covering annuities. A text published in 1776, *Miscellanies or a Miscellaneous Treatise, Containing Several Mathematical Subjects,*[16] treats the configurations in detail, including the number of trials necessary for a rare event to have an even chance of occurring. It is possible to interpret the "rare event" to be the construction of a mansion, and the "less rare events" to be those houses worth $10,000 or more, or even $5,000 or more. Often the solutions for probabilities involved the use of logarithms.

VERIFICATION OF THE MAY 1798 CONFIGURATION

The perception that the coefficients of $(a + b)^{14}$, coupled with a ratio scale, might describe housing in America is significant, whether or not it was a reliable characterization of the actual population (count) of dwelling values. I would be satisfied if we could show that the reality was a unimodal curve with two tails. If the curve were an isosceles or acute triangle, it would capture the idea of a lower tail.

We can do better, however, since the number of houses in each of the nine classes in table 30 is known for 490,000 houses in 15 of the states in 1798.[17] These are shown in table 35. The figures in the table are based on data collected *after* 1 October 1798 and presented to the tax authorities not long after. These data, then, are the reality that provides the statistical verification of the speculative report made in May of that year.

From the data gathered by the tax authorities, the house with the greatest value was the Salem, Massachusetts, edifice designed essentially by Samuel McIntire and built in 1798 for America's first millionaire. At the other extreme were large numbers of humble log huts valued at less than $10. The reports in 1799 (and later) presented by tax authorities show an arithmetic mean only half as large as that implied by Wolcott's May 1798 estimate, but this should not detract from the formulation. The essential fact is that the relative dispersion found in the estimate is almost identical to that found by empirical investigation.

A straight line again appears when the probit values are plotted against logarithms of the lower limits for the nine classes above $100 of the 1799 report. This time the squared correlation coefficient is .9949 and the slope tells us that the standard deviation of logarithms is .5544; the counterpart values for the nine points in the May 1798 report were .9818 and .5624.

TABLE 35
HOUSING VALUES IN FOURTEEN STATES, 1798–1799

Class Rank	Lower Class Limit (X)	Frequencies in Class
1	$30,000	2
2	20,000	12
3	15,000	23
4	10,000	123
5	6,000	842
6	3,000	3,573
7	1,000	19,884
8	500	39,207
9	100	192,259
10	1(?)	234,346
	Total	490,271

Sources: Lee Soltow, "America's First Progressive Tax," *National Tax Journal* 30, no. 1 (March 1977), 53–58; and "Distribution of Income and Wealth," in *Encyclopedia of American Economic History,* ed. Glenn Porter (New York: Scribners, 1980), 3:1087–1119.

Note: The union had seventeen states in this period.

These values are shown in table 36. Any difference could be explained by rounding procedures used in the May report. In any case, there is no question about the authenticity of the empirical data. Authorities spent thousands of hours gathering information in every township in the country, and records of individual valuations have been preserved for a few of the states. I have spent several years developing data for the three states for which no summaries exist, to yield an estimate of 576,600 for the total number of dwellings in the country—little different from the 570,000 total used in the Wolcott report. In addition, my estimated relative dispersion for the 17 states differs little from that determined from the information for the 14 states. The originators of the lognormal curve were able not only to formulate its general shape but also to estimate its essential pattern properly. The Philadelphia group did indeed comprehend that there was relative inequality in America!

How do we explain the flash of brilliance produced in the May report? Were there any further data sets available that Wolcott, Hamilton, Rittenhouse, Joseph Nourse (the registrar), or other men might have seen earlier? Perusal of the *Encyclopædia Britannica* of 1798, of the *Transactions of the American Philosophical Society* before 1799, or of Michael Mulhall's fourth edition of *The Dictionary of Statistics* yields no leads. The British *Parliamentary Papers* for 1797 and 1798 report two distribu-

TABLE 36
DISTRIBUTION OF HOUSING VALUES IN THE UNITED STATES, 1798–1799

	May 1798[a]	1799[b]	Possible DeMoivre
The Top 9 Classes			
Mean	$668	512	728
Probit analysis			
Standard deviation of logarithms	.5624	.5544	.5261
Standard error of slope	.0289	.015	.0096
Correlation coefficient squared	.9818	9949	.9977

All 10–15 Classes

The Top Proportion of Cases (N_x)	Share of All Wealth (A_x)		
.0001	.0051	.0064	.0045
.001	.049	.034	.028
.002	.074	.060	.043
.005	.134	.105	.085
.01	.193	.174	.130
.02	.267	.230	.200
.05	.378	.400	.336
.10	.495	.525	.493
.20	.638	.659	.669
.50	.867	.911	.896
1.00	1.00	1.00	1.00

N	570,000	490,271	16,384
Mean	$592	288	583
Inequality, G	.606	.628	.628

Sources: See tables 30, 33, and 35.

Note: The De Moivre distribution uses coefficients from $(a+b)^{14}$ and class midpoints of 2, 4, ..., 2^{15}. Tests of the difference between sample slopes for the nine probit points reveal no statistical significance.

a. Proposed.

b. Recorded for 14 states.

tions, one for house rents and the other for taxes on houses, windows, and so forth, which in an inadequate way demonstrate a lower tail.[18] These distributions were used in more detail by Sir John Sinclair in a distribution published in 1803–1804; Sinclair was a famous Scottish investigator with whom George Washington corresponded at great length concerning farming experiments.[19]

Perhaps the Philadelphia group had seen the English distributions, but it is more likely that their insight was gained from American sources. Consider an analysis of all of the fireplaces in Connecticut, classified for tax purposes in four categories. (See table 37.) These distributions do convey the idea of a lower tail of a distribution, at least in incipient form. It happens that they display configurations that are almost exactly lognormal when tax rates are used as values, although with far less relative dispersion than is found in the Wolcott report distribution. Note also that the rate schedule of the first, third, and fourth classes conceivably could suggest a ratio scale. A search of the literature of the time produces a few other examples of value distributions for types of property, but they tend to confuse the underlying features of a unimodal curve with upper and lower tails. We can say that the Philadelphia formulators were not operating in an empirical vacuum.[20]

DEFERENCE TO INEQUALITY

We note, finally, that the learned men, officials, and particularly the Congress of 1798 applied their knowledge of inequality wisely. The ingenious form $(a+b)^{14}$ sparked strong congressional discussions about economic classes, particularly in terms of their relative ability to pay a proposed federal tax. Those nine classes quantitatively demonstrated that there were many levels of economic condition, from poor to rich, in this land of equality. Debate arose about "throwing the tax upon that part of the community who are best able to bear it and to avert it from the poor." The leaders groped with the idea of regressive and progressive rates, with terms such as "a tax not merely in an arithmetic proportion to their poorer

TABLE 37

HOUSING VALUES IN CONNECTICUT, AS MEASURED BY TAX ON
FIREPLACES, 1796 AND 1798

Rate Category	Tax	No. in 1796	No. in 1798
1	$2.50	4,883	4,588
2	1.88	6,924	7,839
3	1.25	30,424	33,741
4	.63	25,330	25,372

Sources: Oliver Wolcott, Jr., "Direct Taxes," *American State Papers*, Finance, 4th Cong., 2d sess., 1796, class 3, vol. 1, pp. 443–55; *Return of the Grand List of the State of Connecticut for Aug. 20, 1798*. Connecticut State Library, Hartford.

neighbors," or, more specifically, "a man worth ten thousand dollars a year ought to pay more than ten times the tax than a man pays who is worth only one thousand dollars a year."[21]

The outcome was a House tax law with an astonishing schedule. The rate to be applied to the value of the house for the nine classes, in order from lowest to highest value (and with slightly different class limits), was .002, .003, .004, .005, .006, .007, .008, .009, and .010. The rich owner of a house in the highest class paid a tax five times the rate paid by those with houses in the lowest tax class. The binomial expansion suggests, in addition, five untaxed classes below the nine. This schedule may have produced the world's first effective progressive tax, and certainly one of its most spectacular ones.[22]

The lognormal distribution was not applied in a fashion to convey the superiority of a certain class nor the inferiority of the common man. This was a far cry from the concept that was applied a half century later.[23] Generally, the poor were characterized as rural rather than urban peoples, and, more specifically, as new rather than old settlers. Never was reference made to the idea of a meritocracy; there was only a groping for a fair tax system within a country whose society had experienced vast economic inequality.[24] The lognormal curve, a normal curve, was first formulated as an approximation to empirical data in Philadelphia in 1798. This application in the field of economics was occasioned by a fiscal crisis stemming from the threat of an imminent war with France. Using the lognormal curve for purposes of assessing taxes originated not in a major capital of Europe, but in a remarkable town of 40,000 inhabitants, in a new republic, and in the company of a remarkable group of learned men.[25]

6

Comparisons with Europe

THE SHARES of wealth belonging to various social groups is a strong measure both of political power and of sociological demarcation of those population segments. These wealth shares have economic ramifications affecting income incentives and the degrees of consumption and saving. Another natural approach for studying relative shares within a country is to compare ownership configurations in one country with those of another. We can thereby highlight the distribution of wealth in the United States relative to those for a composite of European countries. There can be little doubt that America's distribution was significantly different from those of Europe. This chapter is devoted to the magnitude of these differences.

From the standpoint of inherent political power, it is convenient to consider four wealth groups: the few at the top; the top several hundred to several thousand, in part delineated as the nobility; the wider group of property owners in the labor force; and the remainder of the population with no appreciable wealth. We have seen that this fourth group, the propertyless, constituted half of the adult males in America. The relative size of the propertyless group in any European country is the most fundamental quantitative distinction that can be made between America and Western Europe. However, the shares of wealth belonging to the other three groups is also of fundamental significance in understanding political and social groups in any society. Does the top group have 10 percent of wealth while the remainder of the top several hundred lay claim to half of the wealth? John Taylor asserted that one thesis proposed by John Adams was tantamount to saying that the top three groups each would have one-third of total wealth.[1] This severe scheme describing inequality was far off the mark in America. Was it more true of Europe?

THE FEW

In England and on the Continent, a few individuals owned very substantial amounts of land at the end of the eighteenth century, as had their fathers and grandfathers in previous generations. The members of this group usually were the select coterie of royalty, the king or queen, their brothers and sisters, and other members of the royal family as well as the top echelon of the nobility. For example, in 1798 in England, the duke of Bedford owned 7 percent to 8 percent of the landed value in Bedfordshire, as did a later duke of Bedford in 1874–1875. Entailed estates and primogeniture helped to cement the proportional shares held by the few from generation to generation. Admittedly, there had been some radical changes in the structure of ownership in the years preceding 1800. In the United States, the large Loyalist estates that had been confiscated during the Revolution were transferred to Americans; and in France, the confiscated church lands essentially were transferred to private individuals; but, in a slightly earlier period, the church in Spain had retained nearly 20 percent of the country's land.[2]

The duke of Bedford was the greatest property owner in England in 1798, as revealed by the land tax books for that year. His extensive collection of estates stemmed from land originally given to the family by Henry VII, and included 1,800 properties in the counties of Bedford, Devon, Southampton, Middlesex, and on the Isle of Ely.[3] Yet the aggregate estate belonging to this wealthiest of individuals constituted only .17 percent of the total number of properties in England and Wales and only .07 percent of aggregate value

Landholding patterns in distant Sweden were of strategic importance in the settlement of America because in the former country the populace was almost without hope of ownership; the prospects of climbing the economic ladder attracted large numbers of Swedes to this country and deprived Sweden of a significant portion of its population over a number of years. A methodical search of the estate inventories of deceased wealthy nobles in Sweden for the years from 1791–1810 gives a strong indication that the nobility held the greatest amounts of wealth in that country. For example, the estate of largest value was that belonging to Count Carl Bonde (and his wife, Countess Högvälborna Ebbe Margarete Bonde) who died in 1791. The 1796 inventory showed that his estate included .1 percent of Sweden's land area and 1.3 percent of its value:

	Carl Bonde, 1796	Sweden, 1800
Area (in *hemman*)	70⅛	70,998
Value (riksdaler banko)	2,192,162	166,126,167

In 1783 Bonde established an entailed estate, Vibyholm in Södermanlands County, consisting of 2,915 hectares and valued at 64 million kronor in 1796. Bonde was the owner of two other entailed estates in Jönköping County, apparently not part of the estate mentioned above.[4]

In the United States, surely Elias Hasket Derby was the most affluent man at the end of the eighteenth century. The value of his estate inventory at the time of his death on 8 September 1799 was $990,882.[5] Derby amassed this wealth as a shipowner, merchant, and trader. His worldwide foreign commerce included dealings in the West Indies, Russia, Africa, China, India, and the East Indies. The Derby estate accounted for .16 percent of U.S. real estate in 1798 and about .13 percent of its total estate values. The estate of George Washington, probably the second or third wealthiest man in America, in 1799 had a value that amounted to just about half of Derby's. While Derby's mansion (described in chapter 4) was most magnificent for this country, it surely did not measure up to the standards of manor houses belonging to the duke of Bedford or to Sweden's Count Bonde. Visits to both of these residences as well as to Washington's home makes one realize that while Mount Vernon has great historical significance, it is no match for the others in elegance. Examples of the shares of wealth held by the richest men in the United States and some European countries are given in table 38.

Generally, the richest individual in a small population can be expected to have a larger share of total wealth than the most affluent person in a large population. Thus, the share of wealth, A_W, in table 38 is misleading unless some adjustment is made by considering N_W. One approximation is to use the lognormal tables, and to find the Gini coefficient table specifying the N_W and A_W given above. This is tantamount to assuming that wealth was lognormally distributed among all adult males or families in each country, county, or parish, extending to the very upper tail above four standard deviations from the mean. The coefficients for England-Wales and for the United States are the same in this case. This approximation test indicates that the share held by the duke of Bedford was in line with Derby's because the combined population of England and Wales was nearly three times as large as the population of the United States. The fact that the Gini coefficients were larger for the richest person in three of the four Scandinavian countries, if

TABLE 38
THE SHARE OF WEALTH HELD BY THE RICHEST MAN IN
EIGHT COUNTRIES, 1770–1814

	No. of Males 20 and Older (1800)	The Top Case as a Proportion of Population (N_W)	Proportion of All Wealth Owned (A_W)	Implied Inequality[a]
England	2,500,000	.0000004	.0007	.79
Sweden	640,000	.0000016	.013	.92
Denmark	277,000	.0000036	.025	.93
Norway	216,000	.0000093	.017	.88
Finland	217,000	.0000029	.007	.73
Belgium	700,000	.0000014	.002	.80
Scotland	316,000	.0000032	.029	.94
United States	872,000	.0000011	.0013	.79

Sources: Lee Soltow: "Wealth Distribution in Denmark in 1789," *Scandinavian Economic History Review* 17, no. 2 (October 1979), 1–18; "The Distribution of Property Values in England and Wales in 1798," *Economic History Review*, 2d ser. 34, no. 1 (February 1981), 60–70; "The Distribution of Wealth in Belgium in 1814–1815," *Journal of European Economic History* 10, no. 2 (Fall 1981), 401–13; "Wealth Distribution in Norway and Denmark in 1789," *Historisk Tidsskrift,* Winter 1981, pp. 221–35; "Wealth Distribution in Finland in 1800," *Scandinavian Economic History Review* 29, no. 1 (Winter 1981), 21–32; "Wealth Inequality in the United States in 1798 and 1860," *Review of Economics and Statistics* 66, no. 3 (August 1984), 444–51; and "The Swedish Census of Wealth at the Beginning of the 19th Century," *Scandinavian Economic History Review* 33, no. 1 (1985), 1–24; Loretta Timperley, "Landownership in Scotland in the Eighteenth Century," Ph.D. diss., University of Edinburgh, 1977, pp. 154, 243–76.

a. Rough guess, using lognormal table, for inequality among all adult males.

not for Belgium, is an indication that the very wealthy in these countries held extremely large portions of relative wealth.

In Scotland land was owned by very few heritors who often did not live in the parish or county where the properties were located. Only 3 percent or less of the adult male population owned landed property, led by the duke of Buccleuch with rental incomes totaling £330,000 a year in 1770, or well over $1 million. His share of the total landed wealth in Scotland is an indication that the inequality of wealth was larger there than in the seven other listed countries.

THE TOP SEVERAL HUNDRED TO SEVERAL THOUSAND

The uppermost fraction of a percent of the population, perhaps one in 10,000 or one in 1,000 families enjoyed an inordinate share of each nation's assets. These included the nobility and a few manufacturers, shippers, and traders in Europe and, in America, shippers, traders, and plantation owners with slaves. The heated writings of some Americans at the turn of the century would lead one to believe that those with "paper" or "money wealth" were among the economic elite, a group who held government and bank securities or were creditors—a class having personal wealth rather than wealth in real estate.

The shares held by the top 100—300 individuals in England during this time are not known exactly. For individuals, no collation of all properties has been made, as has been done in the case of the duke of Bedford. However, we do know something about the largest among the one million English properties, as reported in 1798, which gives us some insight into the magnitudes involved. The top 345 properties in England had values of at least $100,000 each, or possibly $200,000, in 1798, depending on how their rental value was determined.[6] Of these estates, the duke of Norfolk owned five, while the duke of Bedford and the earl of Spencer each owned four. The marquis of Buckingham, the duchess of Buccleuch, the earl of Guilford, the earl of Harborough, the earl of Hardwicke, Colonel Noel, the duke of Portland, and George Sutton, Esq., each owned three. Thus, there was a hierarchy among multiple property holders within this small group of extensive estates that constituted 3 percent of the real estate values in England and Wales.

Some feeling for the grandeur of the living standards of the rich is shown in the list presented in table 39 of window counts in Scotland. The three entries heading the list were each taxed for having 17 male servants. The duke of Hamilton reported four four-wheeled carriages for private use and two other persons reported ownership of three. The majority stated that they owned more than 10 horses while others owned more than 20. A final index stems from a tax on dogs, presumably hunting dogs. One person on the list reported ownership of 41 dogs, and three others declared from 30 to 32 dogs.

Swedish holdings also provide a picture of domination by a select group owning significant shares of wealth. This is best understood by studying the entailed estates, a process founded after 1695 and essentially completed by 1805. In 1880, this institution accounted for 219 estates representing 4.6 percent of the rural land in Sweden and 4.4 percent of the country's tax value. The larger part of the 163–65 owners in that year belonged to the nobility: 37 counts and countesses, 41 barons and baronesses, and 61 others of the noble class. Many of their manor houses are standing today, lasting evidence of the grandiose scale of life that characterized most of these estates.

TABLE 39
Houses in Scotland with 100 or More Windows, 1798

Owner	Manor or Parish	County	No. of Windows
His Grace the Duke of Hamilton	Hamilton	Lanarkshire	336
The Duke of Gordon	Bellcy Parish	Banffshire	250
The Earl of Hopetoune	Abercorn	Invernesshire	216
The Duke of Queensberry	Durrisdeer	Dumfriesshire	185
Hble. William Ramsay Maule	Panbride	Forfarshire	171
Robert May, Dunse Castle	Dunse	Berwickshire	169
Marquis of Tweedale	Gifford	Haddington	168
Earl of Capills	Kirkoswald	Ayrshire	165
George Bailie	Earlston	Berwickshire	158
The Rt. Hon. James Earl of Fife	Banff	Banffshire	150
Earl of Moray, Donybristle	Dalgety	Fife	150
Earl of Haddington	Whitekirk	Haddington	142
Earl of Wemyss, Amisfield	Haddington	Haddington	139
Earl of Leven	Monnymail	Fife	136
R. A. Oswald	St. Evox	Ayrshire	133
	Old		130
Earl of Dumfries	Cumnock	Ayrshire	
William Fairholm, Lauderfort	Lauder	Berwickshire	125
William Ferguson of Raith	Abbotshill	Fife	125
Rep. of Earl of Marchmont	Palworth	Berwickshire	120
Lord Kintore	Keith-hall	Aberdeen	116
General William Wemyss	Wemyss	Fife	115
Earl of Bute	Kingarth	Buteshire	114
J. F. Erskine	Alloa	Clackmananshire	113
Walter Campbell	Bothwell	Lanarkshire	112
Lord Aberdeen	Methlick	Aberdeenshire	110
Marquis Fitchfield, Balcombie	Crail	Fife	110
James Murray of Broughton	Girthon	Kirkcudbrightshire	109
Lad Douglas	Douglas	Lanarkshire	108
General Gordon	Fyvie	Aberdeenshire	108
Sir David Carnigie	Kinnard	Forfarshire	105
Robert David	Newbyth	Haddington	105
Col. Grant of Maie	Dyke	Elginshire	104
William Nisbit	Dirlton	Haddington	102
Sir James Grant	Cromdale	Invernesshire	100

Source: Scottish Records Office, Edinburgh, E326/15. This list of 34 houses is not complete, since many counties are missing. "An Account of the Net Assessment of the Duty on Houses and Windows in Scotland" (June 1812) states there were 23 houses with 150 or more windows and 57 with 100–149 windows.

It seems strange that in a country such as Norway there may have been an upper echelon of wealth holders, since its population was only about one-third that of the United States, and essentially there was no Norwegian nobility. The list of rich in 1789 was led by Frue General Krigs Commissarinde Holter, the widow of Peder Holter, a businessman and estate owner as well as director-general of the war office and collector of customs and excise. His wealth was largely in landed estates such as Hafslund and Borregaard in Østfold and Ljan in Oslo. He was active in the timber trade and owned a sugar refinery. The second wealthiest individual was a large-scale shipowner, timber merchant, and owner of a mining industry. His forest land and sawmills were spread all over Østland. This richest of men in a relatively poor country estimated that about 20,000 people were directly dependent on his business activities for their livelihoods. A list of the top 20 to 40 wealth holders in the country reveals business activities similar to the two stated above. They were merchants, shippers, traders, and landowners; in addition, some maintained high positions within the government bureaucracy or in the military.

The excellent occupational censuses for Scandinavia compiled around 1800 are unique, and in many ways they are the best in the world. They display counts of the various socioeconomic groups, from the multitudes of day laborers to the few "capitalists" and the nobility. There is a remarkable classification of Swedish families as destitute, poor, somewhat rich, or rich, that shows 26 percent and 3 percent, respectively, in the last two categories. *Very* rich persons presumably may have consisted of .3 percent or less of the total, or about 2,000 families in that country whose population was about three-quarters the size of the white population in the United States at the time.[7]

Finally, table 40 notes the occupations of Belgium's richest individuals in 1814, the top .3 percent of the country's 700,000 adult males.

Were the United States' wealthiest 200–2,000 persons significantly different from persons in Europe of comparable rank? Most assuredly, the Americans were different in the sense that there was no nobility in the country, and, just as uniquely, owners of large plantations possessed many slaves. First, by presenting a distribution of slaves for 1790 (see table 41), we can delineate the group that should be considered to be the economic elite.

To be sure, those 1,056 slaveholders who owned 50 or more slaves were a group in many ways as significant as were the elite groups in Europe, described above.[8] Their wealth in 98,000 slaves, valued at $175 per slave, represented 2.3 percent of aggregate wealth in real and personal

TABLE 40
OCCUPATIONS OF THE WEALTHIEST MEN IN BELGIUM, 1814

	N
Proprietor	498
Rentier	266
Merchant or industrialist	307
Official	310
Lawyer	33
Banker	6
Farmer or cultivator	76
Notary	31
Doctor or pharmacist	39
Other	52
Total	1,818

Source: Lee Soltow, "The Distribution of Wealth in Belgium in 1814–1815," *Journal of European Economic History* 10, no. 2 (Fall 1981), 403; basic data are given in F.G.C. Beterams, *The High Society Belgo-Luxembourgeoise au Debut du Gouvernement de Guillaume Ier, Roi des Pays-Bas (1814–1815)* (Wetteren, Belgium: Imprimerie Cultura, 1973).

Note: The table represents the top .3 percent of Belgium's adult males in 1814.

TABLE 41
FAMILY WEALTH, AS MEASURED BY OWNERSHIP OF SLAVES, 1790

No. of Slaves (SL)	No. of Slaveholding Families above SL
300 or over	7
200	45
100	243
50	1,056
20	6,330

Source: U.S. Bureau of the Census, *A Century of Population Growth* (Washington, D.C.: GPO, 1909; rpt. New York: Johnson Reprint Corp., 1966), p. 136.

estate in the United States. In value terms, this 2.3 percent was the equivalent of the 345 landed estates in England and Wales described previously. On the other hand, the 2.3 percent was half of the equivalent value of Sweden's entailed estates.

The American rich in the North are more difficult to quantify. A methodical listing of the top several hundred rich persons could be compiled by examining all inventories of those who died between 1790 and 1810, or preferably, between 1785 and 1815, in order to encompass a generation. However, such a feat has not been performed, to my knowledge; at best, I can report some cases for Suffolk County (Boston). It appears that in the North there were at least several hundred families whose wealth was larger than that of plantation owners. The inventories of deceased in Suffolk County for the 12 years from 1796 to 1807 form the distribution shown in table 42.

The very rich, with property worth over $50,000, constitute .7 percent of the estimated number of Suffolk County's adult males who died in this period.[9] Considering the exchange values, such wealth may have rivaled the holdings of the affluent in Europe, as we shall later see. Each of the 123 above $10,000 had wealth roughly equivalent to 50 slaves; furthermore, the 123 represented .4 percent of the number of adult males in Massachusetts and Maine who died during the period. In terms of wealth, the group is a counterpart to the 1,056 slaveholders in the South with 50 or more slaves who constituted .3 percent of that area's population of adult males.[10]

Among Suffolk County's rich was Thomas Russell, whose total estate worth $480,000 consisted of three farms, buildings, houses, and wharves, and included $108,000 invested in three ships and $172,000 in stocks and bonds, as well as an intriguing number of enterprises such as bridges, locks and canals, banks, and sizable holdings of United States securities. Although Russell's estate dominated the figures from 1796 to 1799, in the next decade we find a half dozen others with inventories of more than $100,000, including John Codman, a merchant who died in 1803, leaving an estate of $640,000.[11]

TABLE 42
ESTATES OF THE DECEASED IN SUFFOLK COUNTY (BOSTON), 1796–1807

Total Estate (TE)	No. of Families above TE
$500,000 or over	1
250,000	3
100,000	6
50,000	17
20,000	57
10,000	123

Source: Lemuel Shattuck, *Vital Statistics of Boston* (Philadelphia: Lea and Blanchard, 1841), pp. 8, 11, 13; U.S. Bureau of the Census, *A Century of Population Growth* (Washington, D.C.: GPO, 1909; rpt. New York: Johnson Reprint Corp., 1966), pp. 188, 224.

Note: It is assumed that 2.1 percent of adult males died each year.

Other prominent examples of wealthy individuals from New England included John Brown of Providence who had prepared a well-organized 14-page inventory of his estate in 1802. The list includes 53 or more major items; table 43 reports about 20 of them in order to convey a general impression of his assets of $785,000 and debts of $195,000.

The 530 letters of administration for deceased in Philadelphia in 1798 show 14 estates with evaluations above $10,000. Considering the numbers of administrations and wills in that county from 1794 to 1810 and the extraordinary number in 1798 when there was a yellow fever epidemic, it appears that Philadelphia's rich were at least as numerous per capita as in Boston. The 1799 assessment roll for New York City's Wards 1–7 reveals 164 persons with total estate greater than $10,000. Such a number is consistent with the list of estate administration bonds for executors in New York City in 1798 which shows 17 persons with holdings above $10,000; 12 of the deceased were merchants, two were furriers, one a printer, and two were listed as "esquire."[12]

A list of the top several hundred landholders throughout America at the end of the century would be difficult to obtain. Some wealthy individuals owned land in several different states or were partners or shareholders in land companies. A further complication arises because some landholders were heavily mortgaged, and not a few individuals prominent in the early

TABLE 43
ESTATE OF JOHN BROWN OF PROVIDENCE, 1802

House & 1.5 acres	$18,000	210,000 acres in New York,	
2.5 acres	2,000	8 townships, considerable	
2 lots	2,000	cleared land	$210,000[a]
Farm, 520 acres	18,760	Bridge at India Point	15,000
Part of 8,100 acres	10,000	Valuable farm, 654 acres	23,000
Air furnace &		Gin distillery pump	13,000
blacksmith shop	1,800	Ship, *General Washington*,	
Lot & wharf (2)	2,000	with cargo, from South	
Land, India Point	7,500	America to Canton and home	120,000
Lots at Clavicack	2,000	Ship *Hope* and cargo	52,000
Ohio Co. bottom land		Bank shares	76,500
(50 cents per acre)	18,900	50 shares, Newport Insurance Co.	6,000
Farm on Prudence island	11,700		

Source: Archives, Rhode Island State Capitol, Providence, R.I.; James Blaine Hedges, *The Browns of Providence Plantation* (Providence: Brown University Press, 1960).

Note: The total list includes over fifty-three major items.
   a. Hedges questions this figure (pp. 224–25).

1790s were bankrupt before the end of the decade. Yet even a sketch of the magnitude of holding conveys the degree of inequality or potential inequality that arose as the population continued its westward movement.

A map of Maine in 1798 prominently displays William Bingham's one million acres in an area of little or no market value.[13] The tax rolls of counties in western Virginia show entries of a half million acres of land purchased at two cents an acre.[14] Many of these entries involved overlapping claims; therefore, it is better to turn to land records that were prepared more carefully. The Pennsylvania patent books for the 1780s and 1790s show Robert Morris, known as the financier of the American Revolution, as the largest multiple-property holder, with 1,024 entries totaling about 300,000 acres in western Pennsylvania. Next was John Nicholson, Pennsylvania's well-known comptroller general, with 464 properties, followed by Jeremy Parker with 245. Other familiar names were Benjamin Rush, with 103 entries, and William Bingham with 101. These were all lands purchased after 1784, at 17 to 27 cents an acre.[15]

The precarious financing of some of these holdings is demonstrated by the fact that Robert Morris was in debtors' prison by February 1798, where he was joined by John Nicholson in 1799–1800; and they were not the only ones who fell upon hard times.[16] Apparently some of their land purchases had been backed by notes that were insufficiently secured by unmortgaged assets. The plight of Morris and his friends resounded far beyond Pennsylvania's borders. In Kentucky, the Morris entries in the tax lists of nonresident land in 1796, in the lists of nonresident land sold for taxes in 1799, and in the more than 1.2 million acres in the 1795–1800 Court of Appeals, with Morris as grantor, all attest to his activities and his economic demise.[17] All of the activities of Morris and his fellow speculators in Pennsylvania itself may have been of rather minor significance, however, since their manipulations caused no more than a ripple in the fundamental transfer of land to private ownership in the nation's first years.

A better approach to judging the effects of land grant policy is to study the distribution of wealth in real estate. This we are able to do with the inventory of land, houses, buildings, mills, and wharves—that is, all fixed assets inventoried in the state at the end of 1798, a time after the spectacular cyclical upturn not only in land speculation but also in real activity between 1792 and 1796. We begin by searching out the assets of the rich insofar as they could be located. Quite understandably, the leader was William Bingham, who had $156,000 in real estate. This value was invested in only 1,300 acres, to yield a rather staggering average value of more than $100 an acre. Bingham's holdings consisted of Philadelphia housing and buildings, mills, and wharves, as well as highly valued land in surrounding counties. His worth in real estate may have been equal to a goodly share of the land held by the patentees in our preferred list of 112. In the list I developed for 1798, I found that the top 100 individuals held 3 percent of the total value of real estate in Pennsylvania and that it was invested in less than 25,000 acres.

The 1798 inventories of land and housing for Connecticut demonstrate that Charles Phelps of Stonington was the state's largest owner, with $74,000 in real estate; his holdings included 1,272 acres, valued at $15 an acre, 17 other properties occupied by various individuals, and 16 houses having values from $20 to $100, as well as 11 houses valued between $120 and $2,730. A record for Jeremiah Wadsworth lists $68,000 in real estate in houses and stores in Hartford in addition to several farms. The document also reports his ownership of 14,000 unevaluated acres in Vermont.[18]

In two of America's newer states, Kentucky and Tennessee, there was considerable inequality of wealth in 1800. The Kentucky tax list for 1800 reveals that John Hunter of Mason County was the largest landholder in the state, with 130,360 acres. The 107 men holding 10,000 or more acres represented less than 1 percent of the total population, yet they reported ownership of one-third of the state's total acreage.[19] In eastern Tennessee, 1 percent of residents and nonresidents owned one-third of the acreage reported for tax purposes.[20]

Finally, we should pay some attention to personal estate, as reflected in government securities. Many persons felt that the new nation's procedures in debt funding and banking made it possible for a relatively small but influential group to obtain significant wealth. As noted in the next chapter, historian Charles Beard gives great prominence to this financial movement. Even John Adams referred to both real and personal estate in his writings, and felt that immense fortunes had been made with one great leap; furthermore, he conveyed the impression that inequalities in wealth had increased dramatically in the 1780s and 1790s.[21]

One statistical body of evidence is the distribution of security holdings for individuals in five states, presented in table 44. We see that 273 persons did own or control extensive securities of $10,000 or more in value. The aggregate amount accounted for in the table was $12.3 million, or 39 percent of the amount stated for the nation's debt of this type.[22] Thus, the total number of individuals involved above $10,000 could have been about 700 rather than the 273 noted on the table. These rich do appear to be a significant group. Yet they represent only 17.5 percent of the 4,000 holding real estate presented in chapter 2; the $31.8 million in securities was only 5 percent of the aggregate value in real estate in the country. Undoubtedly there are other forms of commercial wealth that I have not been able to quantify.

This brief review of American holdings of slaves, of urban and rural real estate, and of some personal estate indicates that in America there were several thousand persons with impressive wealth above $10,000. Several hundred families and individuals in the United States were very rich indeed. Did these affluent Americans, say .5 percent of adult males, have control of one-quarter of America's wealth? Were their shares less than those held by the top .5 percent in European countries? The share of the affluent Americans in the early federal period was far less, as we shall see later in the chapter. Even if the American percentage share of the rich were less, the average wealth of the rich in America conceivably had a market or exchange value as large as that of its European counterpart. We shall see in this chapter, too, that per capita wealth in America generally surpassed that of Europe.

PERSPECTIVE USING A LOGNORMAL CURVE

Before describing the mass of the population, the bottom 99.5 percent, and before distinguishing between those in the group with and without wealth, we might find it fruitful to designate possible shares, as described

TABLE 44
HOLDINGS OF FEDERAL DEBT IN MASSACHUSETTS, MARYLAND, PENNSYLVANIA, AND RHODE ISLAND, AND SUBSCRIPTIONS AT THE TREASURY, 1790

Holdings (H)	No. of Persons Above H
$25,000 or over	96
10,000	273
5,000	500
1,000	1,447
500	1,947
100	2,896
1	3,294
Mean	$3,742
Inequality, G	.766

Source: E. James Ferguson, The Power of the Purse (Chapel Hill: University of North Carolina Press, 1961), pp. 273, 276, 278, 280, 283.

Note: The five distributions have been combined; some include interest, others do not.

by lognormal curves. There is a great deal of evidence that, in some sense, wealth was distributed almost lognormally in many different countries at the end of the eighteenth century.

An extreme example during the period was the distribution of *sakdinah* (dignity) points in the hierarchical society of Siam (now Thailand). Each individual was assigned to a specific category within society, with each category carrying dignity points as defined by law. The king was assigned an infinite number, but his brother was given 100,000 points, the top rating, aside from the king's. Ratings for 1,149 categories were developed that conform very closely to a lognormal curve with a Gini coefficient of .69, or .85 if weighted by possible numbers of persons in each class. The concept of *sakdinah* encompasses more than just possession of wealth, land, or farm animals, or of work duties. The categories partially depended on the strength of blood relationships to the king, but with an adjustment downward from generation to generation; on the other hand, there was an upward merit adjustment for officials highest in the administration.[23] Ranks within a society based on royalty, merit, and tradition, then, can form a lognormal curve. It should not be surprising that wealth distributions, too, can attain the same configuration.

The degree of inequality measured by the Gini coefficient, G, can be used to distinguish one country from another in 1800. There is reason to believe that inequality usually fell between .50 and .95, or was even greater; it was between .70 and .95 for all males 20 and older; it was between .70 and .90 for all families. This range is presented in table 45. I assert that the distribution of wealth in Sweden, Denmark, and probably England and Wales, and Scotland, conformed roughly to the shares in the .90–.95 columns of the table, and that the distribution in the United States was roughly .80. We note first that the share of the richest person out of every 1,000 adult males (say, in a group of those 21 and older) would have had 22 to 38 percent of the wealth in Scandinavia and 10 percent in the United States. This group of roughly 900 men in Sweden and Denmark would have had a proportionate share about three times as large as the same group in the United States. Nevertheless, if average wealth in the United States were three times as large, as we shall see later in this chapter, the average value of wealth for the two groups could have been roughly the same. Going deeper, to the top .5 percent of people, we see that about 4,000 would have possessed half of all the wealth in Scandinavia, but that the same top .5 percent would have owned less than one-fourth of the wealth in America. In absolute terms, this percentage group in America very well could have owned more than its counterpart in Scandinavia.

Proceeding further, we can note that the share of the top 10 to 20 percent encompasses the Gini figure itself ($A_P = G$) and that there is little difference, in percentage terms, between the Scandinavian and the U.S. groups. Finally, it is noted that both in the United States and in Scandinavia the bottom 50 percent had little or nothing. Yet, even in this mathematical framework there is a suggestion of a comparative advantage in America. Suppose the conditions prevailed that are shown in table 46. This lognormal scheme, with the imposed means, translates into very little wealth below the median; the average would be $50 for an American and only $5 for the Swede—a difference between owning and not owning cattle, for example. The lognormal scheme also suggests the proportions of property holders in a country. Suppose $100 were necessary to own 40 acres of

TABLE 45

SOME POSSIBLE GENERALIZATIONS OF WEALTH DISTRIBUTIONS IN EUROPE
AND THE UNITED STATES IN 1800
(using lognormal curves, for lognormal tables with G of .50–.95)

Proportion of Cases above Percentile (N_P)	Share of Total Wealth (a_P)					
	European Countries?[a]		Intermediate Inequality	United States?[b]		Very Modest Inequality
	.95	.90	.85	.80	.75	.50
.001	.38	.22	.13	.10	.07	.02
.005	.58	.40	.28	.22	.17	.05
.01	.67	.50	.37	.30	.24	.08
.02	.76	.61	.47	.40	.33	.14
.05	.87	.75	.63	.57	.49	.24
.10	.93	.85	.76	.70	.64	.37
.20	.97	.93	.87	.83	.78	.54
.50	.99	.99	.98	.97	.95	.83
1.00	1.00	1.00	1.00	1.00	1.00	1.00

Sources: Author; data were derived from a computer program. See J. Aitchison and J.A.C. Brown, *The Lognormal Distribution* (Cambridge: University Press, 1969), pp. 79. See also tables 48 and 54.

Note: The subset of persons above the median has 97 percent of total wealth if the distribution is lognormal, with G = .80 as stated in table 3 in connection with the Adams hypothesis; this subset above the median itself plots essentially as a lognormal curve, except in its lowest portion.

a. High inequality probably characterized Sweden, Denmark, England, Wales, and Scotland.

b. Moderate inequality (about .80) probably characterized the United States during this period.

land. The above specifications for the mean and the Gini coefficient suggest that 56 percent of Americans would be landholders, but only 22 percent of Swedes would hold land.[24] These two speculative percentages are not far from the empirical facts, as we shall see.

PARETO CONSIDERATIONS

The lognormal curve essentially plots as a Pareto curve, at least above the mean, or better, above the median. This means that the finding that income in various countries followed a Pareto distribution having a slope of about 1.5, is not really at odds with the lognormal formulation. The Pareto slopes for various classifications of the lognormal curve are highly suggestive, as is shown in table 47. Pareto's slope (α) is somewhat confusing in this respect since it is inversely related to the level of income inequality. Pareto's formula originally was designed to be only a description of the upper tail of the curve and to be applied to an income, not a wealth, distribution. Yet his finding of a slope of about 1.5 may be found in table 47, namely for the top few percentages in the European case. The squared coefficient, R^2, indicates an almost perfectly straight line in this region of the lognormal curve if $G = .5$. The United States, with its $G = .8$ or less, yields no region with inequality approaching 1.5 in any upper portion of the curve.

Finally, it should be noted that the lognormal curve of .8 for all people can, in a sense, be adapted if we consider only property owners. Consider

TABLE 46
HYPOTHETICAL COMPARISON BETWEEN SWEDEN
AND THE UNITED STATES, 1800
(using lognormal curves)

	Sweden	*United States*
Mean wealth[a]	$258	$708
Inequality, G	.9	.8
Lognormal shares		
% below median	1.0	3.5
Average below median	$5	$50
% below $100	5.6	2.4

Sources: Parameters for the United States are those of the table 9; Swedish parameters appear on tables 54 and 55.
   a. See chapter 2.

TABLE 47

UPPER PORTIONS OF TWO LOGNORMAL CURVES ABOVE SELECTED
PERCENTILES PLOTTED AS PARETO CURVES: RESULTING PARETO SLOPES
(α) AND COEFFICIENTS OF DETERMINATION (R^2)

Selected Percentiles	Lognormal Curve with G = .9		Lognormal Curve with G = .8	
(N_P)	α	R^2	α	R^2
.01	1.60	.993	2.05	.993
.02	1.54	.993	1.97	.993
.05	1.42	.991	1.83	.991
.10	1.40	.989	1.80	.989
.20	1.33	.980	1.70	.980
.50	1.12	.951	1.44	.951
1.00	.82	.867	1.05	.867

Source: See table 45.
Note: The upper portions of lognormal curves plot almost as straight lines on Pareto charts.
A Pareto line has the form log N_P = k$-\alpha$ log P.

a lognormal curve with G = .8 and eliminate all cases below the median
in studying the possible distribution of wealth among property owners.
This subset of the lognormal curve plots more as a Pareto curve than a
lognormal curve since there is no lower tail below the mode. Yet, this
subset is not too far removed from being a lognormal curve with G = .68
as demonstrated with a probit plot. The plot of the subset of the lognormal
curve above the median on a Pareto chart demonstrates a reasonably
straight line, one with a slope of 1.44 and coefficient of determination of
.951 as stated in table 47 (for a lognormal curve with an overall G of .8).
Thus, empirical data for property holder wealth may be roughly lognormal
overall and yet be quite Pareto in shape in its upper regions.[25]

PROPERTY OWNERS

The crucial distinction between the distributions for Europe and for
the United States is that only 10 to 30 percent of adult males possessed
land in such countries as England, Scotland, Sweden, and Denmark, while
half of adult males in the United States owned land. Significantly, the
effects of pressures from population growth and limited land supply were
first enunciated by Malthus in 1798, the very year I highlight in this book.
In Europe at that time the majority of adult males or families experienced

extreme difficulty in obtaining land or even in accumulating a stock of farm animals. I shall discuss their plight, first with data from one parish in England and then for Scotland and Sweden. Both countries sent great numbers of emigrants to America—Scotland about at the time treated in this study, and Sweden, two generations later. Scotland is strategic to this work because of the restlessness pervading the populace in 1798–1800, Sweden because of the data from its marvelous censuses describing the country's various socioeconomic groups. Conditions in both countries not only shed light on later developments, but also stand as a stark contrast to conditions in the United States.

GORRAN PARISH

Some unique 1798 data for Gorran Parish, in Cornwall, help to clarify the distinction between landownership and land use. They also highlight the fact that a strong majority of people in an area can be tenants or subtenants or farm laborers. Finally, the data illustrate the fact that the lognormal curve characterizes both the ownership and the use of land. The data for this study were found within the 121 volumes in which the land tax records for England and Wales are recorded.

The 162 entries for Gorran Parish list 154 persons as possessing acreage. (See table 48.) The distribution of acreage displays a curve very similar to a lognormal table (the probit correlation has an $R^2 = .98$) and has a mean acreage that is rather humble, judged by American standards at the time. Its land is classified as good to medium, from the standpoint of the quality or physical basis for farming, so that acreages can be considered to have provided adequate livelihoods.[26] The inequality level was fairly moderate, with the largest property having 454 acres. If the four properties below two acres are eliminated, the inequality coefficient is the same as for Pennsylvania in 1798, and actually shows less dispersion below the median.

The 1801 census for the parish records 185 houses, 206 families, and about the same number of adult males.[27] Thus, there were about 52 families, or about one-fourth of the labor force, with no land, and one-third of the families lived on less than five acres. Inclusion of the landless in the distribution raises the inequality coefficient from .57 to .68. Even this distribution appears lognormal above $-.5$ standard deviations (with a probit $R^2 = .95$).

An analysis of proprietors indicates that there were but 42 owners of the 154 properties, so the possibility of being an owner was little more

TABLE 48
LAND TENANCY IN GORRAN PARISH, CORNWALL, 1798

No. of Occupied Acres	No. of Occupiers
200 and over	2
100–199	1
50–99	11
20–49	32
10–19	451
5–9	47
2–4	12
1–1.9	2
.1–.9	2
Total	154
Mean (acres)	22.9
Inequality, G	.574

Sources: Lee Soltow: "Wealth Distribution in England and Wales in 1798," *Economic History Review,* 2d ser. 34, no. 1 (February 1981), 69; "The Land Tax Redemption Records, 1798–1963," *Economic History Review,* 2d ser. 35, no. 3 (August 1982), 429.

than one in four among the 154, or one in five among the 206. Here, then, is one example of the ownership proportion being substantially less than it was in the United States. From the standpoint of numbers, the top owner, Thomas Graham, Esq., had 22 properties but did not own as much acreage as did the earl of Mount Edgecombe, who owned 15 properties. These two were followed by an untitled man owning 12 properties, and by a lord with 10; these four men owned just about half of the total acreage of the parish.

The ownership distribution also forms an excellent lognormal curve (with $G = .65$ and a probit analysis with an $R^2 = .97$) for the 42 owners and a not unreasonable lognormal curve when we extend the analysis to all 206 families (with $G = .93$ and $R^2 = .92$). (See table 49.)

Perhaps this picture of Gorran Parish is typical of England as a whole. Certainly the inequality level, with a Gini coefficient of .90–.93, is encountered often in the 1873 Domesday Survey. The level for Cornwall for seven classes, including cottagers with one or more acres, was .92, while that for England and Wales was .949.[28] Finally, we note that the relative inequality of the pound sterling value of acreage parallels almost exactly the analysis made for numbers of acres. The Lorenz curves and Gini coefficients are almost the same, of necessity, since the correlation between acreage and value has a correspondence of almost one to one.

TABLE 49
LANDOWNERSHIP IN GORRAN PARISH, CORNWALL, 1798

No. of Acres	No. of Owners
600	1
200–599	4
100–199	4
.1–.9	7
0	164
Total	206
Mean	17.1
Inequality, G	.928

Source: J. T. Coppock, *An Agricultural Atlas of England and Wales* (London: Faber and Faber, 1964), p. 43.

SCOTLAND

The population of Scotland increased from 1,265,000 in 1755 to 1,608,000 in 1801, partly because of the dramatic increase in food supply due to potato production and consumption, partly because of smallpox vaccination, and because of other reasons not fully understood.[29] At the same time, "clearances" or enclosures were dislodging tenants from the land so that agricultural cultivation was displaced by the raising of cattle and sheep.[30] Pressures on the land were severe, particularly in the Highlands. Tenants were unwilling to become cotters or crofters as a result of the consolidation of farms. Migration to America was strong throughout the second half of the century except when Great Britain was at war with France from 1793 to 1801. Migration surged again from 1801 to 1803.[31]

The hierarchy in the Highlands begins with the laird, the landed proprietor, or more likely the tacksman, the resident member of the upper ranks. Beneath him were tenants or possibly subtenants, but joint tenancy also was very common. Below tenants were the subtenant classes: the crofters, pendiclers, and cotters. Crofters of the eighteenth century in the Highlands cultivated some land but did not have the opportunity to own livestock because often they did not have adequate grazing privileges in outer-lying lands during the winter. This is an important point, since farm animals may have been the sole means of accumulating any wealth beyond subsistence. A cotter occupied a cot (a small or humble dwelling house, cottage, or small shelter) and owned very little, if any, garden land for domestic use. A pendicle was a small piece of land and a cottage, an appendage of an estate. The vast majority in the subtenant class were landless laborers with a little land on which to raise food for home consumption, but the amount of land was insufficient to support livestock, the potential source of a little wealth.[32]

It is unfortunate that no census counts of the various tenant and subtenant classes survive for England and Scotland. To get a feeling for the quantitative importance of these groupings, we must turn to the Scandinavian censuses.

SWEDEN

The socioeconomic classes in Sweden were well delineated by 1805 and even earlier, as can be seen from that most admirable count of wealth classes made in 1805, presented in table 50. The rich were defined as those having a surplus of 500 riksdaler in excess of annual expenditures, the somewhat rich as those with less income but who lived without the need to incur debt.[33] The poor were those "who manage not without difficulty"— and could include property owners whose debts were greater than their assets. The destitute group was sustained by the charity of others. A study of a lognormal curve for these group proportions reveals that the average wealth of each group falls into proportions very similar to my "guesses" shown in the last two columns of the table. The second of the guesses

TABLE 50
CLASSES OF WEALTH IN SWEDEN, 1805

		Assumed Average Wealth	
	Proportion of Families	First Guess	Second Guess
Rich	.03	SD 4,000	SD 6,400
Somewhat rich	.26	400	160
Poor	.55	40	4
Destitute	.16	4	.1
	1.00		
Mean		245	233
Inequality, G		.75	.91

Source: Lee Soltow, "The Swedish Census of Wealth at the Beginning of the Nineteenth Century," Scandinavian Economic History Review 33, no. 1 (1985), 9.
 SD = Specie-daler.

appears to be not far from the actual wealth distribution in Sweden in 1800. Thus, the choices for limits of classes curiously are only a step removed from a lognormal curve.

We can assume, for practical purposes, that the proportion of property holders (POP) was .29 for the rich plus the somewhat rich, a quantification substantiated from an evaluation of estates of all individuals of Sweden. The final results of combining the 1805 census with the 1800 inventory of estates are shown in table 51. The essential facts are that 29 percent of adult males had wealth, that the inequality coefficient was .92 for all, or .73 for property holders. These parameters fit the lognormal scheme of table 45.

Further insight into wealth distribution in Sweden may be gained by examining the occupational classifications given in table 52. In 1805, farmers operating their own farms and new settlers constituted only 27 percent of farmers and peasants [(150,136 + 3,135)/560,690]. Even when we add all possible upper classes, including titled and professional people, burghers, and gentlefolk to the group of farm owners and settlers, we account for only 27 percent of Sweden's population (204,835/762,836); to add to this number the separate and somewhat duplicative counts of manufacturing owners and master artisans does not raise the proportion of this group above 30 percent.

One should ponder each entry among the 560,000 farmers and peasants. It is the cottagers (*backstuga boer*) who appear to have been the most marginal group. The 207,000 farmhands and boys constituted three of

TABLE 51
DISTRIBUTION OF WEALTH IN SWEDEN, 1800–1805
(males 20 and older)

		Property Holder Proportion	Wealth in 1800			
			Property Holders		Adult Males	
	N		Mean	*G*	Mean	*G*
Rural	574,548	.284	SD 743	.696	SD 211	.914
Urban	65,288	.312	2,125	.803	678	.937
Total	639,836	.287	900	.734	259	.923

Source: The 1805 Swedish census has been combined with the 1800 inventory of estates, shown in table 50.

SD = Specie-daler.

TABLE 52
IMPLICATIONS OF POSSIBLE WEALTH HOLDING BY
SOCIOECONOMIC CLASSES IN SWEDEN, 1805 AND 1810
(no. of males 15 and older)

	1805			1810		
	Rural	*Urban*	*Total*	*Rural*	*Urban*	*Total*
All social classes						
Nobility	2,083	936	3,019	1,977	1,089	3,066
Professionals	3,481	1,466	4,947	3,467	1,018	4,485
Rural bourgeoisie	695	20,212	20,907	698	19,072	19,770
Persons of standing	15,569	7,122	22,691	12,136	6,568	18,704
Peasants	559,428	—	559,428	558,876	—	558,876
All others	105,744	46,100	151,844	104,138	46,533	150,671
Total	687,000	75,836	762,836	651,434	74,280	755,572
Farmers and peasants						
Working own farms	150,136			153,792		
Working others' farms	53,008			52,158		
Crofters	63,401			63,461		
Settlers	3,136			4,265		
Hired hands						
Cottagers						
(hired hands)	28,013			25,299		
Live-in workers	15,033			15,332		
Fishermen	5,370			4,393		
Other farmers and						
crofters	34,985			39,557		
Farmhands and boys	207,609			199,196		
Total	560,690			557,643		
Other						
Manufacturers	1,038	572				
Master artisans	2,819	9,342				

Source: Lee Soltow, "The Swedish Census of Wealth at the Beginning of the 19th Century," *Scandinavian Economic History Review* 33, no.1 (1985), 8.

Note: Nobility = *ridderskapet och adeln;* professionals = *låro-ståndet;* rural bourgeoisie = *borgare på landet;* people of standing = *stånds-personer;* peasants = *bonde-ståndet;* farmers and peasants working own farms = *bönder på egna hemman;* working others' farms = *bönder på andras hemman;* crofters = *torpare;* settlers = *nybyggare;* cottagers = *backstuga boer;* live-in workers = *arbetsföre inhyses man;* fishermen = *skår-bönder och fiskare;* other farmers and crofters = *åldrige bönder, torpare;* farmhands and boys = *bondegrånger;* manufacturers = *ågare, bruk, fabrik;* master artisans = *mästare.*

every eight persons and presumably were at the bottom rung of the socio-economic ladder. Just what proportion of them were young is difficult to determine; the total number of rural males age 15–19 was 96,000, a maximum figure since many youths living with their families were classified in the census by the status of their parent. Domestic servants may have been next to the bottom of the ladder because they had had no opportunity to live separately in their own cottages and were unable to marry and to establish families. The Norwegian census of 1801 distinguished between day laborers living in farmhouses, ordinary day laborers, and those receiving alms.[34] In the Swedish statistics there is a very prominent distinction between crofters (*torpare*) and cottagers (*backstuga boer*). Often, crofts were not much different from small freehold farms, while a cottage consisted of a dwelling plus a potato patch. Perhaps more important were distinctions in work rules. Crofters had long-term contracts with rights to the use of their land, for which they worked a certain number of days, often three to six per week. Cottagers paid rent for the use of their land; some of them had no fixed employment. In effect, cottagers were largely untrained laborers who came from the lower servant classes; they were a marginal group—perhaps an index of the pauperization in a society. Yet they did have freedom to work—a privilege not available to the crofter group.[35]

The proportions of crofters, cottagers, and laborers grew during the century after 1751; that is, the proportion of the Swedish labor force that consisted of farmers (*bönder*) dropped from about 45 percent in 1751, to 40 percent in 1801, to a little over 30 percent in 1860.[36] Yet real wages seem to have dropped only to the end of the eighteenth century. In an important study of daily wage rates and prices, Lennart Jörberg found that the real wage rate for agricultural workers in Sweden was at its nadir at the turn of the century, dropping from 1737 to about 1800, and then rising.[37]

An alternative data set that adds the dimension of age is provided by the Norwegian census of 1801. In a society where the land supply was limited, a man may have had to delay marriage until he could obtain at least a home of his own, or until he had access to land sufficient to support a family. In the Norwegian data no distinctions are made between crofters and cottagers, but are made between crofters with or without land (*husmenn med jord/utan jord*). Published information on married couples gives rise to the classifications given in table 53. Unfortunately, no distinction is made for farmers owning or not owning their land. We see that only 50 percent of 31-year-old men were married, whereas after age 36 that proportion rose to 80 percent. This is in significant contrast to marriage rates among rural males in Ontario in 1871 (the earliest and only established marriage rates for America that I have), where half of males were married by age 26, five years earlier than was the case in Norway.[38] The remaining columns of table 53 are designed to show the slow pace of improvement through the life cycle in a European country at the end of the eighteenth century compared to possibilities in America. Since I have no age data for landholders in the United States, I use data for Ontario in 1871. Opportunities for owning land in use were much greater in America.[39]

SUMMARY DISTRIBUTIONS

We have the most complete information about the distribution of wealth at the end of the eighteenth century for the Scandinavian countries and the United States. The bottom row of table 54 shows that the United States was in a far superior position, to the extent that wealth was distributed widely among free men. Granting this first step, what can we say about the distribution of wealth only among those with positive wealth? Here again, we see that America was an egalitarian nation. Only Finland appeared to have had a distribution of property holders resembling that of the United States.

But does this mean that the rich in America suffered in any absolute sense? In terms of American dollars, both Scandinavia and America had a millionaire. There were 4,100 Scandinavians with wealth over $10,000, and there were 4,100 Americans with wealth over that amount. One-third of Americans had wealth of at least $500. However, only 7 percent of Scandinavians had at least $500. This is the evidence to prove that America was indeed a land of opportunity.[40]

COMPARISONS OF AVERAGE WEALTH, 1798–1800

An alternative approach to judging America's position in 1800 is to compare average wealth in the new nation to averages in other countries. Was the average U.S. holding of $708 mediocre or impressive by European standards? If that average was only mediocre, it could be interpreted as evidence that American growth could not have been large. If that average was high by European standards, on the other hand, we may infer that growth had proceeded rapidly.[41]

Two timely data sets can serve as excellent checks on the American average. In Sweden there was a tax census of real estate in 1800, and

TABLE 53

LAND TENURE AND MARITAL STATUS OF NORWEGIANS, 1801

(rural males 16 and over)

Age	N	Proportion Married	Proportion of All Rural Males					Proportion Reporting Acreage in Ontario, 1871
			Total	Farmers	Crofters with Land	Crofters without Land	Other Categories	
16–20	33,333	.005	1.000	.007	.001	.000	.992	.053
21–25	29,447	.112	1.000	.066	.027	.008	.899	.152
26–30	26,695	.427	1.000	.209	.124	.031	.636	.492
31–35	22,157	.694	1.000	.368	.216	.040	.376	.661
35–40	25,379	.815	1.000	.426	.279	.051	.244	.776
41–45	19,525	.877	1.000	.503	.291	.048	.158	.801
46–50	22,660	.891	1.000	.498	.309	.059	.134	.798
51–55	16,058	.891	1.000	.510	.296	.060	.134	.860
56–60	15,036	.867	1.000	.463	.286	.066	.185	.873
61–65	9,557	.828	1.000	.418	.256	.062	.264	.765
66–70	9,424	.770	1.000	.324	.224	.066	.386	.765
71–75	5,142	.618	1.000	.243	.177	.057	.523	.643
76–80	4,297	.618	1.000	.179	.152	.057	.612	.548
81–109	82,384	.618	1.000	.108	.104	.046	.742	.450

Sources: Norwegian Central Bureau of Statistics, Population Census 1801, Reprocessed (Oslo: Norges Offisielle Statistikk, 1980), p. 84, 92, 147–48; special tabulations provided by the Historisk Institutt, University of Bergen, Jan Oldervoll, director; Ontario data are a sample of size 5,709 drawn from census of Canada manuscripts, National Archives, Ottawa.

TABLE 54
DISTRIBUTION OF WEALTH IN FOUR SCANDINAVIAN COUNTRIES, SCOTLAND, THE UNITED STATES, 1770–1800
(wealth holders [W>0] among males 20 and older)

The Upper Proportion of Wealth Holders (N_w)	Sweden (1800)			Finland (1800)			Lognormal Table with $G=.73$	Denmark (1789)	Norway (1789)	Scotland (1770)	United States (1798)
	Total	Rural	Urban	Total	Rural	Urban					
.0001	.045	.021	.029	.023	.006	.022	.015	.057	.042	—	.009
.0002	.057	.031	.058	.032	.011	.043	.024	.082	.059	.041	.014
.0005	.083	.052	.13	.048	.024	.078	.042	.13	.095	.076	.024
.001	.11	.077	.16	.069	.038	.12	.063	.18	.13	.11	.036
.002	.15	.12	.20	.098	.059	.17	.094	.24	.18	.16	.054
.005	.23	.20	.27	.15	.096	.25	.16	.34	.26	.24	.090
.01	.31	.28	.33	.19	.14	.34	.22	.43	.33	.32	.13
.02	.41	.37	.42	.25	.19	.45	.31	.55	.41	.41	.19
.05	.54	.48	.58	.35	.29	.59	.47	.70	.54	.56	.31
.10	.65	.60	.70	.46	.40	.69	.61	.80	.65	.69	.45
.20	.76	.72	.84	.61	.57	.80	.76	.89	.78	.82	.62

A_w, the Proportion of Total Wealth of the N_w Group

.30	.84	.81	.91	.72	.70	.87	.85	.93	.85	.89	.74
.40	.89	.87	.94	.81	.79	.91	.90	.95	.89	.93	.82
.50	.93	.91	.96	.88	.86	.95	.94	.97	.93	.96	.88
.60	.95	.95	.98	.92	.91	.97	.97	.98	.95	.98	.92
.70	.97	.97	.99	.96	.95	.98	.98	.99	.97	.99	.96
.80	.99	.99	.99	.98	.98	.99	.99	.99	.99	.99	.98
.90	.99	.99	.99	.99	.99	.99	.99	.99	.99	.99	.99
1.00	1.00	1.00	1.00	1.00	1.00	1.00	1.00	1.00	1.00	1.00	1.00
N	184	163	21	51	48	3	—	73	77	8	433
Mean	SD 900	743	2,125	541	487	1,325	—	rb1,395	rb487	£470	$1,433
Inequality, G	.734	.696	.803	.588	.549	.776	.73	.853	.740	.77	.588
Proportion of owners	.287	.284	.312	.130	.231	.210	—	.24	.38	.03	.494

Sources: Lee Soltow: "The Swedish Census of Wealth at the Beginning of the 19th Century," *Scandinavian Economic History Review* 33, no. 1 (1985), 15; revised data from "Wealth Distribution in Norway and Denmark in 1789," *Historisk Tidsskrift,* Winter 1981, pp. 221–35; Loretta R. Timperley: *A Directory of Landownership in Scotland,* Scottish Record Society, n.s. 5 (Edinburgh: Econoprint, 1976), pp. 1–428; "Landownership in Scotland in the Eighteenth Century," Ph.D. diss., University of Edinburgh 1977, pp. 154, 243–76; see also Lee Soltow: "Wealth Inequality in Scotland in the Eighteenth Century," working paper, Department of Economics, Ohio University, Athens, Ohio 45701; "The Distribution of Private Wealth in Land in Scotland and Scandinavia in the 17th and 18th Centuries," presented at the Symposium on Scotland and Scandinavia, University of Aberdeen, 1988; "Inequality of Wealth in Land in Scotland in the Eighteenth Century," *Scottish Economic and Social History,* forthcoming, 1990.

SD = Specie-daler.

rb = Riksdaler banco, equivalent to a U.S. dollar.

TABLE 55
Average Wealth in Sweden, Finland, Britain, and the United States, 1798–1803
(among males 20–21 and older)

	N	Aggregate Wealth[a]	Average Wealth
Sweden (1800)	642,902	$165,639,525	$258
Finland (1800)	216,873	27,580,174	127
Total	859,775		225
Britain (1803)			
England			
10% return	2,310,000	1,314,000,000	569
5% return	2,310,000	2,628,000,000	1,140
Wales			
10% return	149,000	72,400,000	486
5% return	149,000	145,000,000	973
Scotland			
10% return	429,000	153,000,000	357
5% return	429,000	306,000,000	713
Total	2,888,000		533–1,060
Sweden (1800)			
Rural	574,548	121,373,521	211
Urban	65,288	44,266,004	678
United States (1798)			
Rural	796,889	531,450,748	667
Urban	80,866	89,678,657	1,109
Free	877,756	621,130,405	708
Free and slave	1,110,000	621,130,405	565

Sources: Swedish data are in riksdaler banco (equivalent to a U.S. dollar) as stated in *Förmögenhets-Uppsakttningen 1800–1803,* vol. 44–109, Riksarkivet, Stockholm; population data are from microfilm 113N–116N of the Swedish Census of 1805, Kung. Statistiska Centralbyraån. See also Lee Soltow, "The Swedish Census of Wealth at the Beginning of the 19th Century," *Scandinavian Economic History Review* 33, no. 1 (1985). On the value of the riksdaler banco, see Joseph Lippincott, *A Collection of Tables* (Philadelphia: Johnson, 1792), p. 40; *Encyclopaedis, or a Dictionary of Arts, Sciences, and Miscellaneous Literature* (Philadelphia: Dobson, 1798), 12:232.

British data are income assessments adjusted to a wealth concept considering alternatively a 10 percent and a 5 percent return, as stated in British Library: S.P.R., BS, Ref. 8 (Population Act, 41, Geo. III, 1800), 1801–1802, 7:452–52 for population and annual value of lands, tenements, and heriditements in 1803, series A for agriculture in *Parliamentary Papers,* 1812–1813, 12:240–81. A pound was treated as $4. See Lee Soltow, "The Land Tax Redemption Records, 1798–1063," *Economic History Review,* 2d ser. 35, no. 3 (August 1982). An alternative estimate, intermediate to that stated in table 38, can be derived from the land tax assessments of 1798; see Lee Soltow: "The Distribution of Property Values in England and Wales in 1798," *Economic History Review* 2d ser. 34, no. 1 (February 1981); "Wealth Distribution in Finland in 1800," *Scandinavian Economic History Review* 29, no. 1 (Winter 1981), 21–32; see also table 9.

Note: An inventory of real estate and some personal estate was made in Denmark and Norway in 1789 yielding wealth averages for adult males 21 and older of $290 and $175, respectively. (These figures have not been adjusted for price changes; grain prices rose about 50 percent from 1789 to 1800.) The overall average for 1,352,000 adult males in Denmark, Norway, Sweden, and Finland was $230 (or $276 as adjusted to populations and prices in 1800 in Denmark and Norway). See Lee Soltow: "Wealth Distribution in Denmark in 1789," *Scandinavian Economic History Review* 27, no. 2 (October 1979); and "Wealth Distribution in Norway and Denmark in 1789," *Historisk Tidsskrift,* Winter 1981.

a. Wealth in Sweden, Finland, and Britain represents real and some personal property; U.S. wealth is measured in real estate.

English authorities enumerated the annual income from lands and buildings in 1803 as well as taking a tax census of the annual income from real estate in 1798. Totals for both countries as well as population censuses are available, so averages can be constructed for comparisons with U.S. averages. The totals are a result of aggregating values of essentially all properties in each country. I have taken large samples from all three data sets for 1798 and 1800, and I know that each was compiled with the view of obtaining the value for each property in the country. Totals include the values for the nobility and at least part of the royalty. Many items of personal estate are included in Sweden's total, such as money outstanding, claims on capital loaned, and shares as shipowners; excluded were the values of farm animals, household items, and clothing. English data in 1803 are for that part of total income derived from agriculture; those in 1798 were based on income and assets described by Adam Smith as "the whole mass of revenue arising from the rent of all the lands, from that of all the houses, and from the interest of all the capital stock, that part of it only excepted which is either lent to the public or employed in the cultivation of the land."[42]

Both Swedish and English definitions of wealth, shown in table 55, were a little broader than those used in the United States. These broader Swedish and English classes lead to an overstatement of from 10 to 20 percent relative to those for the United States, but, on the other hand, we do not know how close to assessed values were market values. Table 55 highlights the fresh valuations of 1803, as distinguished from the 1798 valuations, for England, and capitalizes income liberally at 10 percent and 5 percent in estimating wealth in real estate.

The most startling aspect of table 55 is the calculation showing that the average wealth of the free population in the United States ($708) was almost three times that in Sweden and well over six times that in Finland. This differential existed a full two generations before the mass emigration that began in Sweden in the 1870s. The differential existing in 1800 may have been essential in alerting Sweden's population, at an early date, to the economic opportunities available in the new nation. However, it would take decades for emigrants to grow from a few persons to significant numbers.

It is possible that Sweden's level of wealth was similar to that of Prussia and central Europe. In some areas averages were higher, and in others, lower. The mean for Finland, presented in table 55, was only half of Sweden's average. In Denmark, wealth per adult male was 20 to 60 percent larger than that in Sweden, while Norway's was 20 to 60 percent larger than that in Finland. The 1,350,000 adult males in the four Scandinavian countries had a wealth average of $230–$280, depending on the method of calculation. America's 877,000 adult free males had an average between two and one-half to three times as large; its 1,110,000 free men plus adult male slaves had an average double that in Scandinavia.[43]

Of more consequence is the startling comparison with England, the leading industrial country in the world at the time. Its average probably was no larger than was the average for free males in the United States, although it may have been either somewhat larger or smaller.[44] It is impossible to make an exact statement because the relationship between income and wealth is not known with any degree of precision. A net return of 8 percent for the figures in table 55 and the accompanying note would mean that the U.S. and English averages would be similar and that average wealth among the free population was larger in the United States than in Wales and Scotland.

SUMMARY

America had the lowest degree of inequality of any Euro-American country, yet its average wealth was as large, or almost as large, as that in any country. This suggests the possibility that there could be an inverse relationship between inequality levels and average wealth (between, say G and W). Scotland had perhaps the most inequality, and it was associated with low average wealth. Nevertheless, the experience in other countries demonstrates that this inverse pattern is rather tenuous.

The international comparisons presented in this chapter can lead us to a misinterpretation of the results of this book. Relative inequality was less in America than in European countries; this fact cannot be denied. Nevertheless, America was not an egalitarian nation. Everyone did not have the same income or the same wealth. Inequality in America was substantial in 1798. This is the message arising from the evidence presented in preceding chapters.

7

Changes in Inequality, 1770–1798

THERE ARE VALID reasons for believing that changes during the generation prior to 1798 may have altered inequality significantly. Possibly, these changes were of more consequence than those arising in the generation or two following 1798. The ratification of the Constitution, without its Bill of Rights, has been seen as a step that strengthened both property rights and labor service contracts over a very large area, a step paving the way toward greater multistate landholding by a few and thus to greater inequality of wealth. The onset of speculation in government securities and the establishment of banking after the Revolution signaled the rise of a "paper" moneyed class that may have strengthened materially the degree of inequality in personal estate holdings.

On the other hand, there are equally cogent reasons for believing that inequality decreased during this period. For one thing, the forfeiture of Loyalist estates during the Revolution could have significantly decreased inequality in landownership. In general, primogeniture and entailed estates had been abolished after the Revolution. Jameson makes the case that the systems of land distribution and land use changed greatly between 1775 and 1795. Presumably, the imposition of certain restrictions had placed a greater penalty on lower-income groups relative to groups who were well established, at least for persons who either had moved within smaller areas or who wished to move to the frontiers of settlement. Under the colonial system, the settlement and patenting of land beyond the Alleghenies were forbidden; these restrictions were weakened during the 1780s in Pennsylvania, Virginia, and in other areas further west. By the turn of the eighteenth century, Kentucky and Tennessee had achieved statehood, followed shortly thereafter by Ohio.

Alexis de Tocqueville made by far the most extensive analysis of inequality in America for the generation preceding 1835. His assertion in the opening sentences of *Democracy in America* establishes the tone of his findings: "Among the novel objects that attracted my attention during my stay in the United States, nothing struck me more forcibly than the general equality of condition among the people. I readily discovered the prodigious influence that this primary fact exercises on the whole course of society; it gives a peculiar direction to public opinion and a peculiar tenor to the laws; it imparts new maxims to the governing authorities and peculiar habits to the governed." He goes on to state that the break from colonialism helped stimulate this equality by abolishing the institutions of entail and primogeniture. The rapid establishment of counties and townships stimulated landownership at a rate that allowed no perpetuation of manorial estates, without which no noble class could thrive.[1]

The changes occurring in the generation before 1798 were peculiarly significant in the history of inequality in America. In this chapter, I will discuss a dozen or so factors that influenced the differences between the rich and poor at the time and will attempt to assess their impact on the relative distribution of wealth, especially as measured by the Lorenz curve and the Gini coefficient. Unfortunately, some events are difficult to assess. A land policy may benefit those with no land or little previous ownership of land, but also make it possible for the rich greatly to expand their holdings. An improvement in credit facilities can help a poor individual to acquire assets and a rich man to reap dividends or interest. To disentangle any differences in impact on the rich and poor caused by inflationary or deflationary surges often proves impossible. Fortunately, we can make an overall statistical assessment of the influence of the aggregate affect of all factors on inequality. Inequality of wealth in 1798 will be compared to inequality in 1774, using the colonial distribution developed by Alice Hanson Jones. Inequality in Massachusetts in 1771 will be contrasted to that in northern states in 1798.

FORFEITED ESTATES (DECREASED INEQUALITY)

Many persons living in colonial America who were loyal to Britain had their estates confiscated by the colonial governments during the Revolution. The persons and sums derived were significant and could have materially altered the distribution of wealth in America after 1774. The 2,190 Loyalist claims, as stated in the 1784 Report of Commissioners (available in the British Public Records Office), had a total value of £10.8 million. Although this aggregate undoubtedly was overstated, it must be treated as a significant part of the total wealth in this country. In fact, the total represents 10 percent of the aggregate wealth (including slaves) reported by Alice Hanson Jones for 1774. The wealthiest five on the list are shown in table 56. Those claiming losses of £20,000 or more were as follows:

£ 100,000 or more	2
50,000–99,999	24
20,000–49,999	77
Total	103

Of this number, 23 were from New York and 25 from South Carolina. The distribution of all of the 2,190 confiscated estates roughly represented a lognormal distribution with a Gini coefficient of .70 and a mean of £5,000, 20 times average wealth in 1774. How much of an impact would the forfeiture of these estates have had on overall inequality? Even an imprecise calculation can provide at least some measure of the effect. Suppose one had a lognormal distribution, with G = .60, that included a rich subset constituting .5 percent of wealth holders who held 10 percent of wealth which, in turn, was distributed in lognormal fashion, with G = .70. The resulting wealth distribution of the nonconfiscated cases shows a Gini coefficient of .57, a significant drop. In this case, the share owned by the top 1 percent of persons drops from 13 percent of total wealth to 9 percent.

What happened to the forfeited estates is a question still to be an-

TABLE 56
VALUE OF FIVE ESTATES FORFEITED DURING THE
AMERICAN REVOLUTION, 1784

Owner	State	Amt. of Claim
Archibald John Hamilton, "served the crown"	Virginia	£192,600
William Cunningham	Virginia, Maryland	135,650
George Rome	Rhode Island	98,600
Governor James Wright	Georgia	97,750
Attorney General Jonathan Kemp	New York, New Jersey	97,300

Source: American Loyalist Claims, microfilms AO 12–13, British Public Records Office, Kew, England; these include Exchequer and Audit Department, American Loyalist Claims 1776–1831 and 1780–1835. I have focused on the 1784 report.

swered. A detailed study of 94 confiscations in five counties of New York State shows that they were sold as 592 estates and that as a result relative inequality in the state was considerably lessened. Unfortunately, we do not know about other wealth held by those new purchasers. Yoshpe feels that after several years, redistribution ultimately may have caused inequality to rise to earlier levels. In his view, "most of the loyalist estates fell to wealthy and influential merchants, landowners, army contractors, Revolutionary leaders, and speculators, many already possessed of substantial land holdings."[2] He does point out that there had been a remarkable redistribution of the estates belonging to the two most affluent Loyalists, and this fact should not be minimized. Philipse Manor alone had a value equal to 1.5 percent of the real estate value of the district (comprising the counties of New York, Kings, Queens, Richmond, and Westchester) in 1798. It is interesting to note that there was a conscious effort to sell the lands to patriot tenants in amounts of less than 500 acres.

There were confiscations of other large estates throughout the country, as the individual states tried to meet an ever increasing need for revenues to support the war effort. For Philadelphia County, there are records of agents who sold lands in 1780 whose value amounted to $2.9 million. These included three tracts of 687 acres in Merion County owned by John Roberts that was sold for $725,000.[3] Galloway was sold for $530,000. The Penns received only $350,000 for land reputed to be worth $2,700,000. It is not known just how much these values had been affected by the war-related inflation.[4]

Richard Brown argues that inequality was reduced as a result of confiscations in Massachusetts. The number of property owners rose after the sale of confiscated properties in Boston. George Stiverson presents data on net returns of 96 (noncompany) private confiscated estates in Maryland. This distribution is strikingly lognormal in shape, with a Gini coefficient of .82. Surely the distribution after confiscation should have shown more owners and less inequality.[5]

ABOLITION OF PRIMOGENITURE AND ENTAIL (DECREASED INEQUALITY)

Inheritance laws in many states during the colonial period perpetuated the European tradition of entail and primogeniture. An entailed estate passed from generation to generation within the same family because the designated heir or beneficiary could not be changed; the estate could not be subdivided or encumbered by further debt, but had to remain intact under the direction of one person, according to the stipulated rules of succession. After several generations, such an institution could reverse a trend toward equality if land were relatively scarce. Primogeniture meant that the eldest son received all of the lands, to the neglect of the other children, if the father had not made a will; this institution, too, could create a landless class if there were many intestate administrations and if land were difficult to obtain. At the beginning of the American Revolution, seven states had stipulated that primogeniture was the inheritance procedure to be followed; these seven included all of the southern states, and New York and Rhode Island in the North. In many other northern states there were provisions for double portions for the eldest son, and in a few states a daughter was entitled to only half the amount inherited by a male heir.[6]

The impact of these institutions in America is difficult to trace, since family members who had been deprived either of land or of the prospect of inheriting land could easily have moved elsewhere. Yet the probable consequences of allowing the two inheritance schemes within the same state were apparent to anyone who had observed the effect of such a practice in Europe. Entail led to very large holdings in Sweden as more and more estates became entailed during the eighteenth century, a situation described in chapter 6. Over one-third of Scotland's land was entailed—a condition Adam Smith found troublesome in a description dated 1776. Fewer than 3 percent of adult males owned all of Scotland's land, and there was little alteration in the Scottish pattern of holdings among landowners for at least a century thereafter. Obviously, such concentration was impossible, or at least highly unlikely, in America because there was an excess of available land in almost all states to the west and north.

Nevertheless, Jameson states that at the time of the Revolution, entailed estates and primogeniture were significant factors in maintaining the existing distribution of wealth. The argument has special appeal in the cases of New York and South Carolina. Manors, patroonships, and plantations were numerous in these states and it behooved wealthy legislators to protect their integrity as long as possible. In a later chapter we shall see that in 1798 inequality was greatest in New York in the North and in South Carolina in the South; excluding Rhode Island as a special case, New York was the only northern state that upheld primogeniture until 1786, and South Carolina supported the institution as late as 1791, five years longer than any other southern state.[7]

The quantitative potential of primogeniture can be assessed from the New Jersey inventories of movable estates for two periods, 1770–1774 and 1796–1800. These do not necessarily pertain to primogeniture; on the contrary, they are for all deceased persons reported to have children. The data from these estates have been coupled with wills that reveal the number of children in the family. Summary measures of the estate distributions, classified by number of children per family, are given in table 57.

What happens if the estates of the deceased were to be distributed equally among all the children in the family? What happens if the eldest child gets a double share? Finally, what happens if only the eldest child receives an inheritance? An understanding of the quantitative effects of the three possible procedures also can be obtained from the data about New Jersey movable estates. Using the summary measures of the estate distribution, classified by number of children, means that the three

TABLE 57

PERSONAL ESTATES IN NEW JERSEY CLASSIFIED BY NUMBER OF CHILDREN, 1770–1774 AND 1796–1800

No. of Children	No. of Estates		Average Value 1796–1800
	1770–1774	1796–1800	
1	23	20	$1,300
2	27	51	900
3	34	61	1,300
4	33	82	1,800
5	45	76	1,600
6	44	72	1,100
7	40	52	1,200
8	33	29	1,500
9	15	24	1,200
10	8	15	
11	2	9	1,800
12	1	4	
More than 12	2	1	
Total	307	496	1,400
Mean	5.28	5.18	
Inequality, G	.271	.265	

Sources: Documents Relating to the Colonial, Revolutionary, and Post-Revolutionary History of the State of New Jersey, 1st ser., vols. 33, 38, Calendar of New Jersey Wills, Administrations, etc., ed. Elmer Hutchinson (Newark: New Jersey Law Journal, 1944). Price data from Hearings before the Joint Economic Committee, 88th Cong., 1st sess., April 7–10, 1959, S. Cong. Res. 13, pt. 2, pp. 394–97.

processes can yield significantly different patterns of inheritance, as shown in table 58.

There is a dramatic increase in inequality among children for the listed propositions. In the case of primogeniture, relative inequality remains the same among first children, but these fortunate individuals represent only 20 percent of all progeny; in terms stated earlier, for 1796–1800, G = .20 × .699 + .80 × 1; such an extreme could lead quickly to the Scottish pattern. In New Jersey, the eldest son, in intestate cases, received a double share at the time of the Revolution, and this could have augmented inequality at least a little.

The demise of entail and primogeniture did not mean that large estates were eliminated by 1798. Manors and plantations existed long after 1776, particularly in New York, Virginia, and South Carolina. The institutions had an impact on income as well as on wealth patterns, since some persons were tenants rather than the owners they would have become if estates had been equally distributed. Thus, in 1795, 207 petitioners in Columbia County, New York, complained about the title to more than 175,000 acres held by the heirs and descendants of Robert Livingston. The petitioners called themselves "tenants holding under the descedents [*sic*] . . . upon terms and conditions oppressive" to the point that they felt themselves but "slaves and vassals." Interestingly, 97 of the petitioners signed their names on the document with an X-mark.[8]

TABLE 58

ESTATES AND INHERITANCES IN NEW JERSEY, 1770–1774 AND 1796–1800
(in 1798 dollars)

	1770–1774			*1796–1800*		
	N	*Mean*	*Inequality, G*	*N*	*Mean*	*Inequality, G*
No. of Estates	307	$1,600	.569	496	$1,400	.582
Inheritance	1,620	$ 300		2,567	$ 270	
Inheritance if there had been:						
Equal shares			.586			.603
Double share to oldest			.600			.617
Primogeniture			.918			.919

Sources: See table 57.

Note: A pound-dollar exchange rate of $4.15 was used in 1774. See also Alice Hanson Jones, *Wealth of a Nation to Be* (New York: Columbia University Press, 1980), pp. 9–11.

Scarcity of Land (Increased Inequality)

It is possible to test statistically Jameson's claim that potential settlers were bottled up in the East because the area west of the Alleghenies was not open for settlement. I have studied the land grants issued in Pennsylvania after 1680; these data can be examined for discontinuities. Figure 9 displays time series for the number of properties warranted and patented

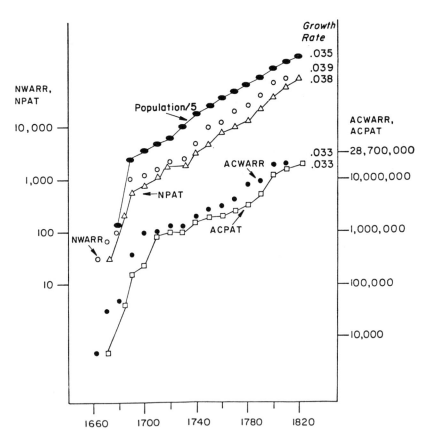

FIGURE 9. Land Grant Warrants in Pennsylvania, 1663–1823

Note: The figure presents the cumulative number of land patents, classified by warrant year (NWARR) and patent year (PAT), and the cumulative number of patented acres, by warrant year (ACWARR) and patent year (ACPAT), as recorded in the Pennsylvania Patent Books, 1663–1823.

between 1663 and 1823 (the entry or warrant year often preceded the year of final transfer or patent year by a decade). There appears to be no appreciable discontinuity in the number of transfers in the 1780s or 1790s, as compared to an earlier period. The long-run pace of transfers, of 3.2–3.9 percent a year, was methodical.

It is true that there was a surge in amounts granted. The average annual change in acreage patented was as follows:

1770–1779	2.1%
1780–1789	5.6
1790–1799	9.2
1800–1810	2.4

The Pennsylvania land law of 1779 clearly expressed the new attitude. Lands belonging to William Penn and his heirs were to be "for the benefit of the settlers as [well as] for his own particular emolument."[9]

The effect of the increasing sizes of granted properties on the overall distribution of wealth is imperfectly understood. Was the wealth inequality level among all persons in Pennsylvania greater in the 1770s than in 1798? I doubt that the surge in purchases arising after statehood caused a change in the proportionate shares held by the relatively affluent people in the earlier time. I have collated Pennsylvania acreage granted to 112 prominent persons from 1788 to 1795 and found that they received 10 percent of the state's patented land. This would have signaled increasing inequality except for the fact that most grants were western land of inferior quality or value and, in any case, may have been resold rather quickly.[10]

POLITICAL CHANGE (DECREASED INEQUALITY)

How revolutionary was the American Revolution? Did it bring about a significant realignment of political power among the rich, the middling, and the poor? If so, did the realignment translate itself into less or greater inequality of wealth? Historians differ widely in their assessments of the impact of the Revolution on various socioeconomic groups and on the degree of change in economic inequality from 1770–1800.

Palmer asserts that our revolution brought about a major political realignment and that it was comparable in magnitude to the initial stages of the French Revolution, but with a more lasting effect.[11] In America, the ratio of refugees or émigrés to the total population was larger than in France. Confiscated property (excluding church land) as a proportion of wealth was similar in the two countries. Palmer maintains that between 1796 and 1800 in America there was a transfer of power from the Federalists to the Republicans, that there was a "Revolution of 1800" in which power was transferred from the High Federalists to the Republican party of Jefferson and Burr, and that the Federalists never again held a majority in Congress. This alleged movement of power from the few to the many may or may not have been accompanied by greater relative economic opportunities for those of little or average wealth—to the lower 80 or 90 percent of the population as opposed to those in the top 20 or 10 percent. Palmer feels that the changes meant greater opportunity for small farmers and possibly for indentured servants, large elements in the population during the colonial period. Let me call this the Palmer hypothesis. A further elaboration of the hypothesis could include an upturn in inequality from 1788 to 1798, as shown in figure 10. The figure considers the period of debt assumption and bank development and ends with the passage of the Alien and Sedition Acts as well as the First Direct Tax of the United States. After this time, John Adams turned to reconciliation with the French, and Jefferson was elected to the presidency.

An alternative hypothesis is that the Revolution had little impact and that the new federal Constitution, without its first ten amendments, was in many ways a conservative document. It established an orderly society dedicated to the preservation of property rights, servant contracts, and debts throughout a large land. Although it devised an open society without

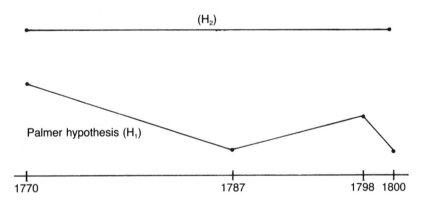

FIGURE 10. INEQUALITY OF WEALTH CAUSED BY POLITICAL CHANGE, 1770–1800: TWO HYPOTHESES

SOURCE: R. R. Palmer, *The Age of the Democratic Revolution* (Princeton, N.J.: Princeton University Press, 1970), 1:185–89, 2:544–45.

a royal family or nobility, such hereditary groups never had existed in this country, even in colonial times. While the new framework made possible great mobility among ranks of wealth from one generation to the next, it nevertheless brought about the same general degree of inequality in each decade and generation. Hypothesis (H_2) holds that the period after 1787 was one of general prosperity, with labor in strong demand; this was an era benefiting both rich and poor. The shift in political perspective after 1798 was nothing more than a complete expression of former underlying political beliefs that were manifested in the full development of political parties.[12]

Statistics cannot demonstrate whether H_1 or H_2 is more likely. My data on wealth and income distributions are for 1798, and not for 1800 or later. The Palmer hypothesis, if true, would have had its strongest effect *after* 1800, as embedded in land purchase laws, poor laws, and laws governing voter eligibility. Yet the openness provided by the new government in the early federal period seems more likely to have increased rather than weakened equality.

Were people even cognizant of political distinctions in 1798? Did voters tend to promote their own economic self-interest? I present data for New Jersey voters in figure 11 and for Pennsylvania voters and congressional voters in appendix 9. As reported in the newspapers of their persuasion, New Jersey Republicans used terminology that attempted to identify them with the common man, that is, the small farmers, mechanics, tradesmen, and the "midling sort." Newspapers commonly denounced the "aristocracy," merchants, lawyers, judges, bankers, speculators, landjobbers, stockjobbers, and swindlers. Evidently journalists thought the power of the Federalists went hand in hand with wealth. In the New Jersey election of 1800, the only evidence of the economic implications of voting is the margin by which one party or the other won in each county. The results clearly demonstrate a linear relationship between the Federalist vote and wealth, as shown in figure 11, with $R^2 = .63$. Also, dwelling house values were higher in the Federalist counties.[13] Similar statistics for all 420 townships in Pennsylvania in 1800 are presented in appendix 9.

OTHER FACTORS LESSENING INEQUALITY OF WEALTH AND INCOME

There are other reasons for believing that inequality may have decreased in the quarter century before 1798. There is evidence that literacy was increasing and that transportation improvements reduced inequalities between areas. The development of the postal system helped disseminate

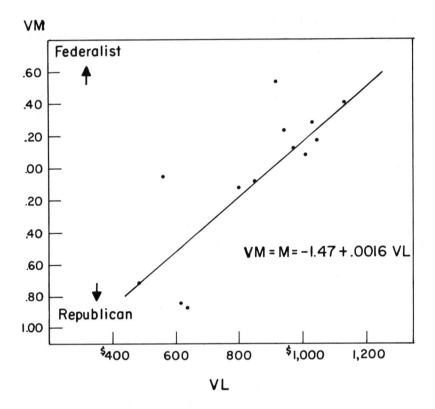

FIGURE 11. The Federalist Vote and Land Values in New Jersey, 1800

Note: The figure shows the vote margin for Federalists as a proportion of the number of white males 26 and older in 1800 (VM), related to the value of land in 1798 per white male 26 and older (VL) for each of New Jersey's 13 counties.

information of all kinds, including knowledge of markets. Any improvements that facilitated greater participation in landownership could decrease the inequality of wealth in the population at large. The spread of knowledge concerning investment or work opportunities, the establishment of credit, including banking facilities, the ability to get goods to markets, all could enhance the wealth holding of lower groups relative to the rich. These changes also enhanced the position of individuals without any wealth. It cannot be denied that some of the same factors (such as those creating banking and making credit available) also enhanced the opportunities for becoming rich and enabled the rich to become richer. It is conceivable that the lower portion of the income distribution may have become more equal while the upper portion became even more unequal. Some of these points have been considered more systematically in my discussions of income distribution, and many of the factors touched on here are examined in greater depth in chapter 4.

DEBT ASSUMPTION (AND INCREASED INEQUALITY)

James Callender wrote in 1798:

> But on tracing the treasury faction up to the fountain head, it is clear that the first bond of union among their leaders was a conspiracy for paper jobbing. To enrich perhaps fifty members of Congress, the whole continent was converted into an immense gaming table, and the wheels of government were clogging and the industry of the country was oppressed with forty millions of domestic debt, instead of ten or fifteen millions. Of their *religion,* the six percent heroes have given many practical proofs. . . . This is a bird's eye landscape of the *truly federal* system and of the precepts and projects of its godly and sanctified conductors.[14]

Any dealings in ownership of government debt created during and after the war might have benefited only the few. At the end of the Revolution, the federal debt existed largely in the form of loan certificates held by investors as well as final settlement certificates issued to army veterans. The former had a market value of 20 to 25 cents on a dollar, while the value for soldiers' certificates was as low as 10 to 15 cents on a dollar. Some states began accepting final settlement certificates in payment for land in 1785–1786 and certificate values increased accordingly; they were of value in purchasing northwest lands after 1787. All of this activity produced a great deal of trading in certificates, especially since soldiers and officers tended to sell to paper speculators.[15] There was a strong feeling that a small group of men had gained very substantially by the time the federal government had funded the debt in August of 1790.[16] By 1791, all of the various types of securities had a market value above par; there was a strong degree of inequality in the total value of these securities held by different persons, as we shall see.

Some observers were extremely agitated by the thought that these events had established what they believed to be an opulent group in the new republic. Particularly were they disturbed that it was made possible by an act of Congress, whose representatives, after all, should foster equality rather than maldistribution. The most articulate complaint appeared in a 1792 pamphlet, *The Path to Riches,* whose title page displayed the following lines:

> Where is the upright man, with skill refin'd
> to check their rage, and cure the public mind
> With honest zeal, to plead a People's cause
> and guard their equal rights, by equal laws?[17]

The author, James Sullivan, believed such injustice was counter to the spirit of equality engendered by the Revolution:

> The men who had risked their lives in the war, or who had parted with their patrimonies or hard earned estates, to save the public liberty stood at a distance, and with astonishment beheld the singular and unexpected phenomenon. The securities which they received for their services and properties, in the place of gold or silver, and had sold at two shillings and six pence in the twenty shillings, resumed their pristine value in the hands of their new possessors, and greatly enlarged their new and unexpected value by the machinery of the American bank.[18]

In another passage, Sullivan went on to explain why large inequality of wealth is undesirable—a topic almost never analyzed by writers at the time. He took the position that inequality caused envy and unhappiness, to the detriment of the majority of the people. Presumably, people could observe the frivolous consumption by the rich, particularly in the forms of clothing and carriages, but most especially housing. He felt that emulation would not goad men to work harder at ordinary endeavors, but would entice them into attempts at financial speculation. "A great part of our wants are factitious, arising from what we see in the possession of others; and therefore, when a few men, by an inequality of operation in the laws of the ruling power, accumulate fortunes, and live in unequalled splendor, it corrupts the taste of the other part of the community, and draws their attention from their ordinary means of business."[19] In some ways the argument yields an end result opposite to that usually given today. In Sullivan's sense, inequality would increase the proportion of income that is consumed because the emulative effect would be strong. It is often felt that great inequality increases the proportion of society's income that is saved because, for the rich, the marginal propensity to consume is low.

The uneasiness expressed by some persons in 1791 and 1792 continued throughout the decade. The assumption of state debts by the federal government and the establishment of banks so enflamed James Callender in 1798 that he wrote, "In attempting to describe our absurdities, one *sinks under the imperfection of human language.* The corruptions of Philadelphia paper-jobbing demand the pencil of a master."[20] Corroborating these 1798 sentiments are the conclusions that we can draw from quantifications of the 1798 distribution of wealth, with and without debt holdings.

By how much might the inequality of wealth have been increased by the security holdings—the paper—that so obsessed Callender? (See table 59.) The number of security holders for the country was about 8,500, as estimated from data reported for five states and the known aggregate funded debt of $32 million. To add this number to the distribution established in chapter 6 is to increase the number of holders by 2 percent and aggregate wealth (adjusted for slave values) by 4 to 5 percent. This addition really has very little effect on the fundamental force of inequality; the Gini coefficient only rises from .59 to .60.

Even to assume that the top 8,500 security holders were also the top real estate holders only increases inequality from .592 to .608. This particular calculation is given in table 59. In this case, the share of the wealth of the top 2 percent increases from 20.5 percent to 23.6 percent. Yet these figures do not provide enough evidence to explain the feelings at the time. Perhaps there was no antipathy against the rich themselves or to becoming rich, as long as the wealth did not arise from information concerning government action or from manipulation stemming from government activities.[21] In this sphere, we should include rising private assets derived from military land warrants, bank stock, securities of private companies and commercial or liquid wealth (such as cash, inventories, and accounts receivable). Data on bank holdings and commercial wealth are difficult to obtain, but some information is available concerning land warrants.[22]

MILITARY LAND WARRANTS (AND INCREASED INEQUALITY)

The debt due to supporting the Revolutionary cause during the war had ramifications other than the creation of a security-holding class. Soldiers were issued military warrants that entitled them to purchase land in the West. By amassing these warrants, often purchased for but a few cents on a dollar in the 1780s, speculators were able to obtain large amounts of land. In 1793 George Logan was particularly disturbed that soldier certificates had risen as much as eight times the value paid to the soldiers. "To satisfy the ambition of one class of men and the avarice of another, the Americans have submitted to a second revolution, by which they have bartered their domestic rights, liberty and equality, for the energy of

TABLE 59
HYPOTHESIS TESTING THE IMPACT OF POSTWAR SPECULATION IN
SECURITIES ON INEQUALITY OF WEALTH
(U.S. wealth altered by boosting the top 8,475 wealth holders
to account for $32 million in securities holdings)

Class	No. of Wealth Holders	Average Wealth in Land, Housing, and Slaves	Average Wealth with the Addition of Securities
1	The top 248	$96,200	$150,000
2	Next 457	42,400	57,700
3	586	29,600	36,600
4	2,442	20,300	32,600
5	1,289	12,700	13,400
6	2,447	20,800	10,500
7	2,026	8,970	8,990
Subtotal	8,495		
8	424,727	1,495	1,495
Total	433,219	1,750	1,823
Inequality, G		.592	.608

Sources: Ferguson's frequencies given in table 44 have been multiplied by the ratio 8,495/ 3,294 to account for data in other states and to give a total debt of $32 million as reported in *American State Papers, Finance,* 2d Cong., 1st sess., 23 January 1792, p. 149. See E. James Ferguson, *The Power of the Purse* (Chapel Hill: University of North Carolina Press, 1961), pp. 273–83. The 1798 U.S. distribution is taken from table 8, adjusted upward to account for slaves, using district and county aggregates given in table D (appendix 6).

Note: It is assumed that the top 248 persons in the distribution of wealth were also the top 248 in the distribution of securities, and so forth. The $32 million is accounted for approximately in the next to last line of the table by 433,219 (1,823 − 1,750).

government and the ettiquette [*sic*] of a court. After having wrested the sceptre from the hand of a British tyrant, they have suffered it to be assumed by a monied aristocracy where it will be found more oppressive and more injurious to the people."[23]

It is difficult to quantify the effects on inequality arising from this type of speculation. I will present the figures for federal land sales in one Ohio district, followed by an examination of state sales procedures in North Carolina and Virginia that were applied to lands in Tennessee, Kentucky, and Ohio by the end of the century.

The Military District (and Increased Inequality)

An example that reflects the quantitative importance of army warrants on land redistribution is the U.S. Military District in Ohio.[24] Under land grant laws passed in 1796 and 1799, military personnel were given land warrants for varying amounts of acreage. Noncommissioned officers received 100 acres, lieutenants 200, captains 300, majors 400, colonels 500, brigadier generals 850, and major generals 1,100 acres. This allocation procedure in itself may have been thought to foster inequality, but the warrants were sold to speculators who registered them for land parcels whose location was determined by lottery. For example, George Skinner registered for 4,050 acres of land for 25 warrants he had purchased from privates, sergeants, and others. Twenty warrants were for 100 acres, one for 200 acres, two for 300 acres, one for 400, and one for 850.

In extant records of warrants registered in the district from 1796 to 1799, there were approximately 500 owners who had obtained 7,957 warrants, presumably from 7,957 officers and enlisted men. The distribution accounts for an aggregate of 1,112,300 acres, as shown in table 60. This level of inequality is not insignificant and indicates the substantial dispersion that existed in the military hierarchy, a fact that is further substantiated by army pay schedules for the period.

In any case, the warrants were sold at low prices to a few individuals, which tended to make the distribution even more unequal than it was originally. Most of the warrants were surrendered, in groups that enabled the acquisition of an average of 4,000 acres, to the approximately 500 individuals who bought them from veterans and their heirs. The distribution of these warrants, after sale, was approximately as follows:

No. of Owners	Average Acreage
262	4,000
238	10
7,957	0

This distribution shows very extensive inequality. If the warrants had been sold at one-eighth of their stated prices in 1788, the distribution might have been as follows:

No. of Owners	Average Acreage
262	3,500 (⅞ of 4,000 acres)
7,957	17 (⅛ of original average of 140)
238	9 (⅞ of 10 acres)

TABLE 60
LAND GRANT WARRANTS REGISTERED IN THE
U.S. MILITARY DISTRICT OF OHIO, 1796–1799

No. of Warrants	Rank	No. of Acres Granted
6,269	Noncommissioned officer	100
98[a]		150
629	Lieutenant	200
626	Captain	300
153	Major	400
78[a]		450
81	Colonel	500
20	Brigadier general	850
3	Major general	1,150
Total 7,957		
Mean		140
Inequality, G .24		

Source: Microfilm #847553, Church of Latter Day Saints Genealogical Library, Salt Lake City, *Army Land Warrants,* Registered under the Act for Regulating the Grants of Land, Appropriated for Military Services, passed 1 June 1796 and 2 March 1799 for the U.S. Military District in Ohio and Reserved Under General Act in 1788.
  a. Unidentified by rank.

Here, the inequality, G, is .84 (or .86, if I array the one-eighth service share as in the original warrant distribution).[25] The calculations help to convey the quantitative importance of the powerful redistribution that took place when the final settlement certificates of military personnel rose to par value with the Assumption Law of 4 August 1790.

Yet one notes that the number of owners and amounts of land involved in this military district represented only 2 percent of the adult male population and less than 1 percent of private acreage (in 1798); more important, the ultimate overall relative inequality was only a little larger than that displayed for the country in chapter 2.

Virginia Military Warrants (Increasing or Constant Inequality)

The original distribution of land warrants to army personnel from southern states established a pattern of strong inequality within the military organization. This was particularly true after 1780 and appears to have been a holdover from the schedules that prevailed during colonial days. The schedule evidently perpetuated the existing level of inequality; a reshuffling by selling warrants could have increased inequality. The Revolution made it possible for many to obtain land but, paradoxically, the imposed pattern was an unequal one.

The North Carolina Act of 1782 stated that men in the army in 1782 should be given land according to this acreage schedule: privates, 640; noncommissioned officers, 1,000; subalterns, 2,500; captains, 3,840; majors, 4,800; lieutenant colonels, 5,760; colonels, 7,200; and brigadiers, 12,000. (Nathaniel Greene received 25,000 acres on Duck Creek in 1784, for example.)[26] Virginia's schedule showed even greater relative inequality for land distributed in Kentucky and Ohio. Awards began at 200 acres for soldiers and noncommissioned officers and rose steadily through nine ranks, to 15,000 acres for major generals.[27]

Virginia's distribution of warrants for land in Kentucky and Ohio, presented in table 61, is an example of very substantial inequality and a distribution shape that was very roughly lognormal. The story does not end with ranks and warrants, however. The veteran of the Revolution or

TABLE 61
LAND GRANT WARRANTS ISSUED IN KENTUCKY AND OHIO
(VIRGINIA MILITARY DISTRICT) BY 1810

| | | Cumulative Proportion | |
| | | --- | --- |
No. of Acres	No. of Recipients	Recipients (N_X)	Acres (A_X)
10,000–15,000	8	.0017	.024 (.08)[a]
5,000–9,999	120	.027	.21 (.35)
2,000–4,999	650	.17	.77 (.65)
1,000–1,999	90	.18	.80 (.68)
500–999	240	.24	.84 (.72)
200–499	1,880	.63	.96 (.95)
100–199	1,700	.99	.99 (.99)
60–99	100	1.00	1.00 (1.00)
Total	4,788		
Mean	827 acres		
Inequality, G	.704		(.72)

Sources: Virginia State Library, Item 99, Register of Military Certificates Located in Ohio and Kentucky, nos. 1–6, 899, 8,701–8,850. See listing in Daphne S. Gentry, *Virginia Land Office Inventory,* Archives Division, 1976. The above distribution is derived from a stratified sample of 586 men, 128 of whom had acreage above 5,000 acres.

a. Lognormal shares if G = .72.

his heir could sell the warrant to someone else. Land inequality arising from the Revolution was large in the states of Kentucky and Tennessee by 1798; it was surprisingly significant even in Ohio, an area that included the Virginia Military District, but a state where sales were conducted largely under federal direction.[28]

The review of statistics dealing with military warrants indicates a pattern of strong inequality and gives no hint that the relative dispersion of wealth declined in the last quarter of the century. One dimension of the overall effect of western lands on inequality is not measured by the statistics for Kentucky, Tennessee, and Ohio or by distributions for western Pennsylvania and New York. The western movement of the population undoubtedly lessened the pressures for land further east. How much greater would the inequality level have been in the East if people had had to remain there? My guess would be that the inequality of wealth would have been somewhat larger. Somewhere between 8 and 15 percent of the population would have had to remain in the East. The proportion of property owners would have been less and the group at the bottom of the distribution of landed wealth would have held smaller amounts of productive land.

DISRUPTIONS OF WAR (AND INCREASED INEQUALITY)

The war had created extreme hardship for some Americans. Many owners' buildings had been burned, while others had lost their cattle. Some had to neglect their farms because of army service. Inequality could have increased to the extent that hardships affected one group more than another. The extreme inflation from 1777 to 1781 obviously benefited some and hurt others who had engaged in land sales or were involved in other financial commitments for several years.

Disruptions in the economy augment relative inequality unless there is a substantially higher percentage of losses among the rich than among those with little wealth. A theorem of mathematical statistics states that if a random shock is applied to a lognormal variable, then the relative dispersion increases.[29] An experiment can be performed with a lognormal distribution of 10,000 items, with $G = .70$. When, as chosen by lot, one-fourth of the items are raised by 50 percent, one-fourth are lowered by 50 percent, and half are left alone, the Gini coefficient increases from .70 to .88.

LIFE-CYCLE EFFECTS (AND CONSTANCY OF G)

The diversity in age groups in a population explains part of the overall variance in statistics on wealth. The average wealth of the young is less than that of the old, and the distribution of wealth adjusted for life-cycle effects shows less inequality, but the adjustment does not account for as much as one would imagine. We can see this in table 62, which uses data from the U.S. censuses of wealth in 1850 and 1860. Average wealth increases with age, as expected, but relative inequality decreases with age, at least until age 50. The average Gini coefficient obtained by weighting age-specific coefficients by their populations is not much less than the overall Gini coefficient. Age, in this sense, explains only a small percentage of the inequality of wealth. The life-cycle inequality displayed in any given year accounts for very little unless one limits the field to, say, only those age 40 to 49.

An investigation of life-cycle effects should not be abandoned because of the apparent uselessness of the evidence for one year. The parameters for 1850 and 1860 may not have been the same as those for 1800 or 1774. The opportunities for accumulating wealth at an early age may have improved after Independence. The strong dispersion of wealth among the young may have lessened if greater opportunities for acquiring land arose or if the proportion of indentured servants in the population dropped. These possibilities were not likely; nevertheless, age data should be mobilized as a check.

Unfortunately, age classifications for the time before 1850 are difficult to find. An exception is a remarkable census for Franklin County, Pennsylvania, for 1821, which yields a complete enumeration of the age and acreage owned for all adult males. The average wealth and inequality of various age groups is strikingly similar to the pattern of 1850, as is shown in table 62. Age data generated by Jackson Turner Main for Connecticut from 1650 to 1753 also appear to show the same patterns for central tendency and dispersion.[30] Finally, we note that the age-specific averages developed by Alice Hanson Jones for 1774 display a similar life-cycle pattern. One can conclude only that the life-cycle effects exerted the same influence on inequality throughout the last half of the eighteenth century and later. The impact of age tended to stabilize long-run inequality. The inheritance mechanism undoubtedly explains part of the phenomenon. A study of the ages of fathers and sons in 1860 illustrates this permanency. The probability was small that a son would inherit property when he was in his twenties; only a few persons of that age inherited substantial amounts, and inequality of inheritance was of the magnitude demonstrated in table 62. A son had a larger probability of inheriting in his thirties, and an even larger probability in his forties. His expectations of inheritance rose along with his age, generating averages and dispersion similar to the figures presented in table 62.[31]

TABLE 62
AGE OF LANDOWNERS, ACREAGE OWNED, AND VALUE OF REAL ESTATE IN FRANKLIN COUNTY, PENNSYLVANIA, AND RURAL UNITED STATES, 1821, 1850, AND 1860

| | Franklin County, Pa., 1821 | | | Rural United States | | | | |
| | | | | 1850 | | 1860 | | |
Age	N	Average Acreage	Inequality, G	Average Value of Real Estate	Inequality, G	Average Value of Real Estate	Inequality G	New England, 1774 Average Net Worth
20–29	93	21	.89	$ 410	.86	$ 660	.90	£ 93
30–39	71	34	.78	1,220	.74	1,220	.76	147
40–49	69	55	.65	1,820	.68	2,870	.69	314
50–99	93	67	.69	2,420	.69	3,220	.70	492
20–99	408	48	.75	1,390	.77	1,890	.78	375

Sources: Franklin County (Fannet Township) data are from the Septennial Census of 1821 and Franklin County tax list of 1822, Division of Archives and Manuscripts, State Archives, Harrisburg; see also Lee Soltow and Kenneth Keller, "Rural Pennsylvania in 1800: A Portrait from the Septennial Census," *Pennsylvania History* 49, no. 1 (January 1982), 42. U.S. data are described in chapter 2. The 1774 New England data are from Alice Hanson Jones, *Wealth of a Nation to Be* (New York: Columbia University Press, 1980), p. 385, cols. 1, 3, a sample of 261 decedents.

INHERITANCE (INCREASED OR CONSTANT INEQUALITY)

Inheritances tend to perpetuate the inequality of wealth from decade to decade and from one generation to another. Because of the death of wealth holders, all assets are transferred every 30 years or so, which brings about either stability or a more gradual change in inequality than would otherwise arise. If inheritance of land were a very dominant force affecting variations in wealth, then the kinds of changes that took place from 1740 to 1770 would be expected to be repeated between 1770 and 1800. The effects of the Revolution and institutional changes that took place during the early federal period would not have had an overriding influence on inequality.

To look at the record of inequality during the three generations of the eighteenth century is beyond the scope of this book. Selected results of probated estates, presented in table 63, provide some insight into the changes occurring over the span of nearly a century. The data seem to indicate stability, with some increase in relative variation throughout the century as assets were transferred to children.[32] It would be of analytical value to establish a distribution of inheritances to children in each generation. These can be simulated by using a distribution of the numbers of children in families, which forms the basis of a simple model of land inheritance that constitutes the remainder of this section.

I will develop a model of land fragmentation that highlights the effects of inheritance and changes in inequality from generation to generation. One could think of the model as beginning in Ohio in 1800 or in western Pennsylvania in 1770. Initially, the land in a township or county could have been transferred from government ownership to private hands very quickly, particularly if there were speculators or absentee owners. The original tracts, in any case, would be subject to fragmentation upon the death of the private owner, and we can posit a simple model for the size of each piece after inheritance as L/CHI, where L is the plot in acres and CHI is the number of children in the family, assuming that each child receives an equal share. This aspect of fragmentation highlights the size of the family, since parcels obviously were subject to a greater degree of division in large families. I will obviate the problems of the future marriages of the children by considering only males as the recipients of land. The distribution of sons presented in table 64 will be employed in this connection.

We are in a position to speculate about the distribution of agricultural

TABLE 63
INEQUALITY OF WEALTH REFLECTED IN ESTATES OF DECEASED IN SOUTH
CAROLINA, NEW JERSEY, AND MASSACHUSETTS, 1720–1861

Charleston District, S.C.[a]			New Jersey[a]			Suffolk Co., Mass.[b]		
	N	Inequality, G		N	Inequality, G		N	Inequality, G
1720–1729	304	.59	1680–1689	33	.51	1688–1708	515	.53
1730–1739	368	.63	1690–1699	74	.60	1746–1750	428	.68
1740–1749	589	.61	1700–1709	210	.57	1767–1769	273	.65
1750–1759	513	.61	1710–1719	99	.60	1796–1807	979	.81
1760–1769	413	.66	1720–1729	129	.57	1829–1831	432	.86
1785–1789	309	.71	1730–1739	155	.56	1859–1861	878	.85
1790–1794	281	.71	1740–1749	396	.54			
1795–1799	249	.71	1750–1759	1,312	.54			
1800–1804	218	.68	1760–1769	1,625	.59			
1805–1809	238	.66	1770–1774	1,076	.59			
			1790–1799	2,812	.62			
			1800	221	.64			

Sources: Suffolk County Probates, County Courthouse, and Massachusetts Dept. of Labor, *Report on the Statistics of Labor 1894,* pt. 2, "The Distribution of Wealth," pp. 216–37; South Carolina Department of Archives and History, and William George Bentley, "Wealth Distribution in Colonial South Carolina," Ph.D. diss., Georgia State University, 1977. Data for 1785–1809 are five-year averages of Gini coefficients computed from annual data; see *Documents Relating to the Colonial, Revolutionary, and Post-Revolutionary History of the State of New Jersey,* 1st ser., Calendar of New Jersey Wills, Administration, etc., vols. 1–11, ed. Elmer Hutchinson (Newark: New Jersey Law Journal, 1944). A few wills have alternate dates.
  a. Personal estate.
  b. Total estate.

landholdings in succeeding generations by using theorems drawn from mathematical properties of the lognormal distributions. Suppose there was no free land, that each original family had 1,000 acres, that land was equally distributed among sons, and that the number of sons in each generation was unrelated to the size of the plot. Now suppose that the number of sons was distributed lognormally, with a mean of 2.7 and Gini coefficient (G) of .26. (The G is 1.0 if one man owns all land and is 0.0 if land is equally distributed among all.) Theorems for the lognormal distribution lead to the following consequences, under such assumptions: The distribution remains lognormal in each generation and is unaffected by whether or not we weight the size distribution by the number of

TABLE 64
DISTRIBUTION OF SONS AMONG FAMILIES IN
WASHINGTON COUNTY, OHIO, 1810

Sons $(X)^a$	No. of Cases	N_x, the Proportion of Cases above X	A_x, the Share of All Sons Accounted for by the N_x Group
7	1	0.011	$0.03 (0.03)^b$
6	2	0.033	0.08 (0.09)
5	3	0.07	0.14 (0.16)
4	19	0.28	0.45 (0.45)
3	21	0.51	0.71 (0.69)
2	28	0.82	0.93 (0.92)
1	16	1.00	1.00 (1.00)
Total	90		
Mean			2.72
Inequality, G			0.258 (0.26)

Source: Washington County, Ohio, 1810 census manuscripts, in the collections of the Marietta College Library, Marietta, Ohio.

Note: Five families with no sons are not included. Presumably, most of the 90 cases represent families with wives near the end of childbearing age (since presumed husbands are over 45) and most of the wives' sons are still in the nuclear family. The proportion of families with stepsons, foster children, or nonrelated boys is unknown.

a. Sons 16 and under in families with one female age 25–44, no female age 45–99, no male age 25–44, and one male age 45–99.

b. Lognormal shares at the selected percentiles for G = 0.26 are given in parentheses.

children.[33] (See table 65.) We note that inequality continues to increase but that it settles down for several generations, to a range of .5 to .7, a level often experienced for the inequality of wealth in real estate, as distributed among men.

The real world is obviously far more complex. The distribution of land does not begin with uniformity. The availability of free land to the west of Ohio lessened inequality, as the decline in the number of sons would do in later decades. Families with greater acreage probably tended to have more children, and this worked against inequality. Finally, we know that the fragmentation of land occurred for many reasons other than inheritance. In numbers, deeds of sale surely far surpassed deeds of gift.

What would tend to impede the increasing inequality suggested by breakage theory? Some sons would sell their shares to a chosen brother. If there were two farms, the third and fourth sons might move west or into town. Potentially small parcels would be shunned. (If one regards the

TABLE 65
INEQUALITY IN LAND DISTRIBUTION IN SUCCESSIVE GENERATIONS,
CONSIDERING VARIATION IN FAMILY SIZE

| | Tract Size (in acres) | |
Generation	Mean	Inequality, G
0	1,000	0.00
1	370	0.26
2	137	0.37
3	51	0.43
4	19	0.49
5	7	0.54
6	3	0.59
7	1	0.63

Source: See ch. 7, n. 33.

propertyless as holding insignificant acreage, we might demonstrate increasing inequality.) The real world also involves consolidations and rearrangements through marriage that I am unable to trace.

A possible adaptation of the model leading to constant inequality is a truncated lognormal process. (See table 66.) Suppose we begin with a lognormal curve with a mean of 30 acres and G = .64, parameters similar to those suggested by Ohio data. Plots of two acres or less constituted 13 percent, or only .5 percent of all acreage. The distribution for X > 2 is still essentially lognormal and it has G (X > 2) = .60. Each stage of subdivision that would increase G from .60 to .64 could be cut back to .60 by eliminating unmanageably small plots. (These could be reabsorbed on a proportional basis among plots above two acres.) This process could continue through many stages, leaving the distribution essentially lognormal, with G = .64. An initial distribution in Ohio with G = .64, .60, or even .50, might have arisen as a reflection of the existing inequality in New England and Pennsylvania where the process had already been taking place for generations and was introduced by the migrants to Ohio. The new settlers and speculators could reflect the economic condition of fathers in the east who experienced greater, but essentially the same kind of inequality.

The distribution of sons g(S) seems to remain essentially a lognormal curve (truncated, as explained below) through time, with a Gini coefficient of about .3 or a little less, even though its mean decreases. This is true for the United States in 1870 and 1966, and may very well have been true in

TABLE 66
Hypothetical Model Maintaining Constant Inequality in Landholding, Assuming a 40-Acre Limit and Curtailment of Population

Step	Type of Distribution	Generation or Period (t)			
		0	1	2	3
1	Truncated distribution of estates $[f(E)]^a$				
	Mean	967	396	204	143
	Inequality, G	0.601	0.601	0.600	0.600
	N	1,000	2,421	4,621	6,502
2	Distribution of sons $[g(S)]^b$				
	Mean^c	2.78	2.27	1.66	1.19
	Inequality, G	0.302	0.292	0.261	0.138
	N	1,000	2,421	4,621	6,502
3	Distribution of inheritances $[h(I)]^d$	348	174	123	110
	Inequality, G	0.642	0.641	0.637	0.649
	N	2,777	5,550	7,656	7,748
	Proportion of cases in which inheritance exceeds 40 acres (b_i)	0.84	0.70	0.54	0.54
	Acre limit above which G = .60	34	25	18	18

Source: Author.

Note: Constant inequality is for a G of .64 to .65.
  a. $h(I_{t-1})$ truncated to LL_{t-1}.
  b. Lognormal in all periods with G = .3 before rounding.
  c. $S_t = X_t b_{t-1}$.
  d. $I_t = E_t/S_t$.

1790, as illustrated by the data for Washington County in table 64. The estate distribution f(E) in any generation might deviate substantially from lognormality[34] if it is fractured and in effect molded again at the death of the landowner. We can hypothesize that the distribution of inheritance, h (I = E/S), would again be nearly lognormal with the impetus stemming from g(S).

The computer simulation given in table 66 tests this hypothesis. It draws randomly the estates of 1,000 from a lognormal distribution with a mean of 1,000 acres and an inequality coefficient of .60. The results in step 1 for the base period do not quite approximate these figures due to sampling error. In any case, this stage would entail land as distributed among settlers, potential settlers, and speculators in a given region in Ohio. The simulation then draws randomly the number of sons for each man from a lognormal distribution with a mean of 2.7 and an inequality coefficient of .3, drawing enough cases to have 1,000 after rounding to integer values and discarding cases with $S = 0$. The resulting inheritance distribution of the 2,777 sons is approximately lognormal, as the theory predicts, in spite of the truncation in $g(S)$.

The distribution of inheritances in the base period has two characteristics that will be employed in succeeding steps: the 2,777 sons include some with minimal farm plots, but 84 percent have above 40 acres. This factor (the $b = .84$ in table 66) is used as a proxy in curtailing the average number of sons in the next generation. The distribution of inheritances demonstrates a truncated lognormal distribution with an inequality coefficient of .6 if we eliminate the few poor having less than 40 acres (the LL in table 66). I assume that they joined the urban population or moved further west, and I do not redistribute their small amount of land among the others.

Period 1 of the table begins with a distribution of estates that is the truncated distribution of inheritances of the preceding period, involving the 2,421 sons with estates of more than 40 acres. I assume they will produce a $g(S)$ with a mean of $2.7 \times .84$, or 2.28 ($\bar{S}_1 = \bar{S}_0 b_0$), and $G = .3$ as a continuous distribution which, after rounding, gives us 2,421 cases. This is a fresh distribution of sons randomly generated in step 2 and it can be coupled with the distribution of step 1 to produce the distribution of inheritances found in period 1. Period 2 applies the same rules by truncating the previous period's inheritance distribution at $G = .6$ and curtailing the number of sons so they have a mean of $2.7 \times .84 \times .70$, the proxy for the scarcity of land. The same rules are again applied in period 3.

When the distribution of inheritances in period 3 is tested, we find that it does indeed conform to the prediction. This was also true at each preceding stage. (See table 67.)

The model given in table 66 is of utmost importance in demonstrating that relative inequality can remain constant because of inheritance, even with a rising population and a decrease in average acreage. It could explain how relative inequality in land would remain constant every generation.

SLAVERY (INCREASED OR CONSTANT INEQUALITY)

The distribution of slaves among slaveholders also may lead to increasing or constant inequality, with very gradual change. The supply of slaves

TABLE 67
DISTRIBUTION OF INHERITANCE IN PERIOD THREE OF THE MODEL
PRESENTED IN TABLE 66

Upper Proportion of Persons $N(I_3)$	Their Share of Total Acreage $A(I_3)$	Share, if Lognormal, with G=0.65
0.01	0.17	0.16
0.02	0.25	0.23
0.05	0.39	0.37
0.10	0.53	0.52
0.20	0.69	0.68
0.30	0.79	0.79
0.40	0.85	0.86
0.50	0.90	0.91
1.00	1.00	1.00

Source: Author.

changed methodically, say 3 percent a year. This change reflected neither cyclical swings nor irregular movements. Nor was it fundamentally affected by disruptions of war. A time series for the South, showing the number of slaves, acres owned, acres cultivated, the number of horses, cows, and other livestock owned for each year from 1770 to 1800, or 1740 to 1800, would be most revealing. I suspect that the series for slaves would show the most stability in growth, but perhaps the ownership of land might increase more. It is true that disease could reduce the number of slaves and that the importation of slaves would cause periodic surges.

The distribution among slaveholders could change if there were shifts in returns to scale favorable to larger plantations or possibly to smaller operations. A shift in the type of crops grown could also alter the distribution of slaves. The invention of the cotton gin obviously introduced some alterations in size after 1792. Rice-growing counties had a smaller concentration of holdings than did the counties in which cotton farming predominated. In spite of this, the inequality of the distribution of slaves among slaveholders in 1790 was appreciably larger in South Carolina than in either North Carolina or Virginia.[35]

Whether relative inequality in slaveholding increased or decreased in the one or two generations preceding 1800 is difficult to determine. Only data for South Carolina are offered in table 68. They lead to the hypothesis that slave inequality was *constant,* neither increasing nor decreasing. A special sampling from the 1800 census allows a comparison with the known distribution of slaves for 1790, as reported in the table. Inequality did not increase after use of the cotton gin became widespread.

ASCERTAINING THE DISTRIBUTION OF WEALTH IN 1774 AND 1798

One must be cautious when making comparisons between the figures in tables 68 and 69. My distribution is derived from a sample of 39,000 living wealth holders adjusted to published aggregate totals for 13 states and the nation. Alice Hanson Jones's information for 1774, given in table 69, is derived from a sample of 919 estates of deceased. The 1774 data represent net worth in land, slaves, nonhuman "portable" or personal wealth and financial assets or, alternatively, total physical wealth including land, slaves, and portable wealth. My sample data include values for land and housing adjusted to aggregate totals for land, housing, and slaves for 687 tax districts. The 1798 data technically reflect the dispersion in the value of property and wealth between districts, but not within districts,

TABLE 68
INEQUALITY OF SLAVEHOLDING IN CHARLESTON DISTRICT,
SOUTH CAROLINA, 1720–1800

	No. of Deceased Slaveholders	Inequality, G	
		No. of Slaves	Value of Slaves
1720–1729	240	.55	.56
1730–1739	267	.64	.57
1740–1749	463	.60	.58
1750–1759	414	.56	.57
1760–1769	323	.59	.60
1798	70	.58	.59
South Carolina census			
1790		.66	
1800		.62	

Sources: South Carolina Department of Archives and History; William George Bentley, "Wealth Distribution in Colonial South Carolina," Ph.D. diss., Georgia State University, 1977; U.S. Bureau of the Census, *A Century of Population Growth,* p. 136 (1790 data); 1800 data are a random sample of 585 families from the census; see also Lee Soltow, "Socioeconomic Classes in South Carolina and Massachusetts in the 1790s and the Observations of John Drayton," *South Carolina Historical Magazine* 81 (1980), 290, 298.

and they understate the importance of wealth of persons owning properties in more than one county and in more than one state; I consider the 1798 distribution presented in table 69 to be a minimum statement of the degree of relative dispersion in real estate and the value of slaves. My distribution describes the number of slaves owned by 877,000 males 21 and older who represented 20.1 percent of the free population in 1800. The Jones distribution is for 435,000 wealth holders representing 23.9 percent of the free population in 1774.[36]

A glaring difference between the two data sets is that Jones has included personal estate and I have not. Had I been able to use data for furniture, clothing, utensils, livestock, and currency, my distribution would have shown a greater proportion of persons having wealth, and the overall distribution probably would have shown a little less inequality. To estimate a distribution of total estate in 1798 would be difficult to do. The data presented in table 72 indicate that in 1860 about half again as many persons owned personal estate as real estate; the inequality in personal estate was the same as for real estate, but the inequality in total estate was somewhat less than in real estate. As but one possible alternative of the 1798 distribution presented in table 69, consider that total estate in 1798 was distributed in the same way as real estate, but among 60 percent of adult males rather than among 50 percent. The Gini coefficient then drops from .80 to .76 for males or .75 to .71 for families.

The comparisons of the relative shares of wealth for 1798 and 1774 shown in the table definitely indicate a greater concentration of wealth in 1798, with or without adjustments for personal estate or for the collation problem of multiple estate holders in 1798. The differences arguably might be due to measurement and sampling errors, but they do seem to be substantial.[37] Had the 1774 data included the estates of royal officials living in the colonies, differences may have been negligible. Nevertheless, I have to conclude that inequality increased during the early federal period. But perhaps not by much. The development of debt holdings, shipping, cotton and the growth of the nation to beyond the Alleghenies introduced a heterogeneity not present during the colonial period.

There is a monumental data set describing the assets of 34,402 individuals or families in Massachusetts and 3,636 in Maine for the year 1771.[38] It yields data for personal estate as well as real estate for rural and urban areas. This set cannot be ignored even though it is only for two states and it has no exact counterpart for the period around 1800. Its distribution of real estate, or land and buildings, for 27,856 families or individuals had a mean value of £116 and a Gini coefficient of .532. The number of

TABLE 69
SHARES OF WEALTH HELD BY FAMILIES IN 1798 COMPARED
SHARES HELD BY TO WEALTH HOLDERS IN 1774

The Top Proportion of Wealth Holders	Shares Held by Families in 1798 (%)	Shares Held by Wealth Holders in 1774	
		Net Wealth (%)	Total Physical Wealth (%)
.00–.0099 (top 1%)	19	15	13
.01–.0199 (next 1%)	8	8	7
.01–.0499	15	16	15
.05–.0999	14	16	16
.00–.099	58	55	51
.10–.199	16	18	17
.20–.299	11	11	11
.30–.399	7	7	8
.40–.499	4	5	6
.50–.599	2	3	3
.60–.699	1	1	1
.70–.799		1	1
.80–.899			1
.90–1.00		−2	
Mean wealth	$1,061	£237	£252
Median wealth	$ 292	£ 83.8	£109
Inequality, G	.75	.73	.66

Sources: See table 9, adapted to 715,000 families, and table F. The 1774 data are from Alice Hanson Jones, *Wealth of a Nation to Be* (New York: Columbia University Press, 1980), pp. 10, 289.

Note: 1798 data are adjusted for slaves but not other personal estate. See text.

property holders as a proportion of an estimated 57,200 males 21 and older was .486—almost exactly the .487 proportion estimated as the property owner proportion (POP) in the northern states in 1798. The Massachusetts-Maine Lorenz curve for 1771 demonstrates a little more equality than does the Lorenz curve of northern real estate in 1798, as shown in figure 12. The difference in Gini coefficients for these two data sets is not large, and can be explained in part by measurement error. If the 1798 mean in each of the other seven northern states is adjusted to the Massachusetts-Maine average, inequality in the northern states is cut from .575 to .54, not really much different from the G = .532 for the two states. Certainly these data

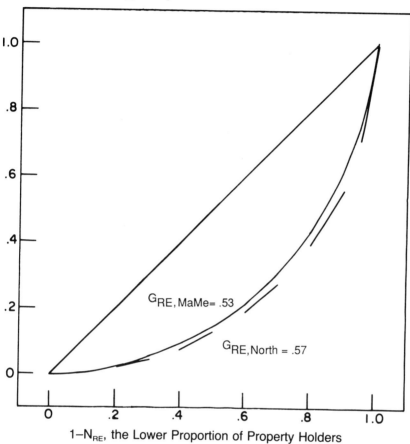

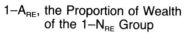

FIGURE 12. THE LORENZ CURVE OF THE DISTRIBUTION OF REAL ESTATE AMONG PROPERTY HOLDERS IN MASSACHUSETTS AND MAINE, 1771, AND IN THE NORTHERN STATES, 1798

are a strong indication that inequality in the northern states was about the same in 1771 and in 1798.

There is some confusion at this point. The comparison of my 1798 data with those of Jones for 1774 shows an increase in inequality, but the tax data for 1771 and 1798 for northern states and the slave data for at least the Charleston area indicate little or no change in inequality. If I had to choose which is more likely to be the case, I must conclude that there was little or no change in inequality. It seems more appropriate to compare tax data with tax data than probate data with tax data.

I conclude that inequality in the North did not change much in the generation before 1800. Possibly personal estate changes might have created some shifts in shares of the rich, but not many. Appendix 8 explores further ramifications of this subject; the fact that personal estate in 1771 was prominent and was very unequally distributed signifies that there could not have been much alteration in the distribution of total estate between 1771 and 1798. I suspect that inequality in the South remained constant during the generation, since the region was so strongly agricultural and the distribution of slaves remained constant.

8

Changes in Inequality, 1798–1860

I S THERE REASON to believe that inequality of wealth changed between 1798 and the beginning of the Civil War? Probably not. While slavery dominated the economy of the South more in 1850 and 1860 than in 1798, nevertheless it was quite prominent in 1798, strengthened in part by the development of the cotton gin. Northern agriculture was influenced by the relative abundance of land in 1850–1860, as in 1800; the development of the Northwest Territory in effect created a new country which by 1850 had many of the characteristics of the original northern states in 1800.

Because of the rise of urban areas, the increasing proportions of immigrants, and the increasing importance of personal estate, one might expect that inequality increased during this time. Can the effects of these dynamic influences be measured? It is possible, but some difficult statistical problems must be dealt with in order to derive adequate measures.

We begin by ramifying aspects of some of the features of constancy in the distribution of land and slaves. We then turn our attention to the 1850–1870 census data and to what the distribution of wealth for those years would have been, had some of the characteristics of the economy in 1800 been in effect in the later years. In particular, we shall try to determine what would have happened if the proportion in the rural sector had continued as it was in 1800, and the land area of United States had been confined to that of the original colonies, and, alternatively, had been confined to its new states in Ohio and to the west.

THE PROPERTY HOLDER PROPORTION, 1760–1870

The cornerstone of capitalism is the private ownership of property. The most simple or fundamental measure of participation in this institution in the eighteenth century and the first half of the nineteenth is the proportion of society owning real estate or land (PHP or PHP_{21}). To restrict ownership to free males 21 and older is to recognize that this was the only group eligible to vote. It also recognizes the fact that 95 percent of all land reported in the early censuses was held in the names of males 21 and older, not by women or children.

The development of a time series for PHP_t ($t = 1760, . . ., 1870$) would be invaluable to the understanding of inequality of wealth in the United States. Few would argue with the statement that a high rate of ownership sustained over a long series of years, would have been desirable for America and its people. Wide participation in ownership would mean that the poor had not been denied an opportunity—that they owned at least some small amount of land; nor would a small, rich group have owned a disproportionate amount, at the expense of the great majority.

The most probable hypothesis is that PHP decreased with urbanization and the movement of the labor force into occupations other than farming. The entire history of the rural-to-urban movement can be seen in the trend away from ownership: sons of farm owners became renters of urban houses. Our investigation of the 1850–1870 data, presented in this chapter and in appendix 12, indicates that the shift of population from rural to urban areas brought about a drop in PHP_{21}, from .49 or .50 to .445, between 1800 and 1850–1860. (I obtained this result by considering the urban residence of those 70 and older in 1850 and adjusting populations 20 and older in 1850 for this lessened degree of urbanity.) This finding is based on data from only two census years at mid-century, not from the full span between 1760 and 1870.

An alternative hypothesis might be that PHP_{21} either remained constant or actually increased through the decades. With the development of better roads, coastal and river traffic, land surveys, land laws, the establishment of courthouses and banks as well as other systems of credit, and with the abatement of the Indian hostilities, it became easier for a greater number of people to obtain land. The increase in literacy, wider availability of newspapers, books, and broadsides all worked together to spread the good news about the availability of land. The ratification of the Constitution in 1787–1788 made land procurement procedures more uniform between states; a uniform currency and government control of land-surveying practices also served to improve the dispersal of land. Even awarding land rights to war veterans served to reduce inequality in landholding, at least in theory. Growth in real income per capita would allow the poor to purchase government land at fixed prices, but only to the extent that the poor shared in economic growth.

Unfortunately, the PHP trend between 1800 and 1850–1860 is not known. At best, there are some tangential time series that allow a glimpse at the process of land accumulation. Table 70 shows that the growth in both land grants and population proceeded at roughly the same rates in the public land states, a signal that there was no increase in the scarcity of land. An ample supply of land meant that relative inequality in a region most likely remained constant, but this is not a certainty. It is conceivable that large landowners had been adding to their shares of the total, thus making it increasingly difficult for the many to advance themselves from renters to owners. There is even some evidence in table 70 that the land/labor ratio began to decrease after 1840, an indication consistent with the adjustment for urban residence applied to the 1850–1870 data.

A means of measuring PHP is to use tax censuses for the various states after 1760. Table 71 provides such a listing for selected states and demonstrates the prevailing stability from decade to decade within each state. Generally, the number of taxable persons (overwhelmingly males) was more than a simple count of property owners. In New York State tax lists, those males paying high annual rents were included with those owning real estate. In Pennsylvania, those paying occupational taxes or poll taxes as single individuals were included. The proportions in the table account for well over 50 percent of adult males, but certainly not all. Because roughly 21 to 25 percent of the total population were adult males 21 and

TABLE 70
INCREASE IN LAND GRANTS AND POPULATION IN
PUBLIC LAND GRANT STATES, 1800–1860

	Cumulative Acres Granted[a]	Population[a]	Acres Granted per Resident
1800	68	60	1.1
1810	3,588	411	8.7
1820	18,434	1,229	15.0
1830	28,235	2,338	12.0
1840	90,858	4,822	18.8
1850	107,794	8,288	13.0
1860	159,001	13,358	11.9

Sources: S. Doc. 246, pp. 6–10, U.S. serial set no. 416, 27th Cong., 3d sess., 5 December 1842–3 March 1843; serial set no. 539, H. Exec. Doc., vol. 3, no. 12, 30th Cong., 2d sess., 18 December 1848, pp. 240–41; serial set 597, H. Doc. 9, 1 July 1849–30 June 1850; serial set 1078, 1 July 1850–1 Janury 1860, p. 93; serial set 1117, pp. 506, 512; *Historical Statistics of the United States, Colonial Times to 1970*, pp. 24–36.
a. In thousands.

TABLE 71
TAXABLE PERSONS IN TEN STATES, 1760–1830

		N	Total Population	Ratio
Pennsylvania	1760	31,669	183,703	.172
	1770	39,766	240,057	.166
	1779	54,683	317,300	.172
	1786	66,925	387,700	.173
	1793	91,147	478,800	.190
	1800	113,355	602,000	.188
	1807	138,285	741,000	.187
	1814	163,780	898,000	.182
	1821	210,441	1,076,000	.196
	1828	254,428	1,282,000	.198
New York	1790	57,468	340,000	.169
	1795	63,774	448,000	.142
	1801	85,844	618,000	.139
	1807	121,289	829,000	.146
	1814	151,846	1,107,000	.137
	1821	202,510	1,420,000	.143
Connecticut	1792	35,400	241,000	.147
	1796	36,002	244,000	.151
	1798	36,432	248,000	.150
	1800	35,312	251,000	.144
	1802	37,498	253,000	.152
Massachusetts	1792	72,365	387,417	.184
Maine	1792	16,106	106,000	.152
Vermont	1800	24,494	154,000	.159
New Hampshire	1794	25,893	157,500	.164
Maryland	1783	31,067	170,689	.182
Virginia	1786	58,169	387,185	.150
Kentucky	1800	31,662	180,000	.176
	1810	55,764	334,000	.167
	1830	91,005	519,000	.175

Sources: Samuel Hazard, *The Register of Pennsylvania*, July 1829, 4:13; *New York Census of 1855*, pp. ix–x for electors owning freeholds and persons not freeholders but renting tenements of 40 shillings annual value; *Grand Lists of the State of Connecticut*, State Comptroller's Office, Connecticut State Library, Hartford, Conn.; Joseph Felt, "Statistics of Taxation in Massachusetts and Maine," *Collections of the American Statistical Association* (Boston: T. R. Marvin, 1847), p. 487; Office of the Vermont Secretary of State, *General List*, Montpelier, Vt., polls 21–64, adjusting with Lycoming ages; Oliver Wolcott, Jr., "Direct Taxes," *American State Papers*, class 3, vol. 1, p. 442, for polls 18–70, adjusted to age 21 and over with county and Lycoming data and p. 460 for Virginia; Maryland Hall of Records, *Summary Accounts, 1783*, Annapolis, Md.; Kentucky *Tax Lists*, Kentucky Historical Society, Frankfort, Ky., and *Journal of the Senate of Kentucky*, 11 December 1811 (Frankfort, Ky.: 1811), p. 74; *Historical Statistics of the United States*, ser. A195–209, Z1–19, interpolated values.

over, their percentages probably should have been significantly higher than those in the last column of the table. But this discrepancy should not detract from the main thrust of the table: there was a strong stability from year to year in this approximation of the proportion of the population owning property until 1830. The evidence in the table provides yet another reason for believing that relative inequality in real estate remained constant in the United States, at least among farmers.

PERSONAL ESTATE

Data for 1800 are particularly sparse in the case of personal estate or assets in movables, including farm animals, carriages, slaves, ships and intangibles, including cash, bonds, and shares in banks, utilities, and manufacturing. It is fruitful to state succinctly some of the inequality relationships in real, personal, and total estate for 1850–1870 and to comment on how they may have differed in 1800. In this connection, a distribution of slaves for 1790 will be presented.

To study inequality in personal estate holdings at the middle of the nineteenth century for whatever clues it may have to offer about 1800 is to overstate the case, since personal wealth grew from about 30 to 42 percent of total estate during the two generations (or roughly 20–33 percent if one excludes slaveholders).[1] Nevertheless, a few indications of relative inequality from the latter period are of some value.

Personal estate in 1860 was defined as the value of bonds, mortgages, notes, slaves, livestock, plate, jewels, and furniture.[2] This was, indeed, a very standard system of accounting, since only clothing seemed to be exempt from the listing. Table 72 shows that the proportion of the population holding personal estate was naturally high; real estate generally was not reported if under $100 in value, while personal estate was reported even for values as low as $10. Nevertheless, relative inequality, as measured by the Gini coefficient, was *roughly the same* for all free males for real, personal, and total estate, as shown in column 2 of table 72. It is important to note that the Gini coefficient in the North for the distribution of real estate (.84) was the same as for total estate (.84), as given in column 2. Inequality of real estate was less than that for total estate for those having such resources (column 3), but there were more persons owning total estate (column 1). In the South, the great inequality in personal estate was overwhelmingly caused by the inequality in slaveholding, which in turn probably resulted in greater relative inequality in real estate holdings than otherwise would have been the case.

TABLE 72
INEQUALITY OF WEALTH IN REAL, PERSONAL, AND TOTAL ESTATE, 1860
(males 21 and older)

| | Proportion of Wealth Holders (1) | Inequality, G | |
		All (2)	Those Reporting a Positive Value (3)
North			
Real	.44	.84	.63
Personal	.64	.83	.73
Total	.74	.84	.78
South			
Real	.45	.87	.71
Personal	.73	.86	.81
Total	.67	.81	.72

Source: See Table 71.

Note: The basic equation relating columns 1–3 is (2) = (1) × (3) + 1 − (1). Thus .84 = .44 × .63 + 1 − .44.

DISTRIBUTION OF SLAVES, 1790–1860

One cannot avoid the importance of slavery in the total picture of wealth held by free males in the United States either in 1860 or in 1800. Slaves represented 19 percent of total wealth in 1860 and, according to one estimate, 12.5 percent in 1800.[3] The value of slaves accounted almost entirely for movable estates belonging to free males in 1860; slaves represented 82 percent of personal estate in the South and 46 percent of all personal estate in the United States. Stated otherwise, for the entire country, the ratio of slaves to free males 21 and older was .56 in 1869 (and, surprisingly, .99 in 1800). Surely the inequality in slaveholding was the primary reason for the inequality in both personal and real estate holding in the South. The larger-scale operations in southern agriculture demanded more acreage as well as more slaves.[4]

The statistics regarding the distribution of slaves are crucial to an understanding of the inequality of wealth in the South from 1790 to 1860; fortunately, such statistics are readily available for selected years. The data of table 73 demonstrate constant inequality for the years 1790, 1830, 1850, and 1860, with the Gini coefficient being about .6 among slaveholders. It should be noted that the proportion of slaveholders actually decreased

TABLE 73
DISTRIBUTION OF SLAVES IN FIVE REGIONS OF THE
UNITED STATES, 1790–1860
(Maryland, District of Columbia, North Carolina, South Carolina, and Virginia)

No. of Slaves (lower class limit)	No. of Slaveholders in Class			
	1790	1830	1850	1860
1,000 and over			2	1
500	2	9	2	7
300	5	43	34	28
200	38	69	89	75
100	198	463	572	601
50	813	1,740	2,194	2,654
20	5,271	9,040	11,565	12,638
10	11,530	18,000	22,170	21,802
5	16,594	26,000	30,933	29,814
2	20,689	30,200	37,252	34,818
1	14,596	17,700	21,666	26,061
Unknown	348			
Total (SH)	70,084[a]	103,000	126,479	128,499
Mean, $\overline{X}_{S/SH}$	8.3	9.6	9.8	10.2
Inequality, G, $R_{S/SH}$	.572	.573	.582	.597
Proportion, SH_{21}	.31	.28	.25	.22

Sources: Bureau of the Census, *A Century of Population Growth from the First Census of the United States to the Twelfth, 1790–1900* (Washington, D.C.: GPO, 1909), p. 136 (1790) and p. 134 for amended figures for slaveholders from 35,710 to 38,946 and 70,084 to 72,972, as stated on those pages. Also see Lee Soltow, "Economic Inequality in the United States in the Period 1790 to 1860," *Journal of Economic History* 31, no. 4 (December 1971), 829.

a. This total does not include a few districts in Maryland and North Carolina; their inclusion would increase the figure slightly.

during this 70-year period, so that when we compute overall inequality coefficients for slaveholders and nonslaveholders (using an adaptation of the equation stated earlier for those with and without property), we see a slight increase in relative inequality. Thus, there is a strong reason to believe that inequality of wealth in the South in 1800 was about the same as that for 1860.

The issue of inequality in the North in 1800 as a result of slave ownership remains an unsettled problem. It is true that there were some few slaves in the North at the turn of the eighteenth century, .07 per adult male in 1800. Nevertheless, slaveholding could hardly have been a major cause of inequality in the North.

A BACKWARD EXTRAPOLATION

The problem is that while we do have data on the nativity and rural/ urban residence of each individual and the amounts of personal and real estate owned by each individual in 1850–1860, such is not the case for 1798, for which we have only rural and urban classifications. Furthermore, the values of the estate owned by each person have been aggregated, since officials asked for the total estate "wherever owned" in the former censuses. In simple terms, this means that the data for 1850–1860 are much more amenable to calculations. One can ask, for example, what the distribution may have been had there been fewer foreign-born or fewer individuals living in towns and cities.

I propose projecting the 1850–1860 distributions backward to 1800 or 1798, adjusting for nativity, urban/rural residence, age, and area of birth and residence. The results of such a projection reveal details about 1800 that otherwise would not be known (such as how many foreign-born there were). These projections to 1800 or 1798 can be compared with actual 1798 data in some cases. This kind of backward extrapolation is anathema to the historically inclined, who generally expound their explanations as time unfolds its story. I must justify my procedure on the basis of the greater availability of evidence from the 1850 and 1860 censuses of population. I cannot use the 1798 data to make a forward projection.

A possibly adequate estimate for 1800 distributions could be made from the distributions of real estate in 1850 or 1860, considering four constraints: limiting the population to (1) males 70 and older (2) who were native-born (3) who lived in the rural sector (4) in the 17 original states. Males who were 20 years old in 1800 and made their living largely as farmers in the East probably saw few changes over a half century. It is very unlikely that technological change could have altered radically the relative inequality of wealth for that age group between 1800 and 1850–1860, an era before the introduction of extensive mechanization and before the significant advent of the railroad (at least in 1850).

A variation of the above plan would be to adjust all populations in 1850 or 1860, weighting each nativity, urban/rural, East/West location group so that its population reflected the relative importance of these groups in the population of males age 70 and over. This feat can be achieved only partially because sample sizes of those 70 and over are small and because the 1850 census does not account adequately for farm laborers. The data sets for old persons in the farm sector in 1860 for residents in the 17 original states and residents in the remaining public land states have particular meaning for our attempt to understand inequality in 1800. Finally, the later censuses not only provide evidence of the rigorous standards of statistical measurement we could have wished for in the 1800 data, but they also indirectly suggest the degree of participation in ownership and inequality at the end of the eighteenth century.

POSSIBLE DISTRIBUTIONS OF WEALTH IN REAL ESTATE IN 1800

The argument can be made that there should have been less inequality of wealth in 1800 than in 1850 or 1860 simply because society was more homogeneous. There were fewer foreign-born with little or no wealth; in addition, there were fewer urban dwellers, who usually represent the extremes of rich and poor commonly found in cities. To mitigate inequality at mid-century first demands an estimate of nativity and urbanity in 1800 and applying these weights to the equivalent groups in 1850–1860.

It is difficult to determine the number of foreign-born persons in the United States in 1800 since no noteworthy immigration data were gathered until after 1820 and no census data pertaining to nativity before 1850. Fortunately, the age classifications in the 1850 census provide strong evidence about nativity if we focus on men 70 and older in that year as a proxy for those age 20 to 30, or even 40, in 1800. Only differential death rates and the arrival of foreigners at older ages might render the results of table P in appendix 12 misleading.

The implication from the ratios presented in that table are that the proportion of foreign-born males 21 and older doubled after the turn of the century, rising from 9 or 10 percent in 1800 to over 20 percent by 1820; the foreign-born proportion ultimately would rise to a stable rate of nearly 30 percent of the nation's white male population.[5]

Rural/urban residence has been measured by considering the number of farmers and farm laborers in 1860. The calculations show that two of every three persons in 1800 were rural (as judged by those 70 and up), as opposed to one in two in 1860.[6] These data furnish a crosscheck since the 1800 census lists only 7.3 percent of the population in towns or cities, leaving a complement of 92.7 percent rural. A large minority of rural persons was engaged actively in some alternative occupation, with farming as a secondary pursuit. Tench Coxe, a leading promoter of manufactures, noted in 1793 that it was common for tradesmen and manufacturers to live on small rural farms which they cultivated in their spare time.[7] In its

1800 census, Pennsylvania provides the only methodical census listing occupations at the turn of the century. Surprisingly, less than half of adult males were designated as farmers or laborers. Prominent were the occupations of carpenter, tailor, weaver, blacksmith, and merchant.[8]

In recently settled areas in central Pennsylvania in 1800, the appelation "farmer" was used in only two-thirds of the cases. Thus, in essence, the composite of America's population included perhaps 65 percent that was strongly rural; in the South and West, the rural proportion was even larger. A large minority of these groups survived on smaller amounts of land— a clue strongly suggesting that the lower tail of the real estate distribution may have been prominent.

Our next task is to apply to the distributions the nativity-urbanity weight of males age 70 and older to those 21 and older in the 1850–1870 censuses (given in appendix 12). One could note that the native-born farmers serves as a limit for what might be expected in 1800. They were a homogeneous *rural* group, not foreign-born and not living in towns or cities. They had a real estate ownership proportion (PHP) of .592 in 1860. Almost 6 of every 10 nonurban men 21 and older owned land, a very gratifying record, indeed. However, the group's inequality coefficient ($G_{RE,21}$) of .77 is quite large, compared to the hypotheses presented in chapter 1. Without regarding other population sectors, this is almost the level of inequality proposed by John Adams. Some emphasis also should be placed on the native-born living in towns and cities, since they should reflect the ownership of houses, lots, other buildings, wharves, and factories; the largest part of such ownership was in housing. The maximum proportion of the population owning property might be set at 35 percent in the urban sector for the United States in 1860, a figure about the same as that found for ownership of houses in Boston in 1798–1800.

How much did immigration contribute to inequality? Among farmers and farm workers, the native-born held almost twice the average wealth of the foreign-born but, surprisingly, measures of inequality were about the same for the two groups. Gini coefficients ($G_{RH,21}$ of .771 and .772 in 1860) are the same, for all practical purposes, and the ownership proportion is .59 for native born and .56 for foreign-born. In towns and cities, the foreign-born experienced greater inequality than did those who were born in America.

What about inequality among city and town dwellers? Urbanity is of much greater consequence than nativity, as revealed in the 1860 statistics. In a society that was 49.6 percent rural and 50.4 percent urban, there was an overall property ownership proportion of $PHP_{21} = .496(.586) +$

.504(.308) = .445. For a society 65.6 percent urban in 1860, as determined from the weight for the 70-and-older group, the formula would have read $REP_{21} = .654(.586) + .346(.308) = .490$ in 1800. This calculation tells us that 49 percent of adult males would have held property in 1800, if we assume that this backward extrapolation is cogent. It would mean that there was a total of about a 4.5 percentage-point slippage in the rate of ownership during the first two generations of the nineteenth century, a drop that can be attributed to the rural-to-urban movement. The extrapolation is fascinating since it would signify that one of the Adams hypotheses introduced in chapter 1 was most accurate, that a minority of adult males were property holders, the justification for establishing a bicameral legislative body at the national level. This finding has been confirmed, indeed, as reported in chapter 2.

The statistics for the full gamut of wealth distributions in 1850–1860 are also strong enough to be projected backward, by considering proportions of individuals in various wealth ranges. The four major distributions of free males 21 and older (native-born farmers, foreign-born farmers, native-born nonfarmers, and foreign-born nonfarmers) have been weighted so that their relative populations are those of males 70 and older, as given in the last column of table Q, appendix 12. This backward extrapolation from the 1860 data produces an estimate having a Gini coefficient of .643 for property holders in 1800, defined as those with positive real estate ($RE \geqslant 0$). Similar projections have been made from 1850 and 1870 data, yielding about the same results for 1800. All three of the distributions of property holders are essentially lognormal.

The homogeneous farmers' sector (excluding farm laborers) for 1850 has a Gini coefficient of .612. In this case, we consider only property holders—only those reporting a positive value for real estate. This distribution is definitely lognormal in shape. Its mean is $2,700 and its mode is $300, a ratio of nine to one. This ratio also holds for an exact logarithmic curve for which the Gini coefficient is .61. There is a lower tail for this frequency curve, imposed partly by relative poverty, but also because some individuals classified as farmers were engaged part-time in crafts, trades, and other occupations.

The information from the 1850–1870 distributions leads to several tentative conclusions about 1800. The proportion of individuals having real estate came very close to 50 percent—very close to Adams's hypothesis that fewer than half of Americans owned property. The distributions for those owning real estate have Gini coefficients from .61 to .65, inequality levels that are quite substantial but definitely closer to .6 than to .7.[9]

In any case, these results suggest, as did those of chapter 2, that in 1800 wealth in real estate was distributed according to the Adams hypothesis. Certainly the real estate distributions suggested for RE$\geq$ 0 have Gini coefficients of about .8 and roughly match the lognormal curve stipulated by the Adams hypothesis. The following relationship holds for an overall set composed of two subsets of the population, one with wealth and the other without:

$$REP_{21} \times G_{RE>0} + (1 - REP_{21}) \times 1.0 = RE_{21}$$
$$.5 \times .6 + (1 - .5) \times 1 = .8$$

If about half of the people had assets, with an inequality coefficient of about .6, and if the other half had nothing, then the overall inequality coefficient was about .8. These are the approximate figures suggested for 1800, as derived from the censuses of wealth in the United States in the middle of the nineteenth century and by the actual data for the country in 1798.

The projected distribution for 1800 showing the Gini coefficient and shares of wealth for various decile ranges is given as table R in appendix 12. This detailed presentation shows the 1800 distribution, as projected from data for 1850 and 1860, as well as from 1870 data. Again, the main point is that overall inequality as shown by the projected distribution is similar to what we have learned about actual inequality in 1800.

THE 17 ORIGINAL STATES

The backward extrapolations to this point have considered only two aspects of change during the first half of the nineteenth century, increased immigration and urbanization. No consideration has been given to a multitude of other influences, most notably the changes in technology, beginning with the impact of the cotton gin in 1793, and ending with the railroad, which was started after 1830 but not really effective until about 1850. Particularly germane to aspects of property holding were the development of roads, canals, and steam transportation that spurred the westward movement. How did these improvements alter the relative fortunes of different economic groups? Did they benefit the rich more than the poor? Some technologies may have been of greater benefit to the small farmer than the large. Increases in real income might well have enabled those without property to purchase land and houses. Development of financial institutions made it easier to obtain credit.

Technological developments often have been studied in terms of gains to the average person, but they are difficult to evaluate from the standpoint of either the poor or the rich. I have no readily available means of isolating any of the factors affecting the distribution of wealth in 1850–1860 except one: analysis by region. It is possible to analyze distributions for the North and South in particular because slaveholding enhanced the inequality of wealth among free individuals in the South. Since slavery exerted a continuous influence until the Civil War, it doubtless was one of the more powerful elements in maintaining constant relative inequality.

More promising analytical tools are comparisons of inequality between East and West in 1850–1860, that is, between the 17 original states and the public land states. Strong hints about the 1800 distribution can be obtained by examining conditions in the original 17 states. In them we are able to establish controls for terrain, fertility of land, and the availability of river transportation, since there were no essential changes in those factors between 1800 and 1850. In turn, conditions in the public land states in 1850–1860 can give some semblance of conditions in the East in 1800. In the middle decades of the nineteenth century, the new frontier to the west in some ways replicated the conditions existing in the original 17 states in 1800. For instance, the average age of a farm (that is, the length of time since the land was granted) in the public land states was 17.2 years in 1850 and 19.3 years in 1860. In 1800, the average length of settlement was similar to this in both Pennsylvania and South Carolina.[10] However, conditions in the public land states cannot be equated with or substituted for those of the earlier time in the East. The newly broken, fertile soil and the new technology used in the West after 1850 far surpassed land conditions and tools available in 1800.

The proportion of adult males holding property in 1860 is shown in table 74. Most striking is the East-West differential in the northern states of .396 − .472, a 7.6 percent net gain that may be attributable to the relative abundance of land in the West. In summary, PHP_{21} in 1860 was .470 in all western public land states, and .415 in the original 17 states. This difference curiously is similar to the 4.5 urbanization effect presented in the previous section. In a certain sense, the differentials measure the same cause, the land supply and its relation to the size of the population. In fact, the number of private acres per person in public land states in 1850 was the same as in the East in 1798–1800.[11]

While in 1860 the relative increase in the supply of land and its recent development may have had an impact on the proportion of property holders, such was not the case for inequality in general. The data of table 75 show, if anything, that in 1860 inequality was as great in the West as in the East.

TABLE 74
PROPORTION OF THE U.S. POPULATION OWNING REAL ESTATE, 1860
(males 21 and older)

	North	South	United States
First 17 states	.396	.446	
Rural	.567	.567 ⎫	.415
Urban	.293	.275 ⎭	
Other states	.472	.462	
Rural	.602	.590 ⎫	.470
Urban	.331	.301 ⎭	

Source: Lee Soltow, *Men and Wealth in the United States 1850–1870* (New Haven, Conn.: Yale University Press, 1975).

Note: Data are derived from a stratified sample of 13,698 drawn from the 1860 census manuscripts; the sample size for free males 21 and older is 13,187. (The data in the table are based on computer runs of the basic data set excluding persons age 20.) It is not possible to classify laborers by urban/rural residence in 1850, which precludes that data set from the table.

TABLE 75
INEQUALITY OF U.S. REAL ESTATE HOLDINGS, 1860
(males 21 and older)

	Mean Value of Real Estate Owned		Those Reporting Real Estate		All	
	North RE	South RE	North G	South G	North G	South G
First 17 states						
Rural	$2,070	$2,300	.57	.69	.76	.82
Urban	1,140	1,050	.71	.71	.91	.92
Other states						
Rural	1,700	2,240	.55	.59	.73	.84
Urban	1,070	1,540	.73	.71	.91	.91

Source: See table 74.

This is a far cry from any misleading preconceptions we may have held about equality at the frontier, and is an indication that differences in asset-holding between individuals were quite significant in the West. Persons living in a region a few years longer than others of the same age had accumulated substantially more wealth.

Ohio in 1835

The investigation of inequality of wealth from 1800 to 1850 is probably only in its beginning stages. One fruitful approach is to scrutinize distributions in an individual state in any given year. One such study is that for each of the 138,785 owners of real estate in Ohio in 1835. The property holder proportion, PHP_{20}, was .542 in Ohio in 1835, compared to a PHP of .494 in the United States in 1798. The distribution for property holders in 1835 was quite lognormal in shape, and with a Gini coefficient of .637. In this case, the share of the top 1 percent of property holders was 20 percent of wealth, and the top 10 percent owned 52 percent of wealth. Chapter 2 shows that the corresponding shares for the United States in 1798 were 13 percent and 45 percent. In 1835, Ohio was surprisingly urban, with inequality among wealth holders being substantially greater in towns. Nevertheless, more town dwellers owned property, so that overall inequality was about the same between the urban and rural sectors.[12]

Surely Ohio in 1835 was in line with the patterns found for the entire period from 1798 to 1860. The influx of persons from the East, the inheritance procedures, the fertility of the soil, the laws regarding ownership of property, the rules derived from the federal Constitution of 1788 as well as those from the Northwest Ordinance of 1787 all played their part in imposing a property holder configuration in this great state in 1835. How could the configuration have been fundamentally different from that in the United States in 1798?

Summary

Details from the 1850–1870 censuses include the variables on age, urban/rural residence, and nativity—dimensions not available for my 1798 data set. Why not adjust the 1850 data to the higher proportions of native-born and higher proportions of farmers that existed in 1800? If this feat could be achieved, we would have a projected 1800 distribution suggesting some rough bounds for estimating inequality in 1800. I did this and found projected inequality to be about the same as actually existed. The upshot of the experiment was to demonstrate that urbanity and nativity did not really have much influence.

Backward extrapolations from inequality in real estate in 1850–1860 lead to an estimate of the proportion of property holders to be .49 in 1800 and inequality, G, to be .61–.64 for landholders, and .82 for all adult free males in 1800. These estimates were made by adjusting for changes in urbanity and nativity during the two generations. An examination of acreage in the public land states in 1850–1860 confirms these estimates, since acreage per capita in those states at the time was the same as in the original states in 1800.

There is evidence that inequality within states remained stable during both the eighteenth and nineteenth centuries. In their censuses, New York and Pennsylvania show constant proportions of property owners after 1760. Finally, the inequality in personal estate probably remained fairly constant in this period, at least in the South. The value of slaves accounted for almost half of personal estate in the United States, and inequality in the ownership of slaves generally remained constant from 1790 to 1860.

The backward extrapolation to 1800 yields an overall inequality coefficient for wealth in real estate of roughly .8. Broken down, it amounts to a proportion of adult males holding wealth (PHP_{21}) of about .5 and the inequality coefficient for those having real estate ($G_{RE>0,21}$) to be approximately .6; these are coupled with the equation

$$REP_{21} \times G_{RE>0,21} + (1 - G_{RE>0,21}), \text{ or } .5 \times .6 + (1 - .5) = 8.$$

This is a very rough generalization of the proportion of haves and havenots, and of inequality among those with property that applies to the entire first half of the nineteenth century. It means that the backward projection from 1850–1860 real estate distributions shows an inequality level in 1800 not far from that suggested by John Adams's hypothesis presented in chapter 1. It also means that relative inequality of wealth in 1860 was roughly the same as it was in 1800.

Data for the state of Ohio in 1835 help fill the gap in our knowledge about inequality in the period between 1798 and 1850. A marvelous data set of all property holders in the state for that year demonstrates inequality in the same degree as existed in the nation at the beginning and middle of the nineteenth century. This is to be expected, since this strategic state was a singularly representative area of the activities of new settlers arriving from other areas of the country.

The findings presented in chapters 6, 7, and 8 lead to the conclusion that there was substantial inequality of wealth in the United States in 1798. U.S. society was not so egalitarian as Franklin or Tocqueville may have led us to believe. In 1798, inequality was a little larger than in the 1770s and almost as large as in 1860. America's relative dispersion of wealth was egalitarian only by European standards. There definitely was homogeneity in America relative to the heterogeneity in Europe.

Inequality remained constant or increased slightly between 1771–1774 and 1798, and between 1798 and 1850–1860. I find that inequality of income has dropped substantially between 1798 and the present time, and perhaps decreased slightly between 1798 and 1860. These results are contrary to the findings presented by Williamson and Lindert.[13]

9

Economic Development
and Changes in Inequality

ONE REASON for believing that inequality of wealth must have increased radically after 1800 stems from the argument that the country was very backward in 1800, that it was a sleepy agrarian economy devoid of activity. This implies that there necessarily was great growth after 1830 or 1840 that made the economy in 1850 and 1860 very different from that of 1800. If such were the case, then one could argue that, earlier, inequality may have been substantially less than in 1850–1860. To some, agrarianism in America means equality, and commercialism or industrialism means inequality.

It is very important that we dispel the view that in America in 1798 there was a traditional agrarian economy that only aped procedures from the past. In reality, the economy was dynamic and experienced growth; it was part of a pattern demonstrating rapid changes similar to those occurring in 1850 and 1860. A demonstration of change is vital in understanding that inequality in 1800 could have been equally large as inequality a half century later.[1] Again, some hold the notion that change is synonymous with increased inequality, at least as applied to the United States. They argue that U.S. history has seen the transformation of a homogeneous agrarian economy into a heterogeneous commercial and manufacturing economy. A few of these notions are found even in Adam Smith's *Wealth of Nations*. The stage of commerce develops from an agrarian stage as specialization proceeds. Surpluses arise from economies of scale and they must be dispersed increasingly among the few.[2]

I will first emphasize activity in the two decades before and after 1800, stressing the dynamic changes that were taking place after the adoption of the Constitution in 1788. I then present several other implications of growth stemming from the regional land and wealth values in 1798 in highlighting changes from 1800 to 1860, as well as trends before 1800.

ECONOMIC GROWTH, 1790–1810

A new country evolving in innovative ways strengthens its communication and transportation systems. It develops improvements in the shipment of goods by land and sea as roads are laid out and surfaced and as its merchant fleet is augmented. The young country also must develop its postal system and, more importantly, strengthen its press with a network of newspapers and imprints in general.

Cultural Development

An intriguing index of development unfolds from counting the numbers of imprints of books, pamphlets, and periodicals published each year in America. The series is plotted as the bottom line of figure 13. There is some irregularity in spite of the fact that the original data have been smoothed by using a three-year moving average. Nevertheless, we can see the strong upward thrust in the 1790s, with lower rates of increase after 1800. If one fits a ratio trend to the data, one finds that the rate of increase was 7.9 percent from 1780 to 1800, and 5.4 percent from 1780 to 1810. The very long-run increase from 1660 to 1830 was 3.7 percent in a period when the population was growing at a rate of 3.0 percent a year.[3]

It should be understood that I did not use a weighting system whereby a book is considered more important than a pamphlet or broadside, nor did I consider the number of copies printed or sold, nor the number of times any particular imprint was read. It may very well be true that a broadside posted in a conspicuous place was read by many people. Those broadsides dealing with petitions sometimes had garnered hundreds of signatures. The main impact of reading of imprints was the transmission of information relative to the commercial, agricultural, and governmental activities of people as well as the dissemination of information about religion, philosophy, science, literature, amusement, and social activities. The number of newspapers increased nearly 9 percent a year from 1785 to 1800, well in excess of the long-run rate of 6 percent a year from 1700 to 1820. This was also true if we weight the newspaper series by frequency of publication for each paper; furthermore, newspapers were becoming larger and more complex. Publications facilitated the acquisition of land by informing people of the availability of land and land prices. Publishing increased the

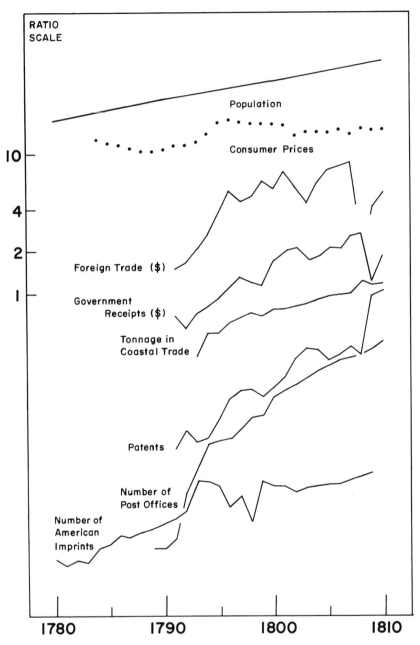

FIGURE 13. TIER CHART OF SELECTED TIME SERIES FOR THE UNITED STATES, 1789–1810

NOTE: Patents and imprints are three-year moving averages. See table 76.

possibility of an individual's becoming a landowner, and probably owning a larger number of acres than would have been possible without the benefit of printed information.

Other Series

There are ten-or-so distinct national series which indicate the upward thrust of the economy in the 1790s and, more broadly, from Independence to 1810. A quantification of the growth is most impressive. (See table 76).

Paul David has produced an outstanding study of the economic growth of the United States after 1790. He holds that there indeed was material betterment in the country, and to a degree that surpassed the increases in

TABLE 76
GROWTH RATES FOR SELECTED TIME SERIES, 1780–1810

	Period Beginning	Annual Increase (%)	
		to 1800	to 1810
Total population	1780	3.2	3.2
Prices	1784	3.1	1.3
Foreign trade ($)	1791	18.0	5.7
Aggregate receipts of government ($)	1791	11.1	6.4
Costal trade (tonnage)	1789	9.6	5.9
Surfaced roads (miles)	1794	85.5	28.4
Post offices (N)	1794	4.9	11.8
Patents (N)	1792	19.5	15.8
Banks (N)	1784	17.3	7.6
Imprints (N)	1780	7.9	5.4
Newspapers (N)	1785	8.8	6.9
Post roads (miles)	1790	26.6	13.6
Postal receipts ($)	1790	18.2	11.4

Sources: U.S. Bureau of the Census, *Historical Statistics of the United States, Colonial Times to 1970,* Bicentennial Edition, 2 pts. (Washington, D.C.: GPO, 1975), see esp. references to series before 1800 at the end of pt. 2; Timothy Pitkin, *A Statistical View of the Commerce of the United States* (1816; rpt. New York: Augustus M. Kelley, 1967), pp. 51–53, 379, 382–83, 389–90. The banking series is from U.S. Bureau of the Census, *Historical Statistics of the United States, 1789–1945* (Washington, D.C.: GPO, 1949), ser. N-13; Clarence Brigham, *History and Bibliography of American Newspapers* (Worcester, Mass.: American Antiquarian Society, 1947); data on imprints are from Clifford Shipton and James Mooney, *National Index of American Imprints Through 1800, the Short Title Evans* (Worcester, Mass.: American Antiquarian Society and Barre Publishers, 1969); post mileage and receipts are reported in *American State Papers,* class 7, vol. 1, Post Office Department, p. 66.

population. Real domestic product per capita increased at an average annual rate of "close to 1.3 percent" within the time interval from 1800 to 1835, and generally from 1800 to 1860. Further, he has found a long-run decrease before 1860 in the labor cost of living, that is, series of price indexes divided by series for wage rates.[4]

The most spectacular growth during the 1790s was in cotton exports, which grew from 10,000 pounds in 1790 to 54,000 in 1791, and then annually from 1792 to 1800 as follows (in thousands of pounds): 76, 93, 159, 1,109, 912, 1,008, 2,476, 2,801, and 6,425. This phenomenal rise, sparked by the development of the cotton gin in 1793, essentially came from land that had already passed into private ownership, since the number of land grants per annum had already reached its apex in 1786. A similar development in the North, of lesser magnitude, was the increase in real tonnage in shipping in Massachusetts, which exactly doubled from 1790 to 1800.[5] Particularly telling was the rise in the number of banks, growing from 3 in 1784, to 6 in 1791, to 16 in 1792, to 25 in 1798, and to 75 in 1805. The need for postal service no doubt provided the impetus in improvement of roads. Post miles increased from 2,000 in 1790 to 36,000 in 1810.

It is possible that the surges in cotton production, shipping, and particularly in banking all redounded to the particular benefit of a small group. There may have been an increase in the number of large-scale plantations at this time. Thus, one can conclude that inequality may have risen a little in the early federal period. This was the subject matter of the previous chapter.

GROWTH OF WEALTH, 1798–1860, AND POSSIBLY 1750–1798

To divide the $620 million aggregate by the 899,000 free males 21 years old or older in the United States in 1800 results in a substantial average for real estate holding of $690 per adult free male. Was this average mediocre or impressive, as judged by earlier or later standards? An immediate comparison between 1800 and a later period is possible with the average for real estate owned by free males in 1850 and 1860, given in the last column of table 77, adjusted to market prices in 1798. The annual growth rate, with this adjustment, is 1.4–1.7 percent a year. This splendid pace is significant, but is less than the 2 percent annual growth that Raymond Goldsmith found for reproducible tangible wealth between 1805 and 1850. The averages in the table have been adjusted by a *consumer* price index in an attempt to understand only the purchasing power of the wealth involved. I employed this technique to determine the purchasing position of wealth holders, were they to sell their assets for cash. I have not utilized price indexes of land values and fixed assets, and can make no direct statement concerning the productivity of assets in real estate.

The figures in columns 3 and 4 of table 77 show strong dollar increases in the real value of per capita wealth in the United States in the first half of the nineteenth century. In 1850, the average adult male could purchase a market basket of consumer goods worth $1,110. In 1800, his grandfather or someone of his grandfather's age typically could command a basket only half as large with his wealth. The annual growth rate from 1798 to 1850 averaged 1.36 percent a year, as stated in column 5 of the table. This rate is intriguing, since it is similar to the long-run growth rate Simon Kuznets found for U.S. per capita *income* after 1840. Yet, income and wealth in real estate are quite distinct concepts; in addition, the wealth/ income ratio need not have been constant through time. The inclusion of privately held land, and, more particularly, uncultivated land, in the wealth measure but not in the income measure, might be the reason for arriving at different rates of growth in private wealth in real estate and in income. The point should be made that *some* part of the growth I have measured is due to the appreciation in land values relative to other prices, not increased output (which real income is supposed to measure). Thus my measures are *not* directly comparable to real national product measures, the Kuznets measures.

The data of table 77 may indicate general gains for a century and a half. Here the gnawing question is, what was the purchasing power, per person, of average wealth in 1750? Was it one-half that of 1798? Was the purchasing power in 1700 one-fourth that of 1798? Or was there little or no growth during the century? To consider a backward extension of the $1,110 and $550 values of column 4 to values of $275 and $138 or, perhaps more modestly, to $400 and $300 for a century earlier, may seem far-fetched. Still, the values were less than $500, as will be indicated. The alternative hypothesis that there was no growth in the purchasing power of private wealth should be considered, however. A colony of ten families in 1630 may have possessed a charter for 1 million irrevocably owned acres having a market value of a half cent an acre, the equivalent of $500 per family. On the other hand, the entire acreage may have been worth only a few dollars to any of the ten families or to anyone in Europe.

To extrapolate from column 4 the trend backward into the eighteenth century raises many questions. Nineteenth-century economic growth arose

TABLE 77
Average U.S. Wealth in Real Estate in 1798 and 1850–1870 and Possible Growth Rates from 1798
(males 21 and older)

	Wealth in Real Estate (1)	Consumer Price Index (2)	Real Estate Wealth Divided by Price Index (3)	(3)× Ratio of Market Prices to Assessed Prices (4)	Average Annual Growth in (4) after 1798 (5)
1798	$ 708	1.48	$ 478	$ 550	—
1850	1,046	.94	1,110	1,110	.0136
1860	1,540	1.00	1,540	1,540	.0167
1870 (whites)	1,960	1.57	1.250	1.250	.0114

Sources: Timothy Pitkin, *A Statistical View of the Commerce of the United States* (1816; rpt. New York: Augustus Kelley, 1967), pp. 377–78. Population censuses are from tables of the Inter-University consortium for Political and Social Research, University of Michigan. Wealth data for 1850–1870 are described in chapter 4. The consumer price index is taken from Paul A. David and Peter Solar, "A Bicentenary Contribution to the History of the Cost of Living in America," in *Research in Economic History* 2 (1977), 16. Deed information is from R. Thomas Mayhill, *Deed Abstracts and Oaths of Allegiance,* rev. and enl., *A through M: 1729–1770* (Knightstown, Ind.: The Bookmark); *South Carolina Deed Abstracts, 1719–1772* (Easley, S.C.: Southern Historical Press, 1983), vols. 1–4, all deeds of sale listed on pp. 1–50, then every other page through vol. 3, and every tenth page of vol. 4. Bailey F. Davis, *Albemarle County, Virginia, Deed Books 1–3,* in collection of the Church of Latter Day Saints Genealogical Library, Salt Lake City. These were supplemented by samples from deed films in the L.D.S Genealogical Library and records in the South Carolina Department of Archives and History, Columbia, S.C. Price data from U.S. Congress, Joint Economic Committee, Hearings, 88th Cong., 1st sess., S. Con. Res. 13, pt. 2, April 7–10, 1959, pp. 394–97; B. R. Mitchell and Phyllis Deane, *Abstract of British Historical Statistics* (Cambridge: Cambridge University Press, 1962), pp. 484–87; Anne Bezanson, Robert Gray, and Miriam Hussey, *Prices in Colonial Pennsylvania* (Philadelphia: University of Pennsylvania Press, 1935); George Rogers Taylor, "Wholesale Commodity Prices at Charleston, South Carolina, 1732–1791," *Journal of Economic and Business History* 4 (1932), 356–77, 848–68; Arthur Cole, *Wholesale Commodity Prices in the United States, 1700–1861* (Cambridge, Mass.: Harvard University Press, 1938). Currency data are from John J. McCusker, *Money and Exchange in Europe and America, 1600–1775* (Williamsburg, Va., and Chapel Hill: University of North Carolina Press, 1978), pp. 183–86, 210–12, 222–24; Joseph Lippincott, "A Collection of Tables" (Philadelphia: Johnson, 1792), pp. 40–41, and unnumbered page; *Encyclopædia: or, a Dictionary of Arts, Sciences, and Miscellaneous Literature* (Philadelphia: Dobson, 1798), 12:230–36; Alice Hanson Jones, *Wealth of a Nation to Be* (New York: Columbia University Press, 1980), pp. 9–10.

Note: Column 4 adjusts the 1798 average of column 3 upward by 15 percent; this is the ratio of market prices to assessed prices discussed in appendix 2.

largely from technical change—scientific or engineering innovations—as well as from changes in market structures, industrial organization, and the training of employees. It is generally thought that there was little or no technical change before 1800; farming and manufacturing procedures then in use had been practiced for decades and generations. Henry Adams, in writing about the American economy in 1800, found little innovative spirit, and certainly no startling discontinuities in the ways of doing things. There was no counterpart even to the sulphur match, first patented in the United States in 1836. "The ordinary cultivator planted his corn as his father had planted it, sowing as much rye to the acre, using the same number of oxen to plough, and getting in his crops on the same day."[6]

There is reason to believe that there were important changes in the eighteenth century affecting land productivity and land values, some of which were quite innovative, even though they weren't so spectacular as the development of the sulphur match.[7] The formation of local government, the passing of laws—especially those concerned with private property, the diminished threat of Indian attacks, the establishment of the federal government and its Constitution, all would enhance the attractiveness of land at or near the frontier of settlement. The ownership of land in fee simple was stronger everywhere, and the flame of private initiative burned brightly. There was greater certainty of a future income flow from a piece of land, and probably a greater desire to own land or to own a larger amount of land. Perhaps there was a shift in consumer spending to land purchases and improvement in dwellings, stimulated by a greater sense of permanence. In any case, the American scene had become more attractive to foreign investors, and this demand helped to augment land values. It is possible that real gains per capita arising from increased stability in the eighteenth century were the counterpart to the real gains from the industrial revolution that came in the nineteenth century. It is likely that the upheaval and losses due to the American Revolution were rectified within a decade after the war. The federal Constitution may have been worth the equivalent of a dozen innovations such as the cotton gin or sulphur matches, having had as strong an impact on growth as did the railroad or electricity.

Nevertheless, the pace of economic activity was quickening in the eighteenth century. Post offices became more common, and by 1798 the postal service reached as far west as Cincinnati. Post roads, bridges, and some few strategic canals made the purchase of land in more distant parts more feasible. There was a continuous rise in the number of imprints, newspapers, broadsides, and books, which outpaced the growth in population. Knowledge about land for sale as well as the availability of markets spread ever more rapidly, and to a greater proportion of the people. Particularly telling were changes after 1780 that surely strengthened 1798 real estate values. In table 77 I have presented statistical verification of these changes for the period from 1789 to 1810. Moreover, the population was pushed or pulled to land of higher productivity in the North as families moved westward. There is no implication that the marginal productivity of labor dropped at the time of westward movement, since there was an ample supply of land. Further speculation about growth must be postponed until more facts about real estate have been presented.

EVIDENCE OF EIGHTEENTH-CENTURY GROWTH: FOUR CONSIDERATIONS

The evidence suggests that per capita wealth in the United States at the end of the eighteenth century was at a most handsome level and, in a certain sense, may have been the highest in the world. This necessarily means that in America there was great growth in the purchasing power or real value of assets throughout the eighteenth century. These are bold assertions that must be substantiated by statistical studies. Four bodies of data will be presented: (1) international comparisons of per capita wealth in 1800, (2) time series of land prices as revealed by deeds of land sales in various decades, (3) the improvement in the quality of soil that came with westward expansion, and (4) implicit growth demonstrated by wealth levels and age of settlement in 687 tax districts in 1798.

International Comparisons, 1798

Evidence given in chapter 6 shows that the average wealth of free adult males in the United States in 1798 compared favorably with that in England. This figure may have been as large as that in England, and for all adult males, average wealth was two-thirds of that in England. The average in the United States was appreciably greater than in Sweden, Finland, and Scotland, countries whose capital structure had been improved for centuries and centuries.

Surely these impressive data signify that there had been an enormous surge in economic activity prior to 1798. Wealth by no means reflected only the fertility of land and the unlikely threat of invasion by European armies. Wealth was a reflection of the construction of dwellings, barns, fences, mills, roads, bridges, wharves, ships, and even community institutions such as churches and schools. The mean, median, and modal value of America's housing, the physical characteristics of its dwellings, described in previous chapters, may easily have surpassed those in Europe. These distinctions rest less on the fact that wood and land were plentiful in America. It meant that there had been a gigantic effort to construct edifices from these natural resources.

One possibility militates against the cogency of the above argument. It is that from the time of settlement, America was always richer than Europe; however, this possibility is difficult to measure. How much was the unimproved land in the original states worth in 1620? How much would it have been worth had it lain contiguous to a European country? How much was Ohio land worth in 1798 or 1788? Some answers to questions concerning variations in land values between regions will be offered shortly.

Deeds of Sale

What solid evidence is there that frontier land was rising in value or that the earliest settled land gained in value in terms of the wholesale and retail goods it would buy? One method of testing the thesis is to investigate records of deeds of sale of land in various counties in the eighteenth century. Unfortunately, such a task is exceedingly difficult for at least two reasons. It is a most time-consuming, repetitious procedure to read deeds of some length in order to abstract prices, acreage, and the dates of sales. Second, it is a monumental task to consider the currencies or commodities in which the prices are quoted and to adjust them in any meaningful fashion for the changing purchasing power of these currencies. Fortunately, three sets of deeds have been abstracted methodically, those for Lancaster County, Pennsylvania, 1718–1769, those for Charleston District and County, South Carolina, 1683–1772, and those for Albemarle County, Virginia, 1740–1769, some 3,600 transactions in real estate. I shall report my results after studying these sets and then compare them to county land prices in 1798.

All published deeds for the three counties have been edited to establish representative market values for farm land. In an attempt to exclude town lots and deeds of gift, I have eliminated entries of less than three acres and those having values of less than £2 "current money." Values have been deflated using the U.S. index of wholesale prices from 1720 to 1800, with 1800 = 100 (thus, in effect, 1798 = 100). This index of purchasing power has been supplemented with a commodity price index for Britain from 1683 to 1720. Further consideration is also given to the pound sterling equivalent of the local currencies, the pounds current of Pennsylvania, South Carolina, and Virginia in each year before 1776. Finally, the deed

TABLE 78
COLONIAL AND U.S. LAND VALUES, 1683–1798

	No. of Deeds	Average Value of Acreage[a]	No. of Acres	Value per Acre (adjusted using wholesale prices)
Lancaster County, Pennsylvania				
1718	3	$ 245	313	$ .79
1720–1724	3	463	316	1.44
1725–1729	3	248	133	1.86
1730–1734	13	1,155	204	5.67
1735–1739	48	687	234	2.94
1740–1744	75	856	204	4.18
1745–1749	156	1,093	182	5.98
1750–1754	171	1,771	163	10.82
1755–1759	144	1,829	149	12.27
1760–1764	344	1,563	130	11.94
1765–1769	139	2,147	144	14.83
1798				24.85
Annual growth rate				
1718–1769		.0437	−.0144	.0590
1718–1798				.0441
Charleston District, South Carolina				
1683–1684	7	$ 656	832	.79
1685–1689	22	750	289	2.60
1690–1694	43	304	314	.97
1695–1699	75	585	732	.80
1700–1704	32	935	594	1.57
1705–1709	56	675	645	1.16
1710–1714	53	875	963	.91
1715–1719	22	959	475	2.02
1720–1724	63	1,083	443	2.44
1725–1729	95	913	426	2.14
1730–1734	79	1,081	442	2.45
1735–1739	171	1,075	516	2.08
1740–1744	110	1,419	615	2.30
1745–1749	83	1,325	453	2.92
1750–1754	163	1,069	423	2.52
1755–1759	196	1,351	372	3.62
1760–1764	210	1,246	381	3.27
1765–1769	158	1,189	366	3.25
1770–1774	63	1,212	528	2.29
1794	103	2,556	663	3.86
1798				4.39
Annual growth rate				
1683–1774				.0134
1683–1794		.0114	−.0015	.0128
1683–1798				.0126

TABLE 78 *continued*

	No. of Deeds	Average Value of Acreage[a]	No. of Acres	Value per Acre (adjusted using wholesale prices)
Albemarle County, Virginia				
1745–1749	74	$636	403	1.58
1750–1754	144	400	288	1.39
1755–1759	117	298	273	1.09
1760–1764	276	325	276	1.17
1798				4.58
Annual growth rate				
1745–1764		−.0462	−.0226	−.0247
1745–1798			.0257	

Source: See table 77. Values have been adjusted by a wholesale price index (1798 = 100).
  a. As shown on deeds of sale.

values in pounds sterling have been multiplied by $4.50, the approximate exchange rate in 1798–1800. This procedure for price deflation and currency valuation yields time series of land values, in dollars, as shown in table 78.

The 1,099 deeds of sale for Lancaster County, Pennsylvania, demonstrate increasing real estate values, decreasing acreage, and increasing prices of land per acre. Averages vary from one period to the next, but long-run trends are readily apparent. The average growth rate for prices per acre was a spectacular 6 percent a year. The more conservative estimate of 4 percent, obtained from sale values given in table 78, is a better approximation of *farm* values, plots decreasing in acreage through the years as sections were sold from the original acreage. In any case, the very rapid growth rates are recorded for this exceptional county, which has some of the richest farmland in the United States. The 1798 inventory of land and dwellings shows values per acre averaging $24.85 for Lancaster County, $8.50 for Pennsylvania, and $3.80 for the country.

Turning next to Charleston District and County, we see much more modest growth. The 1,804 deeds demonstrate annual growth of 1.34 percent in the case of prices and 1.14 percent in plot values. Albemarle County's growth is even more moderate, with rates of 1–2 percent. The data provide strong evidence that assets could have been growing at a real rate of 1.4 percent a year.

Supplementary data relating to grants in Pennsylvania, South Carolina, and western Virginia and Kentucky demonstrate the fact that grant acreage was increasing as rapidly as population, if not slightly more rapidly.

The Population Push to Fertile Lands

As settlers proceeded from the Atlantic coast to the western parts of Massachusetts, New York, and Pennsylvania, they probably encountered soils that were more productive. This phenomenon is difficult to measure, since farmers used different crops, crop rotations, and methods of raising farm livestock in each area. I shall use here only one proxy for productive farm land, the proportion of total farm acres that were plowed, as reported in the 1880 census. This census took place two to three generations after 1800, a period sufficient for the full exploitation of the land in the eastern part of the country. It can provide an index of the potential productivity of the land to the purchaser in 1800.

Consider the index for eight northern states, shown in table 79. The value of agricultural output could have increased with any shift in the numbers of farmers to the west. East coast fishing would have been at least partially counterbalanced by river fishing. Increased transportation costs associated with the western movement could and did negate gains in productivity from the soil in 1800. Nevertheless, there was a new market created with the westward movement of population. There were as many people in Pennsylvania in 1800 as there were in the entire country in 1730. Prospects for future shipment to the East on rivers and canals as well as by the Mississippi were promising. This would have buoyed up land prices in the West.

An index of land fertility can be constructed by weighting the 1880 proportion of land plowed in each state by its population in various census years, as shown in table 80. There was a decided rise in the index for the North at the beginning of the eighteenth century and again in the last half of that century. In the South, the average dropped between 1730 and the end of the century, but was at a level in 1800 where it had begun in 1630. The northern average became larger than the southern in 1760. The northern index would have shown greater increases if the plowed proportion could have been weighted by only rural farm populations.[8] The data of table 80 would have been less spectacular had the 1850 census been weighted rather than the 1880 census. However, it seemed unfair to use this earlier date, since very little clearing had taken place in the West by 1850.[9]

TABLE 79
PROPORTION OF TOTAL FARM ACRES PLOWED IN 1880 AS AN INDEX OF
POTENTIAL LAND PRODUCTIVITY, 1800

Massachusetts	.263
Connecticut	.305
New York	.521
Pennsylvania	.579
Ohio	.576
Indiana	.564
Illinois	.656
Iowa	.632

Source: Tenth Decennial Census of the United States, 1880, *Report on the Productions of Agriculture* (Washington, D.C.: GPO, 1883), pp. 102–03.

Age of Settlements: Implications for Growth

William Ogilvie in 1782 and Henry George a century later were intrigued with land values and what portions of them should be subject to taxation. They felt that the value of land included elements that could be attributed to nature or society and others that could be attributed to the activities of the owner or occupier. Ogilvie stated that value should be portioned into three parts: (1) the original value of the land arising from natural endowment, (2) the value arising from the activity of the owner, and (3) the value that could arise from further cultivation of the land in question. The second portion, if measurable, could, over time, provide an index of economic growth. We are able to measure only the first portion by examining land values at and near the frontier of settlement in 1798.[10]

Suppose that in 1798 farm A is worth more and has been settled longer than farm B, and suppose they have about the same fertility and location. Some measure of economic growth can be implied using years of settlement as a proxy for time. There should be evidence of economic growth in any given year either if some farms are older than others, or if certain districts or counties had been settled longer than others. A remarkable 1764 inventory of 195 tracts of land in Northampton County, 50 miles north of Philadelphia, provides this kind of information, because records show the number of years each farm had been settled. The data indicate that about three acres per farm were cleared during the first year of settlement, with additions of about three acres each year thereafter. For these Northampton farms, a similar linear pattern was found when the values of farms were plotted against years of settlement.[11]

TABLE 80
ESTIMATED POTENTIAL LAND FERTILITY IN AMERICA, 1630–1900

	Average Proportion of Land Plowed[a]	
	North	South
1630	.305	.370
1640	.300	.383
1650	.310	.417
1660	.308	.424
1670	.306	.423
1680	.322	.424
1690	.355	.424
1700	.380	.425
1710	.385	.425
1720	.385	.436
1730	.392	.434
1740	.397	.424
1750	.404	.419
1760	.415	.404
1770	.416	.392
1780	.420	.385
1790	.417	.376
1800	.430	.368
1810	.448	.365
1820	.467	.360
1830	.480	.356
1840	.497	.355
1850	.503	.350
1860	.511	.351
1870	.516	.356
1880	.513	.350
1890	.506	.347
1900	.506	.347

Sources: U.S. Bureau of the Census, *Historical Statistics of the United States, Colonial Times to the 1970* (Washington, D.C.: GPO, 1949), pp. 24–36; see also table 79.

Note: The potential for land occupied in 1630 was substantially less than that for land occupied in 1870 in northern states.

a. The proportion of land plowed in each northern and southern state in 1880 weighted by state populations in various census years.

It is possible to make a more elaborate cross-sectional analysis from the 1798 federal inventory of real estate, with its detail for the 687 tax districts and 359 counties in 17 states and the Federal City. If there had been economic growth, then one district 10 years older than another should display larger per capita wealth in real estate, particularly as reflected in the value of houses and buildings. Just what is the relationship between wealth per capita and the age of the county? Does it in any way demonstrate a growth of 1.36 percent a year? No simple answer to this question can be given because the age of a county in 1800 is only an imperfect reflection of the effects of time, per se. Refinements in the measure produce intriguing results.

Let the age of a district or county in 1800 (age_{1800}) be defined as the difference between 1800 and the year the county was created. This variable is a rough measure of the length of time needed to make improvements to the land. A difficulty arises in those cases where new counties were formed by the division of counties of longer duration, so the county's age is not in accord with the actual settlement date. To accommodate these obvious anachronisms, I made adjustments by using regression equations of age and distance, in miles, from the major city within each of six areas in the country.[12] The procedure leads to the important district/age classification presented in table 81.

The plotting of all 687 districts, in figure 14, reveals an implicit growth rate in land and dwelling wealth per capita of about .67 percent a year, a rate about one-half of that expected for long-run growth. Those living at the frontier in 1800, where county age was zero, had average wealth of about $400, while those living in well-established areas—where the county's age might be 170 years—had average wealth of $1,270. This wealth/age gradient is determined solely from 1798–1800 data, and is not necessarily a reflection of the actual long-run growth in per capita wealth.[13]

One suspects that the wealth/age line, with its gradient, r, shifted upward from decade to decade, or at least from half century to half century, as suggested by the scheme shown in figure 15. The sketch depends heavily on the fact that the wealth/age gradient was .0067 in 1798–1800 and that essentially the same gradient existed for 1850 (.0063) and 1860 (.0062), a fact suggesting that development followed rather parallel lines in different eras. I derived the latter two figures from data for the cash value of farms owned by free males 20 and older for each of 1,564 counties in 1850 and 1,929 in 1860, as reported in the censuses for those years.[14] A line representing overall per capita growth is sketched in figure 15 through the average ages of each gradient (33 years in 1800 and 84 years in 1850), as determined by weighting each county's age by its population size); its growth rate is assumed to be .0136, as determined earlier, in table 76. Frontier land would be at age zero in the figure and would rise at an annual rate of about .0136 to .0067 (or about .007). This later increment conceivably could be

TABLE 81
PROPERTY VALUES IN U.S. TAX DISTRICTS CLASSIFIED BY
AGE OF DISTRICT, 1800

Age of District in 1800[a]	Districts (N = 687)	Minimum No. of Miles from a Major City	Average Values		
			Land	Dwellings	Land and Dwellings
0–9	33	350	$467	$ 31	$498
10–19	36	200	296	66	336
20–29	56	164	504	67	566
30–39	49	145	593	75	689
40–49	48	147	522	69	616
50–59	77	117	592	123	718
60–69	33	81	578	118	702
70–79	129	74	644	164	811
80–89	43	53	619	184	802
90–99	50	44	629	173	800
100–109	50	36	651	191	836
110–119	29	31	487	236	723
120–129	28	21	586	300	887
130–170	26	6	600	425	1,063

Sources: Table 5 and appendix 13; Joseph Kane, *The American Counties* (Metuchen, N.J.: Scarecrow Press, 1972).

Note: Average wealth is clearly larger in older districts.
   a. Adjusted using distances, as stated in ch. 9, n. 12.

called an unearned increment by William Ogilvie, an increment arising without the owner's direct improvement of the land.[15]

What could be the reason for an unearned increment? Could it be the increased value of uncultivated land at the frontier? Surely the ratification of the federal Constitution strengthened the laws with respect to private property as well as contributing to the general stability of the national economy. As the young nation survived from one year to the next, it became increasingly clear that its continued existence was without doubt. Distant frontier land would tend to rise gradually in value in the minds of persons on the eastern seaboard, people in European countries, and those contemplating westward migration. Conceivably there were economies of scale in the building of roads, and a new bridge might open a relatively wide expanse of land to migrants. Both a national postal system and a national currency facilitated commercial enterprise and personal communication. Without doubt, the Allegheny Mountains were a barrier to the

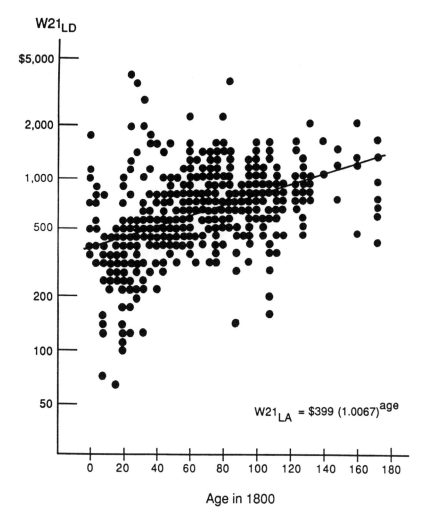

FIGURE 14. AGE AND WEALTH OF THE U.S. TAX DISTRICTS, 1798–1800

NOTE: The light regression line characterizes the overall tendency: a district one year older than another and .67 percent more wealth per capita. See table 81.

shipment of goods. Only when the population west of those mountains matched the population on the east coast decades earlier, could there have been an internal market of any significance. The populations of Kentucky and Tennessee in 1800 were equal to that in all of colonial America in 1710.

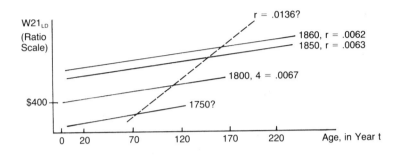

FIGURE 15. U.S. PROPERTY VALUES, CLASSIFIED BY AGE OF COUNTY, IN 1800, 1850, 1860, AND POSSIBLY 1750

ECONOMIC GROWTH AND INEQUALITY, A SIMPLE PRIMOGENITURE MODEL

Evidence does exist that inequality in America was less in the seventeenth century than in the eighteenth.[16] Perhaps these early equalities were more the result of an inadequate account of the wealth of the rich, including that of the colonial officials. It cannot be denied that at least some mechanisms in our society had the effect of strengthening inequality of wealth and that some of these were associated with economic growth. Reasons why an economy might develop greater or less inequality have been given in chapters 4 and 7. Some of the forces augmenting inequality were possibly stronger in the earlier period. While it is difficult to determine the facts, primogeniture may have been an important factor.

It is possible to construct models of changing distributions that result either in increasing or decreasing relative inequality or in little change in relative inequality. This has been demonstrated in the material in chapter 7 dealing with land fracturing. I offer here only a simple model, one stressing economic growth associated with primogeniture. Perhaps it illustrates how inequality could arise, if not in America, at least in Europe during a period of economic growth. Importantly, one adaptation of the model shows the rise of inequality tapering at approximately the actual level in 1800.[17]

In 1798, the average wealth of Americans in real estate was impressively large by European standards. Holdings in land, buildings, and dwellings had grown in number and value to a point where, in terms of possessions, Americans were among the elite in the world. Surely two centuries had seen spectacular growth; at least that is the hypothesis. If average wealth in 1798 was $708 per adult male, and if that wealth grew steadily at a rate of 1.36 percent a year (the rate from 1798 to 1850), for example, then the average in 1630 would have been $71. It is of interest to speculate what this might have meant in terms of wealth accumulation to individuals in this earlier period and the degree of inequality that would have arisen by 1800. Obviously, there are many models that can be specified; I begin with a simple formulation of a primogeniture model. The final result should reveal inequality to have a Gini coefficient between .5 and .8 if it is to be consistent with Franklin's and Adams's hypotheses of chapter 1. The merit of this procedure is that it can help us to understand what conceivably took place in the amassing of wealth by individuals over the next two centuries.

Suppose the net addition to the population each year, starting with 1630, is Δ pop = $pop_t - pop_{t-1}$ (t = 1630, 1631, . . ., 1800) and that a given group settled on the frontier with each person (or adult male) possessing $71. Further, suppose that this group experienced an annual growth rate (r) from that year forward, passing on their accumulation from generation to generation, only to their oldest sons. The father died and transferred his wealth to this one son, as in primogeniture. The other sons constituted the net addition to the population each year, Δ pop; they must each begin at the frontier with estates of $71 each. Each free adult male American in 1800 would possess an accumulated estate, $71(1 + r)^{1800-t}$, beginning in year t, the year he began on the frontier as a second or younger child, the year his father began at the frontier if he had been an eldest son, the year his grandfather began if he had been the son of an eldest son, etc. By 1800, a select few would possess estates accumulated from 1630; the cohort of younger sons beginning at the frontier in 1800 each would have only $71.

Suppose that all those at the frontier accumulated wealth at an annual rate, r*. Further, suppose that the wealth of each father/eldest son grew continuously at the same rate (r*); that is, the son helped to manage the father's estate during the father's lifetime and the son's young adulthood.[18] We can now ask what this rate must be for all cohorts of sons in the total population to yield an average wealth in 1800 of $708, assuming that the net addition of America's population each year can serve as a proxy for sons beginning at the frontier. The process becomes the one displayed in table 82.

The 3.6 percent rate for individuals is necessarily stronger than the growth in the overall average, s = .01364 [in 708 = $71(1 + s)^{170}$]. Each new cohort has a depressing effect on growth because it begins its process at $71. Also, these fresh cohorts maintain their percentage importance

TABLE 82
HYPOTHETICAL ACCUMULATION OF WEALTH AND ITS INEQUALITY BY
1800, A SIMPLE PRIMOGENITURE MODEL

	Frontier Population	Wealth per Person in 1800[a]	Age of Property in 1800
1600–1630	4,646	$71(1.036)^{170} = \$29,000$	170
1631	886	$71(1.036)^{169} = 28,000$	169
1632	1,056	$71(1.036)^{168} = 27,020$	168
.			
.			
.			
1700	4,380	$71(1.036)^{100} = 2,490$	100
.			
.			
.			
1800	157,294	$71(1.036)^{0} = 71$	0
Total	5,310,000		
Mean wealth		$708	
Inequality, G		.77	

Source: Population data are formed by using average annual rates of change for years between census estimates reported in U.S. Bureau of the Census, *Historical Statistics of the United States* (Washington, D.C.: GPO, 1949), pp. 12, 1168.

Note: a 3.6 percent rate (determined by computer) is needed to obtain a $708 average, assumed average wealth per person in 1800.

a. Beginning wealth on the frontier is assumed to be $71 and average wealth is assumed to be $708 in 1800.

among the total population, since the population grew rather constantly at 3.1 percent a year after 1650. The model does not explicitly consider death and inheritance and the timing involved, and we escape reference to marriages by considering the process as solely the result of primogeniture. The cohort with the greatest average in 1800 was that formed in 1630. Each individual need not have had wealth of $30,400; some would have more, and others less, and we need claim only that the force of growth would produce a wealthy group in which about one in every 1,000 had such wealth.

If the model has merit, it must pass several tests, the most important of which is the degree of inequality generated. The sequence leading to the 171 wealth groups shown in table 82 provides a distribution of wealth in 1800 whose inequality coefficient is .77—not far from the .80 suggested by the Adams hypothesis. The distribution is essentially not lognormal, but perhaps is not unreasonable, as is demonstrated in table 83. The fact that the relative dispersion of wealth in 1800 (shown in table 82) is about the same as that for wealth in real estate in 1850, as distributed among both owners and nonowners, signifies that the process has merit.

A basic weakness of the model is that inequality of wealth rises from decade to decade, and the fact that G was .77 in 1800 was only coincidental. A more elaborate model can be constructed in which G rises to .60 or to .70, and then *tapers off* very substantially over the course of a century to .65 or .75. This extended model considers the following elements: (1) The number of children in the family. The number may have been large or small, but each child received an equal share of his or her family's wealth. (The number of children was generated by a Poisson distribution, eliminating cases with a value of zero.) (2) The termination of a family line. It was assumed that, in families with a tradition of legacies, there was a 1 to 2 percent chance that the family's accumulation ceased in a given year, either because there were no children or because of financial mismanagement.

TABLE 83

THE SIMPLE PRIMOGENITURE MODEL IN 1800 COMPARED TO
THE ACTUAL 1850 DISTRIBUTION OF WEALTH, AS ADAPTED TO 1800

Proportion of Persons Owning Real Estate Exceeding a Given Level (N_w)	Proportion of Total Wealth (A_w)		
	Primogeniture Model[a] (1)	A Lognormal Curve[b] (G = .77) (2)	Wealth in Real Estate in 1850[c] (3)
.01	.30	.27	.26
.10	.72	.66	.67
.50	.93	.93	.99
1.00	1.00	1.00	1.00
Inequality, G	.77	.77	.82

Sources: Table 82, a lognormal table (obtained from a computer run), and my 1850 wealth sample using the weights of table 0 (appendix 11).

Note: The generated model (column 1) is tolerably similar to a lognormal distribution (column 2) and a representation of actual distribution (column 3).

   a. See table 82.
   b. A computer-generated lognormal table.
   c. Among owners and nonowners, using nativity and urbanity weights of those 70 and older.

(3) Immigration. It was assumed that a certain portion of population growth in any given year consisted of foreign-born who must perforce have begun life at the frontier with initial wealth of $71. Some simple models considering these three effects did, indeed, generate distributions that produced Gini coefficients that rose rapidly for a century or two and thereafter became stable.

CONCLUSION

The level of per capita wealth in the United States was remarkably high by 1800. The value of land rose rather steadily throughout the eighteenth century in real terms, that is, in terms of the commodities it would buy. Part of this growth in value was due to clearing of additional land and to the improvements in transportation, particularly the road system. Part was due to the perceived increased value of American land—for both Europeans and Americans—after 1775. The winning of the war, the ratification of the federal Constitution, the obviously successful endeavors of Congress and the nation's first presidents meant that the United States would be a viable country. The stability meant that there would be long-run returns for investments made at the time. There is no question that such a momentous document as the federal Constitution was the equivalent of many innovations such as the cotton gin or better farming methods in its impact on the economy. The outcome was an innately workable new system of operation—one certainly qualifying as a Schumpeterian innovation—a radical change in the way of doing things. Furthermore, the increase in population itself may have made possible economies of scale.

We have measured economic growth in several ways. Deeds of sale show growth in real value of at least 1 percent a year. Age and average wealth of U.S. counties in 1800 imply a growth rate of .7 percent a year in the case of land and houses, and 2 percent in the case of houses. The evidence is clear: lands valued at only a few cents at the time of settlement in the seventeenth century had become worth many dollars per acre by 1798.

This kind of growth provides a definite impetus to the inequality of wealth. In general, families who settled first accumulated more than those who settled at a later time. Thus, levels of inequality in 1798 were consistent with the variations in number of years of family accumulation. To be sure, there was substantial variation between regions in the inequality of wealth in 1798; this inequality arose because settlement activity had proceeded methodically from east to west, not as might have occurred had there been more advanced modes of transportation.

10

Ratification of the Constitution and the Distribution of Wealth and Income

THIS BOOK has stressed the fact that there was considerable inequality of wealth and income in America at the end of the eighteenth century. One can ask whether it might have been of any great consequence to society as a whole if the poor had more, and the rich less. On the other hand, the rich might have held even larger proportions if the institutions of entailed estates and primogeniture had continued to exist, and had there been greater taxation of staples as well as lower taxation on luxury items. Had inequality been larger, land might have been distributed in enormous blocks, either as gifts or at nominal cost to a few large patrons, and savings, too, may have been greater. One may properly ask whether the inequality of wealth played a wide role in the nation's social and cultural activities in the early federal period. There is little doubt that the answer must be yes. Inequality played a large part in determining the *extent* of various activities—the participation by groups in the evolution of our culture. An integral part of this movement was participation in the political process.

I propose to highlight but one aspect of this political activity, the ratification of the Constitution. How many persons took part in this process? To what economic and social ranks did they belong? At most, were 25 percent of the people involved? This is the rate suggested by Palmer as the proportion of people participating in revolutionary activities in a half dozen European countries at the end of the century.[1] Did more Americans participate? This chapter explores the relationship of political participation and belief to wealth and income; thus, its material is speculative in nature. At best, it can suggest, albeit with substantial measurement error, how involved Americans were in the functioning of their society.

We begin with an opinion of John Marshall:

> So balanced were parties in some [of the states], that . . . the fate of the constitution
> could scarcely be conjectured; and so small, in many instances, was the majority in
> its favour, . . . that, had the influence of character been removed, the intrinsic merits
> of the instrument would not have secured its adoption. Indeed, it is scarcely to be
> doubted that, in some of the adopting states, a majority of the people were in the
> opposition.[2]

Researchers continue to be fascinated by the reasons why people voted for or against the Constitution of the United States, even though it has been 200 years since delegates to the state ratification conventions cast their ballots. The delegates' motives are usually analyzed in terms of self-interest—their own or those of persons close to them. Often historians have stressed economic motivation as a primary influence on the outcome of the voting. This thesis could be proven by a methodical index of the incomes or accumulated wealth of the delegates, information not generally accessible. At present, the best available indexes have been limited lists of the vocations or the amounts of government securities held by a minority of those men. Little attention has been given to the economic characteristics of the entire labor force within each community who had empowered the delegates to act on their behalf at the conventions.

This chapter addresses the issue by considering the value of houses owned by both the delegates and by all free males age 21 and older in the country in 1798. I use 1798 dwelling values for delegates in 1787–1788 for two northern states and, indirectly (using slaveholdings), for four southern states to project votes as though all free males, or a sizable portion thereof, had voted on ratification of the Constitution. This projection is designed to answer the rather fundamental question, "Would the American populace have accepted the Constitution if they had been allowed to vote?"

DWELLING VALUES AND VOTES, AN ILLUSTRATION

The value of the dwelling unit or partial dwelling unit occupied by a person (DHV) is an excellent proxy for individual income, or more generally, economic well-being. The vote or potential vote of an adult free male in 1788 (YES $= 1$ if in favor of ratification; otherwise, YES $= 0$) will be related to DHV, as measured by the U.S. census of dwelling values in 1798.[3] I shall report the relationship between these values and the vote for 113 delegates in Connecticut and Pennsylvania and, as estimated, for 138 individuals in southern states. We can add another perspective by considering the average DHV of all dwellings and average delegate vote for all 281 counties in the country at the time and, additionally, for 191 voting districts in Pennsylvania. Logistic curves are fitted to the various data sets, and each of these, with its intercept and slope, will be applied to the overall distribution to estimate the results of a national plebiscite.

I will present data on the proportion of delegates voting favorably on the Constitution, classified by their dwelling income, and consider the proportion of all free people who were delegates, classified by income. A technique often used in economics is to classify people by using income as the determining variable; the elasticity of sales of a good with respect to the incomes of individuals is often employed in understanding consumer demand. Yet, voting for the Constitution is a far cry from the purchase of a consumer good. Making a choice on such a fundamental issue is not like buying an automobile. A thorough analysis of the vote would cover such measurable variables as age, number of children, ethnicity, country of birth, religion, occupation, education, and other demographic variables. The analysis would include the individual's wealth (as distinguished from dwelling income) and its form, particularly whether the voter owned public and private securities and whether he had speculated in land.

Jackson Turner Main presents a formidable list of additional variables to consider, such as political experience in local or higher-level offices, military experience in the Continental Army and militia, father's occupation and economic status, intellectual interests, and world view.[4] Other considerations would include any measurable characteristics having a bearing on the person's views on such issues as governmental action, equality, sovereignty, and participation in war. In short, it is a very complex subject.

Nevertheless, I propose studying fervor for the Constitution by considering dwelling income where possible, and when such information is not available, slaveholdings. The procedure will highlight the effects of the wide disparities in income in the late eighteenth century, a dramatic effect brought about by the inequality of income.

An example of a logistic curve is given in figure 16; its data will be explained in detail later. Its shape is a tipped S, becoming asymptotic at yes of 1 and 0. It is an expression describing the probability of voting yes at each level of well-being. We need only two points on the curve to obtain the equation of the curve since it has but two parameters. As an example, if one knows the probability of a yes vote at the median value for well-being and the 99th percentile of well-being, then one can determine the exact equation. I begin my exposition of possible vote outcomes by considering some hypothetical logistic curves; hopefully, these situations provide a range that will encompass possible plebiscite outcomes. In the analysis

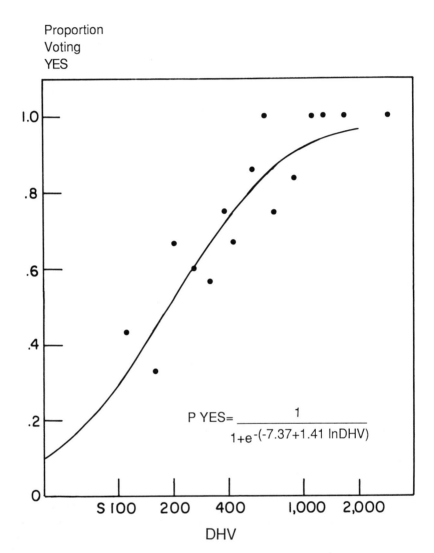

FIGURE 16. THE PROPORTION VOTING YES AMONG 79 CONNECTICUT DELEGATES TO THE CONSTITUTION CONVENTION, 1788, GROUPED BY THEIR DWELLING HOUSE VALUES IN 1798

NOTE: The equation represents a logistic curve.

we will consider not only the probability of voting yes, but also the probability that a freeman would take the trouble to cast his ballot; in addition, we consider his given level of well-being. This latter probability, too, will be described with a logistic curve.

A wide gamut of economic power existed in the country at the time; as we have seen, a few individuals with a great deal of wealth lived in mansions while the many inhabited log cabins or hovels. The distribution of dwelling house values is strikingly lognormal, having a Gini coefficient of .71, a median of $67, and a projected top value of $69,000 in a population of 877,000 free male adults.[5] Suppose the probability of voting for ratification of the Constitution (PYES) was much more likely in the case of the richest man than for the man at the median. Also suppose that at these two levels $(P_{.50}, P_{.999999}) = (.50, .99)$ and that the logistic curve passing through these two points, and indeed specified by them, described the fervor of individuals at each DHV. In this case, if all persons voted, the outcome would be a tie vote (shown as .50 on table 84), as determined from a computer simulation. The rationale for the positive relationship between pro-Constitution fervor and housing values comes from the fact that the rich man perhaps owned land in several states, including land at the frontier. He viewed the Constitution as a means of strengthening property rights throughout the land. The poor man favored no federal government control or, at most, government only at the colonial or state level. This situation provides a hypothesis to be tested,

$$[H_1: R(YES, DHV) > 0].$$

Surely the rich man would be more likely than a poor man to vote at all $[H_2: R(VOTE, DHV) > 0]$. The affluent would have had the resources necessary to make the journey to the state capital to vote; this group also would have had a stronger vested interest in registering its approval. Delegates to the conventions in fact tended to be persons of means. In part, they were prominent and influential because of their wealth in land, houses, slaves, and personal property. These values augmented their incomes—and their ability to live in finer homes. Even if there had been a national plebiscite with polling facilities in the county seats, the poorer man would have found it difficult to vote because of the relatively high cost of having to travel 20–30 miles to cast a ballot.

Table 84 provides four possible cases of voter participation had it occurred in 1798. The first column considers a full plebiscite—where each individual would be required to vote (possibly needing the threat of a fine for not voting). The last column provides a hypothetical case in which only 1.6 percent of adult males vote. This situation is computed by passing a logistic curve through the median and top value, assuming $(P_{.50}, P_{.999999})$ = $(.01, .50)$. This last column of table 84 can be thought of as the case in which only one or two persons—possibly delegates—from each community would travel to a distant polling place somewhere in the country, say, to Philadelphia, for the purpose of casting their votes concerning ratification. These individuals would vote their own self-interest, as measured by their incomes and as demonstrated by the values of their homes. The result in 1798 might not be dissimilar from the tally of delegates to the state conventions in 1787 and 1788. The two intermediate columns represent concepts of plebiscites in which one-half or, alternatively, about one-eighth of adult free males voted in local or county polling stations.

The results of the table can only suggest possibilities. Thus, the second row indicates that in 1798 a small minority of delegates would have voted strongly for ratification ($\overline{\text{PYES}}$ = .61), whereas a plebiscite with a 100 percent turnout might have produced a tie vote. The table assumes that the probability of voting (PVOTE) at a given DHV is the same for one favoring as for one not favoring the Constitution.

POSSIBLE MEASUREMENT ERROR

Three immediate difficulties arise when testing with actual voting data. Delegates to the ratifying conventions may or may not have voted their own self-interest. If the delegate had voted his county's interest rather than his own, then the $\text{DHV}_{\text{county}}$ should be substituted for $\text{DHV}_{\text{delegate}}$. Perhaps some intermediate DHV would be appropriate, say, twice the county average if the delegates lived in houses five times the value of the average person's. Generally, I will assume that the delegate voted his own interest, or nearly so, and I will use $\text{DHV}_{\text{delegate}}$. Some empirical data for one state suggest that this was the case.

A second difficulty arises from the fact that our data about housing are for 1798 rather than for 1788. In some ways, the 10-year lag between the actual vote and my figures is superior as a statistical procedure, since we measure the individual's success in the socioeconomic sense—success proven after a decade. Economic expectations in 1788 could have been a strong influence on a voter's views on the Constitution, could influence how much value he placed on a national order of government.

A further problem is the interaction between PYES and PVOTE. I must assume that PYES at a given DHV was the same for a voter as for a nonvoter, a situation possibly contrary to fact. High-income voters favoring adoption may have been more willing to participate in the ratification process than those with similarly high incomes but who opposed the Constitution. This possibility could arise because people like to participate in movements of positive rather than negative action. My results, unadjusted for this effect, lead to an overstatement of fervor rather than to an understatement. Perhaps the upward bias from this interaction counters the downward bias of the first possible error, the assumption that the delegates voted their own self-interest.

THE CONNECTICUT DATA

Suppose I formalize the investigation of the population in 1798 using the working hypothesis H_1, that there was a positive relationship between ratification fervor and economic well-being. Evidence supporting H_1 is given in table 85. I searched for delegates' names in the dwelling house manuscripts for 1798 in Connecticut and Pennsylvania. Connecticut's case overwhelmingly demonstrates that those living in houses of higher value tended to vote in the affirmative. The logistic formulation

$$YES_{79,CT} = -.7.37726 + 1.40796 \ln DHV$$
$$(2.35868) \qquad (.40000)$$

where $\ln DHV$ is the logarithm of the dwelling house value; (standard errors in parentheses), $n = 79$, $P(\chi^2 = 17) < .0001$. This equation is plotted in figure 16 along with the points describing the average voting result within certain dwelling house ranges. When this formulation is adjusted to dwelling values per adult free male and applied to the lognormal distribution for the United States per adult free male, as outlined in table 84, election results appear as in table 86. Assuming the PVOTE probabilities stated in table 84, the Constitution would have been defeated overwhelmingly (2 to 1) if all free males over 21 had voted; defeated if half the eligible population had voted ($\overline{PYES} = .45$); and easily accepted if only 1 or 2 percent had voted. We obtain similar results if we apply the equation only to Connecticut. An ordinary straight line equation in YES and $\ln DHV$ also gives similar results.[6]

I next establish the hypothesis H_2, that there is a positive relationship between the probability of actually voting and the economic well-being of the individual. Evidence for H_2 is given in table 87. Connecticut's delegates were much more likely to have been rich than poor. The table indicates that the probability of their being wealthy was over 100 times as great as

TABLE 84

EXPECTED PROPORTION VOTING FOR RATIFICATION OF THE CONSTITUTION:
SOME POSSIBILITIES CONSIDERING HOUSING VALUES IN 1798
(males 21 and older)

For Logistic Curves Passing Through	No. of Voters per 1,000 Persons[a]			
	$N = 1,000$ $(1.00,1.00)$	$N = 500$ $(.50,.99)$	$N = 130$ $(.10,.90)$	$N = 16$ $(.01,.50)$
(.50,.99)	.50	.58	.65	.68
(.40,.985)	.42	.50	.57	.61
(.30,.977)	.33	.41	.47	.51

Sources: Computer runs using an adapted distribution of housing values for 1798 in conjunction with an assumed logistic curve for fervor and another for chances of voting.

Note: The distribution of housing values is assumed to be lognormal with a median of $67 and a top value of $69,000 (G = .7). Housing values were generated in a computer program using PYES or PVOTE = $1/(1 + e^{-(a + b \ln DHV)})$, assuming that PYES (proportion voting yes) at a given DHV was the same for voters and nonvoters. Consider row 2 and column 3 as an example for interpretation. Here the logistic curve for *voting yes* is described by two points: the probability of voting yes ($P_{.5}$, where $N_x = .5$) at the median housing value is .40, and the probability of voting yes ($P_{.999999}$ where $N_x = .999999$) for the top person in 1,000,000 is .985. Suppose the logistic curve for the probability of taking the trouble to *vote* is described by $P_{.5} = .10$ and $P_{.999999} = .90$. In this case, only 130 persons in 1,000 would vote and 57 percent would vote for ratification.

a. For logistic curves with probabilities at the median and top value ($P_{.50}, P_{.999999}$), as stated in the parentheses in the stub and in column heads.

for the average adult free male, considering the two outlier classes. The delegate participation rate (DPR) for Connecticut suggests a logistic curve with a very low probability of voting among all free male adults, a configuration similar to the PVOTE formulation in the last columns of table 84 and 86. This can be verified by applying a probit analysis to the six classes of house values or, alternatively, a logistic curve generated from a given multiple of the delegate participation rate. One can only guess what proportion of the population would have voted at various income levels had only half of the eligible population possessed the resources to vote and indeed had voted. Suppose more men in Connecticut had voted than the 80 described in table 87. To multiply the column by 10 produces a new logistic curve with probabilities similar to the last column of table 84, where $(P_{.5}, P_{.999999}) = (.01, 150)$. To multiply Connecticut's 80 delegates by 20 gives probabilities not far removed from the next-to-last column of table 84, using (.10,.90).

PENNSYLVANIA AND THE SOUTH

For Pennsylvania, I could find the names of only 34 individuals among those listed in the 1798 census records for housing; therefore, the

TABLE 85
CONSTITUTIONAL CONVENTION VOTES, CLASSIFIED BY HOUSING VALUES AND NUMBER OF SLAVES, 1787–1798

Dwelling House Value	Connecticut (43 of 67 Districts)			Pennsylvania (13 of 25 Counties)		
	Yes	No	Proportion Voting Yes	Yes	No	Proportion Voting Yes
$1,000 and over	22	0	1.00	9	3	.75
500–999	18	4	.82	8	2	.80
200–499	14	8	.64	6	3	.69
1–199	5	8	.38	1	2	.33
All	59	20	.75	24	10	.71

No. of Slaves	Maryland			Virginia			North Carolina			South Carolina			Simple Average of Four
	Yes	No	Prop. Yes	Yes	No	Prop. Yes	Yes	No	Prop. Yes	Yes	No	Prop. Yes	Prop. Yes
100 and over	5	1	.83	2	3	.67	2	1	.67	34	3	.92	.77
10–99	32	2	.94	39	42	.48	44	65	.40	75	38	.66	.62
5–9	5	4	.57	8	15	.35	13	34	.28	11	11	.50	.42
2–4	2	0	1.00	9	4	.69	4	12	.25	4	7	.36	.57
1	—	—	—	3	2	.60	1	1	.50	2	4	.33	.48
0	15	2	.88	20	7	.74	20	71	.22	19	8	.70	.63
All	59	9	.87	81	71	.53	84	182	.31	145	71	.67	.60

Sources: Public Records of Connecticut, ed. J. Hammon Trumbull (Hartford: 1852), 4:550–53; *Debates of the Convention of Pennsylvania,* from Clifford Shipton and James Mooney, *National Index of American Imprints Through 1800, the Short Title Evans* (Worcester, Mass.: American Antiquarian Society and Barre Publishers, 1969), Evans No. 21365; dwelling house data are from U.S. National Archives and Record Service, *United States Direct Tax of 1798: Tax Lists for the State of Pennsylvania,* pamphlet accompanying microcopy 372 (Washington, D.C.: 1963); data from the Connecticut Historical Society, Hartford (see appendix 13); Forest McDonald, *We the People: The Economic Origins of the Constitution* (Chicago: University of Chicago Press, 1958), pp. 143–47, 155–60, 172–81, 217–34, 269–81; Orrin Grant Libby, *Geographical Distribution of the Vote of the Thirteen States on the Ratification of the Federal Constitution, 1787–1788* (1894; rpt. Franklin, N.Y.: Burt, 1969), pp. 106–16; William C. Pool, "An Economic Interpretation of the Ratification of the Federal Constitution in North Carolina," *North Carolina Historical Review* 27 (1950), 127–41, 288–313, 437–61. (Only the first convention, the Hillsborough convention, is considered in the above table.) Slave data for states are for 1790, as found in U.S. Bureau of the Census, *A Century of Population Growth* (1909; rpt. New York: Johnson Reprint Corp., 1966), pp. 135–36.

Note: In Connecticut, 22 delegates owned dwellings valued at between $200 and $599; 14 of these voted yes.

TABLE 86
PROJECTIONS OF THE PROPORTION VOTING TO RATIFY
THE CONSTITUTION IN VARIOUS STATES
(free males 21 and older)

Delegates Voting Yes	N	No. of Voters per 1,000 Persons[a]			
		N = 100 (1.00,1.00)	N = 500 (.50,.99)	N = 130 (.10,.90)	N = 16 (.01,.50)
Connecticut	79	.33	.45	.56	.62
Pennsylvania	34	.497	.56	.61	.64
Connecticut and Pennsylvania	113	.38	.48	.57	.62
South[b]	152	.39	.44	.48	.51
United States[c]	265	.396	.46	.52	.55

Sources: See the interpretation of table 84 and the sources for table 85.

Note: The interpretation is the same as that given in the example in table 84. In this case, had the actual logistic fervor curve for Connecticut applied and had 130 of 1,000 voted, 56 percent would have voted for ratification.

a. See table 84.
b. Maryland, Virginia, North Carolina, and South Carolina.
c. Based on data for all six states.

information used to estimate the state's ratification vote is much weaker than for Connecticut. Here the predicted result for all persons (table 86) is very close to 50 percent; the proposition would have passed easily if only half of eligible males voted, using the assumptions for PVOTE outlined in table 84. One can make a firmer assertion by combining the 34 Pennsylvania delegates with Connecticut's 79. In this case, the vote is projected to show a rejection if all free adult males voted, or if half voted, as stated in the $YES_{113,CTPA}$ row of table 86. However, the Connecticut results still overwhelmingly tip the scales against ratification.

More comprehensive information for Pennsylvania in 1798–1799 provides a better grasp of anti-Federalist sentiment at that time. The proportion of persons voting Federalist or anti-Federalist (Republican) has been reported for each of 191 of Pennsylvania's 421 townships. I have computed the average dwelling value for each of the 191 townships and fitted a logistic curve. A depiction of the curve, coupled with some average voting results for given dwelling value ranges is given in figure 17.

There is ample evidence that poorer districts were less likely to favor ratification, and that the expected rate would have been 2 to 1 against ratification had all townships voted. However, this evidence must remain

TABLE 87
CONSTITUTIONAL CONVENTION PARTICIPATION RATES,
CLASSIFIED BY HOUSING VALUES AND NUMBER OF SLAVES, 1787–1798

Dwelling House Value	Connecticut (43 of 67 Districts)			Pennsylvania (13 of 25 Counties)		
	No. of Delegates	No. of Dwellings	DPR	No. of Delegates	No. of Dwellings	DPR
$6,000 and over ⎱ 3,000–5,999 ⎰	1	22	.04500	1 2	241 717	.00410 .00280
1,000–2,999	16	510	.03100	8	4,208	.00190
500–999	24	1,570	.01500	9	7,820	.00120
100–499	38	12,024	.00320	14	26,544	.00053
1–99	1	6,532	.00015	0	18,790	.00000
All	80	10,658	.00387	34	58,320	.00058

No. of Slaves	Maryland		Virginia		North Carolina		South Carolina		Simple Average of Four, DPR
	No. of Delegates	DPR	No. of Delegates	DPR	No. of Delegates	DPR	No. of Delegates	DPR	
300 and over	0	—	0	—	0	—	4	.67000	.67000
200–299	2	.67000	1	.08300	1	.50000	11	.52000	.44000
100–199	4	.25000	2	.02700	2	.18000	22	.23000	.17000
50–99	5	.05200	8	.02300	7	.07800	38	.13000	.07200
20–49	21	.02900	44	.01500	47	.06700	37	.04300	.03900
10–19	8	.00440	27	.00420	55	.03100	38	.03200	.01800
5–9	9	.00320	21	.00270	47	.01400	22	.01200	.00490
2–4	2	.00006	7	.00140	16	.00320	11	.00420	.00220
1	0	.00000	4	.00086	2	.00050	6	.00310	.00110
0	17	.00070	22	.00064	91	.00220	27	.00100	.00110
All	68	.00188	136	.00200	268	.00509	216	.00574	.00368

Sources: See table 85.

Notes: DPR = Delegate participation rate, the number of delegates divided by the number of dwellings.

tenuous, since anti-Federalism in 1799 may have been a far cry from antiratification fervor in 1788.[7]

I was unable to find YES-DHV data for the South. Extant housing data for Maryland were not useful in developing equations, since the great majority of delegates favored ratification; in order to develop projections

Proportion
Voting Federalist

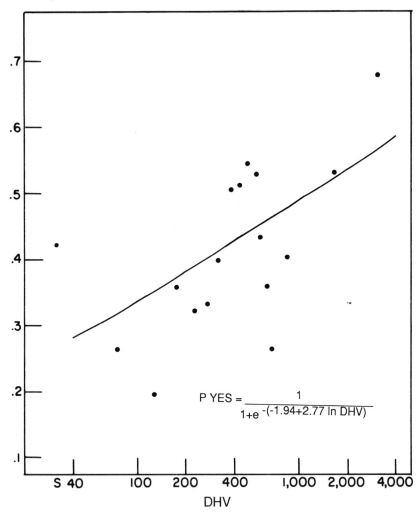

$$P\ YES = \frac{1}{1+e^{-(-1.94+2.77\ \ln\ DHV)}}$$

DHV

FIGURE 17. THE FEDERALIST VOTE IN 191 PENNSYLVANIA TOWNSHIPS,
GROUPED BY AVERAGE DWELLING HOUSE VALUE IN 1798

for the state, I used slaveholder data as a substitute for housing values. For 152 counties in the South, I knew the average number of slaves owned by the delegates (A), the average number of slaves per free male 21 and older (B), and the average dwelling value for each (C). The ratio AB/C was used to estimate the average dwelling value for delegates in each county. Finally, I fitted the data for the 152 counties where YES for a county was considered to be 1 if half or more of delegate votes were positive; otherwise, YES was 0. The projected results for the 152 (given in table 86) show that the Constitution would have been rejected in the South. The vote would have been negative not so much because of a strong economic gradient between rich and poor, but because the intercept, the general fervor for ratification, was lower in the South than in the more urban North.

A Combined Projection

Finally, I pooled the information for the 265 yes votes, and found that the Constitution would have been defeated whether all free adult males had voted or only half had voted, as shown in the last line of table 86. Weighting the data by considering the populations in the northern and southern states does make the vote a little closer than the results given in the table. Logistic curves fitted to the PYES and PVOTE data for the 265 suggest a special case for the United States that could be added to table 86, a situation in which but a fraction of 1 percent of the population would vote.[8] In such a situation, the expected vote PYES would be 59 percent. Here I can obtain a check on whether the 265 for the six states are representative of the 1,111 delegates to all of the 13 state conventions (including the first vote in the case of North Carolina); of the 1,111, 61 percent favored ratification of the Constitution.

County Votes and Wealth

Orrin Libby established a data set encompassing the voting records of delegates for the entire country in 1787–1788, classifying each of 281 counties as Federal, anti-Federal, or as divided.[9] I have determined the average DHV per free adult male for each and called it YES = 1 if it was either designated Federalist or if its Federalist delegates or vote numbers equaled or exceeded those for anti-Federalists. The data of table 88 clearly indicate the fact that richer counties overwhelmingly favored ratification. The vote was largely determined by the delegate and, in this sense, the DHV should be that of the delegate, and not of all persons. The delegate's average wealth in housing was several times greater than the county average. (They were three times as large in Connecticut, a state whose DHV mean was but 8 percent larger than the national average.) Even doubling the DHV of the logistic curve before applying it to Libby's 281 counties in 1798 can lower the overall PYES to .50 or less. Thus, regional data are consistent with the notion that a plebiscite would have rejected the proposition.[10]

The evidence points to the fact that the Constitution would not have been accepted, had there been a plebiscite. Frankly, I felt saddened when I determined these results. Perhaps persons below median wealth would have found the Constitution acceptable, had the Bill of Rights been an integral part of it. In any case, our revered document had a less auspicious beginning in the sense presented here. Chief Justice Marshall was correct when he said that individuals "were disposed to it [a national legislature] with the same sparing hand with which they would confer it on persons not chosen by themselves."[11]

TABLE 88

PROPORTION OF U.S. COUNTIES FAVORING RATIFICATION OF THE
CONSTITUTION, CLASSIFIED BY HOUSING VALUES, 1798

Average Dwelling House Value[a]	No. of Counties	Proportion of Counties Voting Yes
$1,000 and over	2	1.00
500–999	3	1.00
200–499	22	.73
100–199	96	.69
50–99	73	.47
16–49	85	.47
All	281	.57

Sources: Table 23 and Orrin Grant Libby, *The Geographical Distribution of the Vote of the Thirteen States on the Ratification of the Federal Constitution* (1894; rpt. New York: Burt, 1969), pp. 110–16.

a. Average value for males 21 and older.

11

Conclusion

THE FINDINGS of this monograph answer questions dealing with the degree of economic differences between the rich, the middling, and the poor in an exciting time for the United States—the Age of the Democratic Revolution. The analysis consists of a statistical measurement of the degree of economic inequality in the United States in 1798. My major purpose is to determine whether equality did exist and whether economic conditions and opportunities were approximately the same for all free persons when compared to contemporary Europe and to persons in other places and times.

In order to show relative differences in wealth holding, I have compared wealth in America and in Europe at the end of the eighteenth century, in America between 1771 and 1774, 1798 and 1850–1860, and, indeed, I have compared incomes in 1798 with those of 1980.

The views of Benjamin Franklin, John Adams, Alexis de Tocqueville, and others are significant, since their perceptions regarding the inequality of wealth in the young nation form hypotheses that can be tested with statistical analysis. Moreover, their ideas were transformed into policy decisions that influenced existing levels of inequality. The subject of inequality in America did not receive analytical attention until Tocqueville's monumental work, published a generation after 1798, in which he fully explored the consequences of inequality:

> Among the novel objects that attracted my attention during my stay in the United States, nothing struck me more forcibly than the general equality of condition among the people. . . . The more I advanced in the study of American society, the more I perceived that this equality of condition is the fundamental fact from which all others seem to be derived and the central point at which all my observations constantly terminated.[1]

So wrote Tocqueville in 1835, as he observed the new country with the eye of a young European who was himself the descendant of a noble family.

RELATIVE EQUALITY

The hypothesis that there was relative equality of wealth in the early United States is the central and pervasive issue that I have investigated in this book in an attempt to subject the perceptions of Tocqueville and others to quantitative proof. It must be understood that I never expected to find perfect equality, and that any suggestions to this effect were surely rhetorical. Everyone knew that in the early days, the United States consisted of the rich, the poor, and those in between. I am asking, *to what degree* was that society inegalitarian? Tocqueville's expressions about equality were intended to mean that relative dispersion of wealth in America was small, an opinion that could be expected from someone with his aristocratic background.

Other foreign observers also spoke about equality of wealth when they really meant that there was little inequality.[2] In 1845, even the author of *A Christmas Carol* found social equality in the United States to be excessive:

> The Republican Institutions of America undoubtedly lead the people to assert their self-respect and their equality; but a traveller is bound to bear those . . . Institutions in his mind, and not hastily to resent the near approach of a class of strangers, who at home, would be kept aloof.[3]

Nor did our sage, Benjamin Franklin, leave any doubt about his views on the subject when he described the situation as being "the happy mediocrity that so generally prevails throughout these States, where the cultivator works for himself, and supports his family in decent plenty."[4] Many saw only slavery as a deep wound disfiguring America's relative equality.

Tocqueville's equality of condition meant much more than legal equality and the absence of a noble class. It meant *economic* equality or, at least, only mild economic inequality, in a society where poor and rich were not very far apart. It was a land with neither entailed estates nor primogeniture to govern the distribution of estates. It was a land where farms were too small to support a noble class (even if it were socially acceptable), where counties and townships were formed so rapidly that a few individuals could not advantageously hold on to large portions of acreage (except possibly in the South). Smaller farms could compete effectively because of the assiduous efforts of the yeoman class. In Tocqueville's opinion, economic equality could eventually force social and political equality.[5]

Prominent in his analysis was the belief that inequality *was decreasing,* in the main, from generation to generation:

> The gradual development of the principle of equality is, therefore, a providential fact. It has all the chief characteristics of such a fact. It is universal, it is lasting, it constantly eludes all human interference, and all events as well as all men contribute to its progress.
>
> Would it then, be wise to imagine that a social movement the causes of which lie so far back can be checked by the efforts of one generation? Can it be believed that the democracy which has overthrown the feudal system and vanquished kings will retreat before tradesmen and capitalists? Will it stop now that it has grown so strong and its adversaries so weak?
>
> Whither then are we tending? No one can say, for terms of comparison already fail us. There is greater equality of condition in Christian countries at the present day than there has been at any previous time, in any part of the world, so that the magnitude of what already has been done prevents us from foreseeing what is yet to be accomplished.[6]

Tocqueville felt that this tendency toward equality was not just a European trend. True, America had entailed estates and primogeniture in its beginning days, but these laws were abolished with independence. New laws and procedures were established as the country was settled, townships and counties were formed, and society groped its way toward development and equality.

One can contest the Tocqueville thesis. The periods after 1770 or 1798 encompassed the beginning of the Industrial Revolution, a period generating fortunes for industrial leaders and high incomes for skilled employees. A significant laboring or unskilled worker class emerged; immigrants became a more prominent source of labor; and the labor force was increasingly divorced from the land as society became more urbanized. The entire process began in the 1790s with the establishment of banking facilities and when the federal government assumed the revolutionary debt. John Adams felt that there was significant social and economic inequality in America, as elsewhere; he observed that every society, every organization, had a natural aristocracy that would assert itself.

The economic aspects of these alleged trends or, at least, changes in inequality from 1770 to the present are still being investigated empirically and will be a matter of inquiry for researchers for decades to come. The almost continuous series dealing with probates and administration of estates perhaps offer the greatest promise as data sources. To study land grants and patents is another approach. The entire field of demography, including physical height or stature, births, deaths, life expectancy, marriage rates, and fertility, are all most promising avenues that could lead to an understanding of equality of condition in earlier times. Yet another alternative is to concentrate heavily on a single year, uncovering all extant records at the local, state, and federal levels. This I have done by choosing the year 1798, a year highlighted by a national inventory of all real estate. This census of wealth includes the holdings of all individuals in the original 17 states as well as Kentucky and Tennessee.

THE FRANKLIN AND ADAMS HYPOTHESES

Tocqueville's generalizations dealt with observations of social and economic inequality in different places and at different times. (In the case of France, he considered seven centuries of change.) The observations of Franklin and John Adams give us a more specific focus on American inequality in the 1790s. In general, Franklin perceived America as a land of "happy mediocrity," while Adams believed there was substantial inequality, with a very prominent elite of influential rich persons, but no beggars. I have analyzed the quantitative statements of shares held by upper groups in America, coupled them with an assumption of a lognormal distribution, and, on this basis, I suggest two hypotheses:

$G_{RE, Franklin} = .5$, and $G_{RE, Adams} = .8$, where G_{RE} is the Gini coefficient of wealth in real estate ($G = 0$ in perfect equality, and $G = 1$ when one person has all wealth, or there is perfect inequality). Adams felt that property holders constituted a minority, or at least they were not a majority of the labor force; the real estate proportion (REP) was .5 or less, and a senator in a bicameral legislative system was necessary to protect property holders' interests. The Adams scheme leads to a G of .6 for those owning property and to this equation for inequality:

$$G_{RE \geq 0} = REP * G_{RE > 0} + (1 - REP)G_{RE = 0} = .8 = .5 * .6 + (1 - .5) * 1.$$

A BACKWARD EXTRAPOLATION

I made a preliminary estimate of the distribution of real estate in 1800 by using the detail from the censuses of 1850 and 1860. I adjusted these latter data sets by considering the nativity and urban/rural residence of males 70 and older, that is, of those males who were 20 and older in 1800.

The two mid-century sets yield backward extrapolations having results similar to those in the Adams scheme. The proportion owning real estate is .493 in one case and .504 in the other; the inequality coefficient was about .64 for owners and .82 for all free adult males for both extrapolations. The procedure gave me the first suggestion that there was little change in inequality during the first two generations of the nineteenth century. Urban/rural and nativity classifications really did not explain much of the variance in wealth or in logarithms of wealth.

The availability of land played a part in maintaining relative inequality. The average amount of privately owned acreage per person was very respectable in 1800, but the average in 1850, in states joining the Union after 1800, was equally handsome. There was a plentiful supply of land in 1850, and it was relatively more fertile than in the areas of earlier settlement because of the extent of cultivability east and west of the Alleghenies. Slavery also contributed toward maintaining inequality in the South. The relative dispersion of slaves among slaveholders changed very little in the two generations between 1800 and 1860. Finally, there were apparently no significant shifts in returns to scale of farm operation in the two generations.

ECONOMIC GROWTH

An important aspect affecting the level of inequality is economic growth or, at least, the growth in real estate values in their purchasing power—that is, in the commodities they can buy. The earlier a family arrived in the United States, the more likely it was to benefit from substantial growth. In 1798, third-generation families had greater assets than did first-generation families, unless estates had been subdivided among many children. A simple model of immigration, settlement, and primogeniture can be devised that climbs from a G_{RE} of 0 to .6 or .8 after a few generations, given the stimulus of economic growth and including capital gains. Significantly, one variation of the model demonstrates levels of inequality rising after five or six generations only to about the levels for 1798.

What was the level of wealth at the end of the eighteenth century? This we need to know in order to understand the rate of growth in economic well-being in America prior to 1798. Average wealth in real estate in the United States in 1798 was a very respectable $708 for free males 21 and older. This figure is impressive when judged against known averages for some European countries at the time. The average was almost three times its counterpart in Sweden, well over six times that of Finland, and three times the average in the four Scandinavian countries whose combined population was half again as large as the free population in the United States. The U.S. average, for freeman and slave alike, was double that of Scandinavia. More important is the fact that the $708 was probably as large as the average in England, and certainly larger than averages in either Scotland or Wales.

How could America have attained the 1798 level without a rapid surge in economic well-being in the eighteenth century? Certainly yearly average wealth, adjusted by a price index of commodities, was growing rapidly. Just what the growth rate was from, say, 1750 to 1798 is difficult to determine. We do know, however, that the rate from 1798 to 1850 was 1.4 percent a year, based on the census data; surely the rate prior to 1798 must have been at least half this level. Deeds of sale for the whole eighteenth century show the average price of land growing at a spectacular rate of 6 percent a year in Lancaster County, Pennsylvania, and at a more modest rate of 1.3 percent a year in the Charleston District of South Carolina. The frontier county of Albemarle, Virginia, experienced an important rise in land values. The tax valuations of land and structures in Massachusetts and Maine in 1771 and 1798 are evidence that the annual real growth rate was 2.3 percent per adult male. The upshot of these studies is that real land values per adult male were rising at least between 1 and 1.4 percent a year. The increase was due, in part, to innovations such as the cotton gin and to the increasing attractiveness of American land after the Revolution. Both Europeans and Americans were impressed by the stability assured by the new federal Constitution, a gigantic step toward stabilizing the prospects for long-run returns on investments.

Growth was also demonstrated in the 1798 wealth averages by county. In counties that were 120 years old, land values tended to be higher than in those that were younger, as shown below:

Age of County in 1800	Value of Real Estate per Adult Free Male
0–29 years	$482
30–59	678
60–119	793
120 and over	972

The pace of development meant that there was very substantial wealth inequality *between* as well as *within* regions. Modern-day egalitarians in some countries tend to think almost exclusively of regional differences, particularly if some poor regions experienced rapid population loss. Our early history, however, was characterized by the opposite phenomenon. People flowed to areas of low wealth, but their expectations were high.

One of the growth models described in detail in this book generated distributions that may capture much of the history of the seventeenth and eighteenth centuries. In the model, the distribution of wealth demonstrated a rise in G from .00 in 1630 to .75 in 1800, derived from assuming that average wealth grew from $71 in 1630 to $708 in 1800, or 1.4 percent a year. The assumptions for this model are that the population was growing by 3.1 percent a year, and that an immigrant began at the frontier with a wealth average of $71, that his wealth grew 3.6 percent a year, that he left his wealth only to his oldest son, and that his other sons had to begin again at the frontier with wealth of $71. A more elaborate model could incorporate the idea that there might be slippage in the estate of the eldest son. John Adams once stated that if a man distributed his estate equally among his six sons, four would quickly gain the wealth belonging to the other two. Ability and luck cannot be denied as elements in accumulation. Nevertheless, economic growth provided an impetus to equality or inequality, depending on whether the poor gained relative to the rich, or vice versa.

VERIFICATION OF THE ADAMS HYPOTHESIS

I have made an estimate of the wealth distribution in the United States in 1798 by drawing a sample from the extant manuscripts of the census and coupling them with certain regional, state, and national aggregates compiled at the time. The sample included 25,975 persons and 43,245 pieces of property in 62 of the country's 359 counties. The sample was integrated with the population census of 1800 and the aggregates for the 687 tax districts.

The distribution of real estate in 1798 has intriguing attributes. First and foremost is the fact that 433,000—or almost exactly half, of America's 877,000 free males 21 and older—owned real estate. It is astounding to me that John Adams was correct in his curious assertion that property owners were a minority group, albeit by a very narrow margin. The self-interested position of property holders—a minority—was that there was a need for a senate whose members themselves had to be property holders. The distribution of wealth among property holders in 1798 yields the following shares:

N_{RE}, the Upper Proportion of Property Holders	A_{RE}, the Share of the N_{RE} Group
.01	.13
.10	.45
1.00	1.00
G_{RE}	.59

The top 10 percent of adult male wealth holders held almost half of all wealth. The top 5 percent controlled almost a third of wealth. This is substantial inequality. It is true that the top 1 percent did not account for half of all wealth, as would have been expected in a country having a landed nobility. Yet 5 percent is not too far removed from 1 percent. We indeed experienced significant inequality in this country.

Inequality of wealth was greater in urban areas than in rural, greater in the South compared to the North, and in the South, greater in areas closer to the coast than in the hinterland. There is good reason to believe that inequality of wealth in 1798 differed little from that in 1850 or 1860. The relative distribution of wealth among U.S. wealth holders may have remained essentially constant in the first two generations of the nineteenth century. The proportion owning property did decrease from .49 or .50 in 1800 to between .43 and .47 by 1850. Finally, we must accept the Adams hypothesis rather than the Franklin hypothesis, on the basis of the 1798 data. The Gini coefficient for wealth in real estate, considering all adult free males, was about .80 in 1798.

The statistics indicate that there was significant inequality. It was accepted as reasonable, acceptable, and natural in a society that offered personal liberty and accommodated many differing talents. James Madison reported that Alexander Hamilton poignantly stated the proposition on the floor of the Constitutional Convention on June 26, 1787. He paraphrased Hamilton as saying that "it was certainly true that nothing like an equality would exist as long as liberty existed, and that it would unavoidably result from that very liberty itself. This inequality of property constituted the great and fundamental distinction in Society."[7] Timothy Dwight, president of Yale, felt that inequality levels were quite reasonable.

The plenty which I have mentioned has in every period abounded here, with hardly an exception. A scarcity of food has been rarely known, a famine never. This plenty, and indeed the wealth generally, has been more equally distributed than in any other country and, *as equally as probably can be* [the emphasis is mine], amid the present unequal endowments, and exertions, of men. The number of public poor, it is presumed, is not greater than one, out of four hundred, of the inhabitants, a fact equally uncommon and delightful.[8]

Perhaps inequality of wealth was accepted as long as it was not manifested in wealth in consumer durables. In 1799, an editorial in a Philadelphia magazine addressed itself to this issue:

> Equality is a Farce. In the State of Virginia (that state whose citizens are so much famed for their love of *equality* and their simplicity of manners) there are pleasure carriages no less than *three thousand one hundred and thirty nine*. . . . While there is so large a sum of *bona fide* debts still due to the English merchants this expressive stile of living is not quite in character; and totally irreconcilable with Virginia's high toned republicanism.[9]

COMPARISONS BETWEEN EUROPE AND AMERICA

Inequality of wealth in America was accepted largely because it was so much less than in Europe. Did it matter if the top 1 percent of males held 13 percent of wealth in this country when the top 1 percent in Europe held a vastly greater percentage of the total? The prevailing wisdom today concerning the comparative distribution of wealth is that the landed nobility caused the enormous difference between rich and poor. But what are the facts in the case? The extent of landownership was America's outstanding achievement. Half of males 21 and older owned land. The proportion owning property (POP) was 29 percent in Sweden, 24 percent in Denmark, about 10 percent in England, and only 3 percent in Scotland. With such maldistribution, it is no wonder that the emigration rate was so high for Scotland, and later, for Sweden.

America's top wealth holder in 1798 was Elias Hasket Derby, whose inventoried estate totaled $990,882, or about .16 percent of the wealth in the country. Probably George Washington was the second or third wealthiest, with an estate valued at about half of Derby's. The richest man in England at the time, the duke of Bedford, held only .07 percent of his country's wealth, less than the share held by Derby, but his country's population was three times as large. The wealthiest man in Sweden at the time was Count Carl Bonde, who held 1.3 percent of his country's wealth—a share almost ten times as great as Derby's. A study of eight countries shows that Derby's share was not completely out of line, by European standards.

To study the top several hundred wealth holders in various countries is perhaps misleading, since countries varied in size of population.[10] It is better in this situation to study percentage shares at the end of the eighteenth century in each country. (See table 89.) In America a much greater proportion of the labor force owned wealth than was the case in the other countries listed in table 89. Within the wealth holder group, America's rich owned a smaller share; only Norway's POP and Finland's wealth holder shares approached the U.S. configuration.

Another aspect of wealth holding is shown by the data derived from the Swedish census of 1805. One remarkable enumeration classified people in four categories, as shown in table 90. The rich accumulated savings of $500 or more during the year. The somewhat rich had positive saving. The poor were not able to save, and the destitute needed help to survive. No wealth averages for each class were given in the census, but they can be approximated from other data. Let me take some liberties by using the averages of column 2; these yield the known overall mean wealth and follow a lognormal scheme similar to the actual Swedish situation. The figures in the column show a geometric progression, with each average being 40 times the average of the class below it. The results state, in effect, that the average wealth of the destitute (in U.S. currency) was 11 cents, and of the poor, $4—little more than enough to rent, but not to own, a cabbage patch and a cottage.

What might have been the scheme in America at the time? The idea can be conveyed by using the means in column 3 along with the proportions in column 1. These are designed to yield the overall mean and the inequality

TABLE 89

DISTRIBUTION OF WEALTH IN THE UNITED STATES AND FIVE EUROPEAN
COUNTRIES, LATE EIGHTEENTH CENTURY

The Top Proportion of Wealth Holders $(N_W)^a$	Proportion of Wealth Held (A_W)					
	United States	Denmark	Sweden	Norway	Finland	Scotland
.01	.13	.43	.31	.33	.19	.24
.10	.45	.80	.65	.65	.46	.64
1.00	1.00	1.00	1.00	1.00	1.00	1.00
Proportion owning property	.49	.24	.29	.38	.23	.22

Sources: Tables 8 and 54.
a. Males 21 and older.

TABLE 90
DISTRIBUTION OF WEALTH IN SWEDEN AND THE UNITED STATES, 1805

	Proportion of Families	Assumed Average Wealth (roughly approximating the wealth distribution)	
	Sweden (1)	Sweden (2)	United States (3)
Rich	.03	$7,060.00	$12,500
Somewhat rich	.26	176.00	1,000
Poor	.55	4.40	80
Destitute	.17	.11	6
Mean		$258	$708
Inequality, G		.924	.796

Sources: Tables 9 and 54.

coefficient for the American real estate distribution and to form a geometric progression; this time each class mean is 12 times the size of its predecessor and the distribution may better approximate the total estate than do real estate distributions.

The rough schemes for the two countries convey the notion that the "destitute" in America were as well off as the "poor" in Sweden. More startling is the possibility that the "poor" in America may have been almost as well off, or half as well off, as the "somewhat rich" of Sweden. It is at the next level that the scheme breaks down. The "somewhat rich" of America certainly did not have the standards of the "rich" of Sweden! Nevertheless, the richest Americans may very well have had estates having market values as large as estate values of the rich of Sweden. Only very few would have had more in Sweden than they would have had in the United States. To anyone seeing the manor houses and grounds owned by Count Carl Bonde, it is most evident that they far surpassed in magnificence Washington's Mount Vernon.

COLONIALISM AND INDEPENDENCE, 1770–1798

To understand American inequality in 1800 is to appreciate the dynamic changes taking place with the Revolution, the casting off of the colonial framework, and the development of a new government. Was the inequality of wealth in America in 1798 a new phenomenon? Was inequality the same as it was a generation earlier, or had new factors arising with nationhood generated a higher level of inequality than the United States had previously experienced? Developments after ratification of the Constitution led some citizens to become highly agitated. They felt that the assumption of state and federal debts in 1790, the speculation in government securities associated with the debt, and the development of banking all created a moneyed group that had not existed before. The strong speculations in land fueled feelings that a paper-moneyed class was arising in America.

Investigating the various factors influencing changes taking place between 1770–1774 and 1798, particularly as they might influence inequality, helps us to understand the situation in 1800. I have divided factors into three categories: those tending to enhance equality, those stimulating inequality, and those tending to perpetuate colonial levels of inequality.

After the Revolution, Loyalists' estates had been confiscated, a step that tended to decrease inequality. One estimate shows that there were about 2,200 of these estates with a mean value 20 times as large as that owned by all wealth holders. A rough calculation reveals that a G for all wealth holders of .6 is cut to .57 if this top group is eliminated (or redistributed, as was the remainder of wealth), a significant move toward equality. The share held by the top 1 percent would drop from 13 percent to 9 percent, according to this calculation.

The elimination of primogeniture and entailed estates could have had a significant effect in decreasing inequality in each generation. A calculation based on New Jersey data shows that an estate distribution with a G of .700 would climb to .708 if inheritances were distributed equally, to .719 if the eldest son had a double share, and to .941 with primogeniture. There seems to be little evidence, however, that actual inheritance procedures changed in the generation preceding 1800 or that primogeniture was at all prevalent in the United States. The elimination of primogeniture in intestate cases after the war, which occurred in about half of the states, could have been significant in breaking up some large estates, but little change would have taken place by 1798.

Jameson has argued that because potential settlers were kept east of the Alleghenies by British policy, elimination of the restriction against westward settlement after the war enhanced equality in property holding. I have studied the long-run trends in the numbers of land warrants and patents issued in Pennsylvania from 1670 to 1820 and find little evidence of a discontinuity connected with the Revolution. There was a surge in the amount of acreage granted, but this had little impact on the basic distribution of wealth in the state.

The elimination of British colonial rule, the establishment of state and federal constitutions, and finally, the demise of the Federalist party and the rise of the Republican party have been seen by some writers as having a strong positive influence on political equality. Whether this period can be seen as encouraging economic equality is another matter. Tocqueville in the 1830s felt that government in the new nation was run by the poor, to the detriment of the rich. Perhaps passage of the Northwest Ordinance in 1787 can be considered a step toward equality. Perhaps the First Direct tax, with its strongly progressive tax rate, is an indication of the trend. On the other hand, the increased liberty it made possible could have stimulated inequality by allowing each individual to give full expression to his talents. Certainly the comments of Alexander Hamilton and Timothy Dwight, cited above, expressed no fear, and Hamilton thought in terms of a tradeoff between equality and liberty. Dwight felt that a mixture of equality coupled with the inequality created by differences in individual acumen and effort produced unhampered economic activity throughout the land.

Let me now turn to some of the factors tending to increase inequality. The assumption of the debt by the government distressed many individuals who had sold their certificates for as little as 10 or 15 cents on the dollar. By 1792, there was a relatively small group in America owning perhaps as much as $32 million in federal debt. This situation prompted James Callender to state in 1798, "The corruptions of Philadelphia paper-jobbing [had arisen because it was Congress] who voted for the law, with a single view of enriching themselves."[11] Such a position was extreme. At the outside, possibly 8,000 people owned the $32 million. If this group is assumed also to be at the top of the distribution of wealth in land, housing, and slaves, inequality increases from .592 to .608. Its quantitative effect on increasing inequality is about two-thirds of the effect of decreasing inequality caused by confiscation of Loyalist estates.

I investigated the manipulation in land warrants arising with payments to soldiers and officers who had served during the Revolution. The division of military land in several districts in Ohio demonstrated inequality levels similar to those of wealth holders further East. Thus, the system perpetuated the variation already in place. Inequalities arising from the disruptions of war such as the loss of crops, barns, and farm animals by some individuals and not by others, undoubtedly augmented inequality. An extreme calculation in this respect illustrates the magnitude of such a change. Randomly halving or doubling the wealth of half of property holders in 1798 increased inequality from .592 to about .70.

Factors tending to maintain inequality from 1770 to 1798 include life-cycle patterns, inheritance, and slavery. The average wealth of those age

20–29, 30–39, 40–49, and 50–99 was roughly the same in New England in 1774, in Franklin County, Pennsylvania, in 1821, and in rural America in both 1850 and 1860. The life-cycle pattern is reimposed each generation, in part by the inheritance mechanism. A model of the timing of inheritances of sons from their fathers demonstrates this proposition concerning the life-cycle variation. An additional model of inheritances of children, traced for several generations, demonstrates that a large family can cause increased inequality at the frontier, unless children having access to less than a minimum number of acres moved further west or to a city, and the average number of children per family decreases. Finally, the relative distribution of slaves remained remarkably constant in the eighteenth century, as demonstrated by the South Carolina data.

What do all these factors amount to in the end? A comparison between the 1798 family distribution and distributions for net wealth and total physical wealth in 1774, as measured by Alice Hanson Jones, shows mixed results: The figures in table 91 demonstrate some increase in inequality, but measurement and sampling error could account for at least some of the differences.

Another perspective can be obtained from the complete enumeration of real estate in Massachusetts and Maine in 1771, an area that held one-fourth of the North's population. (See table 92.) The proportion owning property was almost identical in the two years. A plot of the Lorenz curves demonstrates no appreciable differences in inequality. Relative inequality *between* regions in Massachusetts would have been less than that between all regions in the North. What little difference there was in Gini coefficients can be explained by the fact that Massachusetts and Maine should be expected to be more homogeneous than all northern states, taken together.

TABLE 91
DISTRIBUTION OF WEALTH IN THE UNITED STATES, 1774 AND 1798

The Top Proportion of All Families (N_W)	Proportion of Wealth Held by the N_W Group (A_W)	
	1798	1774
.01	.19	.13–.15
.10	.58	.51–.55
1.00	1.00	1.00
Inequality, G	.75	.63–.73

Source: Table 69.

Thus wealth in real estate did not change in the North during the generation. It is not likely to have changed in the South, given the dominance of slavery, an institution perpetuating constant relative inequality.

In summary, my investigations of the inequality of wealth in the United States show strong inequality in 1798, with about half of adult males having wealth, and with the Gini coefficient for wealth holders being about .6. Little change in economic inequality took place from 1771 to 1798 or between 1798 and 1860. Possibly, there was a slight increase in inequality in the latter period, since the proportion of people owning property did decrease a little during the two generations between 1800 and 1860. Nevertheless, my working hypothesis is, and has been for the past four years, that inequality of wealth in America remained fairly constant for the century preceding the Civil War. If the Civil War wrought little change in inequality among free men, then the Revolutionary War is not likely to have produced much change either. The relative wealth pattern was rather impervious to new institutional relationships.

DISTRIBUTIONS OF HOUSING AND INCOME

A second theme of this monograph concerns a different aspect of inequality, namely, housing consumption and inequality of income. It

TABLE 92

DISTRIBUTION OF WEALTH IN REAL ESTATE IN MASSACHUSETTS AND
MAINE IN 1771 AND IN THE NORTH IN 1798

Proportion of Property Owners (N_w)	Proportion of Wealth Holders (A_w)	
	Massachusetts and Maine, 1771	*North, 1798*
.01	.103	.116
.10	.456	.424
1.00	1.000	1.000
Mean value	£117	$1,605
Inequality, G	.538	.574
Proportion owning property	.486	.487

Source: Massachusetts Tax Valuation Records, 1771, Bettye Pruitt, Principal Investigator, Inter-University Consortium for Political and Social Research (Ann Arbor: University of Michigan, 1980), ICPSR 7734, table 7.

focuses more on the economic well-being of families or individuals at the median or even at the mode of a distribution of all persons in the labor force. The value of each house in America, in 1798, can tell us not only about those living in mansions, but a great deal about how an ordinary, or even a poor, family lived. We can draw inferences about the incomes of families from the housing data.

The value of the dwelling in which a person lives provides a broader perspective into his well-being than does the value of his real estate. The term "wealth" really tells us only about the rich, since they control so much of it. If 10 percent of wealth holders control 50 percent of wealth, there is little to be learned about the other 90 percent by studying that elite group. Those at the median of the income distribution usually have very little wealth. Housing or income brings into better focus the fortunes of rich, compared to the poor, of the 10th percentile as well as the 90th percentile.

The 1798 census of housing begins with the passage of a bill in Congress calling for a very progressive tax on housing value. A house was a symbol of affluence in a wider sense than land, buildings, and personal estate. A house was a proxy for what a person would or could devote to his personal consumption; more broadly, the house reflected his ability to earn an income. The value was much more than a count of windows or doors; it was a reflection of size, materials, and location. It is quite possible that elasticity of housing value with respect to income ($E_{DHV,Y}$) was 1, or even greater than 1, in our new country. A poor person may have lived in a very rude log cabin. As his income increased by a certain percentage, he may have increased the value of his housing by an even greater percentage.

The earliest housing figures in America take the form of an estimate of the distribution of dwelling house values dated May 1798. This remarkable estimate, prepared under the direction of a most gifted statistician, Oliver Wolcott, was an expression of peoples' beliefs about the conditions of the rich and the poor in our land prior to the generation of any national statistics. Wolcott's estimate was that housing values formed a configuration showing very substantial inequality—a distribution with a G of .65–.70, and one that can be duplicated with a lognormal table with the same coefficient. The distribution was unimodal, and had both an upper and lower tail. It was a skewed curve, with a mode below the median. The fact that there was so much inequality in house values is the truly outstanding feature. And this was from an estimate prepared by an individual who was politically aligned with Hamilton.

DISTRIBUTION OF HOUSING VALUES

Did the statistics derived from the housing census that began in September 1798 corroborate Wolcott's prediction? Uncannily, the answer is yes. Wolcott was off a bit on the mean, but the inequality coefficient, as I have determined it, was between .65 and .70, depending on a continuity adjustment factor. Wolcott knew, of course, the range of housing values. The most conspicuous was the mansion being built for Elias Hasket Derby, in Salem, with a value of between $35,000 to $40,000. The houses owned by William Bingham and Alexander Baring of Philadelphia also were well known. Wolcott also must have seen some very rude log cabins worth, at most, $10, on his trips between Philadelphia and Connecticut.

What was the actual distribution of the value of America's 577,000 homes? I have coupled a sample of 40,000 dwellings with the known totals for 10 tax classes. Its mean was $262, its median was $96, and its mode was the surprisingly low value of $8. Many dwellings were valued at less than $10, indicating that there were many Americans living in very crude hovels. Some had been built in a day or so and had neither windows nor flooring. Owning a dwelling valued at no more than $5 was a distinct possibility in an age when daily wages for laborers were about 50 cents, and wood was abundant. The full distribution is given in table 93.

The fact that urban housing had greater value surely reflects more than the physical attributes of town dwellings. Statements at the time noted that a given house would cost three times as much in an urban area as in a rural

TABLE 93
U.S. HOUSING VALUES IN 1798

	No. of Dwellings in Class		
Dwelling House Value	*All*	*Rural*	*Urban*
$10,000 and over	182	41	141
1,000–9,999	27,868	10,780	17,088
100–999	254,870	226,474	28,396
10–99	244,805	241,990	2,815
1–9	49,073	49,045	28
Total	576,798	528,330	48,468
Mean Value	$262	181	1,150
Inequality, G	.706	.655	.564

Source: Table 10.

setting. Yet the values cannot be dismissed as unimportant. An older person may have been blocked, in effect, from moving to a town or city because of the high cost of houses there. An inheritor of an urban home may have inherited the equivalent value of a farm dwelling and the farm itself.

The data indicate surprising inequality in housing in 1798. This we can say because the distribution of dwelling house values in 1980 is significantly more equal, with a G of .4 instead of .7. Stated otherwise, the transformation $DHV_{1980} = k(DHV_{1798})^{.5}$, where k is a constant, adequately describes the change between the 1798 distribution to the relatively more equal distribution of today. The fact that the coefficient is the square root means that values of \$10 and \$1,000 in 1798 could have their counterparts in houses worth \$10,000 and \$100,000 today. New York State housing data for 1798 and for the 1865 New York State census indicate that some decreases in inequality took place even during the first two generations of the nineteenth century.

INEQUALITY OF INCOME

In the data there is a strong implication that the economic well-being of Americans is much more homogeneous today than it was two centuries ago. While a distribution of *housing* values is not the same as an *income* distribution, the former may not be far removed from the latter. Table 94 estimates the distribution of income among U.S. families in 1798, assuming the elasticity of housing with respect to income ($E_{DHV,Y}$) was 1.0 and 1.2. It is assumed also that a \$35,000 income remained at \$35,000 in moving from the first distribution to the second. Thus, lower incomes have been raised, with the idea that low housing values understated income. The two means imply aggregate incomes encompassing those suggested for 1800, as estimated by Robert Gallman and Paul David.[12] My two income distributions show much more inequality than the 1980 distribution of income in the United States. The Gini coefficient for income is about .42, not the .63–.71, as suggested by the 1798 housing values. This is, then, evidence that Tocqueville's dictum has continued to operate. Inequality of condition in the United States has continued to decrease over the very long run.

INEQUALITY BETWEEN REGIONS

An initial step toward understanding the significant level of inequality in 1798 may be obtained by studying inequality at the regional level. In

TABLE 94
DISTRIBUTION OF U.S. FAMILY INCOME, 1798: TWO ESTIMATES

Dwelling House Value	Elasticity of Housing Values with Respect to Income	
	$E_{DHV,Y} = 1.0$	$E_{DHV,Y} = 1.2$
$10,000 and over	128	352
1,000–9,999	25,000	73,000
100–999	280,000	318,000
10–99	318,000	229,000
1–9	93,000	14,000
Total	715,000	715,000
Mean Value	$211	427
Inequality, G	.711	.631

Sources: Tables 13 and G (appendix 8), and ch. 3, n. 17.

New York, Georgia, and South Carolina variability was greatest among all states, with inequality coefficients of .76, .77, and .83. The manors and plantations existed in part because of primogeniture and entail. South Carolina, for example, codified the common law of England in 1712, and primogeniture was not abolished in that state until 1791. Connecticut, a smaller state with a relatively homogeneous rural economy, had the lowest degree of inequality, with G = .52.

Inequalities in dwelling values can be ascertained in almost incredible detail for each of the 687 tax districts and 359 counties of the United States in 1798, as shown below:

Inequality, G	No. of Districts	No. of Counties
.70–.89	72	63
.50–.69	350	223
.30–.49	257	72
.10–.29	8	1

These data in themselves indicate that there was strong inequality in the dispersion of inequality. Some areas were very homogeneous and others quite diverse in economic condition. The data illustrate how studies of disparities only in individual counties may be quite misleading.

248 / DISTRIBUTION OF WEALTH AND INCOME

The 1798 dwelling data probably provide the best test of the Turner thesis as it applies to economic conditions in the eighteenth and nineteenth centuries. Frederick Jackson Turner argued that the frontier was a force that produced equality in America: "The frontier strips off the garments of civilization and arrays him [the settler] in hunting shirt and moccasin."[13] Based on Turner's thinking, we would expect to find less dispersion, the further west one moved from the coast. The facts prove quite the contrary for the 687 tax districts:

$$G_{DHV} = .47 + .00080 \text{ MILE6,}$$
$$(.00005)$$

where MILE6 is the distance between the area and the nearest of six major east coast cities. Every mile of distance from an urban center was a factor augmenting inequality. An area 100 miles distant showed an inequality level of .55, and not .47. I must admit that a paradox appears to exist. Inequality would have been larger on the coast had there been no frontier as an avenue for escape.

FACTORS IN DWELLING AND INCOME INEQUALITY

We must address ourselves to the fundamental reasons why inequality was so large in 1798. The many factors I have discussed to explain the inequality of wealth obviously are applicable, particularly since they focus on the economic conditions of the rich. A forefeited Loyalist estate involved the potential elimination of a rich person from a distribution. The termination of primogeniture meant that an intestate estate would be more equally divided. The ability to buy government securities at 10 cents on the dollar, shortly before the securities rose above par, was a new governmental action that could create, rather rapidly, a group owning sizable personal wealth. Left unanalyzed are those institutional changes affecting also ordinary individuals, people near the median or even those closer toward the mode, individuals whose wealth was but a bagatelle.

Regions of the country were relatively isolated from each other in 1798; communication facilities were at a minimum. Ordinary individuals had access only to local stores, traders, and businesses that operated under conditions of monopoly. (It is doubtful whether the variation in inequality among the 687 districts in 1850 would have been as great as it was in 1798.) The disparity in average land values in the 359 counties in 1798 was significantly larger than the disparity for the 748 counties in the same 18 states in 1850. Road improvements, the building of canals and railroads, and the development of the postal system and even the telegraph all worked to destroy monopolies of position and knowledge and, thus, tended to promote equality.

There was great diversity in land quality, even within types, such as meadowland, plowed land, mowing and clear pasture, bog meadow mowed and unmowed, bush pasture, and first-, second-, and third-rate unenclosed land. Such a wide range provided a great diversity in the return to owners or laborers in 1798. Variation in weather conditions also caused differences in farm incomes within the various counties and states. Seasonal variation meant that a laborer might be unemployed four or five months of a year, particularly in colder climates. The diversity imposed by nature, such as types and slopes of terrain, the vicissitudes of the weather, and the very strong seasonal variation during the 12 months of the year all contributed to a diversity in income in 1798 that was quite significant. After the onset of the factory revolution, many of these disparities were no longer factors influencing distributions. To be sure, there were strikes that caused disruptions in a laborer's work year, but most strikes were of short duration, less than four months out of each year.

TRADITIONALISM

The claim is made that the U.S. economy of 1800 was quite traditional; most people were engaged in farming and did about the same thing each year. Trade cycles and disruptions allegedly were rather insignificant, compared to those a half century later; there was no basis for dynamic changes that would produce inequality. So runs the argument explaining why inequality should not have been large in 1798 relative to a later period. Yet the Revolution did generate disparities. Farm buildings were destroyed; farm animals were fewer in number in 1788 than in 1779 in some states. The Federal City exploded from an idea, in 1788, to an area, in 1798, whose aggregate housing value was 2.5 times the housing value for the state of Tennessee. America indeed was a country of dynamic growth.

An element introducing significant inequality among ordinary people was illiteracy. Signatures and X-marks on army enlistment papers reveal the extent of this handicap. A sample of 1,800 records shows the following rates of illiteracy:

	1799–1829	1830–1895
Farmers	.46	.28
Laborers	.54	.30
All	.42	.21

Low-income persons were severely handicapped by their inability to read broadsides and newspapers, so that there was a monopoly for literate persons in learning about opportunities for economic improvement. (This monopoly on information weakened after 1800 and was reduced even further after 1830.)

The opportunity to obtain land was greatly enhanced after 1798 when the price of government land dropped. In addition, regulations provided for a decrease in minimum size requirements for the purchasers. Some idea of the degree of inequality engendered by land grants after 1800 can be shown with the following data for Illinois:

	No. of Owners	Inequality, G, in Acreage Granted
1814–1834	72,000	.57
1840–1854	91,000	.59
1855–1899	38,000	.52

The coefficients are reminiscent of those for real estate in the United States in 1798 and, indeed, for Massachusetts and Maine in 1771. The distribution of land in the North maintained rather constant inequality for a century. For the South, slavery created a similar situation.

The factors presented above do not describe adequately the economic activities of lower-income groups in as much depth as I would like. I wish I had access to other information similar to the data on illiteracy from the army records. The army data have an additional variable, the heights of all soldiers, which form a strong lognormal curve; literacy and height were positively correlated. Investigations of mortality rates could prove to be an important source in the study of the distribution of income. For example, the 1805 census data for Sweden demonstrate a significant correlation between the proportions of poor in a county and its mortality rate.

The one solid fact available for those people below the median income level is that their housing distribution varied remarkably. About 8 or 9 percent of American families in 1798 owned housing below the modal value. The mode is significant in the demarcation of a relatively deprived group. These are in the minority; there are more persons above them, on a density-per-dollar basis. But America definitely had a poor group.

INEQUALITY OF WEALTH VERSUS INEQUALITY OF INCOME

It is important to distinguish between the periods of study and the comparisons that have been presented in this volume when considering inequalities in U.S. wealth and income. We have observed the following trends in inequality:

	1771–1774 to 1798	*1798 to 1850–1860*	*1798–1980*
Wealth, in real estate	Constant, or slight increase	Constant, or slight increase	Unknown (constant?)
Income	Unknown	Slight decrease	Strong decrease

Inequality among wealth holders remained rather constant from 1771 to 1860. The proportion of persons with real estate decreased a little, but personal estate may have been a countervailing factor. I have been unable to compare the distribution of wealth in 1798 with comparable data for today because I did not have the distribution of personal estate for 1798. Data for real estate and slave values in Maryland do provide a guide for the effects of personal estate, however. This experience indicates that the inequality, G, for total estate in the country among families was about .75. A federal study of the inequality of wealth in 1962 reported a coefficient of .76. It is quite possible, therefore, that overall wealth inequality in 1798 was about the same as it was in 1962. If this is true, then the inequality of wealth has remained rather constant in the United States during the last two centuries.

Inequality of income may have decreased a little from 1798 to 1860. At least, this is my judgment, based on housing data for the state of New York. More intriguing is the comparison of inequality in 1798 with today, over a period of almost two centuries. Inequality of wealth appears to be at least as strong in 1980 as it was in 1798. By contrast, income is much more equally distributed now than in 1798, as judged from housing data. How inequality in income could change so drastically toward equality while inequality in wealth remained at a constant level is a question with complex ramifications. The importance of capital to income offers one avenue for studying the matter. The ratio of private individual wealth to individual income may have lessened slightly over the last two centuries. The return on capital was less in 1962 than it was in 1798. More significant is the fact that nonhuman wealth has been owned by a relatively small group in any generation. A reshuffling of shares owned at the top does not have an important bearing on income distribution below the 70th percentile. Changes in income distribution below the median are of little importance in the Lorenz curve describing the distribution of nonhuman wealth.

That the income distribution has lessened in inequality over the last two centuries is of major importance. Alexis de Tocqueville was correct in asserting a tendency that has continued, at least in America. "There is greater equality of condition in Christian countries at the present day than there has been at any previous time, in any part of the world, so that the magnitude of what already has been done prevents us from foreseeing what is yet to be accomplished."[14]

To conclude, the main finding of this monograph is that there was surprising inequality of wealth and income in our country at the end of the eighteenth century. Three possible levels of inequality seem to present themselves. They can be stated, with some possible ranges for inequality of wealth and income for free adult males in 1798, as follows:

	Wealth	*Income*
Modest inequality	$G = .5-.7$	$G = .4-.59$
Substantial inequality	.8	.6-.70
Very large inequality	.85-.95	.7 or more

Inequality in America has been found to be substantial in 1798. It was not extreme, as in Europe. Nor was it as egalitarian, perhaps, as Tocqueville suggested. Yet it was considerable.

Appendixes
Notes
Index

APPENDIX 1

The Pitkin Table of U.S. Aggregate Wealth in 1798

TABLE A
A General View of the Assessment and Apportionment of the Direct Tax, Laid by the Acts of Congress of July 9th and July 14th, 1798

	Land		Dwelling Houses		Slaves
	No. of Acres	*Valuation*	*N*	*Valuation*	*N*
New Hampshire	3,749,061	$ 19,028,108.03	11,142	$ 4,146,938.90	—
Massachusetts	7,831,028	59,445,642.64	48,984	24,546,826.46	—
Rhode Island	565,844	8,082,355.21	7,034	2,984,002.87	143
Connecticut	2,649,149	40,163,955.34	23,565	3,149,479.28	654
Vermont	4,918,722	15,165,484.02	5,437	1,558,389.36	—
New York	16,414,510	74,885,075.69	33,416	25,495,631.39	9,994
New Jersey	2,788,282	27,287,981.89	19,624	9,149,918.84	2,433
Pennsylvania	11,959,865	72,824,852.60	51,772	29,321,048.33	1,100
Delaware	1,074,105	4,053,246.42	5,094	2,180,165.83	3,125
Maryland	5,444,272	21,634,004.57	16,932	10,738,286.63	48,254
Virginia	40,458,644	59,976,860.06	27,693	11,248,267.67	153,087
North Carolina	20,956,467	27,909,479.70	11,760	2,932,893.09	59,968
South Carolina	9,772,587	12,456,720.94	6,427	5,008,292.93	65,586
Georgia	13,534,159	10,263,506.95	3,446	1,797,631.25	27,704
Kentucky	17,674,634	20,268,325.07	3,339	1,139,765.13	15,820
Tennessee	3,951,357	5,847,662.00	1,030	286,446.83	5,351
Total N	163,746,686		276,659		393,219
Total Valuation		479,293,263.13		140,683,984.79	

Source: Timothy Pitkin, *A Statistical View of the Commerce of the United States* (1816; rpt. New York: Augustus Kelley, 1967), pp. 377–78.

Note: Subtotals for Maine and Massachusetts (net of Maine) are: acres, 3,839,655 and 3,991,373; land valuation, 13,367,115 and 42,220,217; dwellings, 8,998 and 41,449; dwelling valuation, 2,930,512 and 22,072,703 (Genealogical Society of Boston). Exempt from valuation and taxation were 17.8 million acres and 1,545 dwellings located largely in Maine and western Pennsylvania. (Maine was part of Massachusetts at this time.) Not shown here is an important part of the table stating tax yields separately for lands, dwellings, and slaves for each state.

Appendix 2

Assessed and Market Prices in 1798

The Wolcott inventory of real estate was made by using market prices, a sharp contrast with the practices in at least a few states with assessed values traditionally lower than market values. As secretary of the treasury, Oliver Wolcott worried about this problem and asked officials in his home state in 1798 to make a study of the matter. Among his correspondence there exists a remarkable paper listing the large number of cases he induced the commissioners to uncover. Assessment-to-sale ratios, shown in table B, were largely .80 to .90, and we can consider that the assessment values in our study are about 15 percent less than actual values. We must admire the entire procedure because over 2,500 workdays were spent by commissioners in Connecticut alone to ensure the fairness of the values.

TABLE B
LAND SALES AND TAX VALUATIONS
FOR 518 PROPERTIES IN CONNECTICUT, 1798

	No. of Sales	Amount of Sale	Valuation	Ratio of Valuation to Sale Price
Granby and Hartland	10	$ 3,735	$ 2,527	.67
Symsbury	10	3,587	3,639	1.01
Hebron	9	11,445	11,429	1.00
New Haven and East Haven	15	19,024	17,176	.91
Milford	21	7,018	6,174	.88
Derby	25	9,164	8,197	.89
Waterbury and Wolcott	17	5,674	4,360	.76
Cheshire	10	2,856	2,289	.80

TABLE B *(continued)*

	No. of Sales	*Amount of Sale*	*Valuation*	*Ratio of Valuation to Sale Price*
Hamden and Woodbridge	11	2,871	2,505	.88
Wallingford and North				.84
Haven	8	2,693	2,253	
Branford	21	7,957	5,423	.68
Guilford	22	6,275	5,680	.91
Durham and Haddam	38	16,280	12,195	.75
Middletown	28	19,612	13,375	.69
Chatham	19	10,107	6,922	.69
East Haddam	21	8,674	7,926	.91
Killingworth	16	5,459	4,087	.75
New London and Montville	18	18,429	14,465	.78
Norwich and Bozrah	15	13,004	13,297	1.02
Stonington	7	14,356	8,775	.61
Colchester	13	9,638	7,863	.82
Windham and Hampton	11	6,615	6,942	1.04
Lebanon	16	22,908	20,215	.88
Killingly and Thompson	13	14,072	12,075	.85
Stafford and Union	25	13,348	19,090	.76
Fairfield and Weston	44	30,108	26,667	.88
Norwalk	14	19,374	16,895	.88
Stamford	22	30,556	19,644	.64
Greenwich	20	21,018	18,562	.82
All	518	355,857	300,642	.845

Source: Wolcott Papers, Connecticut Historical Society, Hartford.

APPENDIX 3

Samuel Blodgett's Estimates of Wealth in 1805

Samuel Blodgett, one of America's early statisticians, made estimates of the wealth of the United States for 1805 that look very similar, in some respects to Pitkin's estimates. It can be noted first that Blodgett knew the intimate details of the 1798 tax. He had paid a tax of $278.25 on valuations of $38,551 in land and $19,000 in housing (including a tax of $105 on his own dwelling, which was valued at $15,000).

His 1805 estimates for land values in the United States (excluding the Louisiana Purchase, but including the Northwest Territory) are shown in table C. Blodgett's top two land entries in the table, with a total of 170 million acres, reach a total very similar to Pitkin's 163 million figure. Blodgett's average of about $3.50 for this group is a little larger than the $2.92 average of Pitkin's table for the 17 states, but is, curiously, close to the $3.51 Pitkin average for the 14 states. Blodgett's average house value is $49 larger than Pitkin's for the 17 states, presumably because it includes the value of tools, implements, and furniture, and because of the fact that prices probably were a little higher.

TABLE C
SAMUEL BLODGETT'S ESTIMATE OF AGGREGATE WEALTH, 1805,
AND TIMOTHY PITKIN'S ESTIMATES, 1798

	Blodgett		Pitkin		
	No. of Acres	Price	No. of States	No. of Acres	Average Price
"Lands"	20,000,000	$6.00	17	163,746,686	$ 2.93
Adjoining and near-cultivated lands	150,000,000	3.50	14	119,483,473	3.504
Residue of all lands	451,000,000	2.00			
	No. of Habitations	Price	No. of States	No. of Dwellings	Average Price
Habitations and apparel with shops, implements, tools, furniture	1,000,000	$360	14	490,271[a]	$311
Slaves	1,000,000	$200	17	393,000[b]	$350
	No. of Families	Price	No. of States	No. of Families	Average Price
Other wealth in livestock, turnpikes, canals, bridges, mills, produce, tons shipping, specie, banks, and public buildings	1,000,000	$ 284			
Total wealth per family	1,000,000	$1,603[c]	17	684,357[d]	$1,130
			14	589,095	1,129

Sources: See tables 5 and A; Samuel Blodgett, *Economica: A Statistical Manual for the United States* (City of Washington, 1806), p. 196.

a. Includes dwellings valued less than $100, as described in chapters 2, 3, and appendix 13.

b. Slaves enumerated were in the age group 12–50, almost exactly half the total number. No formal slave price is suggested by the First Direct Tax schedule; the most likely average stems from the South Carolina tax law which was very close to market value because of perceived economic disparities between regions. The stated value was $150 from 1794 to 1798 and $200 in 1799 and 1800 (*The Statues at Large of South Carolina* [Columbia, 1874], 5:250–395). I have chosen to double the value of $175 for slaves age 12–50.

c. This figure does not include the 451 million acres valued at $2—that is, $2,505–902.

d. The number of free males age 26 and older in 1800 is used as the number of families.

APPENDIX 4

The Pitkin-Blodgett Estimates of Wealth in 113 Counties in 1798

The aggregate totals for the United States inventory of real estate in 1798 were reported by Timothy Pitkin in his publications dating from 1815 and 1832. These federal aggregates are of great merit and appear to be those used, earlier, by Samuel Blodgett in his 1805 estimates of wealth in the United States. We can be quite certain of their authenticity for 14 states, since the aggregates also exist, county by county, for 574 tax districts. In the cases of North Carolina, South Carolina, and Georgia, the evidence is much weaker, since valuations were not complete, at best, for three or four years after 1798. I have been unable to find any county totals for those states, except for a housing list for Georgia, and lists for individuals in one county in North Carolina and for two counties in Georgia. Nevertheless, there is reason to believe that the figures are reasonably accurate (the Pitkin table is given in table A, above). It is a most basic reference for the work in this book.

The Georgia list for housing, by county, found in a file at the U.S. National Archives, has a total exactly the same as in Pitkin's table ($1,797,631). The acreage aggregate for North Carolina is quite consistent with a state report in 1808 listing 20.03 million acres as the land taxable under state law. Similar results are found for South Carolina, where the state totals for 1800–1801 are 10.4 million acres. Thus, the 113 counties in the three states have subsets with totals for acreage and land corresponding to the Pitkin tables; it is also clear that the slave totals for the 113 counties revealed in the 1800 census are very highly correlated with Pitkin's totals.

APPENDIX 5

Further Description of the Wealth Sample Reported in Chapter 2

INEQUALITY FOR AREAS AND PERSONS

Some initial notions about inequality among persons may be derived from the area inequalities of table 5. Suppose there were a typical district or county in the United States in which half of the adult males had wealth (a property holder proportion, PHP, of .5) and that the other half owned nothing. Further, suppose that the distribution for those with wealth was lognormal, with $G = .6$. If we assume these parameters for all districts, then the distribution for the United States would appear as:

Within District	Between Districts	United States	United States
G(W>0)	G(W21)	G(W>0)	$G(W \geq 0) = PHP \times G(W>0) + 1 - PHP$
.6	.27	.64	$.82 = .5 \times .64 + .5$

These calculations were obtained by two methods: (1) A simulation was performed by generating a distribution of wealth among men in each county. In a county with 2,000 men, 1,000 had wealth, and the top man was assigned wealth equivalent to 2.8 percent of the aggregate for his county, since $(N_w, A_w) = (.001, .0287)$ for $G = .6$ in the lognormal table. Similar calculations were made at other levels, and the results for all counties were combined by means of a computer run to yield a national distribution with an inequality coefficient, $G = .822$. (2) The results may be approximated from a theorem dealing with the product of two lognormal variates that are independent of each other. If the one has a $G = .6$, and the other G = .27 (see table 5), then their product has a distribution with G = .64. (See Aitchison and Brown, *The Lognormal Distribution,* cited in table G.) It will be shown that the actual distribution in 1798 is not far removed from either the computer simulation or from the mathematical expression. The above two methods lean heavily on lognormal assumptions, configurations investigated in table 5 as well as in later tables. Even more basic to the calculations are the empirical results and statistics derived from the samples taken from the 62 counties.

MILEAGE FROM MAJOR CITIES

My samples had to be drawn from those extant sets I was able to find in various archives; to be sure, I do not claim that the data are representative of the country as a whole, particularly since they tend to overrepresent urban areas. However, a general framework is essential to understanding the sample. To construct such a framework, I first represented the 687 districts as seven distinct areas, as stated in tables 7 and D. Land and property values were strongly related to the three variables: urban/rural location, southern location, and the minimum distance from one of six major cities (Urban, South, MILE6). These are illustrated, in part, in table 7. I computed the distance (miles) of each district from New York City as

$$\text{MilesNYC} = \sqrt{6.0(\text{latitude} - 40.6)^2 + 5.0(\text{longtitude} - .74.0)^2},$$

using the latitude and longitude of the center of the county in which the district lay. The miles were also computed as distances from the county to Boston, Philadelphia, Baltimore, Norfolk, or Charleston. Of the six possible distances, the minimum was selected as the appropriate distance measure. The median minimum distance of about 80 miles was selected in classifying the districts listed in table D.

THE SAMPLE OF 62 COUNTIES

The main objective of the study was to obtain inequality measures for distribution of wealth among individuals, not the variation displayed in table D. I proceeded to gather as much information as I could about individuals and their wealth by going to all the various depositories throughout the country that conceivably would have manuscripts. Several years of endeavor produced information on the wealth of individuals for at least parts of the 62 counties described in table 6 and the seven regions

TABLE D

THE 687 U.S. DISTRICTS, CLASSIFIED BY AREA

Region Code	Region	Total Wealth	Total Wealth Minus Housing Valued over $100	White Males 21 and Older	Average Wealth	Inequal- ity, G	No. of Districts
	Rural North						
1	Within 80 miles	$225,285,257	$181,029,459	270,625	$832	.180	233
2	Outside 80	116,248,574	102,650,344	195,355	595	.209	153
	Rural South						
3	Within 80	67,563,290	50,995,977	92,804	728	.281	70
4	Outside 80	122,353,627	111,508,554	238,103	514	.300	181
	Urban North						
5	Within 80	78,665,705	31,575,660	71,336	1,103	.225	44
6	Outside 80	1,433,714	614,190	1,842	778	.028	2
	Urban South						
7	Within 80	9,588,235	1,906,232	7,688	1,247	.078	4
	All	621,138,405	480,280,416	877,756	708	.271	687

Source: See table 5. In the 50 urban areas adult free males owned an average of less than five acres. Southern states included Maryland, Delaware, Virginia, North Carolina, South Carolina, Georgia, Tennessee, and Kentucky. Distance was measured as the minimum miles to Boston, Philadelphia, Baltimore, Norfolk, or Charleston.

of table E. I then had to estimate the values of parameters for each of the regions in its entirety using the information for the extant counties. Some of these estimates are displayed in table E.

WEIGHTS IN THE DISPROPORTIONATE STRATIFIED SAMPLE OF WEALTH HOLDERS

Seven Areas

A further problem with my sample data has to do with disproportionate representation of the more urban tax districts and points to the vulnerability of county courthouses as repositories for priceless historical data. My weighting scheme, using 687 districts aligned into seven general areas, gives rise to an average dispersion profile consisting of a Lorenz curve with 22 points. These 22 points and arithmetic means for each area were

TABLE E
REAL WEALTH HOLDINGS IN SEVEN AREAS OF THE UNITED STATES, 1798

Region Code[a]	No. of Sample Counties	Size (1)	Mean (2)	Share of Top 1% (3)	Share of Top 10% (4)	Inequality, G (5)	Proportion Owner-Occupied[b] (6)
			An Average County in Each Region				
1	14	370	$1,411	.067	.344	.504	.904
2	19	190	745	.115	.423	.550	.873
3	10	878	1,375	.162	.519	.635	.789
4	5	511	660	.087	.389	.519	.940
5	11	431	1,208	.121	.432	.595	.960
6	2	422	745	.118	.399	.544	.989
7	1	561	1,482	.236	.615	.721	.872
All	62	424	1,084	.113	.422	.561	.892

Sources: See tables 5 and D.

Note: Unweighted averages of county statistics are shown above. Thus the 14 sample means in region 1 were divided by 14 to produce the mean of $1,411. Data are for real estate exclusive of housing valued at $100 or more (W−H) except in columns 2 through 6 in region 7, as derived from the total wealth enumeration (W) of Baltimore City. (The relative variation of columns 3 and 4 and other shares will be used as a proxy for relative variation in total wealth for each tax district in its region.)
  a. See table D.
  b. Owner-occupiers are wealth holders giving evidence of owning and occupying one of their properties; otherwise they rent or leave unoccupied all properties.

computed as simple arithmetic means based on the data from the sampled counties. An example of one point in the first Lorenz curve is the relative share of total wealth of the top 1 percent of wealth holders that was computed for each of the 14 sampled counties; I used the simple average of the 14 to represent the share of the top 1 percent of wealth holders for each of the 233 districts in the area;

$$A_{ik} = \sum_{j=1}^{14} A_{ijk}/14 = .067$$

where $i = .01$, $j = 1, 2, \ldots, 14$, and $k = 1$, an example from a total sample set with ($i = .001, .002, .005, .01, .02, \ldots, .09, 1.0$), ($j = 1, 2, \ldots, 62$), and $k = (1, 2, \ldots, 7)$, or the seven general areas. The arithmetic mean for real wealth among wealth holders in each area is computed as the simple mean of all the sample means of the area. (For example, the simple mean of the 14 sample means in the first area is $1,411.)[1]

687 Districts and Seven Lorenz Curves

Each of the 687 districts was assumed to have the characteristics of the average relative dispersion of its area. In the first area, this yields 233 districts, each with a Lorenz curve for wealth holders, as described by the 22 points. The number of persons having wealth in each district, NPH_{rk} ($r = 1,2, \ldots, 687$) was estimated by dividing total wealth by the sample mean wealth, where wealth excluded houses of $100 or more in value. Further elaboration of this measure is given in the notes to tables 7 and E.[2]

Finally, we have an estimate of the property holder proportion (PHP) for each district, which was computed as $PHP_{rk} = NPH_{rk}/M2199_{rk}$, where $M2199_{rk}$ was the number of adult males in the district. The procedures lead to a computer program of 687 Lorenz curves having 23 points, or 687 times 23 representations of property, weighted by adult population, including the 23 points for the number of classes having wealth in the county, NPH_{rk}, and a 23rd point representing those males with no wealth, $M2199_{rk} - NPH_{rk}$.

1. *Each* county's relative dispersion was considered, whether or not it had a large or small sample size. The average number of owners in a county was 452. In a few counties, the sample size was less than 100.

2. One refinement has been made with NPH by considering the clear evidence of absentee ownership. The small proportion of owners whose collated properties were either all rented to others or left unoccupied (C) was computed for each of the seven sampled areas; the complement of C, averaging about 90 percent, was then multiplied by NPH in the district to obtain a better estimate of the number of owners.

Regional Differences and Inequality Among the 687 Tax Districts

The wealth aggregates compiled for each of the 687 tax districts of the United States in 1798 offer a splendid opportunity for analyzing the inequality of wealth stemming from regional differences, and particularly the variation in regional wealth averages that can be explained by distance from markets. A study can be made of time and distance factors and their impact on the economic growth of private assets and on the inequality of wealth. Each tax district was located in one of the country's 359 counties; each county may be specified by the latitude and longitude of its center and by the year of its creation. From these details, we can state the age of each county in 1800 as well as the minimum distance to a major coastal or port city. These time-distance variables also can be assigned to each of the districts within the country to serve as approximations for mileage and age for the 687 districts.

An analysis of regions is addressed to the analysis of inequality by asking certain questions. How much did regional diversity contribute to the inequality of wealth in America? Was overall variation significantly larger within regions than within a district or county? More specifically, if the Gini coefficient was, say, .6 for wealth holders in a typical district or county, what might we expect it to be for all areas? America certainly was geographicaly heterogeneous; the hypothesis must be that those geographic differences aggravated inequality.

INEQUALITY AMONG THE 687 TAX DISTRICTS

One would expect that inequalities in housing values between regions would be larger than those for land. A new settler would be likely to own a very humble log cabin of low value relative to the value of other real estate; his land may have been worth very little per acre, but the extent of his holdings may have been quite large. The ratio of dwelling values to land values would be relatively low on the frontier as compared to those in long-settled areas.

Inequality of wealth in dwellings should be larger than for land, as revealed in the 687 district averages, and as demonstrated in columns 1 and 2 of table F. Rather startling is the fact that the Gini coefficient was twice as large for the one as for the other. The relative absence of inequality in land stems from the fact that extensive acreage in sparsely settled counties was in private hands. Frontier land might sell for $1 per acre instead of $10, but an individual may have owned 640 or 320 acres instead of 80 or 40. True, a significant portion of frontier land was absentee-owned, but even in long-settled rural and urban areas significant portions were occupied by renters or those farming on shares.

TABLE F

DISTRIBUTION OF WEALTH AMONG 687 U.S. TAX DISTRICTS, 1798

(males 21 and older)

Wealth Category	Land[a] No. of Dist. (1)	M21[b]	Dwellings No. of Dist. (2)	M21	Land and Dwellings No. of Dist. (3)	M21	Slaves No. of Dist. (4)	M21	Land, Dwellings, and Slaves No. of Dist. (5)	M21
$5,000 and over	—	—	—	—	—	—	—	—	1	.00
2,000–4,999	4	.00	—	—	8	.01	4	.00	26	.02
1,000–1,999	38	.04	8	.03	97	.14	22	.03	161	.24
500–999	323	.44	19	.03	397	.56	65	.08	375	.53
200–499	285	.45	86	.14	160	.25	70	.10	118	.20
200–199	29	.05	270	.35	20	.03	58	.12	6	.01
50–99	8	.02	157	.24	5	.01	40	.07	—	—
1–49	—	—	147	.21	—	—	179	.30	—	—
0	—	—	—	—	—	—	249	.30	—	—
All	687	1.00	687	1.00	687	1.00	687	1.00	687	1.00
Average wealth	$536		172		708		156		864	
Inequality, G	.256		.516		.271		.780		.287	

Sources: See table 5 and appendix 1.

Note: The mean and inequality coefficients were computed by weighting each of the 687 averages by the number of free males 21 and older in the district. Estimates for 113 districts (counties) of the 687 were based on the Pitkin aggregates in appendix 1 and from supplementary county data for three states. Further detail is given in chapters 2 and 3.

a. Excludes all housing value.

b. M21 = Proportion of wealth holders in category.

Information on slaves was also gathered in the estate inventory of 1798, since owning slaves was a prominent part of wealth holding in the South. Figures were most complete for slaves age 12–50, almost exactly half of the total number. I assigned a value of $350 for each slave, since a $175 value is suggested by the South Carolina tax law of the 1790s, a sensitive indicator dictated by regional disparities in slaveholding. The value is also suggested by studies of inventories of deceased, and by Samuel Blodgett.[1] The strong inequality between regions shown in column 4 of table F does not appreciably augment the inequality of real estate holdings between regions. Some lower southern averages are raised to offset partially the general thrust toward inequality due to slavery. Conspicuously absent from the table is any other form of personal estate than slaves. Just as housing increased average wealth from $536 to $708 and slavery increased it further to $864, so might personal estate have raised it to $1,000. Whether regional inequality would have been raised to any degree is questionable, at least insofar as can be determined from the data found in the 1850 and 1860 censuses.

INEQUALITY WITHIN AND BETWEEN REGIONS

One can make some estimates of the overall effect of inequality *between* districts if one permits assumptions about average inequality

TABLE G
INEQUALITY WITHIN AND BETWEEN U.S. TAX DISTRICTS, 1798: THREE POSSIBILITIES

	Inequality Between Districts[a]	Estimated Inequality Within Each District[b]	Inequality Among Individual Wealth Holders[c]
Land	.256	.45–.50	.51–.55
Dwellings	.516	.55–.60	.70–.73
Land and dwellings	.271	.50–.55	.55–.59

Source: Author.

a. See table F.

b. Guesses.

c. Column 3 imposes a Lorenz curve of a lognormal distribution with the inequality coefficient of column 2 on each of the 687 tax districts. See also J. Aitchison and J. A. C. Brown, *The Lognormal Distribution with Special Reference to Its Uses in Economics* (Cambridge: Cambridge, University Press, 1969), theorem 2.2, p.11.

within each of the 687 districts, as shown in table G. Roughly speaking, the variation between districts augments inequality from 10 to 20 percent or more. Coefficients of .271 and .50 produce an overall inequality coefficient of .55. The table shows that manmade inequality augments the inequality inherent in landholding, and that variation between districts plays an even more important role. Thus, 25 percent or more of overall inequality in housing values could be explained by differences between districts. The reproducible tangible assets permanently placed on land obviously were important in raising inequality levels. Only the natural fertility of the soil was distributed more equally; in this case, regional differences were not so dramatic.[2]

The relatively undeveloped transportation system in America in 1798 leads one to believe that regional inequality was greater in the new country than in Europe. A tantalizing table displayed in the Musée des Douanes in the Place da la Bourse in Bordeaux lists the "contributions," inhabitants, and per capita contribution for each of the 31 regions of France, including Paris, in 1789, as prepared by the minister of finances in Paris. This distribution generates an inequality coefficient of .29 (weighting the 31 averages by their population sizes). This level is *larger* than the .271 coefficient shown in tables 5 and G. A stratified sample from 494 of 15,000 parish and city assessments of property in England and Wales in 1803 produces a G of .29; yet it is only .19 when computed for the 54 county averages.[3] Results for real estate in 29 counties in Sweden and Finland appear to be similar to those in France (see tables 50 and 51). Perhaps regional inequality in the United States was similar to that in Europe.

1. Lee Soltow, "Kentucky Wealth at the End of the Eighteenth Century," *Journal of Economic History* 43, no. 3 (September 1983), 632, n. 24.

2. What would regional inequality have been if no improvements were made to the land? One approach to an estimate would be to study the per capita value of land (excluding dwellings) in relation to the age of settlement of the county—a technique to be explored presently.

The 1880 census states that proportion of total acreage plowed in each county (Plow/T of table 80). Some counties were almost entirely plowed, while in others there was little tilled land. Weighting Plow/T by the population in 1800 for 388 counties produces a distribution with $G = .245$. This degree of variability in fertility, as measured by plowing activity, is only slightly less than the $G = .256$ displayed by land value in column 1 of table G.

3. *Parliamentary Papers*, vol. 8, *1803–04*, pp. 1–717, and vol. 7, *1801–02*, pp. 1–503.

APPENDIX 7

The Distribution of Wealth
in Housing in 1798

Further evidence of strong inequality of income can be found in the inequality of housing values. This proves to be the case in 1798, since many families were renters rather than owners, and a few owned many homes. The wealth distribution given in table H is not so comprehensive as one would like it to be; in working with the manuscripts, I could collate owners' names only within townships and counties, but not an individual's holdings in more than one county or state. Nevertheless, this table, coupled

TABLE H
DISTRIBUTION OF DWELLING WEALTH AMONG HOUSE OWNERS
IN THE UNITED STATES, 1798
(males 21 and older)

Dwelling Wealth	Cumulative Proportion of Cases in Category		
	All	Rural	Urban
$10,000	.0014	.0003	.011
1,000	.062	.032	.319
100	.535	.486	.962
10	.922	.916	1.000
1	1.000	1.000	—
No. of owners	461,000	431,000	42,000
Mean	$329	221	1,317
Inequality, G	.725	.667	.605

Sources: See tables 5, 10, and A.

Note: Some individuals reported wealth in both rural and urban locations.

with the population totals of table 13, shows that 67 percent of occupants were *owners* in rural districts and over 60 percent were owners in urban districts. The inequality of wealth presented in table H is quite striking, and is further evidence that there were extensive numbers of poor and rich persons in America.[1]

1. Tables 13 and H bear an interesting relationship to each other; a Keynesian cross of consumption and income, with $C = a(DDY)^b$ (where a and b are constants and b is the elasticity coefficient) intersecting DDY at the 33rd percentile of the rural and the 57th percentile of the urban income distributions, generates a relative distribution of savings very similar to the relative distribution for wealth in housing if b is about .90 or .95. Inequality of wealth in table H is similar to that given in table G.

APPENDIX 8

A Possible Relationship Between Wealth and Income Distributions in 1798

The estimates of chapters 2, 3, and 11 can be tested for ramifications of income, saving, and consumption (Y, S, C). Saving will be estimated using the wealth data for real estate only. The lower class limits of selected percentile ranges of the wealth distribution and the preferred income distribution can be arranged as shown in table I. A very rough approximation of an implicit consumption function will be made by assuming saving was 10 percent of wealth, that is, $S = .10W$ and $C = Y - S$. This is estimated in table I, column 4. When C is coupled with the lower limits of column 1, a lognormal probit line appears as a tolerable straight line tapering off some at very high incomes. The inequality coefficient estimated from columns 4 and 5 is .59. (Class means would be technically more appropriate.) The wealth/income ratio of columns 2 and 3 is 2.0, a ratio probably too low. If column 3 were multiplied by .67 (giving a wealth/income ratio of 3), the Gini coefficient for consumption would be .56.

TABLE I
IMPLICATIONS OF DISTRIBUTIONS OF WEALTH, INCOME, AND CONSUMPTION IN 1798

Proportion of Persons Having Wealth Above a Given Level (N_X) (1)	X in Wealth[a] (2)	X in Income with $E_{DHV,Y} = 1.2$[b] (3)	Consumption[c] (4)	Weight (5)
.0001	$ 58,100	$12,400	$6,600	.0001
.0002	44,300	9,840	5,400	.0001
.0005	31,800	8,120	4,900	.0003
.001	21,700	6,770	4,600	.0005
.002	15,800	4,430	2,800	.0010
.005	9,630	4,050	3,100	.0030
.01	7,470	2,890	2,100	.0050
.02	5,320	2,020	1,500	.0100
.05	3,270	1,250	920	.0300
.10	1,920	834	640	.0500
.20	987	480	380	.1000
.30	543	322	270	.1000
.40	271	232	210	.1000
.50	0	155	160	.1000
.60	0	105	100	.1000
.70	0	69	69	.1000
.80	0	46	46	.1000
.90	0	28	28	.1000
1.00	0	0	0	.1000
Mean	$708	$348	$360	
Inequality, G	.797	.631	.59	

Source: Author.
   a. See table 9.
   b. See table 96 and chapter 11, n. 17.
   c. These figures are the result of $(3) - .1(2)$.

APPENDIX 9

The Relationship Between the Federalist Vote and Wealth In the United States, 1798–1800

In 1800, those who voted strongly for the Federalist party in Pennsylvania came from very wealthy townships. The intimate township data (see table J) enable us to consider several other variables and to develop the equation:

Proportion Federalist = .446 − .00028 times Miles (from Philadelphia) − .016 times Mts (one township had mountains) + .025 times Roads (1 if the township had major roads); R^2 = .12.

The variables are designed, in part, to explain the property values which, in turn, influenced the vote. A township with a major road was more likely to be Federalist; one in a mountainous region was likely to be anti-Federalist. Only the coefficient attached to rivers defies economic explanation. River-bottom land was considered in most areas to be superior; an equation available for Georgia certainly illustrates that fact.

TABLE J
WEALTH AND THE FEDERALIST VOTE IN PENNSYLVANIA, 1798–1800
(males 21 and older)

Proportion of Total Voting Federalist (1800)	No. of Townships (N = 420)	Average Land Value (1798)	Average Value per Acre (1798)	Dwelling Value (1798)
.601–.900	35	$3,950	$33.87	$946
.301–.600	81	1,980	8.25	497
.001–.300	75	87	6.86	371
Unknown	229	9	3.08	213

Source: See appendix 13.

Another endeavor using the statistics can be made by focusing solely on the mean dwelling value per nonslave family in a congressional district and the voting records of their congressmen on three key issues in that year. All three supported strong government: the Alien and Sedition Acts, another issue dealing with perceived attacks on government by the press, and the third, with raising revenue in preparation for war. Was the Federalist fervor related positively to income, as measured by housing? The data of table K show that congressmen from the more affluent areas were more likely to favor the issues. We see that economic condition was an explanatory variable; congressmen favoring these issues were more likely to come from regions of higher average dwelling values. It is granted that

TABLE K

HOUSE VOTES ON THREE ISSUES AND

REAL ESTATE VALUES IN CONGRESSIONAL DISTRICTS, 1798

(males 21 and older)

	No. of House Members	Dwelling Value per Occupant (DVO)	Inequality, G, of DVO in District	Value of Real Estate
Alien Act				
For	46	$199	.51	$740
Against	40	145	.62	586
Sedition Act				
For	44	196	.52	737
Against	41	153	.60	596
Direct Tax Act				
For	69	167	.55	669
Against	19	138	.61	637
Party				
Federalist	58	179	.53	712
Republican	49	175	.59	655

Source: Maning Dauer, The Adams Federalists (Baltimore, Md.: Johns Hopkins Press, 1968), appendix III, pp. 305–10.

a. (1) Aggregate dwelling values for a county were first divided by the estimated number of families in the county (estimated no. of adult males × .83). (2) The counties per congressional district were identified and a simple average struck of the mean dwelling values (step 1) to ascertain the dwelling value per occupant. (3) I then found a simple average of those voting yes and no from the district average (step 2). For states without districts, I used a simple average of all counties.

b. Inequality measures were developed in the same fashion, beginning with Gini coefficients of dwelling house values for each county.

the areas tended to be more urban, and were more often located in New England. Yet, in those regions, people generally lived in better housing.

These statistics strongly indicate the positive relationship between wealth, political party affiliation, and congressional voting in 1798–1800. It is presumed that economic conditions determined politics in 1798, and that the shift in political alignment from 1798 to 1800 would redound to the benefit of lower wealth and income groups. Yet there is no cogent reason for believing that political action before 1798 led specifically to greater changes in one period in contrast to another (as in figure 10). Political and governmental changes occurring between 1770 and 1798 undoubtedly had an effect on economic inequality, but it is difficult to judge their overall influence on the positions of the rich and the poor. I treat separately the issues of forfeited estates, land purchases, and so forth—the manifestations of government legislation and administration. Any other issues stemming from the democratic revolution may be presumed to strengthen equality, but one cannot be certain.

APPENDIX 10

Inequality of Wealth in Land, Housing, and Slaves in 1798

The distribution of wealth presented in chapter 2, with inequality, $G = .588$, is based on: (1) Lorenz curves for seven regions of the country reflecting dispersion in land values only, and (2) average values of land and housing in the 687 tax districts. To expand the latter by including slave values increases G to .592. If the former had reflected housing dispersion as well as land dispersion, inequality probably would have been a little larger, say, $G = .590$; there is a suspicion of this, since the inequality in housing wealth was large ($G = .725$ for house owners). To expand (1) to include slaves would change inequality very little; this is known because the 1790 distribution of slaves in the South was essentially the same as for land ($G = .58$ for slaves).

The only real evidence on this issue comes from data for many of the counties in Maryland in 1798. Table L presents the total wealth in land, housing, and slaves reported for each individual in nine counties, including Baltimore City. These results for Maryland demonstrate that concentration was relatively the same for the three levels of aggregation.

TABLE L
INEQUALITY OF WEALTH IN MARYLAND, 1798

	No. of Persons Reporting Wealth	Mean Wealth	Inequality, G
Excluding Baltimore City			
Land	7,308	$ 966	.625
Land and housing	7,745	1,091	.622
Land, housing, and slaves	9,256	1.635	.636
Including Baltimore City			
Land	7,869	1,040	.648
Land and housing	10,055	1,540	.667
Land, housing, and slaves	11,741	1,922	.652

Source: Maryland Historical Society, Baltimore, *Federal Assessment 1798,* microfilms 601–13.

Note: I was able to collate the values from the particular schedules A, B, and C only in the case of Maryland.

Personal Estate in Massachusetts-Maine, Maryland, and the United States in 1798

The 1798 inventory of real estate and slaves is not so complete a statement of wealth as one would like because personal estate, aside from slaves, has been excluded. No national data are available for calculating the dispersion of holdings of farm animals, stock in trade, money at interest, bank stock, or other private securities. (I have discussed the $32 million in government securities held by domestic and foreign bond holders.) Samuel Blodgett estimated personal estate to be about 20 percent of wealth in the United States at the end of the eighteenth century. Slaves accounted for about 40 percent of this personal estate.[1]

We must turn to the accounts of states in determining the importance of personal estate in wealth. The data for Massachusetts and Maine in 1792 (see table M) are by far the best source of this kind of information. Personal estate (excluding the value of slaves) has become an increasingly important part of total estate over the last two centuries. It was one-third of the total in the North in 1860, and roughly half of the total in 1980.[2]

The best evidence of the inequality exhibited in these assets comes from the 1771 Massachusetts-Maine data set, shown in table N. The distribution of the value of farm animals among 24,059 families exhibited the least relative inequality, as might be expected. This was followed by the inequality exhibited in the value of land, excluding buildings and structures. The value of buildings augmented inequality to the point that the G for real estate was .53. Personal estate increased inequality even more, with the value of stock and money loaned at interest being controlled

1. See table C.

2. Raymond W. Goldsmith, *The National Balance Sheet of the United States, 1953–1980,* National Bureau of Economic Research (Chicago: University of Chicago Press, 1982), pp. 5–6.

TABLE M
PERSONAL WEALTH IN MASSACHUSETTS AND MAINE, 1792

	Proportion of Total Value	
	Massachusetts	*Maine*
Real estate	.830	.820
Personal estate	.170	.180
	1.000	1.000
Buildings	.279	.202
Land	.553	.618
Animals	.075	.104
Wharves, vessels, plate	.020	.040
Securities and money	.046	.017
Stock in trade	.028	.020
	1.000	1.000

Source: American State Papers, class 3, vol. 1, 4th Cong., 2d sess., pp. 443–51.

TABLE N
INEQUALITY OF WEALTH IN MASSACHUSETTS AND MAINE, 1771

	No. of Families	*Mean Wealth per Family*	*Inequality, G*
Real estate	27,856	£ 116	.532
Personal estate	25,333	45	.787
Total estate	31,313	145	.614
Animals	24,059	12	.407
Stock	1,704	256	.740
Money	2,509	160	.753
Acreage	22,736	—	.453
No. of males 21 and older	57,000		

Source: Massachusetts Tax Valuation Records, 1771, Bettye Pruitt, principal investigator, Inter-University Consortium for Political and Social Research, (Ann Arbor: University of Michigan, 1980), ICPSR 7734.

Note: I have assumed that annual return on land was 6 percent of value, the usual assumption made in the 1792 tabulation. In computing the value of various types of farm animals, I used the 1792 valuations, assuming their value to be the same in 1771 as in 1792. Similar procedures were used to determine the value of acreage.

TABLE O
Estimated Inequality of Wealth in Massachusetts-Maine, Maryland, and the United States, 1771, 1798, 1860, and 1983
(males 21 and older)

	Mean Wealth	Inequality, G
Massachusetts-Maine, 1771		
Real estate	£ 56.1	.772
Total estate	76.4	.789
Maryland (9 counties), 1798		
Real estate	$6,810	.853
Total estate	9,920	.820
United States, 1798		
Real estate	708	.797
Total estate	—	.76–.80?
North		
Real estate	782	.793
Total estate	—	.76–.80?
South		
Real estate	589	.795
Total estate	—	.77–.82?
United States, 1860		
Real estate	1,490	.853
Total estate	2,580	.832
North		
Real estate	1,380	.840
Total estate	2,040	.813
South		
Real estate	1,780	.872
Total estate	3,980	.845
United States, 1983		
Real estate	77,000	.728
Total estate	120,000	.802

Sources: See table N; see also Maryland Historical Society, Baltimore, *Federal Assessment, 1798,* microfilms 601–13; Lee Soltow, "Wealth Inequality in the United States in 1798 and 1860," *Review of Economics and Statistics* 66, no. 3 (August 1984), 447–50. Data for 1983 were provided by Gregory Elliehausen of the U.S. Federal Reserve Board, regarding *The Survey of Consumer Finances, 1983.*

by a minority of persons. I drew a sample of 362 families from the data set for Massachusetts and Maine in 1792. It generally substantiated the results for 1771, having the same G for acreage and farm animals; the sample was too small to exhibit inequalities in stock, money, and aggregate personal estate.

A list of the inequality coefficients for real estate and total estate, as distributed among *all* free males 21 and older, can help us judge the extent of inequality of total estate in the United States in 1798. This list encompasses the situation in Maryland in 1798; the distribution of slave values serves as a proxy for all personal estate values. These are presented in table O. I have indicated a range of coefficients for 1798, using the data for Maryland in 1798, Massachusetts-Maine in 1771, and for the United States in 1860. It appears that inequality in total estate in 1798 may not have differed much from that in 1983. This cannot be stated with any degree of precision, since there is measurement error in the 1798 data; in addition, there is the collation problem embedded in the sample set, discussed earlier; I was unable to collate the properties owned by rich individuals in different counties and in different states.

APPENDIX 12

Tables Derived from the 1850–1870 Censuses Suggesting Parameters for 1800

TABLE P

FARMERS AND FOREIGN-BORN AMERICANS, 1850–1870

(males 21 and older)

Age	Proportion Foreign-Born			Proportion Farmers and Farm Laborers		
	1850	1860	1870 (Whites)	1850[a]	1860	1870 (Whites)
70–99	.091	.218	.216	.634	.654	.566
21–99	.181	.261	.282	.447	.496	.458

Sources: See tables 74 and Q.

Note: The stratified sample in 1850 is N = 10,393 and includes 276 men age 70 and older.

a. Does not include farm laborers; to have cross-classified this group or the 1860 set by eastern and western, northern and southern states would have left very small samples for those 70 and older. See chapter 3.

TABLE Q
INEQUALITY OF U.S. REAL ESTATE HOLDINGS, 1860
(males 21 and older)

	Proportion Reporting Real Estate	Average Value	Inequality, G	Proportion of Population	
				21 and Older	70 and Older
Rural					
Native-born	.592	$2,110	.771	.413	.534
Foreign-born	.558	1,210	.772	.083	.120
All	.586	1,960	.7746	.496	.654
Urban					
Native-born	.353	1,380	.900	.326	.249
Foreign-born	.224	690	.940	.178	.097
All	.308	1,136	.9144	.504	.346

Source: Computer runs are from the data base described in table 74 and in Lee Soltow, *Men and Wealth in the United States, 1850–1870* (New Haven, Conn.: Yale University Press, 1975), pp. 4–5.

Note: Total N=13,698.

TABLE R
SUGGESTED PROPORTIONS OF THE POPULATION HOLDING REAL ESTATE
AND INEQUALITY IN THE UNITED STATES, 1800
(males 21 and older)

The Top Proportion of Real Estate Holders (N_x)	RE > 0			RE ≥ 0			RE > 0
	1850	1860	1870 (Whites)	1850	1860	1870 (Whites)	1850 (Farmers)
.001	.059	.052	.023	.083	.080	.052	.044
.002	.084	.077	.050	.12	.11	.084	.064
.005	.13	.13	.094	.18	.18	.15	.11
.01	.18	.18	.14	.26	.26	.21	.15
.02	.26	.26	.21	.35	.36	.31	.22
.05	.39	.39	.34	.51	.52	.49	.35
.10	.52	.52	.48	.67	.68	.66	.48
.20	.67	.68	.65	.84	.85	.85	.65
.50	.89	.90	.90	.99	1.00	1.00	1.00
1.00	1.00	1.00	1.00	1.00	1.00	1.00	1.00
REP[a]	1.00	1.00	1.00	.504	.493	.481	1.00
RE[b]	$2,390	3,420	4,080	1,200	1,680	1,960	2,300
Inequality, G	.638	.643	.621	.818	.824	.818	.612

Source: See table 74.

a. REP = Proportion holding real estate.
b. RE = Arithmetic mean of real estate values.

APPENDIX 13

Sources of the Basic Forms Used in the 1798 Study

The Particular Lists A, B, and C, used in the 1798 census (figure A) as well as summary tables derived from them (figures B and C) are scattered in various archives throughout the country. I visited as many locations as I thought likely to have manuscripts dealing with the 1798 inventories. This necessarily included all but one of the states entering the Union before

FIGURE A. BASIC FORMS USED IN THE 1798 CENSUS

FIGURE B. SUMMARY ABSTRACT OF REAL ESTATE VALUES FOR 30
ASSESSMENT DISTRICTS IN NEW HAMPSHIRE, 1 OCTOBER 1798

SOURCE: Oliver Wolcott Collection, Connecticut Historical Society, Hartford.

NOTE: The complete title of the document is: "Summary Abstract of Lands, Lots, Buildings,
and Wharves owned, possessed, or occupied on this 1st day of October 1798 within the State
of New Hampshire."

1803. Particularly fruitful were records found in the Connecticut Historical
Society, Hartford; the Georgia Department of Archives and History, At-
lanta (for data from Burke and Warren Counties); the Genealogical Society
Library, Salt Lake City (for data from Orange County, New York—largely
Minisink Township—and Iredell County, North Carolina); the Maryland
Historical Society, Baltimore; the New England Historic Genealogical
Society, Boston; the Tennessee Historical Society, Nashville (for records
from Davidson County, Tennessee), and the National Archives and Rec-
ords Service, Washington, D.C. (for records from Pennsylvania and the
Summary Abstract for Georgia Housing in 1798).

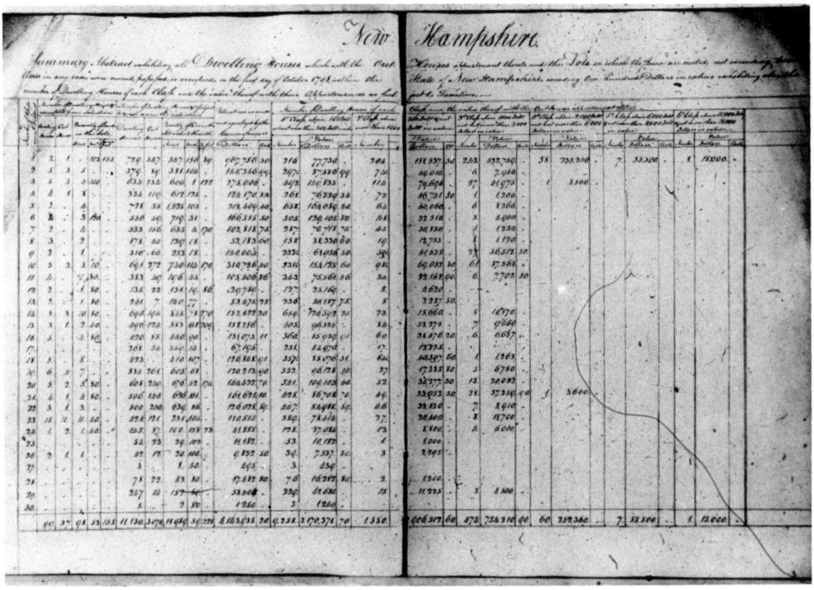

288 / APPENDIX 13

FIGURE C. SUMMARY ABSTRACT OF DWELLING HOUSE VALUES FOR 30
ASSESSMENT DISTRICTS IN NEW HAMPSHIRE, 1 OCTOBER 1798

SOURCE: Oliver Wolcott Collection, Connecticut Historical Society, Hartford.

NOTE: The complete title of the document is: "Summary Abstract Exhibiting All Dwelling
Houses which with the Outhouses appurtenant thereto, and the Lots on which the same are
erected, not exceeding two acres in any case, were owned, possessed, or occupied on this
first day of October 1798 within the 30 Assessment Districts of New Hampshire exceeding
One Hundred Dollars in value, exhibiting also the number of Dwelling Houses of each Class
and the value thereof with their appurtenances as subject to Taxation."

Notes

CHAPTER 1. THE OBSERVATION OF INEQUALITY

1. Benjamin Franklin, *The Writings of Benjamin Franklin,* ed. Albert Henry Smyth (New York: Macmillan Company, 1906), 5:361–63, for the letter to Dr. Joshua Babcock, dated 13 January 1772, London; *The Works of Benjamin Franklin,* ed. John Bigelo (New York: G.P. Putnam's Sons, 1904), 10:398.

2. John Adams, diary entry, 30 December 1779, in *The Works of John Adams, Second President of the United States,* ed. Charles Francis Adams (Boston: Little, Brown, 1856), 3:244.

3. John Adams, letters printed in London in 1786 and reprinted and published in New York in 1789, ibid. 7:305.

4. Thomas Jefferson, *The Papers of Thomas Jefferson,* ed. Julian Boyd (Princeton, N.J.: Princeton University Press, 1974), 8:681–82.

5. Thomas Jefferson, *Notes on the State of Virginia,* ed. William Peden, Institute of Early American History and Culture, at Williamsburg (Chapel Hill: University of North Carolina Press, 1955), p. 133.

6. O.L. Holley, *The Life of Benjamin Franklin* (Philadelphia: John E. Potter, 1860), pp. 272, 285, 295, 299, 320, 372, 450. From 1753 to 1756, Franklin had been in Boston, Albany, Fredericktown, Md., Lancaster, Gnadenhutten, and the Valley of the Lehigh in Pennsylvania; in 1763 he made a tour of the provinces north of Pennsylvania, and in 1776 he went on a government mission to Canada, but in no case do we have much idea about his routes or means of transportation.

7. See Sarah N. Randolph, ed., *The Domestic Life of Thomas Jefferson: Compiled from Family Letters and Reminiscences by his Great Granddaughter,* 3d ed. (Charlottesville, Va.: Thomas Jefferson Memorial Foundation, 1947), pp. 141–42; in a 1790 letter to his son-in-law, Jefferson describes the difficulty in traveling between Richmond and Philadelphia. In 1791 he and Madison set out on a trip to Albany, Lake George, Lake Champlain, "through Vermont, down Connecticut River, and through Long Island to New York" (pp. 166–67), but he mentions nothing about transportation other than

rough weather when they were sailing on Lake Champlain. In a later trip to Philadelphia, he traveled as far as Alexandria in his own phaeton, but went the remaining distance by stagecoach (p. 203).

8. Irving Brant, *James Madison the Father of the Constitution* (Indianapolis and New York: Bobbs-Merrill, 1950). I could find no evidence in the first three volumes that Madison had traveled extensively, aside from what was required in the service of government and his excursion in the company of Jefferson, mentioned in note 7. Brant states that Madison would have declined Washington's appointment to replace Gouverneur Morris in France (Monroe filled the vacancy) because, among other reasons, he was afraid "that ocean travel would bring back the dreaded convulsions of his youth" (3:400).

9. Federalist no. 10, in *The Writings of James Madison,* vol. 2, *1783–1787,* ed. Gaillard Hunt (New York: G.P. Putnam's Sons, 1901), pp. 247–48.

10. James Madison, *The Records of the Federal Convention of 1787,* ed. Max Farrand, rev. ed. (New Haven, Conn.: Yale University Press, 1966), 1:400–01.

11. George Washington, *Maxims of Washington,* ed. John Schroeder (Mount Vernon, Va.: Mount Vernon Ladies Association, 1974), p. 7.

12. George Washington, *The Washington Papers,* ed. Saul Padover (New York: Harper, 1955), p. 398.

13. Duc de La Rochefoucault-Liancourt, *Travels Through the United States of North America, the Country of the Iroquois, and Upper Canada; in the Years 1795, 1796, and 1797,* 2d ed. (London: T. Gillet, 1800), 3:484–85.

14. Ibid. 2:58, 3:54, 119.

15. Isaac Weld, *Travels Through North America and the Provinces of Canada, 1795–1797* (New York: Augustus Kelley, 1970), pp. 146–47.

16. François Michaux, quoted in "François André Michaux's Travels West of Aleghany Mountains 1802," in *Early Western Travels, 1748–1846,* ed. Reuben Thwaites (Cleveland: Arthur Clark, 1904), 3:269.

17. Alas, I cannot locate the name of this observer.

18. Alexis de Tocqueville, quoted in Foster Rhea Dulles, *Americans Abroad: Two Centuries of European Travel* (Ann Arbor: University of Michigan Press, 1964), p. 5.

19. Lee Soltow, "Distribution of Income and Wealth," *Encyclopedia of American Economic History,* ed. Glenn Porter (New York: Charles Scribner's Sons, 1980), 3:1113. Estimates of income will be made from housing data in chapters 3 and 11. An elasticity coefficient between the two variables of other than 1.0 will be employed in raising the incomes of those with low housing values.

20. Francesco dal Verme, quoted in *Seeing America and Its Great Men: The Journal and Letters of Count Francesco dal Verme, 1783–1784,* ed. Elizabeth Cometti (Charlottesville: University Press of Virginia, 1969), pp. 36–37, 42, 56.

21. Henry Wansey, *Henry Wansey and His American Journal: 1794,* ed. David John Jeremy (Philadelphia: American Philosophical Society, 1970), p. 40.

22. Ibid.; Thomas Cooper, an Englishman of means, also found conformity in

America. "There are no men of great rank, nor many of great riches. Nor have the rich there the power of oppressing the less rich, for poverty such as in Great Britain, is almost unknown" (Thomas Cooper, *Some Information Respecting America* [Dublin: William Porter, 1794; rpt. New York: Augustus M. Kelley, 1969], p. 53.

23. Alexis de Tocqueville, *Democracy in America*, ed. Richard D. Heffner (New York: Mentor, 1956), p. 189.

24. Wansey, *Journal*, p. 69.

25. Ibid., p. 105.

26. Robert C. Alberts, *The Golden Voyage: The Life and Times of William Bingham, 1752–1804* (Boston: Houghton Mifflin, 1969), pp. 156, 467–73.

27. Frederick Tolles, *George Logan of Philadelphia* (New York: Oxford University Press, 1953), p. 133.

28. Dulles, *Americans Abroad*, p. 18; Alberts, *Golden Voyage*, p. 154.

29. John Adams, "A Defense of the Constitutions of Government of the United States." "Chapter First, Marchamont Nedham" (*Works* 6:9–10). Apparently this was written in 1787, before Adams's return to the United States in 1788.

30. Lee Soltow, "The Distribution of Property Values in England and Wales in 1798," *Economic History Review*, 2d ser. 34 (February 1981).

31. Adams, *Works*, 10:268.

32. *Letters and Other Writings of James Madison, Fourth President of the United States*, vol. 3, *1816–1828* (Philadelphia: J.B. Lippincott, 1856), pp. 75–99; James Madison, letter to Thomas Jefferson, 19 June 1786, in *The Writings of James Madison*, ed. Hunt, vol. 2, *1783–1787*, pp. 246–49.

33. Adams, *Works*, 1:639. Abigail Adams would have preferred to invest in public securities, "poorly as it is funded, would have been less troublesome to take charge of than Land and much more productive" (*New Letters of Abigail Adams, 1788–1801*, ed. Stewart Mitchell [Boston: Houghton Mifflin, 1947], p. 61).

34. The Boston data are derived from a count of the owners of property enumerated in "A Report of the Record Commissioners of the City of Boston," in *The Statistics of the United States Direct Tax of 1798, as Assessed on Boston*, 22d Report (Boston: Rockwell and Churchill, City Printers, 1890), pp. 1–422. Slave data are derived from a sample of 2,748 families with adult males 20 and older, drawn from the 1800 federal census manuscripts for Maryland, North Carolina, and South Carolina.

35. Adams, *Works*, 6:529–30, a review, apparently written in 1808 and unpublished at that time, in response to a pamphlet published in 1808 titled, "Propositions for Amending the Constitution of the United States, submitted by Mr. Hillhouse to the Senate, on the twelfth day of April, 1808, with his Explanatory Remarks." Robert R. Livingston (1746–1813) was chancellor, or presiding judge, of the New York Court of Chancery, and heir to both name and property (*American Dictionary of Biography*, ed. Dumas Malone [New York: Charles Scribners, 1933], 11:320–24). John Randolph was born at "Cawsons" in Prince George County, Virginia (ibid. 15:363–67).

36. Adams, *Works*, 6:506–07.

37. *Massachusetts Tax Valuation Records, 1771*, Bettye Pruitt, Principal Investi-

gator, data base 7734, Inter-University Consortium for Political and Social Research, University of Michigan, 1980.

38. Adams, *Works*, 6:461–62.

39. Franklin, *Works*, 11:179–80.

40. This calculation is based on the following: (1) The value of lands, buildings, and dwellings per adult male 21 and older was $817 in Pennsylvania in 1798, as will be clarified with Timothy Pitkin's table in appendix 1. (2) The Pennsylvania pound sterling was the equivalent of $2.67 and that Philadelphia wholesale prices rose 54 percent from 1789 to 1798. (See U.S. Bureau of the Census, *Historical Statistics of the United States, Colonial Times to 1970, Part 1* [Washington, D.C.: GPO, 1975), ser. E97–E111.) (3) The ratio of the wealth variate to mean wealth (£ 1,000/£ 173 = 4.72) uniquely determined a particular lognormal table, a table with a Gini coefficient of .5.

41. Since the Gini coefficient is used throughout this book, it would be fruitful to explain its use in further detail. To ramify Franklin's data, we have:

N_X	A_X	A_X if $G = 0$	A_X if $G = 1$
.001	.02	.001	1.0
.01	.08	.01	1.0
.02	.14	.02	1.0
.10	.37	.10	1.0
.20	.54	.20	1.0
.50	.83	.50	1.0
1.00	1.00	1.00	1.00

The shares of the total wealth accounted for by the top classes are fairly extensive. The top 21 percent of persons represented 54 percent of aggregate wealth. If there had been perfect equality, the top 20 percent would have had 20 percent of wealth, as is shown in the next to last column; if there were perfect inequality, this group would have 100 percent of wealth. At the 20 percent level, the A_X of .54 is (.54 − .20)/(1.00 − .20), or a little less than half the distance between the two extremes. It can be determined from all percentile levels that the Franklin wealth hypothesis, with its Gini coefficient of .5, is, on the average, 50 percent of the distance between the two extremes of 0 and 1. Thus, the Gini coefficient is an average of how far actuality is between the two theoretical limits,

$$G = (A_X − N_X)/(1 − N_X).$$

This book on inequality uses the Gini coefficient of inequality almost exclusively, to the neglect of other measures of dispersion. There are three central reasons for using this procedure. The Gini coefficient (G) is by far the most commonly accepted measure in spite of its drawbacks. I know from 40 years of work in this field about what the magnitude of G might be, and I can readily compare any new result with the G that occurs in some situation in a different place, at a different time. The coefficient is intimately connected with the graphic device, the Lorenz curve. The area of inequality described by (N_x, A_x), expressed as a proportion of the area of the triangle traced when there is perfect equality, is a concept often displayed in beginning textbooks in economics, sociology, and political science, if not in history. Finally, the Gini coefficient is intimately connected to the lognormal curve, a concept I have stressed at great length in this book. In this formulation there is a monotonic relationship between G and the variance of the logarithms of the variable; to know G is to know this variance. This is not to minimize the importance of alternative measures. See A.B. Atkinson, "On the Measurement of Inequality," in *Wealth, Income, and Inequality,* ed. Atkinson (Baltimore: Penguin Books, 1973), pp. 46–68.

42. Soltow, "The Distribution of Property Values in England and Wales," p. 69.

43. K.N. Shchepetov, *Krepostnoe pravo v votchinakh Sheremetevykh* (Moscow: 1947), pp. 24–25. I am indebted to Meno Lovenstein for his translation. Also see Jerome Blum, *The End of the Old Order in Rural Europe* (Princeton, N.J.: Princeton University Press, 1978), pp. 25, 479.

44. Thomas Jefferson, *Basic Writings of Thomas Jefferson,* ed. Philip S. Foner (New York: Wiley Book Company, 1944), p. 715.

45. Age explains but a very small part of inequality of wealth and certainly not any sizable portion of that inequality shown in the Franklin hypothesis. The age variable, in general, is not known for the 1798 data, but is available for study in the 1850–1870 data sets. About 4 to 5 percent of total variance or variation in wealth can be explained by age in each of the census years 1850, 1860, and 1870. Inequality of wealth within specific age groups is almost as large as overall inequality.

Age in 1860	Inequality, G, of Wealth, 1860
20–29	.89
30–39	.80
40–49	.77
50–59	.76
60–69	.77
70 and over	.81
20 and over	.832

If the age-specific coefficients are weighted by their populations, an average coefficient of .82 is obtained; this average is only slightly less than the overall coefficient of .832.

Lee Soltow, "Distribution of Income and Wealth," in *Encyclopedia of American Economic History,* ed. Glenn Porter (New York: Scribner's Sons, 1980), 3:1113. For an alternative, but I feel misleading, exaggeration of the effect of age, see Alice Hanson Jones, *Wealth of a Nation to Be* (New York: Columbia University Press, 1980), p. 290.

46. See Norman L. Johnson and Samuel Kotz, *Continuous Univariate Distributions,* vol. 1 (Boston: Houghton Mifflin, 1970).

47. Mary Jean Bowman, "A Graphic Analysis of Personal Income Distribution in the United States," in *Readings in the Theory of Income Distribution,* ed. William Fellner and Bernard F. Haley (Homewood, Ill.: Richard D. Irwin, 1951).

48. Relative distribution of wealth of the lognormal and Pareto forms having the same Gini coefficient may not differ very much, particularly above the mean, if adaptations are made by truncating the Pareto form at some upper limit.

49. Washington, *Papers,* p. 398; Lee Soltow and Kenneth Keller, "Rural Pennsylvania in 1800: A Portrait from the Septennial Census," *Pennsylvania History* 49, no. 1 (January 1982), 25–47. Thomas Slaughter ably describes the issues facing Washington and the complex struggles that ensued in his *Whiskey Rebellion* (Oxford: Oxford University Press, 1986), pp. 175–89.

50. "Prices of Land in Pennsylvania at Various Periods," Bureau of Land Records, Harrisburg; Samuel Shepherd, *The Statutes at Large of Virginia,* vol. 1, *1792–1795* (Richmond: Printed by S. Shepherd, 1835), pp. 64–65; and Lee Soltow, "Land Speculation in West Virginia," *West Virginia History* 44, no. 2 (Winter 1983), 112.

51. Franklin felt that land would be taken up and cultivated as long as it was available, that manufacturing required the poor as a source of labor, and that these laboring poor were available only in Europe, with its scarcity of land (Franklin, *Works,* 9:441).

52. Charles Pinckney, quoted in *The Records of the Federal Convention,* ed. Max Farrand (New Haven, Conn.: Yale University Press, 1966), 1:31. Perhaps Pinckney did hedge a little in discussing the possibility of a nobility of fewer than 100 men arising from the merchant class if under British rule (ibid., p. 35).

53. James Madison, quoted in ibid. 1:422–23.

54. Alexander Hamilton, quoted in ibid. 1:432.

55. Adams, *Works,* 6:509–10.

56. Brian R. Mitchell, *European Historical Statistics, 1750–1970* (New York: Columbia University Press, 1975).

57. "Table of Cases Calling for Relief," *Annals of Agriculture,* ed. Arthur Young, vols. 28–29 *1797,* following p. 426.

58. Adams, *Works,* 6:95. For a definition of elasticity, see ch. 3, n. 14.

59. Claudia B. Kidwell and Margaret C. Christman, *Suiting Everyone: The Democratization of Clothing in America* (Washington, D.C.: Smithsonian Press, 1974).

60. The above calculation assumes that wealth is lognormally distributed, and applies theorem 2.1 from J. Aitchison and J.A.C. Brown, *The Lognormal Distribution, with Special Reference to its Uses in Economics* (Cambridge: Cambridge University Press, 1969), p. 11.

61. "William Manning's The Key of Libberty [sic]," ed. Samuel Morison, *William and Mary Quarterly,* 3d ser. 13 (1956), 202–54. The citation, dated 1/8, is found on p. 220.

62. Adams, *Works,* 6:280.

63. An interesting elasticity was that of land purchases with respect to wealth. If it was 1.0, then the distribution of wealth would tend to be reinforced in spite of the availability of "free" land. If the poor could accumulate relatively more (with, say, an elasticity of .5), then the inequality would drop.

64. Lee Soltow and Aubrey C. Land, "Housing and Social Standing in Georgia, 1798," *Georgia Historical Quarterly* 64, no. 4 (Winter 1980), 448–58.

CHAPTER 2. DISTRIBUTION OF WEALTH

1. The major portion of this chapter appeared in Lee Soltow, "Wealth Inequality in the United States in 1798 and 1860," *Review of Economics and Statistics* 66, no. 3 (August 1984).

2. Lee Soltow, "America's First Progressive Tax," *National Tax Journal* 30, no. 1 (March 1977), 53–58. The progressive tax was prompted by the realization that very few persons in the West, particularly in Kentucky and Tennessee, had adequate cash. The 1798 law also was influenced by struggles over inequitable taxes, a series of background revolts earlier in the decade, and especially the Whiskey Rebellion of 1794. See *Annals of Congress*, Class X, Miscellaneous, 6th Cong., 1799, 10:185–89. Also see Thomas Slaughter, *Whiskey Rebellion* (Oxford: Oxford University Press, 1986), pp. 175–89.

The housing assessment may have been subject to criticism by both rich and poor. It is conceivable that assessors might have underestimated the value of poorer housing, fearing conflict. Yet, the same argument applies to valuations of better housing, particularly that of the rich. Even ten years after 1798 we find that six percent of assessments of all states had not been collected (*American State Papers,* Finance, statements dated 18 November 1803, class 3, vol. 2, pp. 66–67, and 30 September 1809, pp. 388–89).

National Archives and Records Service, *United States Direct Tax of 1798: Tax Lists for the State of Pennsylvania,* pamphlet accompanying microcopy no. 372 (Washington, D.C.: GPO, 1963); *Annals of Congress,* 5th Cong., 3d sess., Acts of July 9 and 14, vol. 9, appendix 3757–86; and Timothy Pitkin, *A Statistical View of the Commerce of the United States* (1816; rpt. New York: Augustus Kelley, 1967), pp. 377–78. Market price data are given in the Wolcott Papers, Connecticut Historical Society, Hartford; data on housing are given in Lee Soltow: "Housing Characteristics on the Pennsylvania Frontier: Mifflin County Dwelling Values in 1798," *Pennsylvania History* 47, no. 1 (January 1980), 57–70, and "Distribution of Income and Wealth," in *Encyclopedia of American Economic History* (New York: Charles Schribner's Sons, 1980), 3:1087–1119.

3. There are essentially no district counts for three states, Georgia, North Carolina, and South Carolina. In these cases I allocated the state aggregates reported in the Pitkin list, presented in appendix 1, among counties, using tax reports prepared by state authorities at that time. The statistics for the number of acres and their values are excellent for the years 1794 and 1800 in the case of South Carolina counties. County classifications for North Carolina acreage are available for 1793 and 1808, and for land values in 1816. Information for Georgia's counties is more tenuous; my estimates are based on the numbers of slaves in 1800 and on distances from Charleston, to which I apply the multiple regression equations established for the 89 counties in the Carolinas. A report of the numbers and values of houses in Georgia's counties in 1798 has been

located; see Lee Soltow and Aubrey Land, "Housing and Social Standing in Georgia, 1798," *Georgia Historical Quarterly* 64, no. 4 (Winter 1980), 448–58. For West Virginia details, see Lee Soltow, "Land Speculation in West Virginia in the Early Federal Period: Randolph County as a Specific Case," *West Virginia History* 44 (Winter 1983), 111–34. Further information for the three states is given in appendix 2. See appendix 3 for corroborating evidence concerning aggregate wealth of $621 million.

4. Raymond W. Goldsmith, "The Growth of Reproducible Wealth of the United States of America from 1805 to 1950," in *Income and Wealth of the United States: Trends and Structure,* International Association for Research in Income and Wealth, 2d ser. (Cambridge: Bowes and Bowes, 1952), p. 269; Raymond W. Goldsmith, *The National Balance Sheet of the United States, 1953–1980,* National Bureau of Economic Research Monograph (Chicago: The University of Chicago Press, 1982), p. 135; Robert Gallman, "Changes in Total U.S. Agricultural Factor Productivity in the Nineteenth Century," *Agricultural History* 46 (1972), 208; Paul David, "The Growth of Real Product in the United States Before 1840: New Evidence, Controlled Conjectures," *Journal of Economic History* 27 (1967), 154–55. Prices in 1798 were 148, based on the index, 1860 = 100; see Paul David and Peter Solar, "A Bicentenary Contribution to the History of the Cost of Living in America," in *Research in Economic History,* ed. Paul Uselding (Greenwich, Conn.: JAI Press, 1977), 2:16.

My data include land as well as structures, while Goldsmith's do not. Technically, the 1798 data do include the holdings of women and children, but their numbers were very few indeed, as reported in the manuscripts.

The original data were almost always reported on forms that listed the name of the occupant or possessor and, additionally, the name of the owner. There was some little ambiguity because of the use of ditto marks, but generally speaking, about 88 percent of properties were owner-occupied. The collated properties produced the distribution of wealth among wealth holders. About 90 percent of these wealth holders gave evidence of owning and occupying one of their properties; otherwise they rented or left unoccupied all of their properties.

To be sure, I do not have the demographic details suggested in the works of Simon Kuznets. For example, see his "Demographic Aspects of the Size Distribution of Income: An Exploratory Essay," in *Economic Development and Cultural Change* 25, no. 1 (October 1976), 1–94; and "Size of Households and Income Disparities," in *Research in Population Economics,* ed. Julian L. Simon and Peter H. Lindert (Greenwich, Conn.: JAI Press, 1981), 3:1–40.

5. A further important distinction involves housing valued at $100 or more, which was subject to the special progressive tax; those houses accounted for the major part of wealth in real estate in urban areas, as well as 23 percent of all real wealth in 1798. Because houses valued at $100 or more were recorded separately in the manuscripts, they pose a special problem in collation.

Some persons prefer to compute inequality coefficients just for families or for those 25–26 years old and over, rather than for those 20–21 and older. I originally used these more restricted measures, feeling that males age 21–24 might very well be part of families, often working on family farms. Later I abandoned these measures for several reasons. Part of the strength of the American economy was in its ability to provide land, a home, and the opportunity for early marriage, in contrast to Europe where the young often remained part of the family. International comparisons do necessitate this broader measure. A second reason for employing the larger set is that statistics for families are less readily available than those for adult males. Another reason is that it was males 21 and older who could vote in most cases. Individuals who feel my Gini coefficients are too large might subtract .10 from my Gini coefficient for wealth. Adult males age 21 to 24 made up 10 to 15 percent of the population, and only a minority of them had wealth. For technical formulations, see Lee Soltow, *Toward Income Inequality in Norway* (Madison: University of Wisconsin Press, 1965), p. 15.

6. My study of *relative* wealth is based on all real estate value except housing plus housing values under $100, except in the case of Baltimore. I apply measures of relative distributions to aggregates based on all real estate including housing. The latter includes estimates only of the number of persons with houses worth more than $100. See also appendix 13.

7. Eugene E. Prussing, *The Estate of George Washington, Deceased* (Boston: Little, Brown, 1927), pp. 71–72. The inventories of other prominent men are found in the county courthouses in Salem, Boston, Philadelphia, and Charleston, as well as in archives in Baltimore and New York.

Collation of values remains a problem even if one has a complete enumeration of all properties (as distinguished from a sample). I have a complete listing of the 175,000 property values, each with the owner's name, for Ohio in 1835 (reported in chapter 8). Sortings by name, without the benefit of genealogical studies for each person, raise serious problems. See Lee Soltow, "Tocqueville's View of the Northwest in 1835: Ohio a Generation after Settlement," in *Essays on the Economy of the Old Northwest,* ed. David Klingaman and Richard Vedder (Athens: Ohio University Press, 1987), pp. 136–37.

8. Lee Soltow: "Male Inheritance Expectations in the United States in 1870," *Review of Economics and Statistics* 64 (May 1982), 252–60; and "Land Fragmentation as an Index of History in the Virginia Military District of Ohio," *Explorations in Economic History* 20 (September 1983), 263–73.

9. J. Aitchison and J.A.C. Brown, *The Lognormal Distribution, with Special Reference to its Uses in Economics* (Cambridge: Cambridge University Press, 1969), theorem 2.1 and appendix A.

10. We know that personal estate represented about half of real estate value in the censuses of wealth in 1860 and 1870; Lee Soltow, *Men and Wealth in the United States, 1850–1870* (New Haven, Conn.: Yale University Press, 1975). See also Goldsmith, "The Growth of Reproducible Wealth"; and Goldsmith, *The National Balance Sheet.*

11. The 21-and-older limit will allow comparisons of U.S. wealth at the end of the eighteenth century with wealth in other countries such as Sweden.

12. Whether Richmond, Alexandria, Charleston, Savannah, and so forth would have had the same average as Baltimore cannot be determined, since the data no longer exist.

13. Under the circumstances, I feel that I have made reasonably accurate estimates. Further details on my methods dealing with the shortcomings are available on request to me in "Working Notes, Wealth Inequality, 1798 and 1860," Department of Economics, Ohio University, Athens, Ohio 45701.

14. An 1860 range of, say, $100 to $625,000 would be compared to an 1800 range of $100 to $300,000, rather than $100 to $200,000 and (log 625,000 − log 100)/(log 300,000 − log 100) = 1.10.

15. See Lee Soltow, "Kentucky Wealth at the End of the Eighteenth Century," *Journal of Economic History* 43 (September 1983), 617–33. Data are derived from a stratified sample of size 5,715. The number of wealth holders for $W_{wherever}$ is 15,167; this is expanded to 17,928 in the case of W_{county}.

16. Aitchison and Brown, *The Lognormal Distribution*, theorem 2.1 and appendix A.

17. See John Adams, *The Works of John Adams, Second President of the United States*, ed. Charles Francis Adams (Boston: Little, Brown, 1856), 6:9–10. An obvious further extension of tables 8 and 9 would be to compare them to the findings of Alice Hanson Jones in *Wealth of a Nation to Be: The American Colonies on the Eve of Revolution* (New York: Columbia University Press, 1980) for 1774. Her distribution of net physical wealth for the United States, based on the estates of deceased, has a Gini coefficient of .73.

CHAPTER 3. DISTRIBUTION OF INCOME

1. John Adams, *The Works of John Adams, Second President of the United States*, ed. Charles Francis Adams (Boston: Little, Brown, 1856), 6:94–95; *Annals of Congress*, May 1798, pp. 1839–41.

2. For more intimate details about regional housing in 1798, the following articles by Lee Soltow: "Egalitarian America and its Inegalitarian Housing in the Federal Period," *Social Science History* 9, no. 2 (Spring 1985); "Wealth Inequality in the United States in 1798 and 1860," *Review of Economics and Statistics* 66, no. 3 (August 1984); "Housing Characteristics on the Pennsylvania Frontier: Mifflin County Dwelling Values in 1798," *Pennsylvania History*, 46, no. 1 (January 1980); "America's First Progressive Tax," *National Tax Journal* 30, no. 1 (March 1977); Lee Soltow and Aubrey Land, "Housing and Social Standing in Georgia, 1798," *Georgia Historical Quarterly* 64, no. 4 (Winter 1980). Data descriptions appear in National Archives and Records Service, *United States Direct Tax of 1798: Tax Lists for the State of Pennsylvania* (pamphlet accompanying microcopy No. 372), (Washington, D.C.: GPO, 1963). Also see Timothy Pitkin, *A Statistical View of the Commerce of the United States* (1816; rpt. New York: Augustus Kelley, 1967).

3. *American State Papers*, Finance, 5th Cong., 2d sess., 1798, class 3, vol. 1, pp. 588–90.

4. In a few of the 70 cells there were no sample items and it was necessary to substitute F_{ij} and X_{ij}. Method A, described above, yields the same mean and almost

the same dispersion and Gini coefficient as do the other two procedures. Method B involved computing a typical Lorenz curve of 13 points for each of the 70 cells. The curve was just a simple average of the various county Lorenz curves in the region. I explored this procedure because of the fear that a given county with substantially more sample items might dominate the pattern unduly. Fortunately, this did not prove to be the case.

Method C was devised as a procedure to develop ownership distributions from the sample data. Manuscripts were in two forms, a dwelling form for homes with a value of more than $100, and a real estate form including land and other real estate as well as dwellings of $1–100 in value. Dwellings of any one owner in a county usually were listed together on either form so that values could be collated by name. In this case, it was necessary to develop not 70, but 14 constants f_{mj} and b_{mj} in blowing up sample data to the population parameters, where m was 1 for the class $1–100, and 2 for classes above $100. Fortuitously, the distribution for occupants in method C was almost identical to that in method A, with G being .707. Method C was employed further in developing ownership distributions.

5. Charles W. Snell, *Historic Furnishings Study, Elias Hasket Derby's Brick House, Salem Maritime National Historic Site, Massachusetts* (Denver: U.S. Department of the Interior, 1974), p. 2.

6. *Annals of Congress,* June 1798, cols. 1917, 1918. Note, in col. 1925, the passage of the inventory law.

7. "François André Michaux's Travels West of the Allegheny Mountains, 1802," in *Early Western Travels, 1748–1846,* ed. Reuben Thwaites (Cleveland: Arthur Clark, 1904).

8. J. Aitchison and J.A.C. Brown, *The Lognormal Distribution, with Special Reference to its Uses in Economics* (Cambridge: Cambridge University Press, 1969), p. 68.

9. U.S. Bureau of the Census, *Census of Housing,* pt. 1 (Washington, D.C.: GPO, 1983), ch. A, p. 61. Values of rental units were assumed to be ten times monthly rentals. The Gini coefficient was computed assuming that class means were 40 percent of the distance between the lower and upper class limits. The open-end class of highest values was assumed to have a mean one-third larger than its lower limit, a procedure suggested by the data in the 1980 income distribution presented in U.S. Bureau of the Census, "Money Income of Households, Families, and Persons in the United States, 1980," *Current Population Reports: Consumer Income* (Washington, D.C.: GPO, July 1982), ser. P-60, no. 132, pp. 70, 74.

10. *New York State Census, 1865.* The Gini coefficient was .65 for the 1865 sample, and in 1798 was .70 for the sample counties and .78 for the state. The implicit rate of growth of the mean value, after adjusting with consumer prices, was 2.5 percent per annum for the sample counties.

11. U.S. Bureau of the Census, *A Century of Population Growth* (Washington, D.C.: GPO, 1909; rpt. New York: Johnson Reprint Co., 1966), p. 100; and *Heads of Families at the First Census, 1790, Massachusetts* (Washington, D.C.: GPO, 1908; rpt. Spartansburg, S.C.: The Reprint Co., 1964); excluded are the populations in the

Northwest and Southwest Territories; Records Commissioners of the City of Boston, *The Statistics of the United States' Direct Tax of 1798, as Assessed on Boston* (Boston: Rockwell and Churchill, City Printers, 1890); *Census of Great Britain, 1801,* Parliamentary Papers, 6:514–17, 533.

12. Records Commissioners, Boston, *Statistics.*

13. Jeffrey G. Williamson, *Did British Capitalism Breed Inequality?* (Boston: Allen & Unwin, 1985), p. 228. The elasticity of Y with respect to X is the coefficient b in the expression $Y = aX^b$, where a and b are constants.

14. Aitchison and Brown, *The Lognormal Distribution,* theorem 2.1, p. 11. To establish a relationship between expenditures and income in 1798 appears to be most difficult. There is some evidence that the rich owned elegant homes that represented neither saturation effects nor diminishing income elasticity. The first consumption study of importance was that for 397 families of wage earners in Massachusetts cities and towns in 1874, where average rentals were $117, average consumption expenditures were $738, and average income was $763. Low-income families did spend somewhat more, relatively, on housing, with the elasticity (E) being .81. However, there is evidence suggesting that the elasticity may have been closer to 1 if allowance were made for owner-occupied (or imputed) rentals among higher-income groups. Budget studies for later years that allow for this effect do demonstrate elasticities averaging about 1. The rent/consumption elasticities were .96, 1.0, 1.24, .88, and 1.37 in studies for 1881 and 1922–1935. See U.S. Bureau of the Census, *Historical Statistics of the United States, Colonial Times to 1970, Bicentennial Edition,* pt. 1 (Washington, D.C.: GPO, 1975), pp. 320–27; S.J. Prais and H.S. Houthakker, *The Analysis of Family Budgets* (Cambridge: Cambridge University Press, 1971), pp. 99–100; and H.S. Houthakker and Lester D. Taylor, *Consumer Demand in the United States: Analyses and Projections,* 2d ed. (Cambridge, Mass.: Harvard University Press, 1970), pp. 176, 260–61.

15. Darrett B. Rutman and Anita H. Rutman, *A Place in Time, Explicatus* (New York: W.W. Norton, 1984), pp. 125–26; Claudia B. Kidwell and Margaret C. Christman, *Suiting Everyone: The Democratization of Clothing in America* (Washington, D.C.: Smithsonian Institution Press, 1974), pp. 19–37; Lee Soltow, "Watches and Clocks in Connecticut, 1800: A Symbol of Socioeconomic Status," *Bulletin of the Connecticut Historical Society* 45, no. 4 (October 1980), 115–22.

16. Simon Kuznets, *Economic Growth and Structure* (New York: W.W. Norton, 1965), p. 305.

17. A house value of $35,000 and an income of $35,000 for the top person, and $8 and $32, respectively, for the modal person, represent two selected points illustrating an elasticity of 1.2.

My elasticities of 1.0 and 1.2 yield an aggregate income for 1798 of between $1.51 and $3.06 million, a range encompassing aggregate income or product estimates made by Robert Gallman and Paul David. My latter estimate is obtained by adjusting the relative distribution for E = 1.2 so the top income is $35,000, the same as it was when E = 1.00; in effect it raises lower incomes. See Robert Gallman, "The Agricultural Sector and the Pace of Economic Growth: U.S. Experience in the Nineteenth Century" in *Essays in Nineteenth Century Economic History,* ed. David C. Klingaman and Richard K. Vedder (Athens: Ohio University Press, 1975), p. 53. Ramifications of the wealth-income ratio for the elasticities of 1.0 and 1.2 are given in chapter 11.

18. *Annals of Congress,* December 1798, p. 3636; *American State Papers,* 5th Cong., 3rd sess., class 6, vol. 1, p. 62; Adams, *Works,* 8:612; Billy G. Williams presents budget estimates for Philadelphia for 1790 to 1800 that imply that ordinary laboring men had food budgets of about £20, say $80, in 1798. These seem quite consistent with the data of table 13 and appendix 8 ("The Material Lives of Laboring Philadelphians, 1750 to 1800," *William and Mary Quarterly* 39 [April 1981], 171, 184).

CHAPTER 4. LOCAL AND REGIONAL VARIATION IN HOUSING VALUES

1. One must always remember that wealth in real estate inadequately measures economic activity in many occupations. Real estate is needed for farming and usually is needed if one is to be a merchant. Yet household manufactures, including that in textiles, provide incomes as real as income from growing crops. For example, see Rolla Milton Tryon, *Household Manufactures in the United States, 1640–1860* (New York: Augustus Kelley, 1966), pp. 140, 288–99.

2. Charles W. Snell, *Historic Furnishings Study, Elias Hasket Derby's Brick House, Salem Maritime National Historic Site* (Denver: U.S. Dept. of the Interior, NPS 516, November 1974).

3. James Wilson, ed., *Memorial History of the City of New York* (New York: New York History Co., 1893), 3:150–52.

4. Records Commissioners of the City of Boston, *The Statistics of the United States Direct Tax of 1798, as Assessed on Boston* (Boston: Rockwell and Churchill, City Printers, 1890).

5. Lee Soltow, "Housing Characteristics on the Pennsylvania Frontier: Mifflin County Dwelling Values in 1798," *Pennsylvania History* 46, no. 1 (January 1980), 57–70.

6. The probit correlation for windows (the technique used for figure 8) has an equation with a slope of .587 ($N = 2,124$, $R^2 = .987$), suggesting an exact lognormal curve with $G = .32$.

7. Both elasticity coefficients are significant at the .0001 level.

I generally consider the property holder to be male. Most women were in the category *feme covert,* and very few females were listed in the inventories. The U.S. censuses in 1860 show only about 5 percent of property holders to be women. The census of Ontario shows that but 3 percent of adult women owned homes; see Lee Soltow and Gordon Darroch, "Ontario Inequalities in 1871," working paper, ch. 6, Department of Economics, Ohio University, Athens, Ohio, 45701; and Michel Dahlin, *Inheritance in America, from Colonial Times to the Present* (New Brunswick, N.J.: Rutgers University Press, 1987), pp. 16–19.

8. A study for Philadelphia in 1769 shows that rents of properties, including dwellings, had a Gini coefficient of .505; see Sharon V. Salinger and Charles Wetherell,

"Wealth and Renting in Prerevolutionary Philadelphia," *Journal of American History* 71, no. 4 (March 1985), 829–30.

9. The inequality coefficient for the 10 classes is G = .61.

10. Henry Adams, *The United States in 1800* (Ithaca, N.Y.: Cornell University Press, 1964), pp. 32–33.

11. *American State Papers,* 2d Cong., 2d sess., 1792, class 3, vol. 2, p. 178.

12. The probit line for carriages for the above 6 classes has a slope of 1.27350, implying that G = .63. The top 6 points trace a line similar to that for the top 22,000 houses with values above $1,000.

13. Perhaps the distributions of values of table knives or forks would yield better estimates. Frequency counts of owners of those items for various estate sizes for 1768–1777 are given in Lois Green Carr and Lorena S. Walsh, "The Standard of Living in the Colonial Chesapeake," *William and Mary Quarterly,* 3d ser. 45, no. 1 (January 1988), 144. Fernand Braudel points out that individuals in earlier centuries often ate without cutting their food (*Civilization and Capitalism, 15th–18th Century;* vol. 1, *The Structures of Everyday Life,* rev. and trans. Sîan Reynolds [New York: Harper & Row, 1981], pp. 195, 206). Also see summaries of consumption patterns presented by Lorena S. Walsh and Gloria Main in *William and Mary Quarterly,* 3d ser. 45, no. 1 (January 1988), 116–23 and 124–34, respectively.

Jackson Turner Main provides a distribution of consumer goods (household items, clothing, and books) in Connecticut in 1765–1774 as well as a distribution for men's clothing. These two have configurations that are remarkably lognormal in shape, yielding Gini coefficients of .47 and .42, respectively. Dispersion for Connecticut surely was less than that for the nation (*Society and Economy in Colonial Connecticut* [Princeton, N.J.: Princeton University Press, 1985], pp. 103, 154).

14. My weights are not far from those given by Paul A. David and Peter Solar, "The History of the Cost of Living in America," in *Research in Economic History,* ed. Paul Uselding (Greenwich, Conn.: JAI Press, Inc., 1977), 2:25. An explanation for greater equality in housing (income) than in wealth is that the wealth measures leave out of account the human capital implicit in the skills of free men.

15. Donald Adams finds surprisingly high levels of saving and in the numbers of savers among DuPont factory workers from 1815 to 1860; see "The Standard of Living During American Industrialization: Evidence from the Brandywine Region, 1800–1860," *Journal of Economic History* 42, no. 4 (December 1982), 915.

16. Quoted in Claudia Kidwell and Margaret Christman, *Suiting Everyone: the Democratization of Clothing in America* (Washington, D.C.: Smithsonian Institution Press, 1974), p. 23; see also Lee Soltow, "Horse Owners in Kentucky in 1800," *Register of the Kentucky Historical Society* 79, no. 3 (Summer 1981), 206, 210.

17. Except for Rhode Island, New York was unique among northern states in having primogeniture in its inheritance laws; South Carolina's primogeniture law survived until 1791, much later than such laws in other southern states. See Lee Alston and Morton Shapiro, "Inheritance Laws Across Colonies: Causes and Consequences," *Journal of Economic History* 44, no. 2 (June 1984), 278.

18. See the following articles by Lee Soltow: "Socioeconomic Classes in South Carolina and Massachusetts in the 1790's and the Observations of John Drayton,"

South Carolina Historical Magazine 81, no. 4 (October 1980); "Land Inequality on the Frontier: The Distribution of Land in Eastern Tennessee at the Beginning of the Nineteenth Century," *Social Science History* 5, no. 3 (August 1981); and "Kentucky Wealth at the End of the Eighteenth Century," *Journal of Economic History* 43, no. 3 (September 1983).

British claim-records of forfeited estates in 1784 show that, of the top 103 estates above £ 20,000, 25 were located in South Carolina and 23 in New York (British Public Records Office, Kew, *Report of the Commissioners,* RGT79 124A). The New York State censuses in 1790, 1795, and 1801 report the number of electors owning freeholds worth $250 or more, those owning freeholds worth $50–249, those paying rents of $5 or more for tenements, and other electors; calculations of inequality based on these data show levels similar to that in New York, shown in table 23 (*New York State Census of 1855,* pp. ix, x).

19. Frederick Jackson Turner, "The Significance of the Frontier in American History," in *Frontier and Section,* ed. Ray Allen Billington (Englewood Cliffs, N.J.: Prentice-Hall, 1961), p. 159. Perhaps this explains why the European traveler found evidence of poverty in the clothing worn by old people at the frontier when they moved there.

20. The inequality coefficients for *wealth* in the seven regions are offered in chapter 2; G was greater in the West than in the East in the rural North, but less in the rural South. Some may feel that consideration of the politics of assessment, the household production, and local exchange along the frontier would mitigate the strength of my results. This I accept, but I am unable to adjust for these factors except as I consider various elasticities of dwelling values with respect to income which I have employed in chapters 3 and 11 and appendix 8.

21. Are there life-cycle effects in my tests that militate against my results? My grandfather lived in a sod hut on the frontier as a young man and in a fine home in the same area when he was an older man. Yet he lived with his older brothers and a father as a young man. Foreign immigrants tended to be in their thirties when they arrived. Data cited earlier show the average age differed little between frontier states and those further east. Only on the very fringe could counties be found with ages averaging 30 instead of 34.

Consider the following data for the number of free males in Kentucky and the United States in 1800:

	Kentucky		United States	
Age	N	(%)	N	(%)
16–25	15,705	(36.8)	371,772	(35.1)
26–44	17,699	(41.5)	425,930	(40.3)
45 and up	9,238	(21.6)	260,029	(24.6)
All	42,642	(100.0)	1,057,731	(100.0)

Surely these distributions are not appreciably different from each other.

It is certainly true that the relative inequality of lifetime incomes is less than relative inequality of income in a given year. (In one case, G for lifetime inequality was 27 percent less than average annual inequality, as given in Lee Soltow, *Toward Income Equality in Norway* [Madison: University of Wisconsin Press, 1965], pp. 101–06.) Yet I have made no pretense of measuring other than inequality. Again, I cannot discount the poor by arguing that some day they will be rich.

Some new counties were formed from older counties as population densities increased. Thus, some counties have a young age even though they are located relatively far east. I have not adjusted for this influence here, but will do so with material presented in chapter 9.

22. *Annals of Congress,* June 1798 (Washington, D.C.: Gae and Seaton, 1851), col. 1917.

23. Eleutherian Mills Historical Library, *Tableau des Valeurs, 1795–1797;* and Lee Soltow, "Oliver Wolcott's Mississippi River Account of 1799," *Journal of Southern Studies* 21, no. 4 (Winter 1982). The number of boats traveling downstream were: 2 in part of January, 6 in February, 58 in March, 50 in April, 52 in May, and 16 in part of June.

Seasonal and cyclical influences on the poor are discussed in Billy G. Smith, "The Material Lives of the Laboring Philadelphians, 1750 to 1800," *William and Mary Quarterly* 3d ser. 38, no. 2 (April 1981), 183–87.

24. Consider the wave of acreage granted that appeared in Pennsylvania in the 1790s and the impact it must have had on the proportion of persons who were property-holders. The average annual change in acreage granted in Pennsylvania was as follows: in 1770–1780, 2.1 percent; in 1780–1790, 5.6 percent; in 1790–1800, 9.2 percent; and in 1800–1810, 2.4 percent (Lee Soltow, "The Long-Run Trend in Pennsylvania Land Grants, 1663–1823," working paper, p. 15, Department of Economics, Ohio University, Athens, Ohio, 47501).

Willard Thorp provides the following description of economic conditions from 1790 to 1805: 1790, revival, prosperity; 1791, prosperity; 1792, prosperity, financial distress; 1793, prosperity; 1794, uneven prosperity; 1795, prosperity; 1796, recession, depression; 1797, depression, panic; 1798, depression; 1799, revival; 1800, prosperity; 1801, mild prosperity; 1802, recession; 1803, mild depression; 1804, revival; 1805, prosperity (National Bureau of Economic Research, *Business Annals* [New York: NBER, 1926], pp. 112–15).

25. Letter from "Academicus" to Thomas Jefferson, American Philosophical Society Library, Philadelphia, archive no. 10.

26. Lee Soltow: "Male Inheritance Expectations in the United States in 1870," *Review of Economics and Statistics* 64, no. 2 (May 1982); and "Land Fragmentation as an Index of History in the Virginia Military District of Ohio," *Explorations in Economic History* 20 (1983), 263–73. New Jersey data are from *Documents Relating to the Colonial, Revolutionary and Post-Revolutionary History of the State of New Jersey,* 1st ser., vol. 38, *Calendar of New Jersey Wills, Administrations, Etc., vol. IX, 1796–1800,* ed. Elmer Hutchinson (Newark: New Jersey Law Journal, 1944).

27. The importance of land supply is highlighted in Stanley Lebergott, "The

Demand for Land: The United States, 1820–1860," *Journal of Economic History* 45, no. 2 (June 1985).

28. Lee Soltow, *Men and Wealth in the United States, 1850–1870* (New Haven, Conn.: Yale University Press, 1975), p. 59.

29. Lee Soltow and Kenneth Keller, "Rural Pennsylvania in 1800: A Portrait from the Septennial Census," *Pennsylvania History* 49, no. 1 (January 1982), 34–37. The directory for Philadelphia lists 903 merchants in its total of 7,154 individuals (*The New Trade Directory for Philadelphia Anno 1800* [Philadelphia: Way and Goff, 1799]). Obviously, persons in rural districts often combined activities as artisans with farming.

30. Jeffrey Williamson and Peter Lindert, *American Inequality* (New York: Institute for Research on Poverty, 1980). My reviews of the Williamson-Lindert and Jones volumes appear in the *Journal of Economic Literature* 20 (March 1982), 92–93, and in *Economic Development and Cultural Change* 32, no. 1 (October 1983), 193–98.

31. Soltow, "Socioeconomic Classes in South Carolina and Massachusetts"; Robert Fogel, "Nutrition and the Decline in Mortality Since 1700: Some Preliminary Findings," in National Bureau of Economic Research, *Long-Term Factors in American Economic Growth*, vol. 51 (Chicago: University of Chicago Press, 1987).

CHAPTER 5. INEQUALITY IN PHILADELPHIA

1. Benjamin Franklin, *The Works of Benjamin Franklin,* ed. John Bigelo (New York: G.P. Putnam's Sons, 1904), 10:398. The passage possibly dates from 1784.

2. For John Adams, the logic of a bicameral legislature hinged on the argument that a house of representatives represented all men, but that the senate would reflect the interests of that minority who owned property. His writings reveal this thinking in many different passages. See, for example, *The Works of John Adams, Second President of the United States,* ed. Charles Francis Adams (Boston: Little, Brown, 1856), 6:9–10.

3. Karl Pearson, "Historical Note on the Origin of the Normal Curve of Errors," *Biometrika* 14 (1924), 402–04; see also the following works by Helen M. Walker: *Studies in the History of Statistical Method, with Special Reference to Certain Educational Problems* (Baltimore: Williams and Williams Co., 1929); "Bi-Centenary of the Normal Curve," *Journal of the American Statistical Association,* 24, no. 185 (March 1934), 72–75; and "Abraham De Moivre," *Scripta Mathematica* 2 (July 1934), 316–33; J.H. Gaddum, "Lognormal Distributions," *Nature* 156 (20 October 1945), 463–66; J. Aitchison and J.A.C. Brown, *The Lognormal Distribution with Special Reference to its Uses in Economics* (Cambridge: Cambridge University Press, 1969), pp. 20–23; see also the articles in the *International Encyclopedia of Statistics,* William Kruskal and Judith Tanur (New York: Free Press, 1978) on Abraham De Moivre, 1:601–04; on Adolphe Quetelet, 2:824–34; on Francis Galton, 1:359–64; on Carl F. Gauss, 1:378–86; on John Graunt, 1:435–37; and on William Petty, 2:704–04.

4. Walker, "Bi-Centenary," p. 74. Further ramifications concerning the 1798 census of real estate can be found in Lee Soltow: "Egalitarian America and its Inegalitar-

ian Housing in the Federal Period," *Social Science History* 9, no. 2 (Spring 1985); and "Wealth Inequality in the United States in 1798 and 1860," *Review of Economics and Statistics* 66, no. 3 (August 1984), 444–51.

5. Erland Hofsten, *Pehr Wargentin, den Svenska statistikens foder* (Stockholm: Statistical Central Bureau, 1983), pp. 168–73. Earlier age ramifications are found in the articles in the *International Encyclopedia of Statistics* on John Graunt (1662), William Petty (1676), and Edmund Halley (1693), and in a Swedish memorandum in 1746. Also see Erland Hofsten and Hans Lundström, *Swedish Population History* (Stockholm: Central Bureau of Statistics, 1976), pp. 81, 169–72. Wargentin, the Swedish statistician, described age and sex distributions in 1754 as a "kind of pyramid or a cone in which the children form the base and the aged the peak." Also see B.R. Mitchell, *European Historical Statistics* (New York: Columbia University Press, 1975).

6. *Population Census 1703*, Statistics of Iceland II, 21 (Reykjavik: Statistical Bureau of Iceland, 1960), pp. 12, 17. The U.S. National Archives collections yield no evidence that a frequency distribution had been constructed at the time.

7. Walker, "De Moivre."

8. *British Sessional Papers*, House of Commons, Accounts and Papers, vol. 11, *1780–1781*, p. 80, nos. 15–17, 20; ibid., vol. 5, *1784*, nos. 54b–59, appendix table, penciled p. 4; Richard Price, *Observations on Reversionary Payments*, 5th ed. (London: T. Cadell, 1792), p. 342.

9. Price, *Reversionary Payments*, p. 384; Price gives frequencies for hearths +1,2,. . .,112; I have combined these into the above six classes. Other historical distributions are given in Robert E. Gallman, "Influences on the Distribution of Land-holdings in Early Colonial North Carolina," *Journal of Economic History* 42, no. 3 (September 1982), 549–75; Raymond W. Goldsmith, "An Estimate of the Size and Structure of the National Product of the Early Roman Empire," *Review of Income and Wealth* 30, no. 3 (September 1984), 263–88; and Peter H. Lindert and Jeffrey G. Williamson, "Reinterpreting Britain's Social Tables, 1688–1913," *Explorations in Economic History* 20, no. 1 (January 1983), 94–109.

10. See letter from Richard Price to Benjamin Franklin, American Philosophical Society Library (file BF85BA), dated 19 March 1783, in which Price refers to page 284 of Price's edition; also see reference to "Essay on the Present State of Population in England and Wales by the Reverend Dr. Richard Price," in William Morgan, *The Doctrine of Annuities and Assurances on Lives and Survivorships Stated and Explained* (London: Printed for T. Cadell in the Strand, 1779); Morgan was actuary to the Society for Equitable Assurances on Lives and Survivorships.

11. For example, I have found counts such as the number of families, by size (class intervals of 1); the number of rainy days and clear days and the "probability" of a rainy day; or the "odds" of winning a tennis game after having won a certain number of points. There are many examples from the physical sciences of classes, or specific values of the variable X and the associated value of some other variable, but no frequency counts, per se, of X within certain value ranges, as in the May 1798 report.

The earliest distributions I can find, where the variable is a monetary or acreage unit with upper- and lower-class limits, are stated in Leopold Krug's distributions for Prussia, *Ideen zu einer Staatswirtschaftlichen Statistik* (Berlin: im Verlage der Realschulbuchhandlung, 1807), pp. 5–6. The income distribution given by Sir John Sinclair in *The History of Public Revenue of the British Empire* (London: A. Straham, 1803–1804), pp. 226–28, uses only a midvalue concept, as do other authors from as early as Gregory King in 1688; see Lee Soltow, "Long-Run Changes in British Income Inequality," *Economic History Review,* 2d ser. 21, no. 1 (1968).

12. *Transactions of the American Philosophical Society,* vol. 4, *1799,* pp. 69–71, and vols. 1–4, *1771–1799, passim.*

13. The Kolmogorov-Smirnov two-sample test is not significant when alpha is 0.5. See Sidney Siegel, *Nonparametric Statistics for the Behavioral Sciences* (New York: McGraw-Hill, 1956), pp. 127–31; H.T. David, "Goodness of Fit," *International Encyclopedia of Statistics,* p. 403.

14. Warren Reininga, Accounting Department, Ohio University.

15. The Gini coefficient for the 167 cases was .45; that for the 160 in the same ward in 1789 was .42.

16. *Miscellanies or a Miscellaneous Treatise, Containing Several Mathematical Subjects* (London: printed for J. Nourse, bookseller in ordinary to His Majesty, in the Strand, 1776).

17. The records available for a few states indicate that there were houses with a value of less than $10, as well as one valued at $2. The summaries for Virginia give no frequency under $100; this has been estimated from acreage and land values given for all states in National Archives and Records Service, *United States Direct Tax of 1798; Tax Lists for the State of Pennsylvania,* pamphlet accompanying microcopy no. 372 (Washington: 1963); and *Annals of Congress,* 5th Cong., 3rd sess., Acts of July 9 and 14, vol. 9, appendix 3757–86. Also see Timothy Pitkin, *A Statistical View of the Commerce of the United States* (1816; rpt. New York: Augustus Kelley, 1967), pp. 377–78. Population estimates come from Dept. of Commerce, *A Century of Population Growth* (Washington, D.C.: GPO, 1909), p. 96; and *Census of Population, 1830.*

18. *Parliamentary Papers,* Accounts and Papers 1797–1798 (45), p. 936; and *Annual Register 1797* (Chronicle), p. 159.

19. Sir John Sinclair, *The History of the Public Revenue of the British Empire* (London: A. Strahan, 1803–04), 2:226–28; Sir John Sinclair, *Letters from His Excellency George Washington, President of the United States of America to Sir John Sinclair* (London: W. Bulmer, 1800), 8 letters. A letter from Washington to Sinclair was published in *Transactions of the American Philosophical Society* 4 (1799), 313.

20. Albert Gallatin, as a congressman from western Pennsylvania, argued in hearings on 30 May 1798 that the secretary of the treasury made estimates ("for which he has no data") that were overly optimistic about values (*Annals of Congress,* 5th Cong., 2d sess., 30 May 1798, col. 1850). The Wolcott report itself refers mysteriously to "information recently obtained" (Oliver Wolcott, Jr., "Direct Taxes," *American State Papers,* Finance, 5th Cong., 2d sess., 1798, class 3, vol. 2, p. 589).

21. *Annals of Congress,* 5th Cong., 2d sess., 30 May 1798, cols. 1840–54; ibid., June 22, cols. 1897–98; and ibid., June 13, cols. 1917–25.

22. Lee Soltow, "America's First Progressive Tax," *National Tax Journal* 30, no. 1 (March 1977), 53–58; and "Distribution of Income and Wealth," in *Encyclopedia of American Economic History*, ed. Glenn Porter (New York: Scribners, 1980), 3:1087–1119.

23. The reasons for the extensive variation in the Wolcott model ostensibly were due to economic factors but these, in turn, were due to settlement history, the geography of regions, and how recently an individual had begun his American experience of wealth accumulation. The explanations given for the wide diversity were considered in a much different context than when Quetelet first proposed, in 1884, the idea that empirical data followed the pattern of the binomial and normal distributions. Quetelet considered variations from the mean more in terms of "accidental" causes. In 1869 and 1887, Galton was to refer directly to Quetelet's work in expounding the "law of deviation" dealing with environment and man's natural characteristics. See articles by David Landau and Paul Lazerfeld on Quetelet and by F.N. David on Francis Galton in the *International Encyclopedia of Statistics*, 1:360, 2:829; Francis Galton, *Hereditary Genius* (New York: 1887), pp. 26–31, 363, 370. An early American presentation of the application of the normal curve to masses of data are contained in E.B. Elliott, Actuary, "On Military Statistics of the United States of America," *Fifth International Statistical Congress, Berlin, 1865* (Berlin: R.V. Decker, 1865), 2:90–155.

24. The belief that the rich should face the responsibility of public burden was held by Federalists such as Alexander Hamilton. See Federalist 36, in *The Federalists*, intro. Edward Mead (New York: Modern Library, 1941), pp. 222–23.

25. The concept applied to anthropomorphic data reached fruition two generations later. See the references to Galton's work, above; see also D.D. Dorfman, "The Cyril Burt Question: New Findngs," *Science* 201, no. 4362 (29 September 1978).

CHAPTER 6. COMPARISONS WITH EUROPE

1. John Taylor, *An Inquiry into the Principles and Policy of the Government of the United States*, ed. Loren Baritz (1814; rpt. New York: Bobbs-Merrill, 1969), p. 88.

2. J. Franklin Jameson, *The American Revolution Considered as a Social Movement* (1926; rpt. Princeton, N.J.: Princeton University Press, 1973), pp. 34–36. Considering that the British Parliament compensated Loyalists with grants for more than £ 3 million and that the claims amounted to £ 8 million, we can say that confiscated estates accounted for from 2 to 5 percent of the $620 million in U.S. real estate in 1798 (A. Aulard, *Christianity and the French Revolution*, trans. Lady Frazer [1927; rpt. New York: Howard Fertig, 1966], pp. 28, 29, 52). A. Matilla Tascón, *La Unica Contribución y el Catastro de la Enseñada* (Madrid: Servicio de estudios de la inspección general del Ministerio de Hacienda, 1947), pp. 185–543, selected tables for each of the 22 provinces in Castile, 1750–1759.

3. Lee Soltow, "The Distribution of Property Values in England and Wales in 1798," *Economic History Review*, 2d ser. 34, no. 1 (February 1981), 68, 70.

4. Lee Soltow, "The Swedish Census of Wealth at the Beginning of the 19th Century," *Scandinavian Economic History Review* 33, no. 1 (1985), 21–22. A *hemman* was about 775 acres. See Lee Soltow, "Inequalities on the Eve of Mass Migration: Agricultural Holdings in Sweden and the United States in 1845–1850," *Scandinavian Economic History Review and Economy and History* 34, no. 3 (1987), 234.

5. Charles W. Snell, *Historic Furnishings Study, Elias Hasket Derby's Brick House, Salem Maritime National Historic Site, Massachusetts* (Denver: U.S. Dept. of the Interior, 1974), p. 5.

6. Soltow, "The Distribution of Property Values in England and Wales," p. 64.

7. Scandinavian countries were not unique in counting populations. The Spanish count of persons in 1797 indicates that 21.7 percent were property owners, 30.2 percent were tenants, and 48.0 percent were day laborers (José Canga Arguelles, *Diccionario de Hacienda* [London: M. Calero, 1826–27], 4:55–57, 353; Richard Herr, *The Eighteenth Century Revolution in Spain* [Princeton, N.J.: Princeton University Press, 1958], p. 94).

8. U.S. Bureau of the Census, *A Century of Population Growth* (Washington, D.C.: GPO, 1909; rpt. New York: Johnson Reprint Corp., 1966), p. 136.

9. It is assumed that 2.1 percent of adult males died each year. See Lemuel Shattuck, *Vital Statistics of Boston* (Philadelphia: Lea and Blanchard, 1841), pp. 8, 11, and 13; *Century of Population Growth,* pp. 188, 224.

10. To consider only Boston as the residence of the rich of the state obviously is too severe. The tax book for Salem in 1798 reveals that this remarkable town had 46 persons, or 3 percent of its population of males 20 and older in 1800, with total estates of more than $10,000. Three-fourths of the town's evaluation was personal estate, and one-fourth real estate (excluding faculty-tax income).

11. Lee Soltow, "Socioeconomic Classes in South Carolina and Massachusetts in the 1790s and the Observations of John Drayton," *South Carolina Historical Magazine* 81, no. 4 (October 1980), 293.

12. Church of Latter Day Saints Genealogical Library, Salt Lake City, microfilm 478,748.

13. *Maine,* entworfen [*sic*] von D.F. Sotzmann (Hamburg: Carl Ernst Bohn, 1798). Map in collections of Widener Library, Harvard University.

14. Lee Soltow, "Land Speculation in West Virginia in the Early Federal Period: Randolph County as a Specific Case," *West Virginia History* 44, no. 2 (Winter 1983), 120; Act passed 17 December 1792, Samuel Shepherd, *The Statutes at Large of Virginia,* vol. 1, *1792–1795* (Richmond: 1835), pp. 65–66.

15. The patent books are housed in the Pennsylvania Bureau of Land Records, Harrisburg.

16. Norman B. Wilkinson, "Land Policy and Speculation in Pennsylvania, 1779–1800," Ph.D. diss., Univ. of Pennsylvania, 1958.

17. L.D.S. Genealogical Library, Salt Lake City, microfilms 174,956 and 174,952; Willard Rouse Jillson, *Old Kentucky Entries and Deeds* (Baltimore: Genealogical Publishing Co., 1969).

18. Archives of the Connecticut Historical Society, Hartford.

19. Lee Soltow, "Kentucky Wealth at the End of the Eighteenth Century," *Journal of Economic History* 43, no. 3 (September 1983), 264.

20. Lee Soltow, "Land Inequality on the Frontier: The Distribution of Land in Eastern Tennessee at the Beginning of the Nineteenth Century," *Social Science History* 5, no. 3 (Summer 1981), 283.

21. John Adams, *The Works of John Adams, Second President of the United States,* ed. Charles Francis Adams (Boston: Little, Brown, 1856), 4:508.

22. *American State Papers, Finance,* 2d Cong., 1st sess., 23 January 1792, p. 149.

23. Lee Soltow, "Long Run Wealth Inequality in Malaysia," *Singapore Economic Review* 28, no. 2 (October 1983), 94–95.

24. These figures understate the case, since Americans were younger, on the average.

25. If a lognormal curve has $G = .9$, then the subset above the 80th percentile has a probit line with a $G = .72$ and an $R^2 = .980$, deviating from linearity essentially only in the lower 15 percent of the curve.

26. J.T. Coppock, *An Agricultural Atlas of England and Wales* (London: Faber & Faber, 1964), p. 43.

27. The 1798 population of adult males 26 and over (or families) is estimated as 39 percent of the total number of males, as based on the evidence for Cornwall in the 1821 census.

28. John Bateman, *The Great Landowners of Great Britain and Ireland* (1883; rpt. Leicester: Leicester University Press, 1971); George Broderick, *English Land and English Landlords* (1881; rpt. New York: Augustus M. Kelley, 1968); *British Sessional Papers,* vol. 80, *1876;* Lee Soltow, "The Land Tax Redemption Records, 1798–1963," *Economic History Review,* 2d ser. 35, no. 3 (August 1982), 432.

29. Brian R. Mitchell, *European Historical Statistics 1750–1970* (New York: Columbia University Press, 1975), p. 34; M.W. Flinn, *British Population Growth, 1700–1850* (London: Macmillan, 1970), pp. 21, 42–48.

30. J.M. Bumstead, *The People's Clearance* (Edinburgh: Edinburgh University Press, 1982). Distributions of wealth in land in Scotland in table 54, below, and in Lee Soltow, "Wealth Inequality in Scotland in the Eighteenth Century," working paper, Dept. of Economics, Ohio University, Athens, Ohio, 45701. Also see Earl of Selkirk (Thomas Douglas), *Observations on the Present State of the Highlands and Probable Consequences of Emigration* (London: Longman, Hurst, Rees, and Orme, 1805).

31. Bumstead, *Clearance,* pp. xii, 35–37, 88, 228–29; Selkirk, *Observations,* pp. 21, 24, 47–57; Malcolm Gray, *The Highland Economy, 1750–1850* (Edinburgh: Oliver and Boyd, 1957), pp. 18–27.

32. I.H. Adams, *Agrarian Landscape Terms, A Glossary for Historical Geography* (London: London Institute of Geographers, 1976), pp. 170–74; Bumstead, *Clearance,* pp. 35–37.

33. The complicated question of the value of the currency is discussed in Lennart Jörberg, *A History of Prices in Sweden, 1732–1914* (Lund, Sweden: C.W.K. Gleerup, 1972), 1:81–85.

A seventeenth-century description of landholding conditions in two parishes in Scotland and developments in America are given in Ned C. Landsman, *Scotland and Its First American Colony, 1683–1765* (Princeton, N.J.: Princeton University Press, 1985), pp. 1–47. Much more to the point is the nationwide study made by Loretta A. Timperley in *A Directory of Landownership in Scotland c. 1770*, Scottish Record Society, n.s. 5 (Edinburgh: Scottish Record Society, 1976), pp. 18–428; see also Timperley: "Landownership in Scotland in the Eighteenth Century," Ph.D. diss., University of Edinburgh, 1977, pp. 154–57, 343–76; "The Pattern of Landholding in Eighteenth-Century Scotland," in *The Making of the Scottish Countryside*, ed. M.L. Parry and T.R. Slater (London: Croom Helm; Montreal: McGill–Queen's University Press, 1980), p. 150.

34. Lee Soltow, "The Distribution of Real Estate Among Norwegian Farmers in 1802," *Historisk Tidsskrift* 3 (1978), 247.

35. Dorothy Swaine Thomas, *Social and Economic Aspects of Swedish Population Movements, 1750–1933* (New York: Macmillan, 1941), pp. 53–55; Florence Janson, *The Background of Swedish Immigration, 1840–1930* (Chicago: University of Chicago Press, 1931), pp. 84, 96.

36. Thomas, *Social and Economic Aspects of Swedish Population Movements*, p. 60; Nils Wohlin, "Faran af bondeklassens undergräfvande," in *Emigrationsutredringen*, appendix 10 (Stockholm: Kungl. boktryckeriet, P.A. Norstedt and Söner, 1910).

37. Jörberg, *A History of Prices in Sweden*, 1:344.

38. A sample of 5,709 rural males 21 and older from the 1801 Norwegian census and the 1871 Ontario census show the following proportions to be married:

Age	Norway, 1801	Ontario, 1871
21–25	.112	.221
26–30	.427	.579
31–35	.694	.766
36–40	.851	.827

(Norwegian Central Bureau of Statistics, *Population Census 1801, Reprocessed* [Oslo: Norges Offisielle Statistikk, 1980], pp. 91–92; Ontario data are from census of Canada manuscripts, in the National Archives, Ottawa).

39. There are numerous data sets for age at marriage in the colonial period that generally show averages for males between 23 and 26. See Philip J. Greven, Jr., *Four Generations, Population, Land, and Family in Colonial Andover, Massachusetts* (Ithaca, N.Y.: Cornell University Press, 1970), pp. 31–37; John Demos, *A Little Commonwealth* (New York: Oxford University Press, 1970), pp. 151, 193; James M. Gallman, "Determinants of Age at Marriage in Colonial Perquimans County, North Carolina," *William and Mary Quarterly*, 3d ser. 39, no. 1 (January 1982), 176–91. Data on age and marriage in the colonial period in Connecticut are given in Jackson

Turner Main, *Society and Economy in Colonial Connecticut* (Princeton, N.J.: Princeton University Press, 1985), p. 21.

40. Evidence of later ramifications due to the disparities in 1800 is given in Lee Soltow, "Inequalities on the Eve of Mass Migration: Agricultural Holdings in Sweden and the United States in 1845–1850," *Scandinavian Economic History Review* 34, no. 3 (1987), 219–26. The inequality of wealth in Ohio in the first three decades after 1800 was very much influenced by the inequality in 1800 in states to the east and south of Ohio. The setting for Ohio in 1835 involving international comparisons in that year is given in Lee Soltow, "Tocqueville's View of the Northwest in 1835: Ohio a Generation After Settlement," in *Essays on the Economy of the Old Northwest,* ed. David C. Klingaman and Richard K. Vedder (Athens: Ohio University Press, 1987).

41. It is possible that America always was richer after its settlement.

42. Adam Smith, *Wealth of Nations,* ed. Edwin Cannan (New York: Random House, 1937), p. 774.

43. The Scandinavian data are discussed further in the note to table 55.

44. Robert Gallman has made international comparisons of per capita national product in 1840. The level in England was 120 percent of that in the United States; the French level was 78 percent of the U.S. level. Ezra Seaman's estimate for the English-American ratio in 1840 was 140 percent, according to Gallman. Seaman offers wealth (and income) averages in 1800 showing those in the Netherlands to be higher than those in England which, in turn, were higher than those for France in the case of wealth (Robert Gallman, "Gross National Product in the United States, 1834–1909," in *Studies in Income and Wealth,* National Bureau of Economic Research [New York: Columbia University Press, 1966], pp. 4–7; Ezra Seaman, *Essays on the Progress of Nations* [New York: Scribner's, 1852], p. 445).

CHAPTER 7. CHANGES IN INEQUALITY, 1770–1798

1. Alexis de Tocqueville, *Democracy in America,* the Henry Reeve text (New York: Alfred A. Knopf, 1966), 1:1, 56. Tocqueville's focus is more on middle- and higher-income groups that generally have wealth in real estate. In "Memoir on Pauperism," Tocqueville emphasizes the lower tail; see *Tocqueville and Beaumont on Social Reform,* ed. and trans. Seymour Drescher (New York: Harper, 1968; and Tocqueville (Cherbourg: 1835, tract in the collections of the Goldsmith Library, University of London).

2. Harry B. Yoshpe, *The Disposition of Loyalist Estates in the Southern District of the State of New York* (New York: Columbia University Press, 1939), pp. 52, 116, and 121–53.

3. Thomas Montgomery, ed., *Forfeited Estates, Inventories and Sales,* Pennsylvania Archives, 6th ser. (Harrisburg: 1907), 12:804–05, 13:179, 307–11, and table, p. 312. The conversion rate is $2.67 per pound sterling.

4. Curtis P. Nettels, *The Emergence of a National Economy, 1775–1815* (New York: Harper, 1969), pp. 138–42; J. Franklin Jameson, *The American Revolution*

Considered as a Social Movement (Princeton, N.J.: Princeton University Press, 1973), pp. 32–35.

5. Richard D. Brown, "The Confiscation and Disposition of Loyalists' Estates in Suffolk County, Massachusetts," *William and Mary Quarterly,* 2d ser. 21 (1964), 534, 546; Gregory Stiverson, *Poverty in a Land of Plenty, Tenancy in Eighteenth-Century Maryland* (Baltimore: Johns Hopkins University Press, 1977), pp. 112–13. I eliminated the stated estates of companies.

6. Lee Alston and Morton Schapiro, "Inheritance Laws Across Colonies: Causes and Consequences," *Journal of Economic History* 64 (June 1984), 277–79; Jameson, *The American Revolution,* pp. 36–37; R.R. Palmer, *The Age of the Democratic Revolution* (Princeton, N.J.: Princeton University Press, 1974), 1:233; C. Ray Klein, "Primogeniture and Entail in Colonial Virginia," *William and Mary Quarterly,* 2d ser. 25 (October 1968), 545–86.

An examination of wills for a state can create the impression that there were very few estates that went to only one child. Yet in the majority of cases subject to primogeniture there would have been no will. In eighteenth-century Scotland, essentially there were neither wills nor probates dealing with land and real estate; only somewhat incomplete records for personal estate have survived.

7. Alston and Schapiro, "Inheritance Laws," p. 278; Jameson, *The American Revolution,* pp. 36–37. Some feel there is little evidence of entailed estates. Primogeniture applied to intestate estates only, and possibly then only to the portion dealing with real estate. Alice Hanson Jones estimates that in the North one-third of estates were probated, and, in the South, two-thirds in the middle and southern counties (*Wealth of a Nation to Be* [New York: Columbia University Press, 1980], p. 45); also see Toby L. Ditz, *Property and Kinship, Inheritance in Early Connecticut* (Princeton, N.J.: Princeton University Press, 1986), pp. 40–42, 188.

8. E.B. O'Callaghan, *The Documentary History of the State of New York* (Albany: Weed Parsons and Co., Public Printers, 1850), 3:499–502.

9. James T. Mitchell and Henry Flanders, eds., *Statutes at Large of Pennsylvania* (Harrisburg: State Printer, 1896–1915), 10:33–39.

10. Lee Soltow, "The Long-Run Trend in Pennsylvania Land Grants, 1663–1823," working paper, Department of Economics, Ohio University, Athens, Ohio, 47501.

11. R.R. Palmer, *The Age of the Democratic Revolution* (Princeton, N.J.: Princeton University Press, 1970), 1:185–89; 2:544–45.

12. One might make a case for increasing economic inequality if the statistical data for colonial America did not include the power or holdings of royal officials living in America in the early 1770s. An American hierarchy of wealth and status after 1787 simply may have replaced a royal hierarchy. If tax data or probate data reflected the latter group but not the former, then statistical data for 1770 or 1774 might show less inequality than do those for 1798 because of this measurement error.

13. Lee Soltow and Kenneth Keller, "New Jersey Wealth-Holding and the Republican Congressional Victory of 1800," *New Jersey History* 100, nos. 1–2 (1982).

14. James Callender, *Sedgwick and Co. or a Key to the Six Per Cent Cabinet*

(Philadelphia: Author, 1798), quoted in Charles Beard, *Economic Origins of Jeffersonian Democracy* (New York: Macmillan, 1915), p. 213.

15. E. James Ferguson, *The Power of the Purse* (Chapel Hill: University of North Carolina Press, 1961), pp. 251–86.

16. Ibid., p. 330. Bills of credit issued by the Continental Congress had a redemption value of only one cent on the dollar.

17. James Sullivan, *The Path to Riches* (Boston: P. Edes, 1792), Evans bibliography no. 24829.

18. Ibid., pp. 39–40.

19. Ibid., p. 40.

20. Callender, *Sedgwick and Co.*, p. 30.

21. Palmer, *The Age of the Democratic Revolution* 1:213.

22. Little is known about ownership in early American banks. The first Bank of the United States, on July 4, 1791, offered $400 shares with a first cash payment of $25. The rights associated with payment rose to $35 in two days, to $50 within a week, and to $150 within a month or two. The bank discounted notes for stockholders so they could pay subsequent installments. No distribution of ownership values is available. See John Holdsworth and Daurs Dewey, *The First and Second Bank of the United States*, S. Doc. 571, 61st Cong., 2d sess., 1909–1910, pp. 24, 30.

23. George Logan (An American Farmer), "Letters Addressed to the Yeomanry of the United States" (Philadelphia: n.p., 1793), Evans bibliography no. 25724.

24. These data come from microfilm 847,553, in the Church of the Latter Day Saints Genealogical Library, Salt Lake City, *Army Land Warrants, Registered Under the Act for regulating the Grants of Land, appropriated for Military Services, passed June 1, 1796, and March 2, 1799, for the U.S. Military District in Ohio and reserved under General Act in 1788.*

25. Final settlement certificates sold at 10 or 15 cents on the dollar in 1788 (Ferguson, *Power of the Purse,* pp. 252–53). The General Act for the U.S. Military District in Ohio was passed in 1788.

26. *Laws, 1800: Laws or Laws Relative to Lands and Intestate Estates* (Knoxville: Roulstone and Wilson, 1800), pp. 35–40.

27. William E. Peters, *Ohio Lands and Their Subdivision* (Athens, Ohio: W.E. Peters, 1918), pp. 126, 254.

28. Lee Soltow, "Progress and Mobility Among Ohio Propertyholders, 1810–1825," *Social Science History* 7, no. 4 (Fall 1983), 405–26.

29. J. Aitchison and J.A.C. Brown, *The Lognormal Distribution, with Special Reference to its Uses in Economics* (Cambridge: Cambridge University Press, 1969), pp. 11, 26.

30. Jackson Turner Main, "The Distribution of Property in Colonial Connecticut," in *The Human Dimensions of Nation Making, Essays on Colonial and Revolutionary America*, ed. James Martin (Madison: Wisconsin Historical Society, 1976), p. 93. See also Main's revisions in *Society and Economy,* pp. 110, 136–39.

31. Lee Soltow, "Male Inheritance Expectations in the United States in 1870," *Review of Economics and Statistics* 64, no. 2 (May 1982).

32. Using data similar to mine, Gloria Main found little or no change in inequality in Massachusetts. See her "Inequality in Early America: The Evidence from Probate Records of Massachusetts and Maryland," *Journal of Interdisciplinary History* 7, no. 4 (Spring 1977), 567.

33. See Aitchison and Brown, *Lognormal Distribution,* theorems 2.1, 2.2, appendix A, and p. 112. The above procedures are considered in much more detail in Soltow, "Male Inheritance Expectations." An alternative might be to use the distributions of family size in 1790 in the two Pennsylvania counties bordering Ohio; the Gini coefficient for Washington County, Pennsylvania, was .24, and that for Allegheny County was .28, levels similar to those presented in table 64. U.S. Bureau of the Census, *A Century of Population Growth* (1909; rpt. New York: Johnson Reprint Corp., 1966), pp. 224–25.

34. Such as the truncation at 2 or even 40 acres, as suggested above.

35. U.S. Bureau of the Census, *A Century of Population Growth,* p. 136. Rice plantations tended to be large, and rice was restricted to a narrow band of land in three states.

36. Jones, *Wealth of a Nation to Be,* p. 37; see also appendix 10.

37. Somewhat astoundingly, the Jones sample (*Wealth of a Nation to Be,* p. 37) consists of only 919 inventories. One must frankly admit that sampling error could exist and that the number of rich people dying in a year may vary substantially. As but one example, the city of Amsterdam has data on deaths of all persons, classified by wealth, for each year throughout the eighteenth century. The numbers in the category of rich, defined as those with wealth greater than Fl 12,000 or annual income greater than Fl 800, was as follows from 1770 to 1780:

	No. of Rich	*Total Deaths*
1770	274	6,503
1771	313	6,765
1772	342	9,226
1773	311	7,221
1774	290	5,777
1775	344	6,899
1776	365	8,926
1777	353	8,077
1778	308	6,858
1779	357	8,059
1780	451	9,051

The number of rich (and by inference the number of very rich) could vary substantially from year to year. My review of Jones's book appears in *Economic Development and Cultural Change* 32, no. 1 (October 1983), 193–98. See also Lee Soltow, "Income and Wealth Inequality in Amsterdam, 1585–1805," *Economisch en Sociaal-Historisch Jaarboek* 52 (1989), forthcoming.

38. *Massachusetts Tax Valuation Records, 1771,* Bettye Pruitt, Principal Investigator, Inter-University Consortium for Political and Social Research, ICPSR 7734, University of Michigan, 1980.

CHAPTER 8. CHANGES IN INEQUALITY, 1798–1860

1. Lee Soltow, *Men and Wealth in the United States, 1850–1870* (New Haven, Conn.: Yale University Press, 1975), pp. 140–42; and Samuel Blodgett, *Economica: A Statistical Manual for the United States* (City of Washington: n.p., 1806), p. 196.

2. Lee Soltow, *Patterns of Wealthholding in Wisconsin Since 1850* (Madison: University of Wisconsin Press, 1971), pp. 18–26.

3. Soltow, *Men and Wealth,* pp. 141–42; and Blodgett, *Economica,* p. 196.

4. We know this is true for 1860 from the fact that the log correlation between real and personal estate in the South in 1860 showed an elasticity coefficient of .55.

5. Some further evidence from the 1870 census indicates that the proportion of foreign-born in 1800 may have been less than 9 percent. A sample of 252 white males age 10 and older in 1870 showed that 6 percent had fathers who were foreign-born.

6. This assumes that 70-year-olds who were rural in 1860 also were rural in 1800, and contrariwise. In a broader analysis, such an assumption has appeared reasonable. See Soltow, *Men and Wealth,* pp. 14–15.

7. Thomas Cooper, *Some Information Respecting America* (1794; rpt. New York: Augustus Kelley, 1969), p. 223.

8. For greater detail on occupations in Pennsylvania, see Lee Soltow and Kenneth Keller, "Rural Pennsylvania in 1800: A Portrait from the Septennial Census," *Pennsylvania History* 49, no. 1 (January 1982), 36–37.

9. It is probably premature to state that the REP_{21} and $G_{RE,21}$ measure found here will not be much different from those to be reported later for 1798 data sets.

10. Walter Smith and Arthur Cole, *Fluctuations in American Business, 1790–1860* (Cambridge, Mass.: Harvard University Press, 1935), p. 185; I have also drawn samples from the land grant records for Pennsylvania, located in the State Archives in Harrisburg; for South Carolina, from records in the British Public Records Office, Kew, ser. CO/5/398, and from records gathered by Marion Chandler in the South Carolina Department of History and Archives, Columbia.

11. *Compendium of the Ninth Census,* table 34, using improved and unimproved acres; Timothy Pitkin, *A Statistical View of the Commerce of the United States* (1816; rpt. New York: Augustus Kelley, 1967), pp. 377–78.

12. Data for Ohio in 1810 and 1825 further substantiate the finding. See Lee Soltow, "Tocqueville's View of the Northwest in 1835: Ohio a Generation After Settlement," in *Essays on the Economy of the Old Northwest,* ed. David C. Klingaman and Richard K. Vedder (Athens: Ohio University Press, 1987). Also see Lee Soltow and Dean L. May, "The Distribution of Mormon Wealth and Income in 1857," *Explorations in Economic History* 16 (1979), 151–62; William H. Newell, "Inheritance on the Maturing Frontier: Butler County, Ohio, 1803–1865" and J.R. Kearl and Clayne

--

Pope, "Choices, Rents, and Luck: Economic Mobility of Nineteenth-Century Utah Households," both in *Long-Term Factors in American Economic Growth*, ed. Stanley K. Engerman and Robert E. Gallman, Studies in Income and Wealth, vol. 51 (Chicago: University of Chicago Press, 1987), pp. 215–306.

13. Jeffrey G. Williamson and Peter H. Lindert, *American Inequality: A Macroeconomic History* (New York: Institute for Research on Poverty, 1980). My views of their findings are given in a review in *Journal of Economic Literature* 20, no. 1 (March 1982). Morton Paglin's review appears in *Journal of Political Economy* 91, no. 5 (October 1983), 900–06. Further material includes Jeffrey G. Williamson and Peter H. Lindert, "Long-Term Trends in American Wealth Inequality," in *Modeling the Distribution and Intergenerational Transmission of Wealth*, ed. James D. Smith, Studies in Income and Wealth, vol. 46 (Chicago: University of Chicago Press, 1980), pp. 1–136, including Robert Gallman's criticism of the work. A statement dealing with distributions in America from its inception, including a bibliography, is given in Lee Soltow, "Distribution of Income and Wealth," in *Encyclopedia of American Economic History*, ed. Glenn Porter (New York: Charles Scribner's Sons, 1980), 3:1087–1119. See also my review of Jones, *Wealth of a Nation to Be*. Edward Pessen has studied the rich in four major U.S. cities in the second quarter of the nineteenth century, and finds that "the egalitarian version of antebellum American society should be discarded" (*Riches, Class, and Power Before the Civil War* [Lexington, Mass.: D.C. Heath, 1973], pp. 306, 321–35, 348).

CHAPTER 9. ECONOMIC DEVELOPMENT AND CHANGES IN INEQUALITY

1. I shall argue that there was as much relative change, qualitatively and quantitatively, in 1798 as there was later, that disruption as a factor in inequality was as large in 1798 as later. See Paul Tillich, "The Decline and the Validity of the Idea of Progress," *Ohio University Review* 13 (1966), 14.

2. Adam Smith, *An Inquiry into the Nature and Causes of the Wealth of Nations*, ed. R.H. Campbell, A.S. Skinner, and W.B. Todd (Indianapolis: Liberty Press, 1979), 2:715; Michael Ignatieff, "Smith, Rousseau, and the Republic of Needs," in *Scotland and Europe, 1200–1850*, ed. T.C. Smout (Edinburgh: John Donald, 1986), p. 190.

3. Lee Soltow and Edward Stevens, *The Rise of Mass Literacy and the Common School: A Socioeconomic Study of the United States to 1870* (Chicago: University of Chicago Press, 1981).

4. Paul A. David and Peter Solar, "A Bicentenary Contribution to the History of the Cost of Living in America," in *Research in Economic History*, vol. 2, ed. Paul Uselding (Greenwich, Conn.: JAI Press, 1977), p. 39; Paul David, "The Growth of Real Product in the United States Before 1840: New Evidence, Controlled Conjectures," *Journal of Economic History* 27 (June 1967), 155. See also Stanley L. Engerman and Robert E. Gallman, "U.S. Economic Growth, 1783–1860," in *Research in Economic History*, ed. Paul Uselding (Greenwich, Conn.: JAI Press, 1983), 8:1–46; Robert

Gallman, "The Statistical Approach: Fundamental Concepts as Applied to History," in *Approaches to American Economic History,* ed. George Rogers Taylor and Lucius F. Ellsworth, Eleutherian Mills–Hagley Foundation (Charlottesville: University Press of Virginia, 1971), pp. 63–86.

5. John Drayton, *A View of South Carolina* (Charleston, S.C.: W.P. Young, 1800), p. 168. The grants are preliminary counts kindly given to me by Marion Chandler of the South Carolina Department of Archives and History. See also ser. U275 of *Historical Statistics of the United States;* and *American State Papers,* 12th Cong., 1st sess., class 4, vol. 1, pp. 895–98. For shipping, data are for registered tonnage employed in foreign trade and enrolled tonnage employed in coastal trade; data for 1790–1792 are from a different collection agency. Lee Soltow, "Socioeconomic Classes in South Carolina and Massachusetts and the Observations of John Drayton," *South Carolina Historical Magazine* 81, no. 4 (October 1980), 283–305.

6. Henry Adams, *The United States in 1800* (Ithaca, N.Y.: Cornell University Press, 1979), p. 13; and Adams, *History of the United States of America During the First Administration of Thomas Jefferson* (New York: Charles Scribner's Sons, 1889), vol. 1, chs. 1–6. By way of contrast, see John J. McCusker and Russell R. Menard, *The Economy of British America, 1607–1789* (Chapel Hill: University of North Carolina Press, 1985).

7. Technological change enhances real income per capita. It also enhances real wealth per capita, as I measure it, but the connection is less clear and direct. Surely the cotton gin enhanced the value of lands, at least in the South.

8. County populations are available for use as weights from 1790 to 1900. When they are applied to the county plowed proportions for 1880, the index is substantially higher, but demonstrates the same upward trends as do the indexes presented in table 80. See also the data in McCusker and Menard, *The Economy of British America.*

9. Regional land qualities have been considered in William N. Parker and Judith L.V. Klein, "Productivity Growth in Grain Production in the United States. 1840–60 and 1900–10," in *Studies in Income and Wealth,* National Bureau of Economic Research (New York: Columbia University Press, 1966), pp. 523–83. They calculate that western growth relative to that in low-yield border states raised average land yields by about 25 percent (p. 541). Robert Gallman has determined that the shift to areas with the higher yields in the West raised land production by almost 13 percent between 1800 and 1850, "The Agricultural Sector and the Pace of Economic Growth: The U.S. Experience in the Nineteenth Century," in *Essays in Nineteenth Century Economic History,* ed. David C. Klingaman and Richard K. Vedder (Athens: Ohio University Press, 1975), p. 45.

10. William Ogilvie, *Birthright in Land,* with biographical notes by D.C. Macdonald (London: J. Walter, 1782; copy, London: Kegan, Trench, Trubner, 1891). A copy of Ogilvie's *An Essay of the Right of Property in Land,* bearing the signature of a former owner, George Washington, can be found in the British Library.

11. Church of Latter Day Saints Genealogical Library, Salt Lake City, microfilm 020,449.

12. One of the six equations employed in estimating age was that for districts that

were closer to Boston than to any other major city; its form was: Creation Date = 1544 + 97.2 × Log(Distance), N = 266, R^2 = .43. Dates from before 1630 were rounded to 1630, and those after 1800 were rounded to 1800. For the six major cities, the distance variable was assumed to be 5 miles. One reader of this manuscript suggested that the procedure is not appropriate for the South, since split counties most often were not near a major city.

13. Could any part of the wealth/age gradient be due to the life cycle? One could argue that it was the young who were further west and the old who were further east. Such does not prove to be the case, as revealed by the census of 1850. The average age in Wisconsin, Iowa, and Dakota was similar to that in Illinois, Indiana, Ohio, and Pennsylvania, averaging ages 36 or 37 for males 20 and older. (Lee Soltow, *Men and Wealth in the United States, 1850–1870* [New Haven, Conn.: Yale University Press, 1975], p. 41). Some evidence of a small age gradient is found for Wisconsin counties in 1850, with ages varying between 30 and 34 for counties with low and high population densities, respectively (Lee Soltow, *Patterns of Wealthholding in Wisconsin Since 1850* [Madison: University of Wisconsin Press, 1971], p. 85).

14. Log (Cash value per adult male) = 7.1235 − .002427 Year of formation, N = 1,564, and R^2 = .087 (standard errors in parentheses), using data for 1850. Results are very similar for the 1,929 points in 1860.

15. Ogilvie, *Birthright in Land,* pp. 13–15.

16. Lee Soltow, "Distribution of Income and Wealth," in *Encyclopedia of American Economic History,* ed. Glenn Porter (New York: Charles Scribner's Sons, 1980), 3:1101–03.

17. Primogeniture could have been rare in many regions of this country. This certainly was true for testated estates in New Jersey. See tables 58 and 63.

18. Perhaps the vigor of the son cancels the weakness and conservatism of the father, and perhaps the efforts of the two help to provide $71 for each of the other sons. Yet the initial gift of frontier land may have been the gift from the government.

CHAPTER 10. RATIFICATION OF THE CONSTITUTION AND THE DISTRIBUTION OF WEALTH AND INCOME

1. R.R. Palmer, *The Age of the Democratic Revolution, A Political History of Europe and America, 1760–1800* (Princeton, N.J.: Princeton University Press, 1959 and 1964), 1:365–67; 2:572–74. Also see Crane Brinton, *A Decade of Revolution, 1789–1799* (New York: Harper, 1963), pp. 22, 69, 213, 280, 283.

2. John Marshall, *The Life of George Washington,* 2d ed. (Philadelphia: Crissy & Markley, 1833), 2:126–27.

3. Lee Soltow: "Wealth Inequality in the United States in 1798 and 1860," *Review of Economics and Statistics* 66, no. 3 (August 1984), 444–51, and "The Distribution of Income in the United States in 1798: Estimates Based on the Federal Housing Inventory," *Review of Economics and Statistics* 69, no. 1 (February 1987), 181–85.

4. See Jackson Turner Main, *Political Parties Before the Constitution* (Chapel

Hill: University of North Carolina Press, 1973), pp. 25–27; Robert A. McGuire and Robert L. Ohsfeldt, "Economic Interests and the American Constitution: A Quantitative Rehabilitation of Charles A. Beard," *Journal of Economic History* 44, no. 2 (June 1984), 509–19; McGuire and Ohsfeldt, "An Economic Model of Voting Behavior at the Constitutional Convention of 1787," *Journal of Economic History* 46, no. 1 (March 1986), 111; Gordon S. Wood, *The Creation of the American Republic, 1776–1787* (Chapel Hill: University of North Carolina Press, 1969), pp. 519–615; Richard K. Matthews, *The Radical Politics of Thomas Jefferson, a Revisionist View* (Lawrence: University Press of Kansas, 1984), pp. 53–58, 106; and John Ashworth, *Agrarians and Aristocrats* (Atlantic Highlands, N.J.: Humanities Press, Inc., 1983), pp. 100–11, 316–17.

5. The distribution for 576,798 dwellings and for 715,000 families appears in Soltow, "Income in 1798," pp. 182, 184. I extended my "crowding" procedure in order to derive a distribution for 877,560 adult free males.

6. The logistic curve for Connecticut using not only DHV but also the average dwelling value per adult free male in the tax districts (DHV21) demonstrates that delegates voted their own interests, and not that of the populace.

$$YES_{79,CT2} = -3.70382 + 1.55268 \ln DHV - .91653 \ln DHV21;$$
$$(.44049) \qquad (.96341)$$

$N = 79, P(\chi^2 = 18) < .0001.$

7. I can provide the data and methods in more detail, on request.

8. The equation employed in table 86 for the dwelling distribution is

$$YES_{265,US} = -2.70044 + .50583 \, DHV;$$
$$(.88390) \quad (.13884)$$

$N = 265 \, P(\chi^2 = 14.4) < .0001.$

The last column, DPR, of table 86, considering all houses, yields

$$VOTE_{265,US} = -11 \qquad .93814 + \qquad .79337 \, DHV;$$
$$(.27503) \qquad (.04368)$$

$N = 576,798$ and 265 delegates $P(\chi^2 = 326) < .0001.$

9. Orrin Grant Libby, *The Geographical Distribution of the Vote of the Thirteen States on the Ratification of the Federal Constitution, 1787–1788* (1894; rpt. Franklin, N.Y.: Burt, 1969), pp. 110–16.

10. Further analysis demonstrates the ratification fervor to be positively associated with the urbanity of the county. (Urban = 1; otherwise, = 0) and weakly with location (South = 1; otherwise, = 0.)

$$YES = -2.2310 + .3744 \ln DHV + 3.9935 \, Urban + .1581 \, South$$
$$(1.5084) \quad (.2262) \qquad (2.9041) \qquad (.3326)$$

$N = 281, P(\chi^2 = 9.6) < .023.$

11. Marshall, *George Washington*, p. 127; Beard, *Economic Origins*, pp. 1–3.

CHAPTER 11. CONCLUSION

1. Alexis de Tocqueville, *Democracy in America,* the Henry Reeve Text, rev. Francis Bowen, ed. Phillips Bradley (New York: Alfred A. Knopf, 1966), 1:3.

2. The term *equality* must continue to be ambiguous unless one qualifies it by speaking of perfect equality or at least of relative equality. Persons in England are not averse to speaking of "increasing equality" whereas I might tend to use "decreasing inequality" in describing a diminution in the value of the Gini coefficient.

3. Charles Dickens, *American Notes, in Reprinted Pieces* (London: Chapman and Hall, 1868), p. 147.

4. Benjamin Franklin, *The Works of Benjamin Franklin,* ed. John Bigelo (New York: G.P. Putnam's Sons, 1904), 10:398.

5. Tocqueville, *Democracy,* 1:10–11, 28–29, 49–51, 53.

6. Ibid., 1:6.

7. James Madison, in *Notes of Debates in the Federal Convention Reported by James Madison,* intro. Adrianne Koch (Athens: Ohio University Press, 1966), p. 196.

8. Timothy Dwight, "A Discourse on Some Events of the Last Century," a speech delivered in New Haven, January 7, 1801, in Rare Books Section, the Library of Congress.

9. *The Philadelphia Magazine and Review,* February 1799 (Philadelphia: printed for Benjamin Davies, 1799), p. 120.

10. Studies of distributions of wealth and income of the past may very well be only in their infancy. It is to be hoped that students will continue to investigate these subjects, not only for countries and regions within countries but also for larger areas. Two important works are Jean Sentou, *Fortunes et groupes sociaux à Toulouse sous la Révolution (1789–1799), Essai d'histoire statistique* (Toulouse: Édouard Privat, 1969); Catharina Lis and Hugo Soly, *Poverty and Capitalism in Pre-Industrial Europe* (Brighton, Sussex: Harvester Press, 1982). Three forthcoming studies are Lee Soltow: "The Rich and the Destitute in Sweden, 1805–1855: A Test of Tocqueville's Inequality Hypothesis," *Economic History Review,* 2d ser. 42, no. 1 (1989); "Income and Wealth Inequality in Amsterdam, 1585–1805," *Economish- en Sociaal-Historisch Jaarboek* 52 (1989); and "Life Cycle of Ownership in Norway, 1664–1930," *Journal of European Economic History,* issue 2 (1989).

The basic weakness in most studies is the absence of detail about the poor and destitute and their position relative to those at higher levels. We need to know more about those near the modal income and below.

11. James Callender, "Sedgwick and Co. or a Key to the Six Per Cent Cabinet" (Philadelphia: Author, 1798).

12. Further detail is given in ch. 3, n. 17; corroborating evidence of the reasonableness of aggregate income in the $E = 1.2$ distribution is given in Robert Gallman, "The Agricultural Sector and the Pace of Economic Growth: U.S. Experience in the Nineteenth Century," in *Essays in Nineteenth Century Economic History,* ed. David C. Klingaman and Richard K. Vedder (Athens: Ohio University Press, 1975), p. 53.

The wealth-income ratio (W/Y) for 1798 was very similar to the same ratio in

1962. The two income averages presented in table 96, when coupled with an estimate for total estate of $1,050, yield a W/Y of 2.5 to 5.0. If the income average was $300, W/Y is 3.5. In 1962 it was 3.3, as presented in Dorothy Projector and Gertrude Weiss, *Survey of Financial Characteristics of Consumers,* U.S. Federal Reserve Technical Papers (August 1966), pp. 30, 110, 151.

13. Frederick Jackson Turner, "The Significance of the Frontier in American History," in *Frontier and Section,* ed. Ray Allen Billington (Englewood Cliffs, N.J.: Prentice-Hall, 1961), p. 39.

14. Tocqueville, *Democracy,* 1:6.

Index

Pittsburgh Series in Social and Labor History

Maurine Weiner Greenwald, Editor

And the Wolf Finally Came: The Decline of the American Steel Industry
John P. Hoerr

City at the Point: Essays on the Social History of Pittsburgh
Samuel P. Hays

The Correspondence of Mother Jones
Edward M. Steel, Editor

Distribution of Wealth and Income in the United States in 1798
Lee Soltow

Don't Call Me Boss: David L. Lawrence, Pittsburgh's Renaissance Mayor
Michael P. Weber

The Shadow of the Mills: Working-Class Families in Pittsburgh, 1870–1907
S. J. Kleinberg

The Speeches and Writings of Mother Jones
Edward M. Steel, Editor

The Steel Workers
John A. Fitch

Trade Unions and the New Industrialisation of the Third World
Roger Southall, Editor

What's a Coal Miner to Do? The Mechanization of Coal Mining
Keith Dix

Women and the Trades
Elizabeth Beardsley Butler

Other titles in the series

The Emergence of a UAW Local, 1936–1939: A Study in Class and Culture
Peter Friedlander

Homestead: The Households of a Mill Town
Margaret F. Byington

The Homestead Strike of 1892
Arthur G. Burgoyne

Immigration and Industrialization: Ethnicity in an American Mill Town, 1870–1940
John Bodnar